International Marketing Strategy 1998–99

The Chartered Institute of Marketing/Butterworth-Heinemann Marketing Series is the most comprehensive, widely used and important collection of books in marketing and sales currently available worldwide.

As the CIM's official publisher, Butterworth-Heinemann develops, produces and publishes the complete series in association with the CIM. We aim to provide definitive marketing books for students and practitioners that promote excellence in marketing education and practice.

The series titles are written by CIM senior examiners and leading marketing educators for professionals, students and those studying the CIM's Certificate, Advanced Certificate and Postgraduate Diploma courses. Now firmly established, these titles provide practical study support to CIM and other marketing students and to practitioners at all levels.

 The Chartered Institute of Marketing

D1741558

Formed in 1911, The Chartered Institute of Marketing is now the largest professional marketing management body in the world with over 60,000 members located worldwide. Its primary objectives are focused on the development of awareness and understanding of marketing throughout UK industry and commerce and in the raising of standards of professionalism in the education, training and practice of this key business discipline.

 The Chartered
Institute of Marketing

 BUTTERWORTH
HEINEMANN

The CIM
Student Workbook Series

CERTIFICATE

ALL PRICED AT £15.99

Business Communications 98/99
Shashi Misiura
0750640359

Marketing Fundamentals 98/99
Geoff Lancaster
Frank Withey
0750640340

Sales & Marketing Environment 98/99
Mike Oldroyd
0750640367

Understanding Customers 98/99
Rosemary Phipps
Craig Simmons
0750640375

ADVANCED CERTIFICATE

ALL PRICED AT £16.99

Effective Management for Marketing 98/99
Angela Hatton
Mike Worsam
0750640324

Management Information for Marketing & Sales 98/99
Tony Hines
0750640332

Marketing Operations 98/99
Mike Worsam
0750640308

Promotional Practice 98/99
Cathy Ace
0750640316

DIPLOMA

ALL PRICED AT £17.99

The Diploma Case Study Workbook 98/99
Paul Fifield
0750640383

International Marketing Strategy 98/99
Paul Fifield
Keith Lewis
0750640286

Marketing Communications Strategy 98/99
Tony Yeshin
0750640294

Strategic Marketing Management 98/99
Paul Fifield
Colin Gilligan
0750640278

ALL WORKBOOKS AVAILABLE JUNE 1998

International Marketing Strategy 1998–99

Paul Fifield and Keith Lewis

Published on behalf of
The Chartered Institute of Marketing

OXFORD BOSTON JOHANNESBURG MELBOURNE NEW DELHI SINGAPORE

This book is dedicated to our partners, Jan and Jane,
without whose support and encouragement not a single
page would have been produced.

Butterworth-Heinemann
Linacre House, Jordan Hill, Oxford OX2 8DP
225 Wildwood Avenue, Woburn, MA 01801-2041
A division of Reed Educational and Professional Publishing Ltd

ℛ A member of the Reed Elsevier plc group

First published 1998

British Library Cataloguing in Publication Data
A catalogue record for this book is available from the British Library

ISBN 0 7506 4028 6

Composition by Genesis Typesetting, Laser Quay, Rochester, Kent
Printed and bound in Great Britain by The Bath Press, Bath

Contents

A quick word from the Chief Examiner

I am delighted to recommend to you the new series of CIM workbooks. All of these have been written by either the Senior Examiner or Examiners responsible for marking and setting the papers.

Preparing for the CIM Exams is hard work. These workbooks are designed to make that work as interesting and illuminating as possible, as well as providing you with the knowledge you need to pass. I wish you success.

Trevor Watkins,
CIM Chief Examiner,
Deputy Vice Chancellor,
South Bank University

Preface

The development by the Chartered Institute of Marketing of Syllabus '94 has led to a far greater emphasis at the Diploma level upon the strategic aspects of marketing, a move which is reflected in the refocusing of all four of the Diploma syllabuses – including International Marketing Strategy. In writing this workbook we have paid particular attention both to the strategic aspects of the subject and to an exploration of the strong linkages which exist – and which students are expected to demonstrate – between the International Marketing paper and the other papers in the Diploma examination.

Students will note that International aspects have been known to form a major part of the Analysis and Decision paper in recent years. It must, however, be recognized from the start that candidates for the Diploma are expected to demonstrate a depth and breadth of their understanding of marketing and this workbook alone will be insufficient to meet a candidate's needs for the Diploma examinations.

Important Note

This workbook has been designed to complement, not substitute for, a wider programme of reading, research and individual study. It is for this reason that throughout the text you will find references to four other books that you will be told to read. They are:

International Marketing, S. Paliwoda and M. Thomas, Butterworth-Heinemann, 1998

International Marketing Strategy, I. Doole, R. Lowe and C. Phillips, Routledge, 1997

Global Marketing Strategies, J.-P. Jeannet and H. D. Hennessey, Houghton-Mifflin, 1998

International Marketing, V. Terpstra and R. Sarathy, The Dryden Press, 1997

Further, this workbook has concentrated on exploring the major differences in International Marketing Strategy from Domestic Marketing Strategy. Students will need a sound basis of understanding in domestic marketing strategy if they are to gain the full value from this workbook. Four other books that you will do well to read are:

Strategic Marketing Management: planning, implementation and control, R. M. S. Wilson and C. Gilligan, Butterworth-Heinemann, 1997.
Marketing Strategy, P. Fifield, Butterworth-Heinemann, 1998.
Strategic Marketing Management 1998–99, P. Fifield and C. Gilligan, Butterworth-Heinemann, 1997.
Marketing Communication Strategy 1998–99, T. Yeshin, Butterworth-Heinemann, 1998.
International Marketing (Marketing in Action series), K. Lewis and M. Housden, Kogan Page, 1998.

We wish you success in the examinations.

Paul Fifield
Keith Lewis

How to use your CIM workbook

The authors have been careful to structure your book with the exams in mind. Each unit, therefore, covers an essential part of the syllabus. You need to work through the complete workbook systematically to ensure that you have covered everything you need to know.

This workbook is divided into 15 units each containing the following standard elements:

Objectives   tell you what part of the syllabus you will be covering and what you will be expected to know having read the unit.

Study guides   tell you how long the unit is and how long its activities take to do.

Exam questions   are designed to give you practice – they will be similar to those that you will be faced with in the examination.

Exam answers   give you a suggested format for answering exam questions. *Remember* there is no such thing as a model answer – you should use these examples only as guidelines.

Activities   give you the chance to put what you have learned into practice.

Exam hints   are tips from the senior examiner or examiner which are designed to help you avoid common mistakes made by previous candidates.

Definitions   are useful words you must know to pass the exam.

Extending knowledge sections   are designed to help you use your time most effectively. It is not possible for the workbook to cover *everything* you need to know to pass. What you read here needs to be supplemented by your classes, practical experience at work and day-to-day reading.

Summaries   cover what you should have picked up from reading the unit.

A glossary is provided at the back of the book to help define and underpin understanding of the key terms used in each unit.

Introduction

The International Marketing Strategy component of the Diploma in Marketing has two concise objectives:

1 To enable students to acquire expertise in developing marketing strategies for countries other than their own and thereby to extend their range of marketing understanding, to deal with both international marketing to suit the situations in non-domestic markets and the impact of international competitors on their domestic market.
2 To promote an understanding of the factors determining the extent to which standardization in strategy implementation is appropriate for success in international markets.

This is achieved by focusing on a number of key issues that logically follow each other in the strategic marketing process:

Stage 1: Where are we now and where do we want to be? (Strategic financial and marketing analysis followed by strategic direction and strategy formulation.)
Stage 2: How might we get there? (Strategic choice.)
Stage 3: How do we ensure arrival? (Strategic implementation and control.)

At the same time, the content of the module has been designed to complement the syllabuses for the other three Diploma papers, Marketing Communications Strategy, Strategic Marketing Management – Planning and Control and Strategic Marketing Management – Analysis and Decision (see Figure I.1) and to build upon material at the Certificate and Advanced Certificate levels.

Given its structure, and in particular the nature of the interrelationship between international marketing strategy and the other aspects of marketing strategy, this workbook has been designed to provide you with a clear insight into the analysis, planning and control processes in international marketing and the ways in which these can be best applied within the international business and commercial world as well as, of course, to the CIM's Diploma examination paper.

In doing this we give considerable emphasis to the three elements that underpin all the CIM's syllabuses: knowing, understanding and doing. Thus, in each of the units we outline and discuss the relevant concepts so that your knowledge and understanding is increased. We

Marketing Communications Strategy	International Marketing Strategy	Strategic Marketing Management	
		Planning and Control	Analysis and Decision

Figure I.1 Diploma in Marketing

then address the issue of 'doing' by means of a series of exercises and questions and, of course, through the mini-case study that forms Section 1 of the International Marketing Strategy exam paper. It needs to be recognized from the outset however, that a workbook cannot explore the complexity of concepts in the same way that a textbook can. For this reason, we make reference at various stages to two books that you may well find useful. These are:

International Marketing, S Paliwoda and M. Thomas, Butterworth-Heinemann, 1998.
International Marketing Strategy, I. Doole, R. Lowe and C. Phillips, Routledge, 1997.

Both books were written specifically for the CIM's International Marketing Strategy syllabus and with the needs of the prospective students in mind.

International marketing strategy

International marketing strategy has always been a major factor in the success of important trading nations such as Britain. Now that membership of the EU has been secured, international marketing skills are becoming even more important to marketers. In this unit you will:

- Understand the range of tasks involved in international marketing strategy
- Review the strategic process
- Understand the Diploma International Marketing syllabus
- Understand what is meant by international marketing

Having completed this unit you will be able to:

- Explain how to avoid problems in international marketing
- Appreciate the key questions involved in 'going international'
- Advise an organization on whether to go international and the key questions involved in this strategic decision
- Explain the role of international marketing in the overall international business process

This workbook is critical to an overall understanding of the International Marketing Strategy process. The key:

- Development of international marketing strategy
- Implementation of strategy
- Evaluation and control of strategy

come from an understanding of the organization's objectives and ambitions for its international operations.

The organization may treat its international business as an 'add-on' to its domestic operations or as an integral part of its mission. This will influence the importance that international marketing has in the organization, the resources allocated to it and the control systems applied to support implementation.

As you work through this unit, remember that:

- Domestic and international marketing work on the same principles – customers must be satisfied
- Customers in foreign markets may have different needs and may become drivers for different marketing policies
- The biggest problem in international marketing is often not the foreign customer but the international marketer.

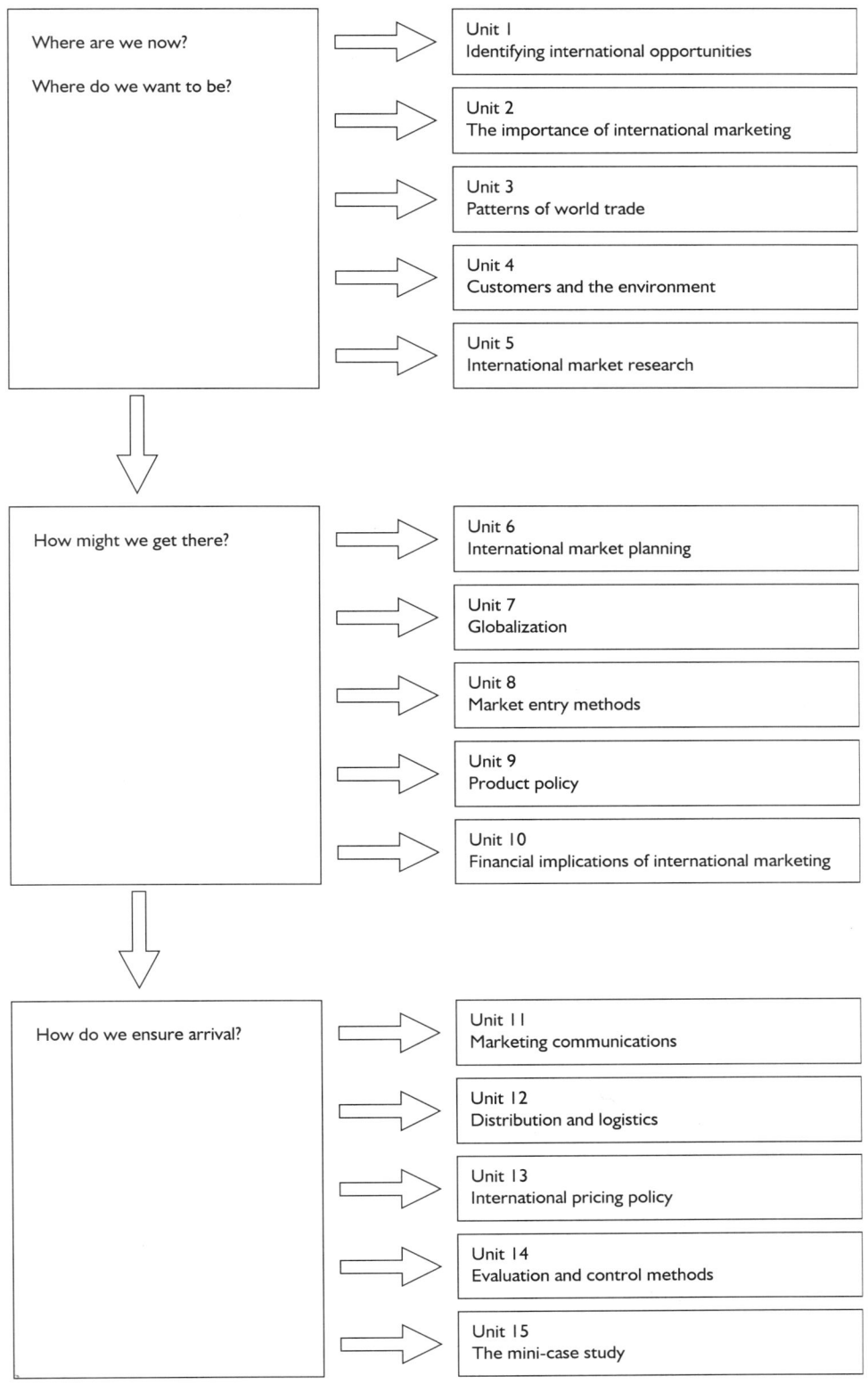

Figure I.2 The International Marketing Strategy syllabus and the structure of this book

We commented earlier that the International Marketing Strategy syllabus focuses upon three key issues: these are illustrated in Figure I.2.

In Units 1–5 we are concerned with the various ways in which managers might identify their organization's current position and assess its true level of international marketing capability. The assessment of the organization's capability and the options open to it in its marketplaces can be seen as one of the principal foundation stones for any strategic planning process – domestic or international – since it determines exactly what the organization is or should be capable of achieving. Marketing capability by itself is, of course, only one part of the planning process and needs to be looked at against the background of the organization as a whole as well as the nature and shape of the international environment in which it is or might choose to operate. Units 3 and 4 concentrate on the nature of the international trading environment and the all-important influences upon customers that may create opportunities for the organization.

Having assessed the current capability of the organization and the opportunities and threats in the international marketplace, in Units 6–10 we start to consider practical ways in which the organization can start to turn its international opportunities into profits.

Units 11–14 assess the all-important question of how we manage, evaluate and control our marketing activities in the international environment in order to achieve the pre-set strategic plans.

Approaching the International Marketing Strategy examination

The syllabus for International Marketing Strategy is very detailed in its approach and has a number of clear and distinct learning outcomes that emerge from a successful completion of the programme. This means that at the end of your course you should be able to:

- Understand the changing nature of the international trading environment
- Understand differences in business and social/cultural conventions which affect buying behaviours and marketing approaches in international markets
- Differentiate between marketing strategies appropriate to industrialized, developing and less developed economies
- Identify sources of information, methods of information collection and methods of information analysis suitable for international marketing operations
- Compare and contrast strategies for export, international, multinational and transnational marketing
- Identify the major organizational changes to be made when a company moves from national to international to global marketing
- Evaluate the factors which influence the implementation of a product, price, distribution and marketing communication mix in non-domestic markets
- Understand the financial implications of different international marketing strategies
- Evaluate the suitability of specific international marketing strategies.

After each examination the senior examiners write a report for the Chartered Institute in which they discuss how the students coped with the examination and highlight any particular problems that have been experienced. In looking back at the reports which have been written over the past few years there are several issues which have been referred to on almost every occasion. Obtain a set of examiner's reports for yourself and make sure that you don't forfeit marks needlessly.

What is international marketing?

International marketing may appear, at first glance, to be an impossibly complex subject involving all functional areas of management. In fact, there is surprisingly little extra knowledge or specific management technique required. International marketing differs very little from domestic marketing in that the objective of the marketer is the same – to understand customer and market needs and strive to meet them with the capabilities which the organization has at its disposal. Internationally, the organization must strive to understand its international marketing environment and then be able to adapt familiar techniques to possibly unfamiliar circumstances.

The organization feels the effect of its international environment in a number of ways, not only in its approach to its overseas customers but also in its raw material or component sourcing, in its financing requirements, in its domestic market through international competition and in its general business level which is affected by the world trade cycle.

One of the most important factors in international marketing, and in international business generally, is not the new and different techniques which have to be learned to deal with overseas markets but in the mindset of the managers attempting to satisfy overseas or international market needs. Every manager or marketer is the product of his or her own culture. The end result of centuries of conditioning in what our domestic culture considers to be acceptable and non-acceptable modes of behaviour colours all our perceptions of foreign market and customer behaviour. The single most important problem any organization faces within its international setting often comes not from the environment but from its own reactions to that environment.

> 'The self-reference criterion is the unconscious reference to one's own cultural values, and is the root cause of most business problems abroad.'
> (James A. Lee)

James Lee refers to the self-reference criterion (SRC) and compares this 'cultural conditioning' to an iceberg: we are not aware of nine-tenths of it. The sequence of comments uttered by many domestic marketers considering international markets for the first time is often as follows:

'That's interesting!'
'That's different (from what we do at home).'
'That's wrong! (it's not what we do at home).'

The third comment is driven directly by the manager's SRC and often results in the application (normally unsuccessful) of domestic marketing policies in overseas market situations. In order to avoid errors in business decisions, the SRC must be recognized and isolated so that its biasing effect is minimized, if not eliminated completely, from international marketing strategy decisions.

The key questions in international marketing
As can be seen from Figure I.3, there are four broad questions which are relevant to the international marketer. These questions can be addressed in a sequential order.

Whether to go international?
There are between 190 and 200 countries in the world with governments which can lay claim to being independent – the number tends to change on a weekly basis! Although they are often classified as being either 'industrialized', 'less developed' or 'advanced' such simplicity is misleading to the international marketer. Organizations operating internationally must analyse the environment in which they will be working; how people think and act – be they customers, agents, employees or governments. It is the organization's international environment which will largely determine the actions that can be taken and the kinds of adaptation that must be made in international operations. In Units 3 and 4 we will look in detail at the ways in which the international environment can be analysed and in Unit 5 we will spend some time considering the mechanical approaches of market research that may be required to uncover the important parameters of the international environment.

Where to operate?
Of all the various markets and the different opportunities that appear to be open to the organization, where should the marketer concentrate his or her efforts? Despite talk of collapsing national boundaries and the global information infrastructure, the world still remains a very big place. Rather than spread the resources of the organization too thinly (the Marmite approach!) it is important that the international marketer is able to focus the

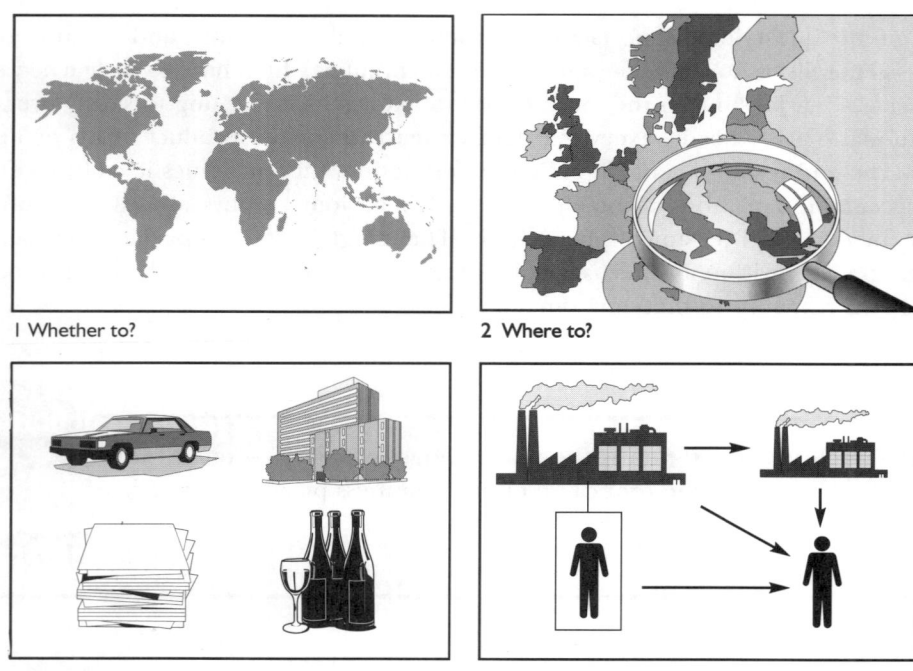

1 Whether to?

2 Where to?

3 What to?

4 How to?

Figure I.3 The key questions in international marketing

resources of the organization on the market or markets where it is felt the returns may be the most promising. How can these markets be selected? In Unit 4 specifically we will address the question of target markets selection and the basis upon which an informed choice might be made.

What to market in the overseas environment?

Although most organizations would prefer to market a single product or service to all international markets, the market pressures are such that some adaptation will often have to be made. These adaptations may be caused by differing use conditions, tastes or habit or government regulation. Other areas of product mix may need modification, for example packaging (language or literacy requirements and different transport and distribution systems) or brand and trade marks (may not travel well due to differences in language, idiom or aesthetics). In Unit 9 we will discuss the implications of product policy for overseas markets in more detail.

How should we operate internationally?

Once the organization has decided where it will operate and concentrate its effort, and what the market requires from it, the final decision is how to operate in those overseas markets. Decisions such as method of market entry and whether to use local agents, distributors or develop a wholly owned subsidiary will be considered in greater depth in Units 6, 8 and 12.

EXAM QUESTION

Examine the steps taken by a firm moving from a domestic business to an international business (December 1992).
(**See** Exam answers at the end of this unit.)

Understanding the international marketing strategy process

In order to understand the international process it needs to be viewed schematically from the first decision-making processes through to implementation and control. This entire process is outlined in Figure I.4 which can be explained in more detail as follows.

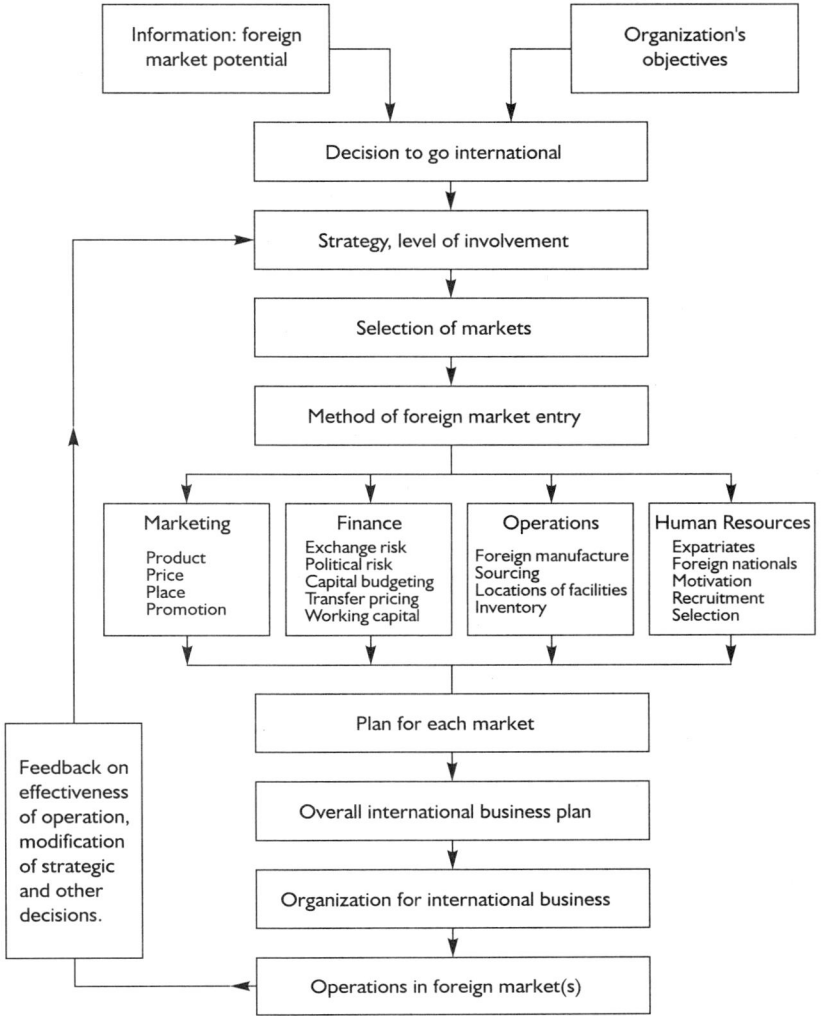

Figure I.4 The international business process

Information: foreign market potential

Any decision to go international must be based on solid and reliable market information on the potential to the organization from the foreign market.

Organization's objectives

A clear understanding of the organization's corporate and marketing objectives will help the marketer to understand whether international marketing and/or the selection of particular key markets is in line with the organization's objectives and ambitions for the future.

Decision to go international

The difference between an organization deciding strategically to take an international role in its business rather than opportunistically following up the odd foreign sales lead has a very different effect on the organization and the way it approaches its international markets. With a corporate decision to take international business as a serious activity, the organization is likely to put the resources required behind the effort and to treat it as a key activity in the future.

Strategy 'level of involvement'

The first strategic decision the organization makes on its route to internationalization, is to decide how deeply involved it wishes to become in the international marketplace. The organization's chosen level of involvement in international business will determine (at least in the short term) the marketing, financial, operation and human resource strategies that can be employed. The different levels of international involvement range from active exporting through joint ventures to marketing subsidiaries overseas as far as foreign production and foreign marketing. These options will be analysed and described in more detail in Units 6 and 12.

Selecting the markets

The organization should resist the temptation to attack too many markets thereby spreading effort and resources too thinly to be successful. The most successful international operations often come from making an initial effort into a single market and then extending this to other possibly neighbouring markets as learning in international business increases. Market selection can be based on three criteria: market potential, similarity to home or other foreign markets and market accessibility. These methods of market selection will be considered in more depth in Unit 4.

Method of foreign market entry

Unlike domestic marketing, the organization often has a clear choice of how it proposes to enter overseas markets. How the method of market entry is selected will determine the freedom of action the organization has over the various elements of the marketing mix. As with level of involvement, method of entry may dictate marketing activities in the short term. Alternative methods of market entry will be considered in more detail in Unit 8.

Foreign market planning

Although the international marketing strategy syllabus is primarily concerned with marketing activities in overseas markets, the modern marketer can ill afford to ignore the international aspects and pressures upon other functional areas of the business. Not only must decisions be made on the marketing mix most appropriate to international markets but also the other functional requirements of the organization must be considered if any strategic marketing activity is to be successful. Financial considerations of international operations are considerable and will cover issues such as exchange risk, political risk, capital budgeting, transfer pricing and working capital requirements. These will be considered in more detail in Unit 10. International operations may also represent a major cost centre and questions such as foreign manufacture, working stock and location of facilities will be considered in Unit 12. Human resources are an equally important area and these will be considered in Units 6, 11 and 12.

EXAM QUESTION

Examine the importance of self-reference criteria in international marketing. Use examples to illustrate your answer.
(**See** Exam answers at the end of this unit.)

Plan for each market

In order to control the marketing and business operations in overseas markets it is important that a plan is developed for each individual market based upon the differing marketing characteristics and customer expectations from that marketplace (see Unit 6).

Overall international business plan

International business planning requires that the individual market plans be coordinated and controlled for international operations. Unlike the domestic situation where there is a single market and easily understood planning parameters, the international environment tends to be much more fragmented and may require differing resources at different stages and levels of allocation. It is important that the organization attempts to remain in control of the situation and the coordination of (often diverse) national or market plans becomes a major strategic activity.

Organization for international business

Structure can be a severe brake on any organization's international ambitions and new organization structures may be required in order to facilitate and promote international business. This will be discussed in more detail in Unit 6.

Operations in foreign markets

As operations and activity 'on the ground' begin to unfold it is important that evaluation and control methods be in place for the organization continually to improve its activity in international markets. Evaluation and control methodology will be considered in more detail in Unit 14.

Summary

In this introductory unit we have considered the format and approach that this book will take in addressing the international marketing strategy syllabus and the importance of using this book in conjunction with other international marketing texts recommended for the examination. We have also considered the detailed analysis of the syllabus as well as the all-important learning objectives and outcomes required for a successful attempt at the examination itself. Finally, we considered the overall nature of the international marketing strategy tasks and we concluded that:

- There is little conceptual difference between international marketing and domestic marketing.
- The focus of the international marketer's activity is the customer (as in the domestic situation), but the customer happens to be in a foreign market with all that that entails.
- A primary problem in successful international business is the social/cultural conditioning of the international marketer (remember the SRC).
- International marketing consists of four interrelated questions: Whether to? Where to? What to? How to?
- The international marketing strategic process can be seen as a logical series of steps which will take the business from a domestic organization to an international organization and possibly to a global organization.

Questions

As a check on your understanding of what has been covered in this unit, consider the following questions:

- How is the organization affected by international business trends?
- How can the international marketer's own cultural background affect the organization's international market strategy?
- What are the four key questions in international marketing?
- What are the two key drivers which may start off an organization's entry into foreign markets?
- What is meant by 'level of involvement'?
- What tactical effects will the strategic decision on 'how to enter a foreign market' have?
- What are the three criteria for foreign market selection?
- What are the special factors to be taken into account when planning for international marketing strategy?

For a more detailed treatment of what international marketing strategy means, read:

International Marketing, S. Paliwoda and M. Thomas, Butterworth-Heinemann, 1998.
International Marketing Strategy, I. Doole, R. Lowe and C. Phillips, Routledge, 1997.

December 1992 Moving from being a purely domestic business to an international one can be both a lengthy and painful process for the organization involved. Rarely, if ever, is this transformation achieved 'overnight'. More often the process is one of a gradual evolution through a number of distinct stages or steps.

(a) *Purely domestic*

The first stage is where a company operates only in domestic markets and hence requires no skills, staff or procedures to investigate and explore international opportunities. No doubt many companies have been and will continue to be content to operate on a purely domestic basis. However, even the smallest company these days can no longer afford to ignore the international aspects of production and trade, and the opportunities and threats which are presented by these aspects. In particular, the company that wishes to expand and grow beyond a certain size will almost certainly have to become international.

(b) *Experimental/'passive' involvement in exporting*

Most frequently the purely domestic marketer starts on the process to becoming an international marketer through experimental and/or 'passive' involvement in exporting. Very often this is as a result of, say, a casual enquiry from a potential overseas customer or possibly due to, say, an overseas agent spotting an opportunity after attendance at a trade fair. Whatever the impetus to become involved at this stage, commitment and involvement on the part of the exporter are likely to be low. Much of the 'marketing' will be passive and/or left to intermediaries. Time horizons will tend to be short, with little or no systematic market selection – other than perhaps on the grounds of physical proximity – and with the dominant objective of immediate sales. Very few, if any, changes will be made to the planning process and/or structure of the organization.

(c) *Active involvement/exporting*

If the results of being involved in exporting are perceived to be beneficial the emphasis may then switch to a more active involvement in export markets. At this stage commitment to export markets begins to grow. As a result more resources will begin to be devoted to this area of the firm's activity together with a more formal approach to planning. The company will now begin to become more systematic in country/market selection. Specialist staff might be employed and the company will begin to explore how to secure more control over its exporting activities.

At this stage, the company has moved beyond being a purely passive exporter. The company may well have a specialist export marketing function and/or some sort of overseas investment in one or more markets. However, even at this stage international markets and marketing are still viewed as being of secondary importance to domestic ones.

(d) *Total involvement/international marketing*

Although often subtle in difference and hence difficult to spot compared to the previous stage, in fact the international marketer has evolved to look at international markets and marketing as being central to the company's future and growth. Put another way, at this stage of development, there is total commitment to the development of international markets in company strategy. Planning horizons now become long run. There is systematic selection of target markets and entry modes. Resource commitment and organizational structures are focused on international market opportunities. Perhaps the most important and telling feature of the truly international company can be found in the attitudes and outlook of its management, and particularly its most senior personnel. In a company which is truly international, opportunities are examined and acted upon in an international context with little or no distinction between these and purely domestic opportunities. The company that has reached this stage is probably ready to take the final step in the process of evolution by becoming 'global' in outlook.

James Lee (1966) used the term SRC to characterize our own unconscious reference to our cultural values and the tendency to want to impose them on others (foreign customers). Textbooks have been written on culture, its importance and relevance, especially internationally. Put succinctly, culture is 'the way we do things around here' – here being any market/country. Failure to address this will reduce the chances of success for any organization planning expansion into overseas markets.

Lee suggested an approach to eliminate SRC:

1 Define the problem/goal in terms of home country cultural traits, habits and norms.
2 Define the problem/goal in terms of the foreign culture, traits, habits and norms.
3 Isolate the SRC influence and examine it carefully to see how it complicates the problem/goal.
4 Redefine the problem/goal without SRC influence and solve for the foreign market situation.

It is very important to regard the culture of a foreign country in the context of that country – being different from rather than better or worse. The key is to identify similarities and to isolate differences so that the principles of marketing can be applied correctly to a given situation. In summary, cultural sensitivity underpins international marketing.

The importance of SRC

1 SRC influences the ability to evaluate objectively and to determine consumer demand – the inability to see the market place from the perspective of the local consumer, e.g. washing powders in the UK are sold predominantly in boxes. A study of the Indian market based on number of boxes sold would indicate a small market. Yet the market is huge – supplied by small sachets, sufficient for one wash, and what is more, specially formulated to wash clothes in cold water. Secondly, an analysis of the UK market for motor cars might not unearth the fact that over 60% of new car sales are bought by companies not individuals. Thus a foreign motor car manufacturer wishing to launch into the UK might completely misread the size of the market.
2 *SRC and cultures that appear similar.* Many UK companies have failed to succeed in entering the US market. Largely they make the error that the US is very similar to the UK (speaking the same language). In fact, the US is culturally very different. Those UK companies that do succeed – Bodyshop and Hanson – do so because they allow the business to be run by Americans, thus leapfrogging the SRC barrier. Businesses such as Sock Shop failed when market conditions appeared, on the face of it, similar to the UK.

   It is worth noting that Australia too is culturally unlike the UK. Likewise, Marks & Spencer, struggled in Canada, and subsequently decided not to launch in the US, although they did buy Brooks Brothers, a US up-market clothes retailer.
3 *SRC and the difficulties with major cultural differences.* Cultures have been defined as low context and high context. Austria, Germany and Switzerland are low context cultures described in terms of being direct in communication – 'What you see is what you get.' High context cultures rely on subtlety in communication, e.g. Japan, where details are often more important, such as in the exchange of business cards. Here the etiquette is fine tuned.
4 *SRC and distribution.* Beware the assumption that the sophisticated UK distribution system is replicated in other markets that, on the face of it, are sophisticated. In the UK, direct delivery from factory to end retailer is commonplace. Japan, rich and sophisticated, has an archaic distribution system with many intermediaries each taking a margin, thus escalating costs.
5 *SRC and marketing communications.* The field is rich with embarrassments. UK comedians earn a living from showing foreign advertisements on TV. Advertising is very culturally sensitive, e.g. the 'Come Alive with Pepsi' slogan of a few years ago

invariably translates into 'Return from the grave with Pepsi' – not the desired message, I feel.

6 *SRC and human resources*. The UK is driven by an Anglo-Saxon Protestant ethic. Transferring UK management systems, techniques and methodology overseas has not been a universal success. Others do things differently and are equally, if not more, successful. Employment law is very ethnocentric, even in neighbouring countries.

In summary, SRC remains the biggest pitfall in international success. Sensitivity to others is not just important but is the building block. However, there is evidence (some) that cultural differences are, if not disappearing, at least converging. McDonald's is an example where cultural differences have been put aside in a wide variety of countries – although when considered under the microscope, fundamental differences persist. A Big Mac may be the same everywhere, but the augmented product frequently differs, e.g. mayonnaise on chips in Belgium, beer in Germany, etc.

Identifying international opportunities

OBJECTIVES

In this unit we will consider how the organization might identify opportunities for itself in overseas markets. We will consider the risks inherent in an international marketing operation and how these might be assessed alongside the opportunities to give a balanced view on any likely strategic planning. In this unit you will:

- Understand the reasons why organizations 'go international'
- Review the principal forms of financial risk for the international organization
- Consider the role of the Marketing information system in reducing the risk of international expansion
- Review the range of models that may be of use in assessing foreign market opportunities.

Having completed this unit you will be able to:

- Identify the key drivers behind an organization's international strategy.
- Evaluate the main areas of risk in international operations.
- Establish ways of reducing risk in planning an organization's international marketing strategy.

STUDY GUIDE

This unit sets the scene for understanding the international environment and the organization's position within that environment. This unit, together with Units 2, 3, 4 and 5, account for 30% of the International Marketing Strategy syllabus.

This introductory unit is key to your understanding of how to position the organization to take advantages of its international opportunities. We will also consider the not inconsiderable risks in international operations.

Once you have completed this unit, read through a few of the mini-cases at the end of the book and try to identify the key international opportunities/threats facing the organizations described.

This unit explains the essential balance that needs to be struck between 'Sales' and 'Profits'. Too many markets still operate at primarily a tactical level, believing that their only responsibility is to bring home maximum sales revenue or market share to their organization. No business lives and grows just by market share but needs a consistent flow of profits.

International opportunities must be assessed by both sales potential and the likely potential for repatriated profits that can be obtained from the activity. Operating just to maximize sales or market share, perhaps at the expense of profitability is not necessarily good marketing.

Some reasons for 'going international'

There are many reasons why an organization might consider going international and the following are some of the most common:

1 *Saturated home market* If the home market for an organization's products or service is saturated or competition is so intense that it can no longer gain any significant market share improvement it might consider extending its market activity to overseas markets. This move might be considered under market extension or even diversification strategies in the Ansoff matrix. Remember that success in international markets will depend on whether the products and/or services offered by the organization are attractive to the international customer. Success in the home market does not, of itself, guarantee this!

2 *Competition* There are two separate but interrelated reasons why an organization may decide to go international in this instance. The first case is that competition may be less intense in overseas markets than in the domestic market. Competition, as we all know, may have benefits for customers but it is always extremely expensive for the organization. Despite the often increased risk of operating overseas it may be that the organization faces a better potential return by operating in markets where there is less intense competition for its products and services. A second competition related factor in moving internationally may be that an organization is faced by particularly virulent international competition in its domestic marketplace. In some instances it is difficult to compete from a domestic base against international competitors. In such cases the organization may consider moving internationally in order to be able to compete on a more equal footing with the opponent organization.

3 *Excess capacity* Where an organization is operating successfully in its domestic marketplace but is operating at below optimal capacity levels there is excess capacity available for production. In these instances it may be wise to consider international operations where the product or service can be costed at marginal cost, thereby giving a potential price advantage for overseas marketing operations. Because the organization can produce at marginal cost does not, of course, mean that it ought to enter foreign markets at a lower price. It could decide to use the extra margin for marketing support. Big price differences may, too, produce the risk of parallel imports back to the home market and could disturb prices there.

4 *Comparative advantage in product, skill or technology* The organization may discover, when analysing overseas market opportunities, that it has a comparative advantage against local competition in the foreign market. This advantage might be in product, skill or technology but, always subject to local market demand and tastes, it could be the makings of a profitable venture. Comparative advantage is often the case when organizations are based in advanced countries and consider marketing internationally to lesser developed countries.

EXAM QUESTION

Examine the factors that would influence a multinational enterprise to export (December 1993).

(**See** Exam answers at the end of this unit.)

5 *Product life cycle differences* As you will know from studies in domestic marketing, as a product or service progresses through the life cycle it often changes in style, performance or efficiency. When considering international markets the marketer may discover that foreign markets are at a different point of development in the product or industry life cycle. The marketer may decide to exploit these differences, either by exporting product which is no longer suitable for the domestic market place (the life cycle requirements have moved on) or by entering the foreign market with a more advanced product than the local competition has yet developed.

EXAM HINT

The product life cycle is probably one of the best known but least understood concepts in marketing. Do you know how to apply the product life cycle concept in domestic marketing? Do you know how to extend the product life cycle applications into international marketing?

There has also been some debate over recent years about the continued relevance of the product life cycle as a planning model. Are you aware of this debate? What side of the argument do you favour? Why? What is the relevance of this debate to use of the model in *International Marketing Strategy*?

6 *Geographic diversification* Linked to items above, an organization may discover in its domestic marketing strategy that either its market is saturated or competition is becoming more intense in established markets. To continue to grow and develop it must extend its operations in terms of either products or markets. The classical development of the Ansoff matrix (see *Strategic Marketing Management 1998–99* workbook) normally considers just domestic operations but international options can be considered too. When considering 'market extension' strategies the organization can include international markets as well as other domestic markets for further growth. A number of companies have preferred to focus their attention on a single product or very limited range of products in a number of markets for growth rather than take on the risk of developing new products or extending their activities into markets that they do not understand.

7 *Organizational reasons* Often an organization may find itself haphazardly involved in international business and marketing operations through the acquisition of random activities during acquisition and merger operations or through the organically grown exporting activities of its own subsidiaries. Soon a point in the organization's development arrives when it is time to put order into the previously piecemeal approach to international operations. This often results in the creation of an international marketing division where the various activities are brought together, rationalized and coordinated. This 'house keeping' often provides areas of significant international potential.

8 *Financial reasons* There are a range of financial reasons why an organization may decide to take the international route to its business and these might include investment incentives in overseas markets and the availability of venture capital as well as the option to maximize profits or minimize losses through international rather than simple domestic operations.

Whatever the original reason for considering international operations, no organization should forget the golden rule: international marketing will prove to be a more successful venture for the organization that is exporting a positive advantage than for one exporting to cover a domestic weakness.

Financial risk in international operations
One major difference in operations carried out internationally rather than domestically is that the funds flows occur in a variety of currencies and in a variety of nations. These currency and national differences, in turn, create risks unique to international business which are explored in greater detail in Unit 10.

There are two types of financial risk unique to international marketing operations:

1 *Foreign exchange risk* This arises from the need to operate in more than one currency.
2 *Political risk* This is a term used to cover those risks arising from an array of legal, political, social and cultural differences. Political risk normally produces losses when there is a conflict between the goals of the organization and those of the host government.

Home country (domestic) law is also important in that it defines acceptable behaviour for the organization in all its activities – whether at home or abroad. Figure 1.1 demonstrates the nature of this relationship between the organization, the host government and the home government.

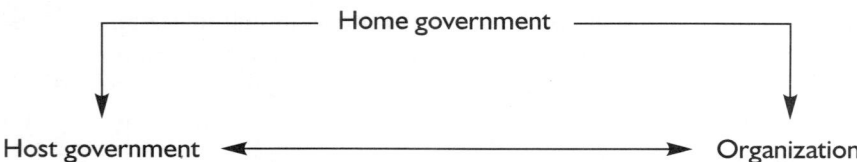

Figure 1.1 The organization and 'political risk'

The international management information system (MIS)

It will be seen from the above that the establishment and maintenance of a high-quality management information system is essential for two primary reasons:

1 Helping the organization to decide whether to follow an international route by quantifying opportunities
2 Helping management to develop and implement suitable marketing strategies and programmes that will allow the organization to exploit the foreign opportunities to the full.

These two key drivers create the need for two different types of data:

1 *Feasibility Data* The decisions which the organization needs to make in terms of whether it should go international and if so which markets it should enter are all to be captured under the title of feasibility data collection. Data in this area will facilitate decisions such as whether to go international or not, where to go, what to offer.

What information does your company collect for its international markets? What gaps, if any, can you identify?

2 *Operational Data* The second form of data required by the organization is that which will allow it constantly to offer the products and services that the markets require, and according to terms and conditions which the local customers and governments find acceptable. As we will see, market conditions and governmentally imposed regulations are subject to regular change. Long-term profitability depends upon the organization's ability to anticipate and, if possible, avoid such restrictions. The operational data collection process should highlight the likely imposition of such restrictive measures in time for the organization to take action.

The market information and analysis process will be discussed in more depth in Unit 5.

Models to assist in the assessment of risk and opportunity

There are a number of models that have been devised over recent years in order to help organizations assess the opportunity/risk in international markets. This workbook is not designed to be a complete international marketing textbook so we have not analysed or explained the most popular models here. As part of your preparation for the Diploma exams you will need to be reading widely and from the recommended texts you will be able to identify the various approaches and advantages/disadvantages of each of these models. The models you may come across might include:

- The Sheth–Lutz model
- Business Environment Risk Index (BERI)
- Litvuk and Banting model
- Good, New and Hausz model
- Gilligan & Hird model
- Harrell & Kiefer model

In your studies you are likely to encounter a number of different models which apply to various areas of international marketing. You should bear in mind when assessing these models that many have been developed not with a larger view of international or global strategy in mind but to meet the specific needs of a particular market or industry or product sector. Greatest success is likely to come if you are able to tap into the models at a conceptual level, understanding what they mean in broad strategic terms rather than treating them as a blueprint for guaranteed success under any circumstances. Often you will find that blending one or two models will give you a greater insight into the existence (or not) of international marketing opportunities for your organization or the case study.

EXAM QUESTION

> In reviewing the international capability of a company, what competencies would you expect to find and who would you expect to be delivering those competencies? (December 1994)
> (**See** Exam answers at the end of this unit.)

Summary

In this unit we have seen that there are a number of very good reasons why organizations may decide to 'go international'. The opportunities and potential profits for an organization can often be quite sizeable. At the same time, there are some significant risks in such operations, particularly foreign exchange risk and political risk. In any event, some detailed market research and analysis is required in order to uncover likely marketplace opportunities for the organization and a range of models exist to help you in this evaluation process.

One final word of warning is that you should bring some common sense to bear on the market research data when available. The data analysis and scanning may identify gaps in the marketplace – the international marketer has to decide whether there is a market in the gap!

Questions

As a check on your understanding of what has been covered in this unit, consider the following questions:

- What are the main reasons that an organization might consider going international?
- How might intense domestic competition encourage an organization to develop markets abroad?
- How can we apply the concept of the product life cycle (PLC) in international business?
- What are the two main forms of financial risk in international business?
- What are the two particular management decisions that research can help support?
- What are the two types of international data that might be collected by an organization?

For a more detailed review of international opportunities, read:
International Marketing S. Paliwoda and M. Thomas, Butterworth-Heinemann, 1998.
International Marketing Strategy I. Doole, R. Lowe and C. Phillips, Routledge, 1997.

EXAM ANSWERS

December 1993 A multinational enterprise (MNE) is an organization with marketing activities in more than one country. It will have direct investment in at least one other country in addition to the home country. These direct investments would include sales and distribution facilities and might include production plants. The Japanese car manufacturers Nissan and Toyota have invested in the UK to set up the manufacture of cars. The multinational enterprise (MNE) will gain its profits and sales from more than one country. It will gain profits and sales from a variety of sources. Product sales, remittance of profits from subsidiary companies and licensing revenues are three possible sources. The MNE will have a level of experience in international business which is usually in excess of smaller companies whose experience of international marketing is limited to the physical movement of goods across country boundaries (exporting).

The factors that influence an MNE to export can be divided into internal and external factors.

Internal factors

The MNE may wish to concentrate production in certain countries for cost and logistics reasons. In their case it will export products to the countries in which it is not producing.

Lower costs are generally obtainable through economies of scale and through the experience curve effects. The concentration production in a limited number of countries will encourage standardization and the associated lowering of unit production costs. In the past the tendency for MNEs to operate with a polycentric orientation encouraged a multi-location approach in which adaptation to country markets became the norm. If this extent of adaption occurred, it would reduce partially or completely the benefits of the increased scale of production.

Logistics reasons would encourage the export of goods to countries that are physically close or to those countries where established modes of transport allow the efficient movement of products.

In addition to cost and logistics, the MNE is concerned with risk management. It is risky to invest in certain countries. For these countries the mode of market entry is safer through exporting. If things go wrong the MNE loses its products but does not suffer the much greater costs of losing its investment in sales and distribution or production facilities.

Senior Examiner's comments

The answer shows a range of factors that influence MNEs. MNEs are large companies but they will be involved in export activities from some countries. The amount of exporting will be influenced by a number of corporate decisions related to production cost and risk management. The decisions on standardization/adaptation and the type of organizational culture (for example, geocentric or polycentric) will have an influence on the number of production plants around the world and will influence the extent to which exporting rather than host country marketing will be used by the MNE.

December 1994 **Note to candidates**: This is a very broad-based question and it can be tackled from a number of perspectives. One approach is to consider the question from the perspective of a modest exporter, whilst another might take the viewpoint of a multinational or global corporation. Either is acceptable. What is essentially required is an **understanding** that to succeed internationally the firm must have competencies distinctive from those required to operate domestically. How these are expressed if of less importance. In this respect this is a 'catch-all' question that allows candidates to write either in general or specific terms.

International competencies	*Responsibility for delivering*
• Commitment	The main board of directors
• Flexibility	The HQ management team
• Strategic thinking	Senior international management to main board level
• Cultural adaptability	Local management level
• Recognition of SRC	At headquarters
• Languages	Divisional HQ management training
• Personnel	Strategically at HQ
	Tactically locally
• Finance objectives/prudence	Established at HQ
• P&L responsibility	Local management team
• International controls	Performance standards set at HQ
	Monitoring and control, local implementation
• International information	Local implementation
• International experience	Both HQ and local management

An additional competence is the ability to recognize what it is that the company can provide and what else needs to be bought in, e.g. skills and expertise in appointing professional collaborators ranging from the appointment of distributors to the management of international advertising campaigns.

Note: It is anticipated that many candidates will add to this list. What is important is not just to write a list but to explain to the examiner why the points made are important in developing international expertise.

The importance of international marketing

In this unit we highlight the growing importance of international marketing and the changes that are accelerating its importance. Understanding the changes that are underpinning the development of world trade – events that are shaping everyone's life wherever they might live and work. In this unit you will:

- Appreciate the growth and scale of world trade.
- Consider just how 'international' our everyday lives are

- Understand the macro forces at work shaping the business world of today and the future.
- Study the factors that are increasingly important in defining success.

Having completed the unit you will be able to:

- Identify the key drivers in world trade
- Appreciate what is creating convergence in consumer behaviour
- Understand the changes in international business
- Recognize that domestic horizons are increasingly meaningless in the fast-changing 'global village'.

International marketing does not begin or end with the activities of the firm – it happens within the environment. Whereas companies and individuals have a sound understanding of their domestic or home market, few take sufficient time to consider events worldwide. It is these that are the basic business drivers and will make increasing impact on the domestic firm. The term 'global village' is familiar to many – that it has arrived and what its impact might mean (in terms of opportunities and threats) has been considered in depth by few. From an examination perspective Syllabus '94 requires candidates to have a broad view of the macro/strategic forces in the world marketplace.

Much of what is considered in this unit is not necessarily contained in the recommended textbooks. International business and the marketing ramifications appear daily as news. Good students will buy a quality daily newspaper and create a file (or series of files) covering key events in, for example, Europe, South-east Asia, North America. From time to time all the quality press run features on countries (e.g. South Korea). Keep these – they are useful references to be used as examples in support of your answers.

Understanding changes in international business factors underpinning international and global marketing

The 1990s saw the world trade in goods accelerate – rising by more than 12 per cent per annum. A comparison with earlier years shows a clear upward trend and, despite the current recession in South East Asia, there seems no reason to suppose that growth will not continue.

World trade in services – financial services, travel and tourism, banking etc. referred to as 'invisible trade', although lower in value than visible goods, is set to grow even faster. The global market for financial derivatives has doubled to £20 million in only 2 years. Even education is an important service export with approximately 50 per cent of CIM Diploma candidates studying overseas and increasingly UK students are studying for part of their degree in foreign countries.

These figures in themselves represent meaningless statistics to most of us. Perhaps a more meaningful perspective of the impact of the international and global market can be taken from an observation of our lives. Look at it this way:

Woken in the morning by Sony alarm radio, usually hurrying through toiletry routine using on the way a Bic razor, Gillette foam, Imperial Leather soap, Head & Shoulders shampoo and Colgate toothpaste. Gulping down a cup of Nescafé and rushing through a bowl of Kelloggs cereal, donning a Hugo Boss suit and setting off for work in a BMW. On arrival, checking the NEC fax machine, switch on the IBM clone and get working.

The description could easily continue with what is a pretty mundane everyday life but the point is that executives are surrounded by international products produced by multinational or global corporations. The products portrayed are the fabric of many people's lives. Furthermore, entertainment and leisure is also similarly inclined, be it a Hollywood movie, a foreign holiday or even a 'foreign meal' (this could include McDonald's and Coca-Cola); usually wearing Levis and Timberland shoes.

What's actually going on here? It's evident that internationalism is all-embracing. The description above is not exclusive to the UK. Any international executive can observe the same broad activity taking place. There are no national boundaries or chauvinistic tendencies at work here. This is the 'global village' in action! Why is this so?

Macro factors in international marketing

The 'global village' – a phrase coined in the 1970s – has arrived and it is here to stay. It's a relatively new phenomenon. After all, Levitt penned his now classic article on Globalization as recently as 1983 and even today many still challenge his views (rightly). The 1960s saw the massive development of multinational companies but at that stage they were more concerned with acquisition and geographical spread than the internationalization of the marketing of their products/services. International marketing, management and control is a later development for most, i.e. treating large sections (or regions) of the world and addressing consumers' needs on the basis of similarities. The forces underpinning the rapid development of international marketing can be summarized as follows.

Population explosion

The world population is growing faster than at any time. The UN population fund estimates the current world population as 5.7 billion and projects this will rise rapidly to 7.1 billion within 20 years. Cold statistics such as these never seem to register much but consider the growth as equivalent to the creation of a city such as Los Angeles every 5–6 six weeks – that's arround 5–6 million a month! Setting aside the obvious implications in terms of over-population and the resultant strain on the world's resources, in marketing terms this means more consumers, potentially bigger markets and profits. But this growth is not uniform. Post-industrial countries have stabilized their population while others are growing at an accelerating rate. The British with an average family size of 2 children is effectively 7 + children at a global level. Fast-growing populations are reflected in growing demand which stimulates rapid economic growth. A good example of this is Thailand and Malaysia, where much of the 8–10 per cent annual growth rate is internal and not export driven. So from an international perspective why aren't you considering operating in these fast-growing markets? Tom Peters wrote recently: 'The population of Indonesia is edging close to 200 million. Is your company represented there? If not – why not?' Instead, companies focus their efforts on Hungary and other East European countries, failing completely to capture the main business opportunities.

Increasing affluence

Not simply the rich are getting richer, but everybody's getting richer albeit with some notable exceptions and these, in the main, are in Africa. Global wealth is increasing and this is again reflected in higher demand. Increasing affluence and commercial dynamism has seen new nations such as Singapore overtake the UK in terms of GDP per head. Increasing affluence and demand simply means that consumers will actively seek choice with the result that competition is emerging as companies compete to win the battle for disposable income. Countries or at least large sections of them are moving into a world away from commodity purchase – maize or rice – into consumer goods, i.e. packaged and marketed to their citizens' personal needs.

A one-world youth culture

Population and affluence together with other macro forces has helped create a 'one-world youth culture'. In many countries, particularly the newly industrialized countries (NICs) more than half the population is pre-adult, creating one of the world's biggest single market – the youth market. Everywhere adolescents project worldwide cultural icons – Niké, Coke, Marlborough, Benetton, Sony Walkman, Michael Jackson and now Sega, Nintendo, etc. This is new, it is only just beginning in the timescale of new 'market' development. Ten years from now when 'virtual reality' is commonplace the one-world youth culture market will exceed all others as a general category for marketers. Parochial, local and ethnic growth products will, with exceptions, cease to exist. We will have created the global youth village. I recently heard that one US toy manufacturer tested new products on over 1000 children a week to determine their opinions and in the last five years or so Toys 'R' Us have spread across much of the world (or at the very least the key nations).

An additional viewpoint is that one of the international icons of the last 5 or 6 years, the pop star Madonna, has virtually made a market for herself by symbolizing current cultural status – Madonna the Material Girl. An offshoot from this is that women's role and their perception is changing rapidly just about everywhere. Not everyone (governments or religions) approves but the changing role of women is going to be a powerful force for change. It is happening here. I would guess there are more female brand managers than male and the trend is continuing upwards.

Global consumers

As an offshoot from the previous point, older consumers will be increasingly non-national in their identity – not from their personal identity, as I am sure the Scots will remain Scottish and the French will likewise resolve to hang on to their cultural heritage, but from the perspective of the consumable fabric of their lives; driving increasingly international cars, watching international programmes on television, using international hardware and software, one of which may have little or no 'nationality' in terms of corporate ownership. (Does anyone know or care that Reebok sneakers are American-owned, made in South Korea?) This general point has been made earlier, i.e. that our whole lives are taken up with global corporations and that we are global consumers to a greater or lesser degree. International consumption is accelerating and boundaries of product ownership are increasingly blurred.

ACTIVITY 2.1

To reinforce the points made so far, wander around your home and list how many international products or services are part of your everyday life. Give thought as to where they come from ie country of origin. Ask yourself the question 'Could I get by without international products/services?

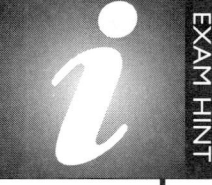

EXAM HINT

Very frequently examiners ask questions demanding that you demonstrate your knowledge via examples. So, at the end of this unit or major activity, write down examples and commit them to memory. This will save you desperately trying to 'think on the spot' in the examination. International Marketing Strategy, on average, requires more examples than, say, Planning and Control.

Multinationals and transnational/global corporations

The message here is again simple. The big are getting bigger. Consider the following. The top 500 world corporations account for

- 30 per cent of gross global product
- 70 per cent of global trade
- 80 per cent of international investment

Stop! Don't just gloss over these figures. five hundred – that's a very small number of firms who dominate the world. Take the figure of 80 per cent of international investment. That leaves practically nothing in terms of global investment for other companies (some of them large). For example, how many UK companies are there in the top 500 world corporations? What hope do small companies have? Plenty, providing they are extraordinarily special. Without being special and occupying a particular niche they have little hope to succeed on a large scale into the next century. That small firms will succeed is stating the obvious – but the leap from small to large will be more difficult.

Here's another powerful fact. The UN Conference on Trade and Development (1994) found that sales from transnational corporations were now worth $4,800 billion – bigger than total national trade – and formed the productive core of the globalizing world economy. Furthermore, 65% of the parent firms were from 14 wealthy countries, concentrating economic power in even fewer hands. In addition, the top 100 firms control over one-third of the world stock of direct foreign investment. Six companies control 63 per cent of all aluminium production, and in general (there are always exceptions) the major primary and secondary markets for products and services are dominated by a handful of multinational or transnational organizations.

A third and final fact for the moment, for we intend to return and discuss multinationals later:

$1 trillion cross national boundaries daily

Money is a commodity, traded 24 hours a day. It has no home and is the fuel of international business.

ACTIVITY 2.2

Write a list of multinational/global corporations. What products/services are they famous for?

Shrinking communications

Nowhere and nobody is far away! Take a walk down your High Street. Check out your local travel agent. Bali, Mexico, Beijing are now as commonplace as Benidorm, Marbella and Blackpool. Check the prices. Even impecunious students frequently return from the summer break having visited India, Thailand, California, etc. Winter holidays in skiing resorts now challenge the traditional summer break. We are international in terms of our travelling. As a guest lecturer, I frequently travel to Singapore for the weekend. Fax, mobile phones and other technology-led creations keep us constantly in touch anywhere in the world. (Incidentally, for the record, the fax machine has been around for 100 years or so – that's how they transmitted the 'Wanted Dead or Alive' posters in the Wild West. It is modern technology that has miniaturized it to a desktop communications tool.)

We do not labour the point that communications are breaking down narrow local thinking in international business. British Airways operates its worldwide 'exceptional request' facility such as wheelchair assistance needed for a passenger from a centre in Bombay. Indian universities are turning out computer-literate graduates by the hundred. They are intelligent, capable and keen and they are inexpensive to hire as is local property to rent. The cost of transmitting data processing from London to Bombay, a distance of some 7000 miles, is no more than sending the same information 7 miles. It is suggested that British Airways plans to run its worldwide ticketing operation from Bombay soon. This has serious implications for the owners of high-rise and expensive tower blocks in the suburbs of London. There is no earthly reason why Barclays Bank, shall we say, shouldn't do much of its data processing in New Delhi. (India, incidentally, is now the No. 2 producer of computer disks.) Dell Computers, by the way, has its European helpline in Ireland. Just use the 0800 number.

Communication companies are taking the lead in global development. It is no accident that Atlanta was chosen to host the 1996 Olympic Games. Atlanta's competitive advantage over other cities bidding for the Games was that it was the home of Ted Turner's organization CNN – a company you'd never heard of 10 years ago. CNN offered global communications and transmisson of events more efficiently than by the alternative route of negotiating with separate countries with their 'local' television networks.

Today tourism is probably the world's No. 1 industry. Growing affluence and cheaper/ faster communications have revolutionized what was until recently the pastime of the relatively rich. For the UK, tourism accounts for 12% of economic output and 12.5% of employment – £100 billion a year and 3 million jobs. New growth world-wide will come from affluent Asians. Being the fastest growing region in the world, it is believed that within just 3 years 500 million newly affluent middle-class tourists from China and the Pacific will be on the move, spending their newly acquired disposable income.

The information revolution

Following on from shrinking communications it is apparent that information is power. At the touch of a button we can access information on the key factors that determine our business. News is a 24-hour a day service. (Each morning my radio informs me of the US, German and Japanese currency rates and world trading fortunes.) Manufacturers wanting to know the price of coffee beans or the relevant position of competitors in terms of their share price or in terms of new product activity have it at their immediate disposal.

Another factor for consideration. Newly emerging countries are abandoning thoughts of investing in land-based technology for communications. The technology of satellite communication has made land cables and telephone lines redundant. The telephone has leapfrogged technology and enabled developing countries to catch up and even be ahead!

Time! The competitive differential

To succeed in tomorrow's even busier crowded world market, success will come from firms that can adapt to change. The past (and present) is full of firms that aren't going to make it. Cantor wrote: 'In the future we will all have to enjoy dancing on the moving carpet.' Note, Cantor does not say dance on the moving carpet but enjoy dancing. *The Economist* recently said something pretty sensational: 'The humbling of big firms has only just begun.' The future lies in the hands of the flexible organization that sees time as its competitive differential. Today's crowded marketplace has little place or sympathy for me-toos. Ever fickle consumers (that's you and me) are demanding new, interesting products. Tom Peters recently spoke of buying his first lap-top computer. He took it home and showed it proudly to his 26-year-old son who replied: 'Dad, you bought one of the old ones (practically an antique), it's been out four months already!' Well, Peters told it as a joke but the thought behind it was deadly serious.

Bill Gates has come from a zero base to being the richest man in the world via the creation of Microsoft. He knows that without huge investment in R&D, and just as importantly in intelligent and imaginative thinking of what the world might be like 10 years hence, his business could be blown away as fast as it arrived.

For those organizations who slavishly follow current marketing theories about focusing on lowest cost, a word of warning. Just think of how the biggest and most cost-effective producer of radio and television valves felt when somebody discovered the transistor.

ACTIVITY 2.3

Select an area where technology is leading product development. Try to identify a company/product that made a breakthrough in the way Sony did 10 years ago with its Walkman. Work out how long it took for competitors to imitate.

Global product standardization

This is really one of the outcomes of the macrofactors underpinning the rapid evolution and development of international marketing. The opening to this chapter aptly demonstrated the recent spread of global products. Levitt in his 1983 article on Globalization describes modernity as the technological driving force towards the world of global products. True enough, but it is the speed of technological advancement that is the initiator of standardization. Microsoft Windows, for example, has universal application. Soon other newly emergent technological standards will make their impact and, being new, will form the single standard(s) for the next century. In service technologies and telecommunications it is inevitable that global standards will prevail. Following on, software and other spin-offs will also adopt a world standard approach from the outset.

Take the position of multinational organizations. They will be the organizations that will dictate the adoption of standardized hardware and software applications so that their information and reporting systems will be standardized from Argentina to Zimbabwe. Most multinationals already have standardized systems in operation.

World brands

Everybody is now familiar with world brands. Examples abound. However, they are, in the main, a new phenomenon. Microsoft, Sega, Nintendo, McDonald's, Niké, etc. did not straddle the world 10 years ago, or even 5 years ago in the case of Sega and Nintendo. The creation of World Brands is a relatively new development. The point is that world brand development is in its infancy, not its maturity. To quote a famous former US president, 'You ain't seen nothing yet!'

It is safe to say that 10 years from now, one quarter of the world brands will be for companies you may never have heard of today. The leaders of this development will come from the world of communications. I've already spoken briefly of CNN and they're just one of dozens of global communication companies that will develop over the next decade (e.g. Viacom).

EXAM HINT

Write down a list of world brands. There is frequently a question on globalization in the examination.

Urbanization

Changing tack for a minute. We've discussed population and affluence. There is another change occurring in this area, the rise of urbanization. With some exceptions in the post-industrial world, populations are migrating from the countryside to the city seeking work and hoped-for prosperity. The world is moving into gigantic conurbations. The population of Greater Tokyo is soon to be close to 30 million; Mexico, 15 million already. Cities such as Lagos, Buenos Aires and Djakarta will outstrip cities such as Paris, London, Rome if they haven't already done so. Currently no European city appears in the top 12, and by the year 2015 none will be in the top 30, all of which will almost certainly have populations in excess of 10 million. By voting with their feet, 17 of the world's mega cities of 10 million plus will be in the Third World. This has powerful implications for marketers. Urbanization equates to simplifying the marketing environment. Urban dwellers require similar products (packaged conveniently and easy to carry). Similarly, they demand services (telephones and transportation of all kinds – commercial vehicles, buses, trains, taxis etc.). Additionally, they crave modern visual communications such as television. Obviously I could continue. The second spin-off of urbanization is, of course, that customers are accessible. We know where they are and can communicate with them efficiently via supermarkets and advertising and other marketing communication tools.

ACTIVITY 2.4

Consider, from a marketing perspective, the significance of a nation's population growth to the international marketer. Identify countries with the fastest-growing population (in overall terms and also in percentage growth) and compare them with some of the world's stable populations)

Global capital

The point has essentially been made. Money is sourced from anywhere round the world. To quote Kenichi Ohmae – money is a truly global product. It has no direct home and money lives in a borderless world. For students of globalization, Ohmae's book, *The Borderless World*, is essential reading.

Consider next the flow of international funds. The emergence of China has radically altered world capital flows. US investment in China has progressed thus:

1992	1993
$11 billion	$111 billion

You don't have to calculate the percentage to see the rate of growth over one year alone. The USA is not the only country investing in China. All the major industrial countries are pouring in money. But hold on, money is limited – it's not in an inexhaustible supply so capital flowing into China must mean capital (or potential capital at least) not flowing into other countries. So China's gain might be the UK's loss as US corporations globalize and move to where production is cheap and efficient. There is no doubt that China's gain is hampering the regeneration of Russia and Eastern Europe.

The enormous infusion of capital into China has helped make it the world's third largest economy in 1994 (after purchasing power – parity adjustment) United States and Japan topping the league.

Globalization of marketing skills

Time was when marketing skills were in the hands of a few well-educated individuals in Western countries. How things have changed. Goldstar, Samsung, Daewoo from South Korea and Proton from Malaysia have all captured marketing know-how. The introduction of Proton cars into the UK has proven to be the most successful new car company launch ever. Certainly they needed our help but the strategic thinking was theirs. Marketing skills are becoming universal business tools. Around half of the CIM Diploma candidates are non-UK based.

Development of world technologies and global industries

This point has largely been dealt with under the headings, Global product standardization, World brands and with reference to multinationals and the information revolution. But it is worth noting that corporations are simplifying their manufacturing operations to take advantage of convergence of global consumer needs. Ford, for example, in its Project 2000 initiative is concentrating its production into five critical regions each of which is coordinated in its development of a world car. This is not to say that they intend to build one single global vehicle but that the technology underpinning production and operation will have worldwide application.

Strategic and transnational cooperation/Corporate mergers and acquisitions

Not a week goes by without some announcement in the quality press of a strategic alliance. Although disagreement exists on the precise definition of a strategic alliance (e.g. are they long-term commitments or stop-gap tactics?) it is safe to say that developments in the modern business world will proceed faster if major organizations cooperate rather than seeking breakthroughs on their own.

The sheer cost of creating technological innovation, the development time involved, and the marketing and distribution costs preclude many companies from going it alone. Instead they form partnership agreements often developing value chains (see Porter for value chain structures)) for the purpose of achieving competitive advantages. Toshiba has strategic alliances with Motorola, Olivetti, AT&T, RSI Logic Corporation, General Electric, Siemens, and probably others.

The basis for alliances is not to subvert competition but rather to create additional value to each firm's offering as it finds its own individual position in the marketplace. Why spend billions perfecting flat-screen technology for computers and televisions when you can cooperate with others in its development, which can be exploited by all parties involved in the strategic alliance?

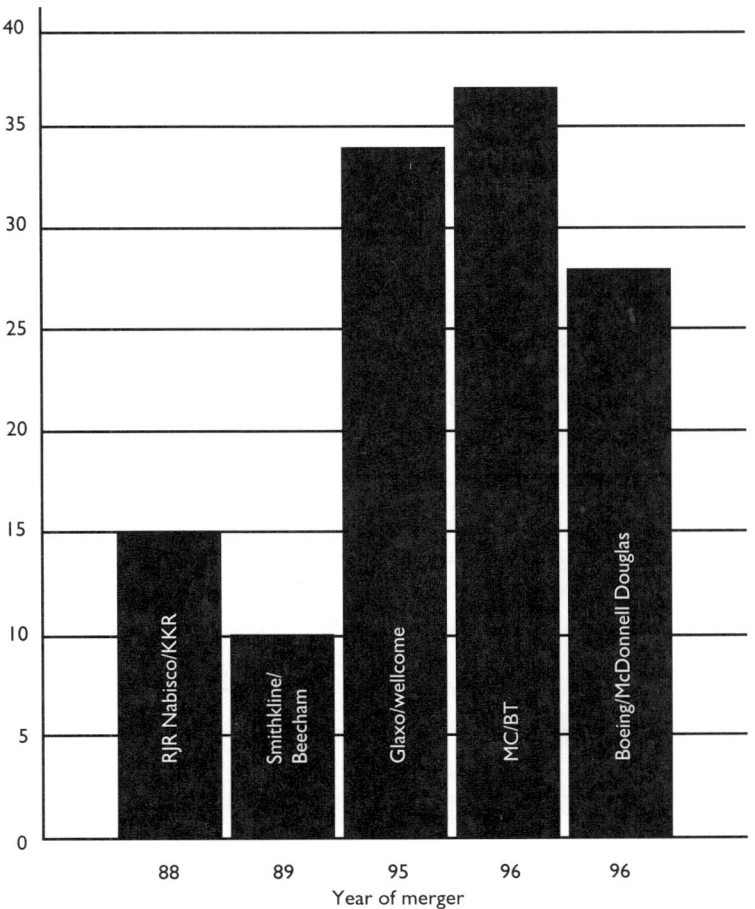

Figure 2.1 World's largest mergers (£bn) (*Source*: *The Guardian*)

Adding further fuel to the debate, the seemingly never-ending business development of acquisitions and mergers will inevitably drive convergence. For example, Boeing and McDonnell Douglas are creating a merger that could steamroller world aircraft competition.

EXAM HINT

It is essential that you identify recent examples of strategic alliances. This area is a high-profile topic in International Marketing and knowing what is going on can gain valuable marks. The source for this information is not the textbooks but the quality newspapers.

Some examples of the basis of alliance include:

- Technology swaps
- R&D development
- Manufacturing (e.g. the development of a common car platform for Saab, Fiat and Lancia)
- Distribution relationships
- Cross-licensing
- Marketing relationships
- Government cooperation

Government cooperation can now be added to strategic alliance in that in the move towards regionalization (e.g. the European Union) has developed several instances of government cooperation. The most celebrated of these is the European Airbus created to challenge the global domination of the passenger aircraft industry by Boeing.

Success factors in strategic alliances are:

- Alliances survive as long as each party regards the other as its best partner. Ideally (though this is seldom achieved) some equity ought to be exchanged. But key factors include
- Mutual need. This is more important than who controls the alliance (or think they control it). Each partner must take whatever steps it can to ensure that the other continues to need mutual benefit.
- Shared objective. Agreement reached on what it is they intend to 'maximize' together.
- Shared risk. No loading of the risks onto one partner.
- Relationship and trust. This is the heart of the alliance, but companies don't invest enough in building trust – which takes years. Honda were particularly upset at British Aerospace's decision to sell Rover cars to BMW after 15 years of close cooperation. Alarmingly, for UK companies, the Japanese as an industrial nation will have taken close note of this behaviour by a major British firm.

EXAM QUESTION

Identify the key changes that have occurred in the international trading environment in the last decade. To what degree have their changes affected the strategies adopted by companies involved in international trade? Illustrate your answer with specific examples (December 1994, Question 5).

(**See** Exam answers at the end of this unit.)

Summary

Having read this unit you should be in no doubt that international marketing is a driving force in developing world trade. Fewer firms can restrict their thinking to the narrow confines of domestic marketing. International influences are affecting everyone's behaviour. Reliance on a 'home' market can only be sustainable where government protection prevails

– and that is in decline. Facing up to international trends in planning for inward competition is an essential prerequisite of every organization.

Questions

To check on your understanding of what has been covered consider the following questions:

- Why is international marketing so important to UK firms?
- Identify five prominent UK companies seriously involved in worldwide marketing. Choose one, preferably one close to your town/city. Study the comments made by the chairman about international marketing – examine its importance to the firm.
- In what way is your life, particularly your business career, related to development on international marketing? Think personally on how events might shape your future career. What will your firm/industry look like 5 or even 10 years from now?
- The big are getting bigger – the paradox is that this leaves more opportunities for small, nimble organizations to prosper. Identify a industry (market). Plot the shapers in terms of macro factors, then see if you can come up with ideas for niche operators.

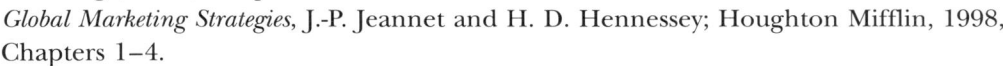

For a more detailed study of this unit read:

International Marketing Strategy, I. Doole, R. Lowe and C. Phillips, Routledge, 1997, Chapter 2.
Global Marketing Strategies, J.-P. Jeannet and H. D. Hennessey; Houghton Mifflin, 1998, Chapters 1–4.
International Marketing, V. Terpstra and R. Sarathy; The Dryden Press, 1997, Chapters 1, 2, 18.
International Marketing, S. Paliwoda and M. Thomas, Butterworth-Heinemann, 1998, Chapter 1.
The quality press; *Financial Times, The Economist, The Guardian, The Times*, etc.

December 1994, Question 5 This is a wide-ranging question, designed to allow candidates to express their knowledge of an awareness of the major/macro factors influencing world trade. Answers should, however, respond directly to the question and be structured into two key areas:

(a) key changes
(b) influences of the changes on marketing strategies.

Your answer must be supported by examples if it is to gain a good grade.

Key changes

- Phenomenal growth in international trade, 7.5% per annum over the past decade.
- Fast growth of services, already up to 25% of world trade. Services are growing faster than products
- Changes in composition of world trade with its developments of the trade markets. Western Europe accounts for 46%, Asia 22%, North America 17%, i.e. 85% of world trade. Consider carefully where future growth is coming from, i.e. Asian Tigers/NICs.

Forces at work
A good answer will discuss the forces underpinning this position and discuss (briefly) each of the following:

- Global consumers
- Multinationals

- Shrinking communication gaps
- Global product standardization
- Growth of world technologies
- Globalization of marketing skills
- Growth of regionalism
- Transnational industrial cooperation

Institutions underpinning the growth

- GATT, renamed WTO (World Trade Organization)
- IMF
- World Bank
- etc.

It is important to include a brief paragraph on the role and significance of these three key institutions, recognizing their contribution to the liberalization of world trade.

Influences on marketing strategies

Factors that should be considered include:

- Greater financial freedom
- Influences concerning siting of subsidiaries, e.g. low cost/labour locations versus high skill locations
- Influences on broader sourcing away from national sourcing towards regional and even global supply
- Wider range of markets – former Comecon, China, India
- Increasing range of market entry possibilities
- Separation of functions – development of NPD and operational processing into South East Asia

All of this should be supported by relevant examples, e.g. British Airways is moving its ticket processing to India and ICL computers is also relocating its 0800 helpline to India, where skilled computer technicians earn less than their UK counterparts.

Patterns of world trade

The preceding unit outlined the major forces that underpin world trade. This unit reviews patterns of world trade and the key institutions that are important in facilitating its development. In doing so the unit:

- Presents a brief overview of world trade – this examines the linkages between nations
- Considers the balance between exports versus imports among the world's leading nations
- Reviews the development towards regionalization and the possible creation of the Triad economies
- Considers the position and growth of China and, briefly, India as they advance towards being key players in the future world economy
- Briefly comment on the impact and relevance of the EU. (Candidates should be well versed and knowledgeable in the development of the EU. Therefore it is proposed not to consider this important item in this text.)
- Reviews the facilitators of world trade.

Upon completion of the unit you will be able to:

- Explain the essential balance of trade between the key trading nations.
- Discuss potential future developments and the impact of the emergence of new giant economies.
- Debate whether regionalism will be a force for good or bad.
- Understand barriers to trade and their impact.
- Initiate discussion on the role of the key facilitating agencies, (e.g. GATT/WTO) and relate their relevance to the nation state and the individual firm.

STUDY GUIDE

Nation trades with nation. They exchange values. It is extremely useful to understand in outline the balance and, indeed, the overall scale of world trade. It has increased faster than the rate of increase of most individual countries. We consider the issues of impediments to its growth – which in effect are impediments to our continual prosperity as a nation. In your study you will realize the importance of the continued interaction of trade between nations.

STUDY TIP

Though the unit contains some data on size and movements, etc. it is important that students read widely around this unit as support to their study. The cutting edge of discussion and decision is in the daily press. All the subjects raised here are intensely topical. Make sure you are abreast of development.

Start today by building a series of files created by cutting articles from the quality press. Create two sorts of files:

1 *Country files*   Here it is a good idea to build information on types of countries, e.g. NICs, Third World countries, advanced industrialized nations. For example, frequently the quality press e.g. *The Times,* will have features on South Korea, India, China, Nigeria, Mexico, etc. This information base will be of considerable value if you use it as an example.

2 *Activity files*   Create a series of headings relating to this unit. (e.g. The European Union, GATT/WTO. World wage comparisons, International mergers, etc.). Once again this will be a helpful aid in the examination in addition to building your knowledge from a work perspective.

Nations trade with nations

Countries, like individuals, are not completely self-sufficient; they exchange 'values' – goods, services, money, etc. We have already highlighted that foreign goods are indispensable to living standards everywhere. However, there is considerable variation among countries concerning the scale of and their reliance on international trade. Table 3.1 illustrates some of the gaps between imports and exports.

The table makes interesting reading for it shows the internal economy as the real engine of growth for the two major countries which are largely self-reliant. It shatters or seriously dents the myth that Japan is a nation of exporters. Germany is the world No. 1 exporting country. Obviously, smaller nations (e.g. Holland and Belgium) have to export and import in order to survive. They cannot specialize in everything. Similarly, many developing countries have a high export and import ratio in their economy.

Table 3.1   Import and exports as percentage of GDP, 1990 estimate $billion

	GDP	Imports/GDP %	Exports/GDP %
Industrialized countries			
USA	5550	9	7
Japan	2932	8	9
Germany	1617	21	25
Holland	272	47	48
Switzerland	228	32	29
Developing countries			
Korea	235	30	28
Mexico	230	12	11

Source: EIU, January 1991

Table 3.2   Leading Exporters of Commercial Services 1988 (% of Total Exports)

USA	22
France	26
UK	25
West Germany	12
Italy	21
Japan	11
South Korea	13
Mexico	21

Source: *The Economist,* 1990

But services are also an important and rapidly expanding part of world trade, accounting for approximately 20 per cent of total exports. Services account for around 60 per cent of GDP in the UK and the figure for USA exceeds 70 per cent (and over 75 per cent of US employment is in services).

At the recent GATT/WTO round pressure mounted to bring services into the agreement but it failed. But it is anticipated that services will at some stage be incorporated into the set of principles.

Growth in world trade: the Triad economies and regionalism

Growth in world trade has been discussed earlier but the principle of free trade as evolved under GATT/WTO has led to the building of country interdependence. With the world fast becoming a 'global village' current thinking is that the faster-growing and most dynamic trading nations will join together in a series of regional trading areas. This has been under development for the past 25 years. The European Union is the most familiar but others include ASEAN (Singapore, Malaylsia, Indonesia, Thailand, Philippines, Brunei and latterly Vietnam and Myanmar) and NAFTA (the USA, Canada and Mexico – created in 1994). It is believed possible that by the end of the decade three 'super blocs' will emerge. The EU, the Americas, and South-east Asia. These three trading blocs are referred to as the Triad economies. Each bloc will develop its own internal market with varying degrees of political, economic and monetary union between the member states.

Figure 3.1 shows the development of three major trading blocks (with the rest of the world, included to illustrate the power of the Triad). The implication of this diagram is that the Triad economies now account for approximately 85 per cent of world trade growing from 70 per cent a decade ago. A further point for consideration is that around 90 per cent of world trade is accounted for by fourteen countries.

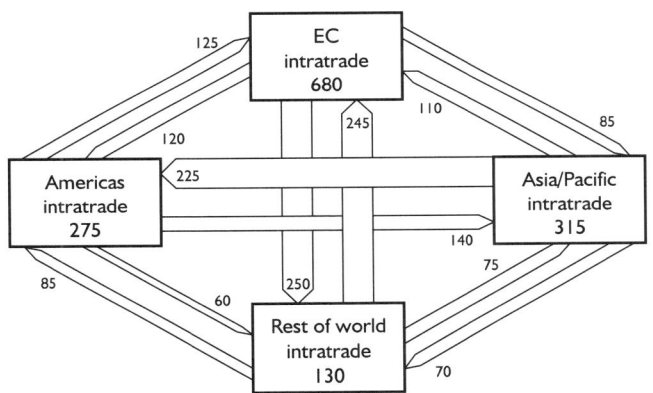

Figure 3.1 World trade flows, 1989 (billions of dollars). (*Source*: 'The world economy', *The Economist*, 5 January 1991, p. 22. © The Economist Newspaper Ltd. Reprinted with permission)

Figure 3.2 shows the distribution of trade (in goods) based on the value of export and imports of the different regions of the world. From this we see that Western Europe alone accounts for nearly 50 per cent of world trade volume with the EU accounting for 46 per cent of world trade. However, this proportion is expected to shift (downwards) as China and the Asian Tigers raise their performance from 12 per cent in 1993 to a likely 20 per cent (or more) a decade hence.

It is interesting and important to note the development of APEC – Asian Pacific Economic Council – embracing 18 member countries surrounding the Pacific Rim from New Zealand to Japan on the Western side of the ocean and Canada southwards to Chile on the Eastern Pacific. Currently differences exceed similarities to forge an agreement but the determination exists to create a vast trade free zone by 2010 – a date that is not far into the future in many companies' planning cycle, e.g. airplane manufacturers – the prime movers of both people and cultural assimilators.

Further examination of the Triad suggests that it is either going to fuel a rapid expansion of world trade or the opposite. The danger is the creation of a fortress mentality with each trading bloc being capable of producing, internally, virtually all its needs; it might well build

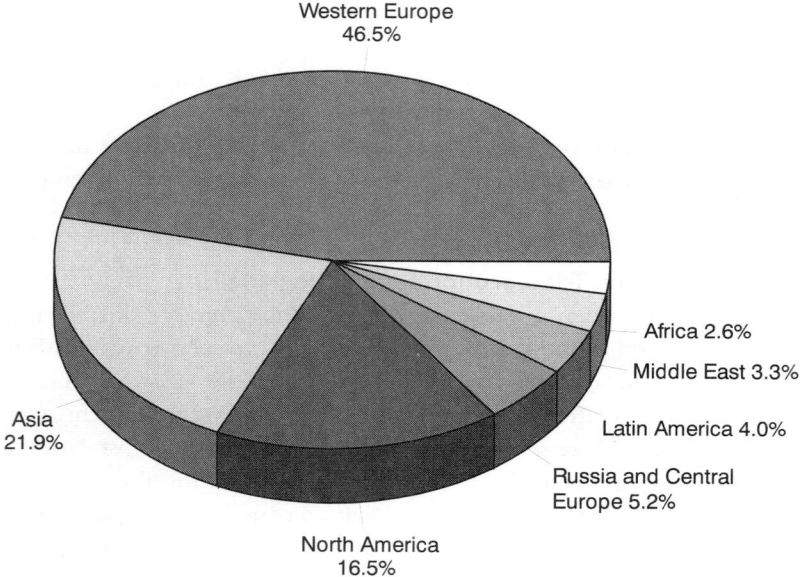

Figure 3.2 Distribution of international trade in goods, 1993. (*Source*: GATT)

barriers to prevent competition from eroding the economies and industrial bases of member states. However although this might be speculation, the long-term planning horizons for major industrial corporations needs to take all views into account.

ACTIVITY 3.1

Reread the data in the text so far. Grasp the importance of the scale of world trade.

Of the regions the EU is most familiar. Currently intratrade, i.e. trade between the 15 countries of the EU, accounts for approximately 70 per cent of EU trade and in the North American Free Trade Area (NAFTA) intratrade accounts for 42 per cent of all trade.

Data and information on the EU abound and students are expected to acquire knowledge of the scale and strength of the European economy and the advantages accruing from the establishment of the EU. For those who are unfamiliar, here is a list of the key benefits of the Single European Market:

- The removal of tariff barriers
- The removal of technical barriers
- The opening up of public procurement
- The free movement of labour
- The opening up of the professions
- The harmonization of financial services
- The removal of border transport documentation
- The removal of restrictions on capital flows
- The standardization of company law
- The removal of fiscal barriers
- More consistent environmental protection

ACTIVITY 3.2

To reinforce what has already been said it is imperative you create a file on the EU. The subject is topical and examinable.

Americas to establish largest free trade bloc

Monstrous disparities create a problem for treaty negotiators, **Martin Walker** in Miami reports

STILLING their suspicions of US economic and cultural dominance, its anti-immigration and drug control policies, the 33 other countries of North and South America agreed at the weekend to establish a Free Trade Area of the Americas.

They also decided to maintain its momentum with biennial summits, and to complete negotiations by 2005.

President Clinton, whose strategy is to place the US at the heart of the vast new trading blocs of the global economy, hailed the FTAA yesterday as a historic step that will create the world's largest market.

The US had to overcome its own doubts, and accept vaguely worded assurances on human and worker's rights, and on environmental protection, as the price of dominating the new economic order for the two continents.

But the unity on display among the 34 leaders in Miami disguised a monstrous disparity in size and in economic prospects, far sharper than the fast-track, slow-track divisions in

Europe. The North America Free Trade Agreement states — the US, Canada, Mexico and soon Chile — are the dominant and most developed partners, with about 40 per cent of the population of the two continents and more than 80 per cent of their wealth.

The multiplicity of treaties threatens to create a real Tower of Babel

Argentina and Brazil form a secondary weaker grouping, the Mercosur group, with which the EU is to open trade co-operation talks. Then comes the medium-sized economies like Columbia and Venezuela, the little ones like Peru and Ecuador, and finally the small fry of the Caribbean islands.

The 'Caribbean nations raised concerns that free trade not swamp their own industries nor hurt their access to US and

Canadian markets', a Canadian official said, 'Many of these economies are very fragile.'

They are particularly at risk from non-tariff barriers, like the legal suits being brought by US agribusiness against the privileged access of Caribbean bananas to Europe. The US trade representative, Mickey Kantor, had to promise an immediate review of the matter to stop the summit stalling.

A series of regional trade groupings like Nafta, Mercosur, the Andrean Pact, the Central American Common Market and Caricom, the Caribbean community, are in place, pursuing their own agendas and their own separate agreements with Japan, the Apec-Asia Pacific group, and the EU.

'This evident multiplicity of treaties, both bilateral and multi-lateral, threatens to create a real Tower of Babel for trade,' warned Chile's president, Eduardo Frei. The real job of the FTAA would be to integrate these regional groupings, he said, while also opening economies to the rest of the world.

'We have pledged that our FTAA will not raise new barriers to nations outside our region and will be fully consistent with the rules of the World Trade Organization,' President Clinton said yesterday.

Figure 3.3

It may be of interest that the North American Free Trade Area (NAFTA) established as recently as 1994 is planning to expand and become the Free Trade Area of the Americas (FTAA) by the year 2005, embracing 34 countries. In a decade it plans to be the world's largest market. The article shown in Figure 3.3 reinforces the point.

- Identify three different types of trading blocs in the world. Take one specific trading bloc and examine how changes that are taking place will influence marketing opportunities within and outside that trading bloc (June 1994, Question 10).
- For a trading group of your choice, discuss the likely changes in trading patterns between the trading group of countries and the rest of the world. How might these changes affect a company wishing to trade with some members of the group (December 1992, Question 10).

China

While on the subject of trading blocs it is worth exploring developments in China. This is probably more fruitful than a discussion on the future expansion of the 'Tiger' economies of South-east Asia (Singapore, Hong Kong, South Korea, etc.). Remember these countries' economies have been growing at an average rate of 8–10 per cent per annum for a decade or more compared with European countries' growth at less than half that rate. But successful though they are, they are all relatively small countries whereas China, the global giant in population, is about to surpass all known growth records. Its potential is awesome. To begin with, far from being a slowly emerging force, China is already the world's third largest economy. The IMF now calculating GDP in terms of a currency's purchasing power at home suggests that China outstrips all European countries. The article shown in Figure 3.4 shows this.

The message is again simple. The Pacific Rim is the region for the new millennium and it begs the question to UK companies. Are you there? If not, you'd better have a good reason

---

Zooming Up in the Charts

TWO WEEKS AGO, China had the 10th largest economy in the world. This week it junmps to third, behind the US and Japan. India, formerly No. 11, leaps to No. 6. Mexico climbs from No. 12 to No. 10.

What has been going on? A stunning advance in Third World productivity? The sudden arrival of a new Green Revolution in the agricultural sector? No, something more mundane but almost as far-reaching is taking place as the Washington-based International Monetary Fund switches to a different system for estimating the size of each country's economy. Those most affected are rapidly industrializing nations such as Mexico, Brazil, India, Indonesia and Thailand, and their upgraded status is likely to change perceptions of the world's economic balance of power. Says Robert Hormats, vice-chairman of Goldman Sachs International: 'This new accounting underscores in quantitative terms just how powerful China, India and other developing countries are today, both as markets and as competitors.'

The IMF's latest calculations replace an accounting technique that valued in US dollars the output of goods and services in every nation. That system, still widely used by economists as well as by multilateral lenders like the World Bank, produces swings in a country's gross national product, its total output of goods and services, every time the value of its currency

shifts in relation to the US dollar. If the Chilean peso, for example, loses 5 per cent of its value against the greenback, estimates of the country's growth – 10.4 per cent in 1992 – are automatically reduced by the amount of the devaluation, as is the economy's total size. When currencies are kept in an artificial relation to the dollar, as in many of Asia's developing economies, wild distortions can occur. By the dollar-based method, the economic output of Asia, excluding Japan, accounts for only 7.3 per cent of the world total, less than the Asian share of 10 years ago. 'That's absurd given that Asia is the fastest growing region of the world,' a senior IMF official points out. Distortions of that sort argued for a change.

The IMF's new gauge relies on 'purchasing-power parity,' a means of calculating national income that many economists believe should have been put into practice long ago. Rather than GNP being measured in dollars, a national basket of goods and services encompassing the likes of transport, food, clothing and shelter is tallied in local currency and compared with purchasing power of similar goods and services in other parts of the world. This method provides a more accurate assessment of the value of what each person is able to buy, a figure that is multiplied by a country's total population to reach an estimate of national output. Using this standard, the IMF pegs China's output at $1.7

trillion last year, far above the $400 billion used in earlier estimates China's per capita income rises from $370 to $1600. Taken as a whole, the developing world's share of global output expands from 18 per cent to 34 per cent.

While the higher IMF estimates may be better yardsticks of economic progress, they have also aroused Third World concern that some hard-pressed developing nations may suddenly be seen as too well-off to receive needed World Bank loans. Under current rules, only countries with a per capita GDP of less than $765 qualify for 35-year interest-free loans, the most favourable terms available. World Bank officials insist that they have no plans to change their own measuring techniques to match the IMF's revised numbers. So the worries in some countries may be justified.

The IMF's new tallies are still controversial, some economists believe that in a number of cases, the value of goods and services in different countries cannot be meaningfully compared. But a majority of economists seem to applaud the change. Nor is the end in sight, forecasters who use IMF methods in adding the economies of Hong Kong and Taiwan to that of China – envisaging a greater China, so to speak – calculate that that total output will exceed the US's in less than a decade.

–By Adam Zagorin/Washington

Figure 3.4

24

not to be! For example, Guandung Province alone with tens of millions of consumers already represents Procter & Gamble's second largest market for shampoo, while there are 14,000 Avon ladies in the province selling cosmetics. In Shanghai to the north this growth is being repeated. Here a city of 13 million people has 2 million enter and leave it daily. One retail development estimates it serves 1 million customers daily. Along the Chinese coastal belt alone live 300 million people whose income is set to grow at 11 per cent per year for the next 10 years. Never in human history have so many grown so rich so fast! It will be the biggest economic player in the history of mankind, says Lee Kuan Yew, former Prime Minister of Singapore. China with 1.2 billion people, 25 per cent the world's population and a rapidly expanding economy (10 per cent+ per annum), offers the single greatest opportunity and threat for Western products.

In airport construction China intends to build 500 new airports over the next 15 years. Its planning in terms of the purchase of new aircraft is equal to the rest of the world combined over the same period.

India

India, already Asia's third strongest economy and with a population of over 900 million, is also posing great opportunities and threats. What's significant here is that 150 million Indians fit into the emerging educated and prosperous middle class. Internal domestic growth alone will see India make major advances in the world's economic success league. Just to meet its energy needs India is building ten major power stations each year until 2007.

Stop and think what you have learned so far. Reread the first part of the unit. Be sure you understand what is happening in terms of the patterns of world trade before you go on to discover the facilitators.

ACTIVITY 3.3

The facilitators of international trade

Barriers to trade

One of the difficulties in international trading is that each nation, or rather its government, feels it needs to exercise control over its trade and, through its trade, its economy. This will vary from country to country depending on the percentage of the GDP associated with export/import flows. Traditionally, either to protect mature (moribund) industries from foreign competition or to encourage infant industries that might be still-born under the pressure from foreign competition, governments have resorted to manipulate imports by imposing barriers in the form of tariffs or non-tariff restriction. A tariff is simply a tax levied on volume (e.g. on a 70cl bottle of wine) or alternatively on value (i.e. *ad valorem*). A further reason for imposing restrictions may be to earn revenue and, as mentioned above, to nurture and/or protect domestic industries. The recommended textbooks cover barriers to international trade in considerable depth. However, government additionally enforce what are known as non-tariff or invisible barriers which are far more difficult to detect and lead to a feeling of natural distrust between nation states. Invisible barriers may include:

Technical specifications
- Packaging regulations
- Size and weight regulations
- Health and safety regulations
- Product design specifications
- Manufacturing specifications

Government regulations
- Boycott
- Government procurement
- Granting of credit lines/subsidies for local producers

- Unnecessary and complicated administration
- Complicated local documentation
- Centralization of documentation
- Sample shipments to be sent in advance

More formal restrictions
- Special insurance requirements
- Special transport
- Port taxes and border surcharges and deposits

Quantitative restrictions
- Quotas
- Embargoes
- Licensing regulations
- Restrictive business conditions
- Exchange control

Again the recommended texts elaborate on invisible barriers. However, it is worth noting that protectionist methods taken by one country have traditionally produced retaliation by others. The overall conclusion of this activity is that *it does not work* (although there are exceptions – but even these ultimately are temporary restraints as consumers invariably seek out superior product offerings and are prepared to pay the price for superiority).

EXAM HINT

The subject of protection against foreign competition appears with some regularity in examination papers. Make sure you not only understand the means through which countries endeavour to restrict foreign imports but are fully cognisant with the impact and outcomes of such activities.

GATT (General Agreement on Tariffs and Trade) (now renamed World Trade Organization – 1995)

Back in the 1920s and 1930s world trade was practically brought to a halt by protectionist methods with all the major countries imposing barriers to prevent 'foreign' competitors entering their home markets and destroying jobs. The term 'beggar my neighbour' was coined. After the Second World War, GATT (General Agreement on Tariffs and Trade) was formed following the Bretton Woods Economic Conference in 1944. Beginning in 1947/8 with 23 countries it has expanded today to over 100 (including associate members such as Russia). The purpose of GATT was to reduce tariff barriers and to ensure that trade should *not* be discriminating with preference given to developing (Third World) countries. Under the terms of GATT, tariffs should either be non-existent or be at the lowest tariff rate for member countries – special tariff rates for countries needing special help. These are accorded Most Favoured Nation (MFN) status. In fact MFN has become a political weapon. For example the USA removed it from Poland and other East European countries over human rights violation in the early 1980s and periodically threatened China over its trading policies. Despite undergoing traumas at its regular meetings GATT has been astonishingly successful. Tariffs have been reduced from 47 per cent in 1948 to approximately 5 per cent today with firm proposals following the Uruguay round of talks to reduce this to 2.5 per cent over the decade. The reduction of tariffs and the resulting freeing of the flow of goods has increased world trade by 500 per cent and global output by 200 per cent. Signatories to the GATT agreement today account for 90 per cent of world trade.

The most recent GATT round began in 1987 in Uruguay and concluded late in 1993 and is still being ratified by member countries. GATT's very survival was under threat. Had it failed after 7 years of discussion the prospects for world trade into the next century would have been grim with the world retreating into trading blocs (EU, NAFTA, etc.). As mentioned previously the EU is largely self-sufficient with nearly 70 per cent of its trade as intracountry member trade and hypothetically Europe can provide over 90 per cent of its needs inside the Union – albeit at a cost. The major losers would have been the multinational and transnational corporations which spread their production facilities and supply chains around the world. It is clear that the major winners from the GATT agreement are not just the 100 or so countries but multinational corporations. Incidentally, the stumbling point in the 1993 talks related not to manufactured goods but to agricultural policies (probably of greater psychological concern to nation states than real trading importance). The other area of contention, still unresolved is the establishment of principles of trade applied to services. This is of growing concern as services account for an ever-increasing proportion of world trade.

The USA is particularly anxious to tackle the issue of services for its economy is now dominated by service industries which increasingly look to export as a source of growth. Between 1980 and 1992 US exports of services increased by 115 per cent whilst product exports lagged at 70 per cent. The French, taking a chauvinist view, feel threatened by American cultural imperialism – their film and television industries being vulnerable to Hollywood are resisting liberalization of trade in services.

Longer term the major threat to GATT is the trend towards regionalism and the creation of fortress mentalities among powerful nations or Triad economies. In fact one commentator remarked that it was the creation of NAFTA that spurred on the conclusion of the Uruguay round in 1993.

> GATT is being renamed as the World Trade Organization (WTO). Being up to date and abreast of current developments, show a keen interest in the subject. This is a specific point but the general one of being on top of the subject matter – through the use of examples – will be rewarded by the examiner (e.g, NAFTA possibly being FTAA by 2005).

EXAM HINT

International Monetary Fund (IMF)

Founded at the same time as GATT from the same Bretton Woods conference in 1944, the purpose of the IMF was to give stability to exchange rate fluctuation. Although the notion of pegged currency rates is now largely dead (except in the minds of certain European countries) the IMF remains. Having said that, it is still conceivable that monetary union could happen among some members of the EU, notably Germany, Austria, Belgium, Holland, Luxembourg and France, before the end of the decade.

The IMF's current role is essentially to provide a forum for international monetary cooperation, lessening the chances of nations taking arbitrary action and returning to the financial chaos of the 1930s. Additionally its role is to offer financial support to nations whose economies and currencies are in turmoil (e.g., Mexico in Spring 1995). In that respect it operates like a bank helping a business over a temporary crisis.

Like any prudent banker, the IMF generally imposes (or threatens) draconian conditions on borrowers which are unpopular to the citizens and politicians of the affected state. This has given the IMF the reputation of the bank of last resort – and the bank one loves to hate.

The World Bank (International Bank for Reconstruction and Development)

The IBRD or the World Bank is yet another Bretton Woods creation. Its impact differs from that of the IMF. Whereas the IMF involves itself with short-term financial crises the World Bank underpins long-term aid via capital loans to further economic development providing, over $10 billion per year. Its 'soft' loans with long-term payback supports many of the world's major developments (e.g. infrastructures, agriculture, tourism and population control initiatives).

Organization for Economic Cooperation and Development (OECD)

This is a United Nations (UN) offshoot comprising 24 leading economies. Its role is basically of providing bi-monthly statistics on the performance of the world's major trading nations and indication of future performance. Its views are respected by governments and multinationals for directional advice.

United Nations Conference on Trade and Development (UNCTAD)

This is a permanent organ of the UN comprising 160 countries. Its aim is to further the development of emerging nations by concentrating on commodities and primary products. If the commodity-producing nations who are mainly in the Third World could organize themselves into some form of co-operative, then prices would rise to the benefit of their countries. UNCTAD's progress has been modest. Commodity prices (in real terms) have fallen consistently over the past two decades.

- 'How have GATT and its successor the World Trade Organization (WTO) contributed to the development of world trade,' is the title of a talk you have agreed to give to your local branch of The Chartered Institute of Marketing. Explain the main elements in your proposed talk (June 1995, Question 4).
- Define briefly the role and the contribution of three of the major organizations in developing world trade (December 1996, Question 3).

Regional Economic Associations

Earlier we spoke of the development of the Triad economies and the implications for international business. We return to the subject under the banner of regionalism to distinguish between the different types of regional cooperation. Regional groupings result from countries agreeing to cooperate in various economic (and sometimes political) matters. Although some political corporation is unavoidable, how else can the region otherwise be created? Our role as marketers is confined to economic benefits. Regionalism is an attempt by nations to achieve goals they could otherwise not achieve by 'going it alone'.

Some principal regional economic associations

- EU (Economic Union): The UK, France, Denmark, Germany, Italy, Spain, the Netherlands, Portugal, Spain, Ireland, Belgium, Luxembourg and (in 1995) Austria, Finland and Sweden
- ASEAN Association of South-east Asian Nations): Indonesia, Malaysia, Singapore, Philippines, Thailand and Brunei. As of 1995 Vietnam and Myanmar (formerly Burma) have joined, and it is only a matter of time for Laos and Cambodia. ASEAN's population exceeds that of the EU, and whilst they are considerably less affluent, the potential is enormous, with average annual GDP growth rates in low double digits
- NAFTA (North American Free Trade Association): The USA, Canada, Mexico

There are others, of course, embracing West Africa (ECOWAS), Western South America (ANCOM), North Africa (AMU) and Central America (CACM).

Types of regional groupings

Broadly, the different types of regional groupings can be described under the following headings:

- *Free Trade Area* (e.g. NAFTA) The simplest level of corporation in which member countries agree to free movement of goods among themselves. (i.e. no tariffs or quotas). EFTA (now defunct) was a European equivalent.
- *Customs Union* Before 1992 the then European Community (EC) was an example with uniform tariffs as trade with non-members presenting a united front to the rest of the world. Its advantages are in stronger economic interaction accelerating intranations trade. However, it necessitates higher levels of political integration and some loss of sovereignty.
- *Common Market* The current EU aim is such with harmonization of internal tariffs, leading to their abolition in the future and a free flow of all factors of production

between members including materials, services and people. In fact the closest example of a Common Market is the USA, but even here the model is not complete. Within Europe there is much debate over the Maastricht agreement which sets out the defined stages towards the Common Market (i.e. United States of Europe) with its development of the single currency and political union (both of which are inextricably linked).

- *Political and Economic Union* Where countries seek out complete unification, submerging their political processes and currencies into one common system. This is the stated long-term goal of the European Union. A recent example of this development is the joining together of East and West Germany in 1992. In the historical perspective the USA and the joining together of Scotland and England are two additional examples.

- *Other Groupings* ASEAN, for the record, is different again being in effect a force for collaboration between its member states. It is early days to see if ASEAN will develop into something more positive and effective.

Summary

Trade between nations is the engine that drives the world economy. It needs supporting otherwise the alternative (i.e. a breakdown in international trade) will result in misery for everyone. Yet unfettered trading can also create a perilous scenario. Of crucial importance is balance – equilibrium with openness and liberalization held in perspective by world forces. But this balance is constantly under threat as individual nations protect and encourage home industries. Tensions are forever arising as nations expand or decline on the world scene. World trade is not static, it is forever changing.

Questions

Having completed the unit, check your learning by considering the following questions:

- From an international perspective, what can be learned from an examination of the make-up and patterns of world trade?
- What is GATT (now renamed the World Trade Organization)? What is its role in international marketing – and what factors threaten its future?
- South-east Asia seems the growth market for the twenty-first century. What advice might you give to the UK firm in:
  (a) Entering the region?
  (b) Facing competition at home from it?
- Why might a UK company deeply involved in international marketing feel threatened by the formation of the Triad trading blocs? How might it react?
- Who/what are the major institutions facilitating world trade? What are they there for? do we need them?
- Why is trade in services so difficult to manage? What do you think will be the future reaction of nation states to the accelerating growth of international services? What in your opinion should happen?
- In terms of their impact on your nation's economic well being explain the similarities and differences between tariff and non-tariff barriers.

There are probably many gaps to fill in your knowledge base in the unit. It is important you read widely as the syllabus is now more strategic.

International Marketing, S. Paliwoda and M. Thomas, Butterworth-Heinemann, 1998.
International Marketing Strategy, I. Doole, R. Lowe and C. Phillips, Routledge 1997.
International Marketing, V. Terpstra and R. Sarathy, The Dryden Press, 1997.
Global Marketing Strategies, J.-P. Jeannet and H. D. Hennessey, Houghton Mifflin, 1998.

EXTENDING KNOWLEDGE

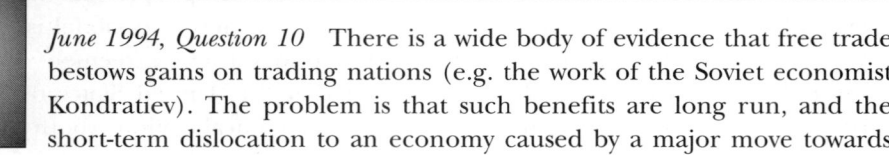

June 1994, Question 10 There is a wide body of evidence that free trade bestows gains on trading nations (e.g. the work of the Soviet economist Kondratiev). The problem is that such benefits are long run, and the short-term dislocation to an economy caused by a major move towards reducing protectionist barriers is often unacceptable. Thus a gradual step-wise move towards free trade is often adopted, resulting in several progressive forms of free trade agreement.

Free trade areas

Nations agree to reduce barriers between member states, but to maintain their own independent relations with other countries, which may or may not involve barriers to trade. No attempt is made to create a 'level playing field' within the area and member states are free to decide local taxes, health and safety, consumer legislation, etc. No attempt is made to aid the flow of goods or to maintain exchange rates. That is, there is little or no economic integration.

Customs unions

These build on the FTA concept, to include a common external (i.e., non-member) tariff or trade barrier, adopted by all the members of the union. That is, whereas FTA members are free to decide trading policy with non-members, CU members agree a common trading policy with the rest of the world.

Common markets

In addition to the coordinated approach to external trade relations exhibited by the CU, the common market seeks to integrate internal trading relations as well. A common market attempts to ensure the free movement of capital and labour and to move towards common tax and welfare systems to ensure all trade partners are equally advantaged.

Monetary and political union

The final and logical progression is the creation of a full monetary and political union, involving agreed economic and political goals, with a common currency and legal system. To some extent the United States might be regarded as a confederation of individual states who have fully integrated their political, legal, economic and monetary systems. Basically, such unions are super-states to all intents and purposes.

Discussion of the implications for a specific trading bloc – the European Union

The European Union currently may be described as a common market, although the full implementation of the Maastricht Agreement will, for most countries, lead to closer political, economic and monetary union.

Within the EU, trade between member states has grown rapidly. Not only is this due to the lowering of trade barriers, but also due to international business outside the EU attempting to avoid the common external tariffs by manufacturing and sourcing within the EU. Some 60% of UK trade is now within the EU. This, of course, means that economic interdependence is being established, raising the desirability of closer relations between members.

The development of easier cross-border movement of goods, capital and labour has undoubtedly been a major factor in this growth. Industrialists in member states are no longer thinking in a local market but in a Europe-wide market.

Outside the EU, a major effect of the existence of the EU has been the leverage applied to the GATT Uruguay round of tariff reduction talks. Prior to the establishment of the EU, Japan and the USA were by far and away the largest economic superpowers. The creation of the EU with over 400 million population in advanced economies gave the EU a negotiating strength that individual member nations did not have. The resultant agreement probably did more to reduce Japanese and US barriers to European countries than any previous round of negotiations.

The success, and subsequent threat to other nations, of the EU has resulted in a plethora of attempts to set up similar blocs elsewhere. However, the basic requirements for such agreements – political stability and common economic and social goals – are often lacking. Recently the creation of NAFTA (North American Free Trade Area) involving the USA, Canada and Mexico, is an example.

Such 'clubs' obviously provide advantages for their members, but instead of protectionism on a country by country level, we are now developing a system of regional protectionism and the need for GATT to avoid escalating external barriers will still be there.

What such blocs will encourage is the dispersion of multinational companies across the globe, to locate inside the blocs, thereby gaining the 'free trade' status. Marketers will thus have to think not on a global basis but perhaps on a regional basis within an overall global strategy.

December 1992, Question 10 One of the most significant changes which has taken place in recent years in terms of its immediate and potential future effect on patterns of world trade and marketing has been the virtual collapse of the communist system in Eastern Europe. There are many reasons for this collapse, not the least of which were the Gorbachev policies of *glasnost* and *perestroika* together with the democratic liberalization of countries such as Poland. Whatever the reasons, there is little doubt that the effects will be far-reaching.

Prior to this collapse of the communist system in Eastern Europe most of the international trading that the Eastern European communist countries carried out was within the framework of the Council for Mutual Economic Assistance (CMEA). Although by no means anything like as fully developed, the CMEA was essentially the Soviet counterpart of the European Community, though its purpose was probably as much ideological as commercial. The members of the CMEA included Bulgaria, Czechoslovakia, German DR, Hungary, Romania and Poland in Eastern Europe, plus Cuba and Vietnam.

Like the EC, the CMEA was to encourage free trade amongst member countries and to control trade with outsiders, i.e. Western non-communist countries. As a result, and again in large measure due to ideology, the volume of trade between members of the CMEA and Western countries, i.e. essentially East–West trade, has until recently been very small in terms of the size of the two groups. However, with the collapse of the Eastern communist bloc and with it most of the vestiges of the CMEA, East–West trade has begun to flourish.

A company wishing to trade with former European members of the CMEA group will now find much greater opportunity and willingness to trade. In turn, as consumer interests awaken in Eastern Europe there will be growing markets for consumer-orientated Western firms. Industrial- and knowledge-based industries such as computer manufacturers have already found substantial market opportunities.

In short, a company wishing to trade with these Eastern European, former communist countries will find few, if any, formal barriers to trade. However, at the moment consumer spending power is still very limited in many of the Eastern bloc countries.

Similarly, many of the indigenous manufacturers in these countries are short of capital investment in plant and, above all, marketing skills and expertise. For many companies therefore the key to trading with members of the group lies in helping them overcome these weaknesses. We are therefore likely to see much inward investment, licensing and joint ventures.

Approached carefully and with tact and skill the prospects for East–West trade have probably never been better.

June 1995, Question 4 **Note:** Your answer should begin with some opening remarks setting the scene, e.g. 'Note for a brief talk to local CIM branch'.

GATT (General Agreement on Trade and Tariffs) was founded in 1944 at the Bretton Woods Conference set up to discuss what should be done to facilitate the growth of world trade following the end of the Second World War. The intention was to prevent the world sliding into a 1930s type world recession/depression. GATT is not an organization but an agreement between nations to reduce tariff barriers. It began in 1947 with 23 nations and today has over 100, including associate members such as Russia. In 1995 it was renamed the World Trade Organization (WTO). GATT (WTO) has been astonishingly successful in that tariffs have been reduced gradually from an average of 47% to 5% and the intention is to reduce barriers to $2\frac{1}{2}$% early in the next century. But such progress has not been easy. Being an agreement between nations, having over 100 members each with its own international agenda, it is hardly surprising that negotiations are long and protracted. The most recent – the Uruguay round – began in 1987 and only reached agreement in 1994. Even so, not all the key issues were resolved. Outstanding are agreements on how to manage the principles of trade when applied to services – of particular importance as services account for an ever-increasing proportion of world trade. For example, between 1980 and 1992 US exports of services increased by 115%, whilst product exports lagged at 70%.

The success of WTO has been obvious to all. The reduction of tariffs has seen the flow of world trade increase by 500% and global output by 200%. Signatories of the WTO agreement account for 90% of world trade today.

But all may not be straightforward. Potential problems lie ahead. First, the deregulation of services (already mentioned). Nations remain chauvinistic – the French in particular are extremely concerned about the growing threat of American cultural imperialism, particularly via the film and television industry. The growth of regionalism – EU, ASEAN, NAFTA – are all potential threats to the liberalization of a free flow of trade. It is clear that these major regions/trading blocs might develop a fortress mentality; for example, the EU has the potential to be virtually self-sufficient, albeit at a price. And it is feasible that these regions might form bilateral agreements on trade.

Therefore, in summary, GATT/WTO ranks among the foremost facilitators of the growth of world trade but care and most importantly, vision is essential if it is to continue its good work.

December 1996, Question 3

Candidates might begin with demonstrating knowledge of world trade and even possibly note the importance of exports to the GDP of major trading nations. They might express the importance of world trade as the engine of prosperity.

Key facilitators include:

WTO
IMF
World Bank
OECD
TRIAD economies

What is expected is a brief description of each and a supporting statement of the contribution made.

A more detailed appreciation of the role and contribution of the facilitators appears in this unit.

Customers and the environment

Customers and an understanding of customer needs and motivations are key to any successful marketing strategy – domestic or international. In international marketing strategy the problem is made more complex for two reasons. First, customers tend to be in different countries and different markets with different environmental effects acting upon them. Second, the self-reference criterion makes it difficult for marketers of a different culture to understand fully how and why a given customer in an overseas market may act differently to the same marketing stimulus. In this unit we will look at the key factors which impinge upon customer behaviour in overseas markets and we will attempt to build a picture of how the international marketer must go about trying to understand the nature and complexities of the foreign market selected.

The best way to understand customers (or to attempt to!) is to analyse and identify those factors of the environment that affect the way that they think and behave. In this unit you will:

- Review the factors that affect buyer behaviour
- Evaluate the key elements of culture
- Consider the main aspects of the international legal environment
- Consider the main aspects of the international political environment
- Consider the main aspects of the international economic environment
- Review the process of international market selection

Having completed this unit you will be able to:

- Understand the differences in business and social/cultural conventions which affect buying behaviours in international markets
- Understand how different stages of economic growth affect buying behaviours
- Appreciate how marketing approaches for different foreign markets are driven by local needs and environmental conditions
- Prioritize and select foreign markets

This unit might be considered to be the most important in the whole question of forming international marketing strategy. Good marketing (international as well as domestic) must begin with the customer – not the product.

Success in international operations comes not from skilful manipulation of product or promotional strategies but from a good depth of understanding of what our customers want, what drives them and how to read the local environment to understand customers.

The candidate should read this unit more than once. It should be worked in conjunction with all the other units in this book.

Once you have completed this unit, try to apply the data as a key to understanding a foreign market that you know, perhaps one that you have visited on holiday. What can you see from an analysis of the market? Can you place some of the 'different' behaviours in context? What special aspects of the local environment are driving the different behaviours?

Environmental factors

The comparative analysis of world markets is concerned with the environment in which international marketing takes place. The kind of steps that the international marketer can take and the adaptations that organizations must make will be determined largely by this environment. In this unit we will be primarily concerned with the international marketer's sphere of operation, dwelling particularly on the uncontrollable variables and how they affect the international marketing task.

There are a number of ways of categorizing the environment and in international marketing strategy the SLEPT method is preferred (i.e. social, legal, economic, political and technology factors).

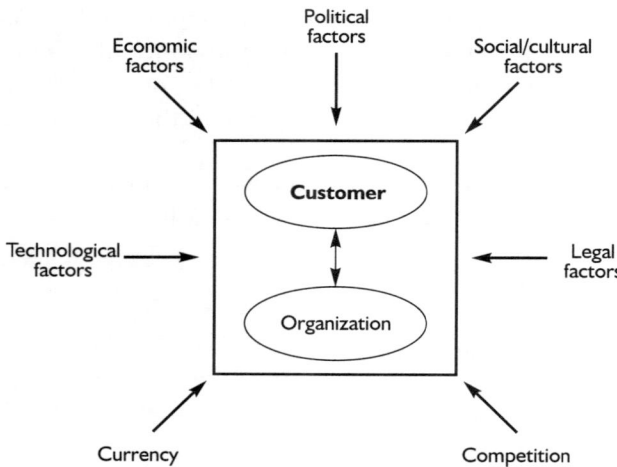

Figure 4.1   Environmental factors in international marketing

Figure 4.1 identifies these various factors which are the most important variables that affect the relationship between the organization and its customer in the foreign market operation. The rest of this unit will consider these factors separately and intends to identify how they impinge upon the international marketers task.

Culture is notoriously difficult to define and many people have tried. Kluckhohn in fact published a book with 257 different definitions. His best composite of all these definitions is:

> Patterned ways of thinking, feeling and reacting, acquired and transmitted mainly by symbols, constituting the distinctive achievements of human groups, including their embodiments in artifacts; the essential case of culture consists of traditional ideas and especially their attached values.

More usefully (perhaps) culture has been described as 'the way we do things around here'.

Figure 4.2 The components of cultures (adapted from Terpstra)

The social/cultural environment

It is only in relatively recent years that socio-cultural influences have been identified as critical determinants of marketing behaviour. In other words, marketing is a cultural as well as an economic phenomenon. Culture is so pervasive yet so complex that it is difficult to define in short, simple terms. The easiest way to grasp the complexity of culture is to examine these varied aspects. Up to 73 'cultural universals' (human behaviours that are to be found in all cultures in the world) have been identified, but we have reduced these to eight 'cultural components' for our purposes (see Figure 4.2). While this brief survey is not sufficient to convey any expertise in the area, its main purpose is to alert the prospective marketer to the kind of cultural parameters that can affect international marketing programmes.

The key components of culture in the international marketing environment are as follows.

Language

Foreign markets differ from the domestic in terms of the language which the people speak and the language which is written. In some markets the official language differs from the actual one used, in other markets there is more than one language to deal with in the same population. Countries with more than one official language are relatively easy to spot (Switzerland has four), other countries with widely differing dialects are sometimes more difficult (India = 500, Papua New Guinea = plus or minus 750). In other markets there are differences in the language spoken by the males and the females of the population (Japan).

Language differences will affect not only the organization's promotional strategy in international markets, but will add complexity in interpersonal relationships and internal written/spoken communications.

Religion

Religion is a major cultural variant and has significant if not always apparent effects on marketing strategy. For example, the identification of sacred objects and philosophical systems, beliefs and norms as well as taboos, holidays and rituals are critical for an understanding of marketing interest in a given product or service. Religion will affect the food which a people eat and when they eat it as well as people's attitudes to a whole range of products from deodorants to alcoholic drink.

Values and attitudes

The values that a market has towards things such as time, achievement, work, wealth, change and risk taking will seriously affect not only the products offered but also the packaging and communication activities. 'Old' and 'New' have quite different meanings in the East and in the West. Motivation of the organization's personnel is also strongly influenced by the local culture and practice. Encouraging local sales forces to sell more by offering cars and more money, for example, may not work in all cultures. The SRC is a major obstacle in this area.

Education

The level of formal primary and secondary education in a foreign market will have direct impact upon the 'sophistication' of the target customers. A simple example will be the degree of literacy. The labelling of products, especially those with possibly hazardous side-effects, needs to be taken seriously for a market that has a very low literacy rate.

Social organization

This relates to the way in which a society organizes itself. It should consider kinship, social institutions, interest groups and status systems. The role of women and caste systems are easily identifiable examples. If your organization has a history of successfully marketing to 'the housewife/homemaker' life becomes more difficult where women have no social status at all. An example close to home would include Switzerland, where the majority of people rent rather than own their houses and expect to rent property with domestic appliances installed – in this case the banks are the largest single purchasers of washing machines!

EXAM HINT

In case you are asked to quote an example, it can be useful to try to understand, in reasonable depth, one or two international markets (culture/technology, etc.) and how things really work. One advanced and one less advanced market is usually enough. Depth knowledge used in one question could make all the difference.

Technology and material culture

This aspect relates not to 'materialism' but to the local market's ability to handle and deal with modern technology. Some cultures find leaving freezers plugged in overnight and servicing cars and trucks that have not yet broken down difficult concepts to manage. In instances such as these the organization is often faced with the choice of either educating the population (expensive) or de-engineering the product or service (often unpalatable to domestic engineers).

Law and politics

The legal and political environments in a foreign market are often and rightly seen as consequences of the culture of that market. Legal and political systems are often a simple codification of the norms of behaviour deemed acceptable by the local culture. These two aspects will be dealt with in more depth below.

Aesthetics

This area covers the local culture's perception of things such as beauty, good taste and design and dictates what is acceptable or 'appealing' to the local eye. An organization's decision as to aspects of the product or service involving colour, music, architecture or brand names needs to be sympathetic and acceptable to the local culture if purchase is to take place. For the unwary there are many, many traps in this area. Colour means completely different things in different cultures and brand names often do not travel well!

The political environment

The political environment of international marketing includes any national or international political factor that can affect the organization's operations or its decision making. Politics has come to be recognized as the major factor in many international business decisions. It is a major factor in whether to invest and how to continue marketing. The best way to deal with this problem is for management to become fully informed of the situation and the firm must go beyond traditional market research to include the political environment.

There are a number of aspects to the political environment that should serve to guide you through this area and they are as follows.

The role of the government in the economy

What is the role of the government in the targeted local marketplace? Is it primarily undertaking a 'participation' role (strongly involved in the day-to-day activities of the economy) or is it primarily a 'regulator' (fixes the rules and regulations but tries to leave the market open to local competition and market forces)?

Ideologies and marketing

The ideological background of the government can give good insights into how it is likely to act/react with a foreign company operating in its marketplace. Ideologies such as capitalism, socialism and nationalism will clearly affect the way the government deals with overseas organizations and its likely approach to your marketing programmes when they are implemented. Beware new 'labels'. The recent (so-called) collapse of communism may have produced apparently new capitalist markets to explore – it normally takes more than a declaration for managers and customers to behave differently. Change certainly doesn't happen overnight.

Political stability

How stable is the government? Here much depends upon the organization's level of involvement and the amount of risk that the organization is prepared to take. Pure exporting is a very low-risk scenario and the political stability is of minor concern. If the organization is planning longer-term involvement and higher investment in the market, longer planning horizons may require a more rigorous analysis of government stability and governmental policy.

International relations

Two forms of international relations are important here: first, the relationship between the home government and the various host government or governments and second, the ongoing relationship between different host governments in those markets in which the organization wishes to operate. In the 1980s owning a subsidiary which operated in apartheid South Africa was a major liability for many international organizations. In the 1990s organizations thought to be supporting the apartheid regime might have similar problems dealing with the new government.

If you work in an organization, find out how well your managers know the cultural aspects of their target markets. How well is this knowledge used in international marketing planning? Alternatively, analyse a well-known company and assess how well they do it.

The political threats

The primary consequences of wrongly assessing the political environment can prove extremely costly for the international organization. In the event of a serious 'falling out' between the organization and host government, local officials may have the power to confiscate company assets, expropriate them or simply increase governmental controls over the company assets located in their country. There are a number of instances where these actions have been taken and, despite loud voices and sabre rattling on the part of the home government, the costs to the international organization have been significant. White farmers in Zimbabwe are now facing the threat of nationalization despite previous assurances from the government.

The legal environment

The legal environment is generated from the political climate and the prevalent cultural attitudes towards business enterprise, that is, the nation's laws and regulations pertaining to business. It is important for the firm to know the legal environment in each of its markets because these laws constitute the 'rules of the game' for business activity. The legal environment in international marketing is more complicated than domestic since it has three dimensions: (1) local domestic law, (2) international law and (3) domestic laws in the firm's home base.

There are a number of key aspects to the international legal environment:

- *Local domestic laws*   These are all different! The only way to find a route through the legal maze in overseas markets is to use experts on the separate legal systems and laws pertaining in each market targeted.
- *International law*   There are a number of 'international laws' that can affect the organization's activity. Some are international laws covering piracy and hijacking, others are more international conventions and agreements and cover items such as IMF and World Trade Organization (WTO formerly GATT) treaties, patents and trademarks legislation (some differences by markets) and harmonization of legal systems within regional economic groupings such as the growth of EU laws which bind member states.
- *Domestic laws*   The organization's domestic (home market) legal system is important for two reasons. First, there are often export controls which limit the free export of certain goods and services to particular marketplaces and second, there is the duty of the organization to act and abide by its national laws in all its activities whether domestic or international.
- *Laws and the international marketing activity*   It will be readily understandable how domestic, international and local legal systems can have a major impact upon the organization's ability to market into particular overseas countries. Laws will affect the marketing mix in terms of products, price, distribution and promotional activities quite dramatically. 'Ignorance is no defence' tends to be a universal in all markets.

EXAM QUESTION

Should an international marketing manager concentrate upon customers or quality or competition when developing strategic plans? Justify your answer (December 1993).

(**See** Exam answers at the end of this unit).

The economic environment

The economic environment has long been recognized as an uncontrollable factor in the task of marketing management generally. The economic environment of international marketing is peculiar in two ways. First, it contains an international economic structure that affects marketing between nations, and second, it includes the domestic economy of every nation in which the firm is attempting to market. Thus the international marketer faces the traditional task of economic analysis but in a context that may include a hundred countries or more. This investigation will be directed towards two broad questions: (1) how big is the market and (2) what is the market like?

The first issue confronting the international marketer is to identify the likely size of the target market or markets. We can assess this in a number of ways:

- *Population size and growth*   How big is the population and how fast is it growing? This will give an indication of likely current and future demand.
- *Population density and concentration*   Where is the population located? How dense is the population and is the population concentrated in specific areas? Population concentration is important for two reasons. First, there are obvious questions of distribution and logistics. Second, when population becomes concentrated it often tends to take on a separate character. 'Urbanization' (see Unit 2) produces the need for different products and services.
- *Population age and distribution*   How old is the average population and what is the distribution among the various age levels? The advanced economies of the West have rapidly ageing populations that offer certain market opportunities for particular products. Some African countries, on the other hand, have 50 per cent of their populations below the age of 15. This offers a completely different market opportunity for the international organization.
- *Disposable income and distribution*   What is the available income in the population? Can enough people afford the proposed products or services that the organization can provide? Equally important, is the income concentrated into particular groups of people or is it widely distributed through the population? Remember that even in the poorest markets there are often pockets of extreme wealth that can afford and demand certain high quality luxury goods.

As well as the market size the international marketer should also try to understand the nature of the economy in which he or she proposes operating. There are a number of dimensions to this question:

- *Natural resources*   What resources are available in the local marketplace that the organization may wish to use for its production? This may include natural resources (raw materials) as well as local management ability. Some countries require an agreed amount of local content as a basis for foreign investment in the first place.

ACTIVITY 4.2

Spend some time with an atlas. Look at the world and at the natural topography. Even today these features can affect marketing plans and implementation. Can you see how?

A few hours' study of a good atlas will almost certainly pay dividends on the day of the examination. Geography lessons at school are long forgotten and population figures change rapidly. Newer atlases will be needed to show up states in the former USSR and the exam could ask questions based on the new, emerging nations.

- *Topography*   This relates to the physical nature of the marketplace, rivers, mountains, lakes and the like. Natural features such as mountain ranges and rivers can provide serious barriers to communication, both physical and electronic in even the most advanced markets.
- *Climate*   The climatic situations prevalent in a marketplace may require adaptations to product or to services from the domestic standard. Climate can affect both the delivery and the operation of the product and service. Consider water-cooled engines in drier climates and the management siesta in the Mediterranean!

- *Economic activity* What is the primary economic activity of the marketplace? Is it basically agricultural or is it industrial? Such indicators will give a good key as to the likely demand, lifestyles and product/service requirements.
- *Energy and communications* Energy sources and communications infrastructures that we take for granted in the advanced Western economies tend to be less readily available or less reliable in underdeveloped or less-developed markets. If the organization's business relies strongly upon speedier reliable communications then overseas markets need to be assessed carefully before entry is made.
- *Urbanization* To what extent is the local market urbanized or rural? The level of urbanization will affect not only the types of products and services that are demanded but also the way in which these are delivered.
- *Differential inflation* What is the level of inflation relative to that of your domestic market or another market with which the target will be linked? If the organization is used to operating in areas and markets of low inflation, annual inflation rates of 500 or 1000 per cent may be beyond the realm of management expertise.

A number of models exist to classify various markets around the world according to different stages of economic growth and development. Examples of these classifications would be:

1(a) Less developed countries (LDCs)
  (b) Newly industrialized countries (NICs)
  (c) Advanced economies
2(a) Self-sufficiency
  (b) Emergence
  (c) Industrialization
  (d) Mass consumption
  (e) Post-industrial society

Many of these classifications are useful shorthand and give an instant view of the various economic marketplaces throughout the world. However, it is difficult to capture the special characteristics of individual markets in this way and oversimplification of this sort can be dangerous in any depth analysis. For example, the second model (Figure 4.3) is based strongly on the natural evolution of economies through a regular and understood industrialization process. It has difficulty in dealing with economies which are either artificially distorted by, for instance, sudden oil revenues or even those markets that are, or have been, artificially controlled by Communist governments. For example, many oil rich states in the Middle East seem to display characteristics of stages 1, 2, 3 and 4 at the same time! The moral here is to treat such models as useful guidance but to temper this approach with some degree of commonsense.

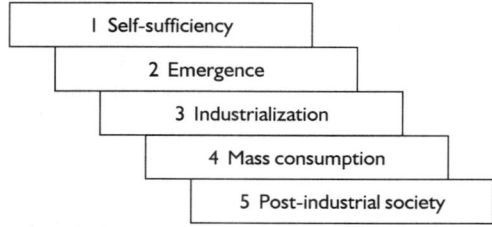

Figure 4.3 Stages of economic development

The technological environment

Technology is no longer subject to national boundaries although it is, to some extent, still subject to economics – not every company can afford to purchase the very latest technology. Technology can be very expensive for a number of organizations and countries, certainly if they wish to acquire state-of-the-art technology which is often necessary just to keep in the race as products and services become more and more developed. On the other hand, technology is also reducing the barriers to entry to many industries by reducing the necessary scale of operations required to reach economically competitive cost levels. Therefore we are seeing smaller markets and smaller countries becoming more feasible for the installation of local operations.

Examine how the country of origin effect might influence the marketing of consumer durable products in three different countries of your choice (December 1994).

(**See** Exam answers at the end of this unit.)

The final important aspect of technology, as it increases its worldwide reach, is a tendency on a global scale for production and services to increase. As a result, pressures on price and margins at a global level increase apace.

The competitive environment

Competition worldwide is increasing at both a global and a local level. Local markets are increasing by subject to international and global competition and, in addition, technology is facilitating competition from previously unexpected quarters. No longer are LDCs satisfied merely by exporting raw materials, they also want the additional margin that comes from manufacturing.

For a company and a market of your choice, can you identify:
- All the different forms of competition they face?
- Exactly how competition affects the development of international marketing plans?
- Can you name the five different competitive forces?

At an international level advanced markets are seeing significant competition from both LDCs and NICs who are using modern technology and lower labour prices to compete in hitherto 'protected' marketplaces.

Competition is critical to the development of any form of marketing strategy – including international. Are you confident that you can apply Porter's competitive forces model to international marketing? You need to know how.

The complexity of international competition has been heightened by the strategic use of international sourcing of components to achieve competitive advantage. (Reference the Japanese electronics industry.)

The currency environment

The world currency environment, stimulated by worldwide trading and foreign exchange dealing, is an additional complication in the international environment. On top of all the normal vagaries of markets, customer demands, competitive actions and economic infrastructures, foreign exchange parities are likely to change on a regular if unpredictable basis. Such changes can be stimulated by a number of different factors, most of which are completely out of the control of the international marketing organization.

Difficult as it may be, foreign exchange movements need to be understood and, to some extent, predicted where possible. With increasing levels of competition and the consequent reduction in international margins, unpredicted exchange movements can, at a stroke, turn a brilliant strategy into a shambles – and profit into loss.

The question of currency also raises the issue of the EU and the 'Euro' or common currency. Whether or not the UK enters the first round of EU members who drop their own currencies in favour of European Monetary Union (EMU) is far from clear. Whether the EMU takes place at all is being debated. Although the issues are still far from clear, the international marketer needs to be prepared for any eventuality and a new currency is no small matter, especially for multinationals or financial services organizations. The Diploma examinations could ask a question in this area, do you have a view?

Foreign market selection

In too many instances the selection of foreign markets, often for considerable investment, would appear to be an informal process. Since a firm's resources are limited it is essential that enough resource is concentrated in a small enough number of markets to have an effect. Resources spread too thinly will not only fall short of 'critical mass' but will also serve to inform competitors of your intentions. Foreign market selection should be a prioritizing activity based on the three rules of 'potential', 'similarity' and 'accessibility' (see Figure 4.4).

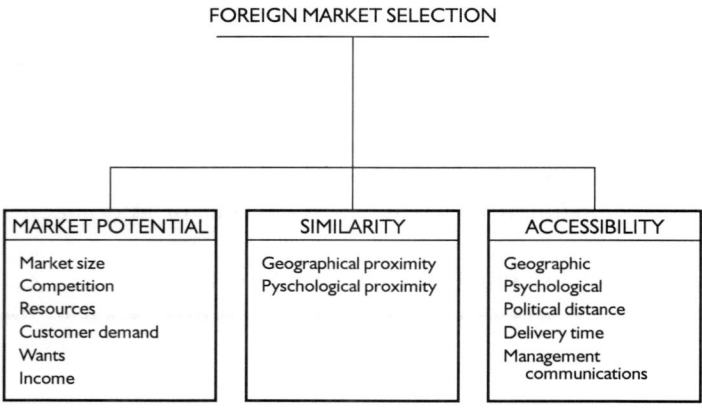

Figure 4.4 Foreign market selection

An organization should resist the temptation to attack too many markets at one time thereby spreading effort and resources too thinly to be successful. The initial effort is often better directed at a single market and extended to other, possibly neighbouring markets later.

Market potential

The first critical measure of foreign market attractiveness is to try to assess the potential of the foreign market for profitable operations. There are a number of aspects to this question:

- *Market size* How big is the market for our intended product or service? Remember that a straight reading of population may not be enough. We are interested in identifying the size of the market which could be potential purchasers for the product or service in question.

- *Competition*   How strong is the competition in the proposed marketplace? What is the picture of domestic and international competition either operating or contemplating entry into the marketplace? Will there be enough competition to stimulate growth but not too much competition to restrict profits to a possibly untenable level?
- *Resources*   What resources are available within the marketplace to support our entry and operations there? What resources ideally do we need? If the resources are not there at the moment can they be brought in from neighbouring markets at reasonable cost?
- *Customer demand, wants, income, etc.*   What do customers actually want? What is the level of demand? To what extent are current needs and wants being met by local or international competition? Is there available income to create profitable demand that the organization can meet? Remember, prospective customers who can't afford to pay is business we can find anywhere in the world!

ACTIVITY 4.5

For your company/a company of your choice what criteria did management actually use to select target foreign markets? How would you suggest improving the selection process?

Similarity (to home or other foreign markets)

In addition to the financial parameters of the marketplace it is important to understand whether the target market is close enough to either our home market (which we ought to understand) or to another foreign market which we understand because we are successfully operating there already:

- *Geographic proximity*   Is the intended market geographically close for us to access it with our products or service and with the management expertise needed to satisfy customer needs?
- *Psychological proximity*   Do we understand how the people in the marketplace think? Do we have a degree of rapport with the local culture? Will we understand management attitudes and activities in the local marketplace? Will they be able to interact with our organization's established culture and norms of behaviour?

Accessibility

Can we get to the marketplace? Accessibility can be judged on a number of different parameters, all of which are equally important to the development of a successful international marketing strategy:

- *Geographic accessibility*   Can we physically reach the marketplace and the separate segments or parts of the market within the local marketplace? Can we meet the lead times and delivery times required by the local customers to at least match, if not improve upon, competitive performances? Are there any physical or communication barriers which will stop us achieving these needs?
- *Psychological access*   Do we understand the local culture and buyer requirements and needs sufficiently to be able to position the products or service to be relevant to local market conditions? Are we able to meet local buyers at an emotional as well as a rational level? (Remember, the majority of purchase decisions are taken on an emotional basis and not rationally – much as we might like them to be so.)
- *Political distance*   How far away is the political system and government ideology and activity from what we are used to dealing with? Do we understand the political motivations and are we able to predict activities in the future? Is there a solid rapport between the home government and the host government and between the host government and other markets in which we operate?
- *Management communications*   Any international marketing operation will require a level of local management in order to implement its plans. This may be carried out by local

agents and/or distributors or local or expatriate staff employed by the company. In any event, the local management will have to be part of the local culture in order to implement any marketing strategy properly. Management attitudes, behaviours and motivations tend to differ quite markedly among different cultures and it is important that the organization be able to communicate effectively with people on the ground. No international marketing strategy can be successfully implemented without this level of communication.

Summary

In this unit we have considered the various environmental factors which act upon the customer in a given or prospective foreign marketplace. We have seen the heavy impact of culture on buyer behaviour and perceptions as well as the infrastructure constraints delivered by legal, economic and political systems.

Technology, competition and currency are all moving to global stages and are having serious effects on international business worldwide. Although often difficult to predict, these effects cannot be ignored or international profitability will suffer badly.

Finally we considered how to select target markets on the basis of this analysis and the broad parameters required for successful marketing strategy implementation which follows.

Questions

As a check on your understanding of what has been covered in this unit, consider the following questions:

- What are the key aspects of the 'environment' which affect the foreign customer?
- What are the eight key aspects of culture?
- What effects can 'language' have on our international marketing strategy?
- What effects can 'religion' have on our international marketing strategy?
- What effects can 'values and attitudes' have on our international marketing strategy?
- What effects can 'education' have on our international marketing strategy?
- What effects can 'social organization' have on our international marketing strategy?
- What effects can 'technology' have on our international marketing strategy?
- What effects can 'aesthetics' have on our international marketing strategy?
- What are the two main roles of government in the economy? How will our international operations be affected by foreign governments?
- What are the main aspects of the international legal environment? How will our international operations be affected by these?
- What are the key aspects of the international economic environment that the organization should consider? How will these affect our international operations?
- What role can models of economic growth and development play in the formulation of international marketing strategy?
- What are the main aspects of the international technological environment? How will these affect our international operations?
- What are the main aspects of the international competitive environment? How will these affect our international operations?
- What are the three parameters by which we can prioritise and select foreign markets?

For a more detailed analysis and explanation of customers and their environments, read:

International Marketing, S. Paliwoda and M. Thomas, Butterworth-Heinemann, 1998.
International Marketing Strategy, I. Doole, R. Lowe and C. Phillips, Routledge, 1997.

December 1992 Immediately a company crosses national boundaries with its marketing strategies it has to be able to plan for and cope with cultural issues. In the case of the company employing foreign nationals as employees in varying capacities, not only will the company have to understand and deal with the cultural issues of customers but also those of employees.

To deal first with some of the cultural issues connected with its customers. The first point for managers in international companies to recognize is that each nation has its own values, customs and taboos. As a result, customers may have very different needs, perceptions, attitudes, product usage patterns. The international marketer ignores or neglects these cultural differences at his peril. For example, women in Tanzania believe that eating eggs can make children bald or impotent. Freezer ownership is currently 31% in Italy compared to 71% in Sweden – a difference explained more by cultural values and lifestyles than climate or income levels. The English say 'lorry' and 'petrol' whereas in the United States they are referred to as 'truck' and 'gasoline'. The colour black signifies mourning in Western countries whereas white is often the colour of mourning in Eastern nations.

The importance of these cultural variables to the company marketing internationally is that they represent extremely powerful influences on customer behaviour. The marketer, therefore, must take them into account in planning marketing strategies and particularly the elements of the marketing mix. One central issue in international marketing which is a direct result of cultural differences amongst consumers is the issue of standardization. We are all aware that there are a number of potential advantages to be gained by the international marketer if the marketing mix is standardized across international markets; even better is if the basis for this standardization can be that of the domestic market. In other words, the marketer simply markets products and services across international markets with no adaptation to domestic strategies.

Although there are a number of advantages to such a standardized approach, and in particular the potential for lower costs, the greatest potential disadvantage is that such a standardized ethnocentric approach is likely to 'clash' with a different culture. It is largely because of cultural differences and the potential for clashes to which a standardized approach gives rise, that mainly international marketers are now adapting their marketing strategies to the culture of each of the countries in which they operate. Often termed a 'polycentric' approach, this non-standardized approach to marketing can be used to minimize many of the customer cultural problems.

International companies must also learn to deal with employee cultural problems. For example, an American company establishing a production and marketing operation in another less developed part of the world may find that cultural differences give rise to a need for, e.g.

- Different systems of motivation
- Different working hours
- Different employment practices *vis-à-vis* sexual equality...

Just as the marketer will probably find it most appropriate to adapt the marketing mix to the local culture, so too must the local and different needs of employees be considered. This must not be at the expense of company policies and objectives, but with sensitive management, careful selection of local employees, and adequate training and education, most potential cultural difficulties from non-domestic employees can be minimized.

June 1997 Answers should begin by reflecting on the rapid growth and development of global brands. Candidates are expected to illustrate this point with examples, e.g. McDonald's with 20 000 outlets has developed a global perspective in the past two decades.

Factors underpinning the recent phenomenon of global branding should be referred to. The development is much in its infancy. McDonald's, Nike, Coca-Cola and Marlboro now head the world symbol recognition.

Why do companies do it? The factors are numerous but the underlying principle is that the pursuit of globalization is appropriate only to the extent that it has a positive influence on financial performance, i.e. profit.

Why then do companies adapt global brands to local needs? The reasons are again numerous but should include the following:

- Consumer preferences, taste, name, colour, design, sizes, i.e. cultural imperative.
- Competitive stance, candidates who recognize this and its role in creating success need rewarding.
- Legislation, affecting all aspects of the mix.
- Product life-cycle differences.
- Target market specifics, niche versus mass market.
- Technological shifts, high-tech shift favouring standardization, low-tech favouring customization (although this is not always true).
- Market sophistication, technological, infrastructure, and after-sales service capabilities.
- Level of economic development, ability to pay etc.
- Climate, geography etc.

This list is by no means complete. Also you will see that each point added together totals more than 20. What is important is that pass grade answers contain around eight to ten points but the quality grades will reflect:

- that some points are more important than others;
- good examples;
- a clear recognition of the development of global/branding;
- the global brands do vary in the details of the product 'offer' but within the global positioning, i.e. McDonalds stands for the same values worldwide but what it delivers to its customers varies according to need.

December 1997 This is a catch-all question that all candidates should be capable of answering. However, this is not an opportunity for candidates to write 'everything I know about culture'. The question demands a more sophisticated management perspective relating to strategic aspects. The good quality answers will create a balance between understanding foreign customers and their needs, together with the firm's capability to deliver, i.e. the internal management audit resulting in an appreciation of the 'match' between the attractiveness of a market/country and the company's compatibility with the market (the Harrell and Kiefer model).

Essentially the core of the answer is contained in Unit 6 where the differences between domestic and international planning are spelled out in depth. They include (from a UK perspective):

Domestic planning	*International planning*
In general a single nationality and language	Multilingual, national cultural factors
Relatively homogeneous market	Fragmented, diverse markets
Data availability	Data collection a formidable task
Political factors relatively unimportant	Political factors very important
Financial climate including currency stable	Financial climate extremely volatile
'Rules of the game' understood	'Rules of the game' unclear, changeable
Management by objectives, shared responsibility, financial controls	Management autonomous, few budgets, controls etc.

The above list is not complete nor is the following one dealing with International Planning Problems. The complete list is on pp. 72–3.

International Planning Problems

Headquarters management	*Overseas subsidiary management*
Unclear allocation of responsibility	Resistance to planning
Lack of international orientation	Lack of qualified personnel
Unrealistic expectations	Inadequate abilities
Unclear guidelines	Misunderstanding of requirements
Insensitivity to local needs	Lack of strategic/international thinking

Process	*Process*
Excessive bureaucracy	Poorly developed procedures
Excessive constraints	Lack of trust
Insufficient involvement of subsidiaries in planning	Lack of loyalty

What is required from candidates is not a series of lists but an explanation of the problems and issues facing international planners. Lists in themselves are not acceptable answers but merely provide a framework from which answers can be developed.

December 1993 I strongly believe that an international marketing manager has to concentrate upon all three elements of customers, quality and competitors. Each is linked and each affects the extent to which the organization can achieve its objectives.

The customer

The customer is at the heart of the marketing concept. It is difficult to understand customer requirements in domestic markets but even more difficult in international markets. The customer will be different in terms of social, cultural and economic backgrounds. The international marketing manager must not be hampered by the self-reference criterion. It is essential to know and to satisfy and anticipate customer demands in a timely and profitable way.

Quality

Customers are influenced by the quality of the product or service. In particular, Japanese manufacturers have made high quality, with very few or no defects in the product delivered to customers, an important part of their offering. Customers have responded favourably to high quality products. Whilst high and improving high quality standards will be important in international markets, not all customers have the ability to pay for some of the features of high quality. In lesser developed countries the quality requirement might be for basic products which can be repaired by local people with basic tools. In more advanced economies, in which labour costs are much higher, high quality might demand very infrequent servicing intervals and the ability to use computer diagnostics to identify faults. For the LDCs, high quality has to revolve around the ability of the customer to pay whilst at the same time performing the main functions of the product. In more affluent countries, customers have the ability to consider value in the wider context of the lifetime cost of ownership in which maintenance costs are an important element.

Competitors

In developing international marketing plans, managers have to know who their competitors are and what are their strengths and weaknesses. In the spread of countries it is often difficult to build a detailed understanding of competition. The way in which competitors develop their marketing will influence the success of other players in the market place. Some competitors will concentrate on low prices; others on high quality; others on developing new and improved products. Some competitors will benefit from favourable movements in the foreign exchange markets. Local competitors might be favoured by their own government passing laws to protect local industries from foreign competition. The link between customers, quality and competitors is through satisfying customers. Your competitors will be attempting to satisfy customers better than your own company. In the spread of markets around the world it will be very difficult to know customer requirements at a consistently higher level than your competitors.

Conclusion

International marketing is a difficult and complicated activity. The international marketer must build an entire picture – the customers, the market, the products and the main competitors.

The financial situation relating to different combinations of marketing plans in different countries must be calculated. The changing requirements of customers and the environment in different countries and trading blocs must be regularly monitored. Each of the three areas is important. In the marketing concept, the customer will be regarded as the most important. The quality of the product must be appropriate for the customer both in terms of the type of 'quality' provided and in terms of the customer's ability to pay the higher prices necessitated by the higher costs to achieve the higher quality product. If the company can produce products that satisfy the customer, then they will have little to fear from competitors. In the increasingly competitive market places in the world, it is becoming more difficult to demonstrate clearly that your product is better than the competition. It is, therefore, necessary for the international marketer to consider competitors very carefully when developing strategic plans.

Senior Examiner's comments

The answer given provides a good balance between the three elements of the question. The competitor issue could be developed further to show that competitors will often exist at different levels and pursue different competitive approaches. The main types of competitors are national, world region/trading bloc and global. They might be exporting, producing and marketing in the country, using a joint venture or an alliance, or perhaps franchising or licensing. Some competitors will develop competitive moves based just on one particular country; other companies are beginning to coordinate their marketing plans and their competitive approaches across a number of different countries and sometimes in a coherent global way.

December 1994 **Note to candidates**: Candidates are asked to explain the country of origin effect and then go on to apply it in three different countries using as the basis a consumer durable. Wise candidates will choose three countries at differing stages of economic development, i.e. advanced, nearly industrialized, Third World stages. The consumer durable selected here is a washing machine.

Country of origin effect

Put simply, where a product is produced influences consumers' perception. Perfume labelled 'Made in France' has a very different cachet from perfume made in Hong Kong. In other words, certain countries have developed a reputation over time, e.g. Germany for engineering excellence, Japan for quality consumer electronics, Sweden for cool simplistic design, France for food and wine, Scotland for whisky. Countries without this perception can suffer in the harsh competitive world of international trading. However, the country of origin effect has limitations. Being perceived as 'good' in one category can have a negative effect in another. Additionally, the values attached can and do change over time. Chauvinism can often hinder. Plastering products with the domestic flag can be a major negative. British Telecom changed its name to BT simply because the word British proved to be a handicap in some markets. For the same reason, British Petroleum changed its name to BP.

In positive terms, the country of origin effect can be extremely positive. It can communicate quality, innovation, design and other positive values. In an ever-more competitive market it can provide reassurance for consumers who otherwise might not be able to differentiate between products. In the competitive consumer electronics market, e.g. hi-fi, a 'Made in Japan' label can provide the final impetus in the consumer purchasing decision. Some companies have deliberately branded their own label products with names that have connotations with specific countries, e.g. Dixons, the leading UK consumer electronics retailer's house brand is Matsui – named so as to convey Japanese origin when, in fact, the products are multi-country sourced.

Country of origin applied to a South Korean washing machine marketed to:

(a) Singapore – an advanced country
(b) Thailand – an NIC
(c) China – a Third World country

Korea is itself in the NIC stage of economic development. Its reputation is for producing products that are reliable and good value for money. Its products are not 'state of the art' or at the cutting edge of technological development. They might be described as 'worthy'.

Marketing to Singapore
The emphasis here would be on the robustness of the machine. Price would be less of a consideration but the consumer would expect guarantees of service and after-sales service. To a Singaporean the development of a brand name would be more important than the country of origin. Korea is known as a country where products deliver what they promise – but that apart, Korea is not seen as a centre of excellence.

Marketing to Thailand
Korea has a reputation for success and its goods are admired. 'Made in Korea' would be used as a platform for marketing the product. Additionally, a Korean product would be seen as good value for money. However, price would be a major consideration.

Marketing to China
To Chinese consumers Korea represents 'state of the art' technology. 'Made in Korea' would be an important selling point and therefore be highlighted in marketing. The washing machine would be low tech, basic and functional.

In summary, country of origin can and is a powerful marketing tool. The skill is in recognizing its strengths yet minimizing the negatives and adapting and emphasizing perceptual values to the selected market place.

International market research

Knowledge is power. In this unit you will study the key issues relating to gathering information on the international front. The scale of the task is wider and the problems in collecting data multiply as markets and customers differ. The major thrust of the unit is not concerned with the specifics and technical details of gathering information but discusses the management perspective. You will:

- Understand issues relating to scanning international markets to decide initially where we should go in the broadest terms
- Examine models of how to approach the broad tasks of identifying market/product combinations and on to prioritize opportunities
- Study the sources of international data and have to deal with such issues as researching within numerous markets
- Understand the difficulties involved in comparing data across countries/markets – both primary and secondary data
- Know the basic principles of appointing an international market research agency

Having completed the unit you will be able to:

- Explain the difference between gathering data from an international market(s) and that of a domestic one
- Apply the process of narrowing down broad-scale international opportunities and identify specific countries for further more detailed examination
- Match sources of data to specific problems
- Identify the resource implications of international market research.

International market research needs to be considered stage by stage. It is unfeasible for even the major global players to be totally global in their research. Time and the scale of the task dictates a measured approach. Costs are equally important. The unit takes the approach that information searches begin on the broad scale and subsequently narrow down. Initially the question is 'Where should we go?' With as many as 200 countries to select how does one go about prioritizing? Think about the implication of planning and control against this background. Remember as you work through this unit that the biggest problem is not so much obtaining data but being selective about what data is essential rather than 'Let's collect everything we can'. Again, consider the issues surrounding the comparability of data, e.g. specific words are culturally loaded. What is a 'small business'? What does 'healthy' mean or 'leisure', 'home owner' etc.? These words in common use nonetheless mean different things in different countries.

International market research

As international marketing has developed rapidly in recent years so has the need for information and knowledge. For example, international marketing research, (i.e. research into the application of the 4/7 Ps to a market) is taking an increasingly important role in strategic planning. It is estimated that the 1990s have seen its growth exceed 30 per cent per annum – twice the rate of UK domestic research growth.

When discussing the changes taking place in world trading in an earlier chapter it was apparent that information, knowledge gathering and transference attains critical importance in decision making. Peter Bartram, of Applied Research and Communications, identified three key areas of development:

1 Development of improved techniques, data availability and research supplier networks in developing countries. (e.g. India and the Pacific Rim.)
2 In more developed countries where market research is more established the key competence will be:
    - Development of pan-regional or global surveys allowing a comparison of data
    - The identification of niche markets across national boundaries creating clusters of customers with similar motivations and needs
    - The specialization of research organizations on a regional/worldwide basis. The more detailed your knowledge search, the greater will be the need for appropriate expertise
    - Rapid defusion of new products internationally will dictate faster research delivery.
3 In mature markets the forefront of research may move into the development of database market research via electronic transfers and the deeper involvement of research into 'value' discriminators in identifying segments within markets.

This unit adopts the outlook that the decision has been taken to 'go international' and, furthermore, our view is to concentrate on the information gathering that relates to marketing issues (strategic and tactical).

The scale of the task: personnel and money

With around 200 countries to aim at even the Coca-Cola's and McDonald's of this world would find it a challenge to undertake research everywhere. For those medium to large UK companies who in the normal course of events conduct, shall we say, ten pieces of research per annum in the UK the task of replicating that in Europe alone would require a budget way in excess of most companies' resources to say nothing of the organizational and operational ramifications. Clearly there has to be a systematic approach at conducting international marketing research.

What information?

1 *Where to go?* Having decided to internationalize, the first critical consideration is the need to rank countries in order of priority or attractiveness.
2 *How to get there?* Having decided where to go, the next decision area is how to access the market(s), i.e. exporting, licensing or local production, etc.
3 *What shall we market?* Should we modify our product or service, in what way and to what degree, i.e. the start of the application of the marketing mix, the product P.
4 *How do we persuade them to buy it?* The development of the mix via the necessary Ps (place, price, etc.) and incorporating all four or seven depending on the nature of our offer (product or service).

The information stream

What information should market research provide? The following list sets out the least intelligence needed.

1 *Where to go?*
   - Assessment of global demand
   - Ranking of potential by country/region
   - Local competition
   - Political risk
2 *How to get there?*
   - Size of market/segments
   - Barriers to entry
   - Transport and distribution costs
   - Local competition
   - Government requirements
   - Political risk
3 *What shall we market?*
   - Government regulations
   - Customer sophistication
   - Competitive stance
4 *How do we persuade them to buy it?*
   - Buyer behaviour
   - Competitive practice
   - Distribution channels
   - Media and other promotional channels
   - Company expertise

Table 5.1 augments this abbreviated list and embraces the point that in today's challenging environment the successful domestic firm cannot ignore international market research for

Table 5.1 The task of global marketing research: what should it determine?

	Differences across countries and regions of interest			
The marketing environment	*The competition*	*The product*	*Marketing mix*	*Firm-specific historical data*
Political context: leaders, national goals, ideology, key institutions	Relative market shares	Analysis of users	Channels of distribution: evolution and performance	Sales trends by product and product-line, salesforce and customer
Economic growth prospects, business cycle stage	New product moves	Who are the end-user industries?	Relative pricing, elasticities and tactics	Trends by country and region
Per capita income levels, purchasing power	Pricing and cost structure	Industrial and consumer buyers	Advertising and promotion: choices and impacts on customers	Contribution margins
End-user industry growth trends	Image and brand reputation	Characteristics: size, age, sex, segment growth rates		Marketing mix used, marketing response functions across countries and regions
Government: legislation, regulation, standards, barriers to trade	Quality: its attributes and positioning relative to competitors	Purchasing power and intentions	Service quality: perceptions and relative positioning	
	Competitor's strengths: favourite tactics and strategies	Customer response to new products, price, promotion	Logistics networks, configuration and change	
		Switching behaviour		
		Role of credit and purchasing		
		Future needs		
		Impact of cultural differences		

Source: Terpstra and Sarathy (1994)

inbound competition is accelerating. This is particularly true within the EU, which should be viewed increasingly as a domestic market.

Research methodology

Scanning international markets/countries
In the initial stage countries are scanned for attraction and prioritization. The search may be extremely wide covering many countries, and three criteria lend themselves to this exercise:

1 *Accessibility* Can we get there? What's preventing us? Trade barriers, government regulations, etc.?
2 *Profitability* Can 'they' (i.e. potential customers) afford our product? Is competition too entrenched? Is the market ready? What is the likely payback? Timescale? Will we get paid? Remember, unprofitable business we can get anywhere!
3 *Market size* Present and future trends.

Gilligan and Hird (1985) identified three types of market opportunities:

1 *Existing markets* Markets already covered by existing products/suppliers making market entry difficult without a superior offering
2 *Latent markets* Evidence of potential demand but with no product yet offered, making entry easier. No direct competition
3 *Incipient markets* No current demand exists but condition and trends suggest future emergent demand.

Figure 5.1 allies the three types of market opportunities to three types of products:

1 *Competitive product* A 'me too' offering with no significant advantages
2 *Improved product* While not unique has a discernable advantage over present offerings.
3 *Breakthrough product* An innovation with significant differentiation.

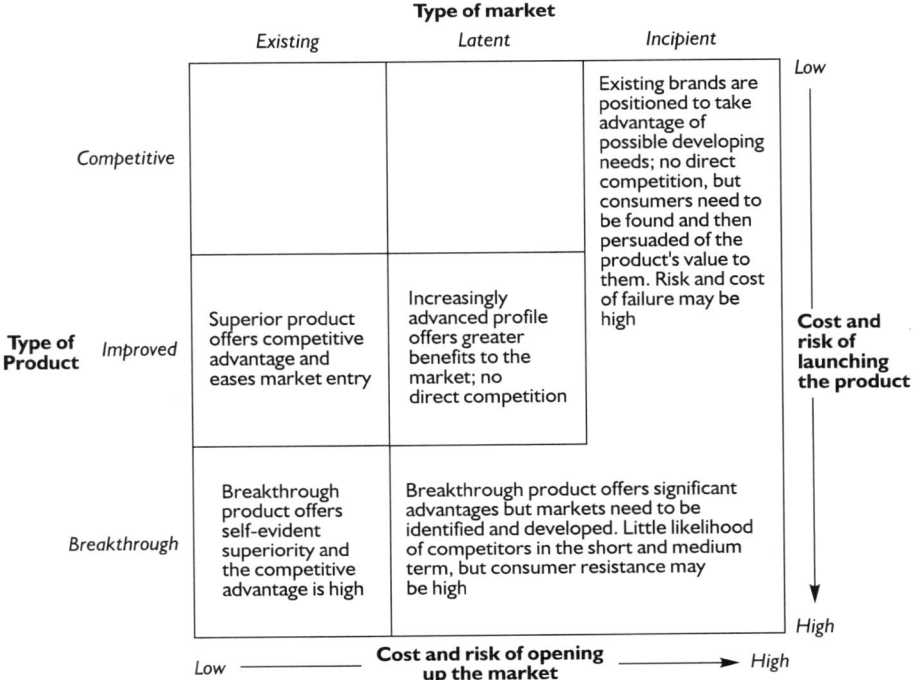

Figure 5.1 Product/market combinations and the scope for competitive advantage on market entry. (*Source:* Gilligan and Hird, 1985)

Figure 5.1 provides an insight into the nature of the marketing task needed. It forms the basis for further detailed investigation (e.g. the degree of competitive advantage and other dynamics).

Method of scanning in underdeveloped countries

Frequently in international marketing it is not easy to obtain relevant information directly, or without resort to expensive research methodologies. When a broad overview only is required/sufficient at this stage and concern is mainly to eliminate non-starters other methods of scanning markets, particularly in developing countries, include the following.

Analogy estimation

Given the absence of significant hard data researchers might rely on analogous countries by either a 'cross-section comparison' of economic indicators, disposable income or a 'time series approach' estimating that country B is developing or following a similar pattern of development (and therefore product usage) as country A. The limitations of analogy estimation is to assume linear patterns of development and should be used as a first stage and inexpensive screening.

Regression analysis

A more sophisticated development of the analogous method involves studying, for example, the relationship between economic growth indicators and demand for specific products in countries with both kinds of data (country A), then transferring it to countries with similar economic growth data, but no product data (country B). For example, if £100 equivalent in per capital GNP in country A resulted in an increase of 10 cars, 20 fridges, 8 TV sets, etc. per 1000 population, the same might well occur in country B. The limitations of this approach are also obvious as no two countries are totally alike.

Cluster analysis

Using macro economic and consumption data is a popular technique of identifying similar markets, for example:

- *Infrastructure dynamics* energy consumption, urbanization, motorway and other transport facilities such as airports, containerization etc.
- *Consumption variation* numbers of cars, telephones, educational level
- *Trade data* import and export figures
- *Health and education* life expectancy, number of doctors.

Improvisation

This is literally extrapolating data between broadly similar countries and in a way 'second guessing' the potential product need and demand in those countries (Table 5.2).

Finally, there are other methods that may warrant your attention. For example, risk evaluation is obviously important (see political risk).

Table 5.2

Level of institution	Potential markets
1. Market Square	Cloth material (not made up), a village economy
2. Church, elementary school	Small forms economy, packaged goods, radios, bikes, garage, petrol, etc.
3. Secondary school, police, government building	Urbanization (first steps), social dresses, fridges, plumbing, etc.
4. Higher education, sewage system	Factories, office supplies and service industries

Source: Terpstra 2nd edn

International market segmentation: prioritization

The scanning method represents phase 1 in international marketing research. The next stage is to evaluate markets/countries in order to prioritize them for still further investigation. The key issue here is not simply to list countries in terms of priorities, but to group them in clusters or segments. We are searching for *similarities* more than differences. Similarities provide:

1 Economies of scale
2 Optimization in marketing
3 Easier diffusion of products
4 Ease of operation, management and control
5 Greater profitability

Unfortunately marketers spend too much time highlighting differences between markets/ countries and forget to identify the areas of similarity and convergence. It is similarities that determine whether a pan-regional or global approach is possible. This is becoming increasingly critical for companies particularly in the EU, where harmonization is under way.

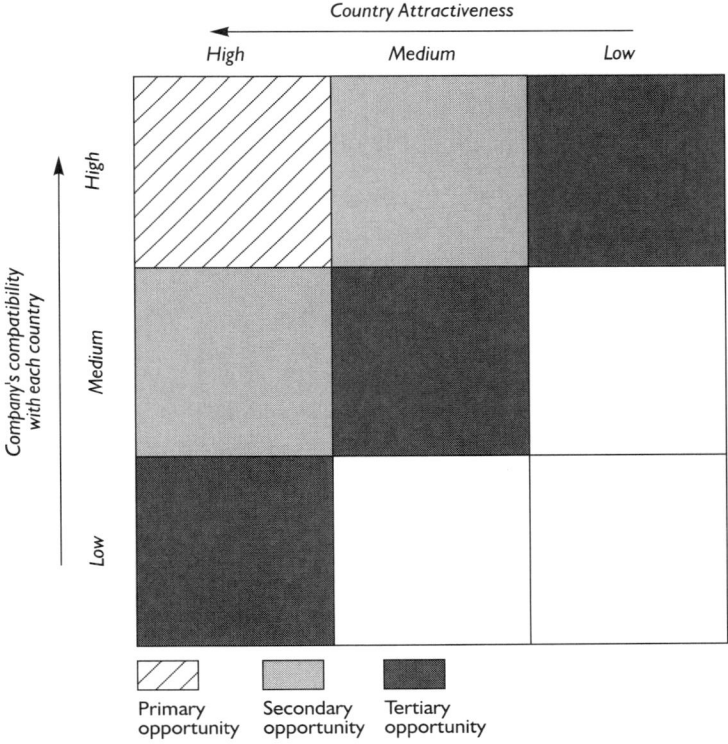

Figure 5.2   Business portfolio matrix (*Source:* Harrall and Kiefer, 1993)

The major methodology is to classify countries into categories as illustrated in Figure 5.2. Broadly, countries fall into three groups:

1 *Primary markets*   where high attractiveness coincides with a high degree of company strengths. This might lead to the company investing heavily within the country(ies)
2 *Secondary markets*   riskier but where there is still significant business to be gained albeit through a lower level of strategic investment
3 *Tertiary markets*   business gained via short-term, *ad hoc* and opportunist activity with no serious commitment in an operational sense. However, good profit may be earned here and it is no reason not to do business providing the level of financial investment and risk to exposure is low.

Once key markets/countries have been identified and prioritized further market research is necessary to identify customer segments within the chosen countries using the recognized and standard quantitative and qualitative research techniques – demographics, buyer behaviour, consumer motivation, lifestyle, etc. This further research is critical for although the international segmentation model described above identifies clusters of countries, the key to successful international marketing is discovering clusters or segments of customers. Country segmentation is therefore often oversimplistic, for it pays insufficient attention to customer similarities across national boundaries.

Kole and Sudharshan (1987) speak of firms needing to achieve strategically equivalent segments (SES) that transcend national boundaries. They contend that to achieve SES companies need to:

1 Identify countries with sufficient infrastructure to support its product and that are lucrative to the company
2 Screen those countries to arrive at a realistic short-list (e.g. those countries with a sufficiently large segment)
3 Develop micro-segments within those countries identified by product characteristics required
4 Identify the key characteristics of the demand of each micro-segment searching for similarities in terms of behaviourial pattern
5 Through cluster analysis identify meaningful cross-national segments which would respond similarly to a consistent marketing mix strategy.

The search is under way to unravel customer behaviour and response similarities across Europe. The major European multinationals (e.g. Nestlé) are fast acquiring and developing Euro brands. To achieve synergies in marketing they are seeking Euro consumers. It is early days but Euro Mosaic is claimed as the first pan-European consumer segmentation system to classify consumers on the basis of neighbourhood having identified ten Euro neighbourhood classifications:

1 Elite suburbs
2 Average areas
3 Luxury flats
4 Low-income city
5 High-rise social housing
6 Industrial communities
7 Dynamic families
8 Low-income families
9 Rural/agricultural
10 Vacation/retirement

As can be seen, the segmentation is broad – and, frankly, is at an early development stage. However, in the absence of more sophisticated approach it is a start.

Nielsen has introduced Quartz, its first pan-European research service, which provides simulated market tests based on consumer reaction in five European countries. Procter & Gamble, Nestlé and in total 25 multinationals subscribe to the service. Europanel, a pan-European panel consortium, checks 55 000 households monitoring the movement and consumptions of consumer goods. Ipsos, a French company, evaluates consumers' viewing and reading habits in major EU countries. The demand for quality multi-country research is still in its infancy and we can anticipate rapid growth in, for example, pan-European quantitative and qualititative comparative research across national boundaries.

EXAM QUESTION

Examine the ways in which an international company should identify and analyse opportunities across a wide spread of country markets (June 1995, Question 3).

Explain why market segmentation developed within country boundaries is different from segmentation that transcends nations. Which method of market segmentation would you recommend and in what situation? Justify your answer and show how marketing research can be used in the segmentation process (December 1995, Question 9).

Many companies are looking to emerging markets in their internationalization programmes. What are the problems involved in researching these markets? How, if at all, might they be overcome? (June 1997, Question 6)

The international marketing information system

Doole, Lowe and Phillips (1997) refer to the 12C analysis model for creating an information system:

Country
- General country information
- Basic SLEPT data
- Impact of environmental dimensions.

Choices
- Analysis of supply
- International and external competition
- Characteristics of competitors
- Import analysis
- Competitive strengths and weaknesses.

Concentration
- Structure of the market segments
- Geographical spread.

Culture/consumer behaviour
- Characteristics of the country
- Diversity of cultural grouping
- Nature of decision-making
- Major influences of purchasing behaviour.

Consumption
- Demand and end-use analysis of economic sectors that use the product
- Market share by demand sector
- Growth patterns of sectors
- Evaluation of the threat of substitute products.

Capacity to pay
- Pricing
- Extrapolation of pricing to examine trends
- Culture of pricing
- Conditions of payment
- Insurance terms.

Currency
- Stability
- Restrictions
- Exchange controls.

Channels
- Purchasing behaviour
- Capabilities of intermediaries
- Coverage of distribution costs
- Physical distribution infrastructure.

Commitment
- Access to market
- Trade incentives and barriers
- Custom tariffs
- Government regulations
- Regulations on market entry.

Communication
- Promotion
- Media infrastructure and availability
- Which marketing approaches are effective
- Cost of promotion
- Common selling practices
- Media information.

Contractual obligations
- Business practices
- Insurance
- Legal obligations.

Caveats
- Factors to be aware of.

Without doubt, collection of this information is a formidable task – well beyond the resources of all but the largest firms. Even these will find difficulties in drawing the comparison and making the necessary links between countries to assist in the creation of potentially profitable segments. Having made this point a list is useful as a consistent point of reference.

EXAM QUESTION

?

Identify and justify the marketing research approach you would recommend to a company that wishes to assess global market potential (December 1994, Question 6).

Identify the principal methods that companies might use in assessing and reviewing underdeveloped country markets, and suggest how the information generated might be used to prioritize countries for decisions on market entry (December 1997, Question 7).

(**See** Exam answers at the end of this unit.)

Sourcing international market research

Where and how do we find international information – and the problems involved? Terpstra and Sarathy state that because of its complexity international market research generates more and different problems than domestic research. Because countries are different, each poses its own set of problems. Furthermore, how does one deal with gathering information from dozens or up to a hundred countries?

The breadth of the task

International market research covers macro economic, micro economic, cultural, political and a host of other variables. Also, because of the drive towards internationalization, markets can no longer be studied individually – they must be screened for similarities to develop pan-regional or even global markets. It follows that the international market researcher (or the division) has a far wider remit than any domestic research organization making the creation of an MIS system even more important.

The problem of numerous markets

Besides such important considerations as cost and because countries are different the international researchers must take into consideration various problems in designing and interpreting multi-country research. Mayer identifies some basic considerations:

- *Definition error*   countries often define markets and categories differently, e.g. the term 'small business' varies across Europe
- *Instrument error*   arising from the detail written on questionnaires
- *Frame error*   sampling frames vary by country. The UK socio-demographic definitions of A, B, C1, C2 etc. will have little direct equivalent overseas. Even within the EU, whilst there is a very broad equivalent the differences remain substantial.
- *Selection error*   problems arising from the way the actual sample is selected from the frame
- *Non-response error*   the cultural variance.

Returning to the issue of costs, how much research can we afford? A sense of realism must prevail, we can't research everything and the organization must refer to its resources and the timescales involved.

Secondary data – acquiring them and problems with them

With so many markets to consider it is essential that companies begin their international market research by seeking and utilizing secondary data, i.e. data that already exists and is generally available at low cost. For those who are unclear in terminology secondary research is frequently referred to as desk research.

Many countries are awash with secondary data but, in general, there is a correlation between the stage of economic development and the availability, depth and accuracy of information. Where it is available it is generally plentiful, cheap and accurate; where it is not its quality is variable, its relevance dubious and its accuracy flawed. As a preliminary stage of investigation secondary research can quickly unearth general background information to eliminate many countries from the scope of enquiries. Such information might include:

- Population, language(s), ethnic differences
- Type of government, political stability and that of neighbouring countries, risk of war, etc., social policies
- Location, geography, topography, climate
- Basic economic data, income and its distribution, employment, industry versus agriculture, policy towards businesses, tax structure, private versus government sector split
- Legal information, regulations, barriers to entry and exit (of profits), member of GATT, etc.
- Overseas trade patterns, with UK, other nations, importance of exports and imports to the economy.

All this material forms a good solid basis for initial screening purposes but falls some way short of providing marketing information to help pinpoint real customer needs and wants. Most of the above information can be unearthed on the majority of countries but it is only in the more sophisticated countries that you might discover the following:

- Size of market (as defined locally), its make-up and structures
- Who are main customers, who buys what (what are the available products) and, very importantly, why they buy (motivations for purchase)
- Competition, scope and practices (marketing mix)
- Promotional practices – availability, sophistication, legal restrictions
- Distribution patterns – where customers buy (supermarkets or market squares), intermediaries (choice and number of stages)
- Pricing, how much customers pay, what the trade structure is in terms of mark-up, margins
- Service element; after-sales guarantees, who fixes the product if/when it breaks

Note: The list is not complete, it is indicative of the broad range of data services available in the UK.

Problems with secondary data are as follows:

1 The non-availability of data. Westernized countries apart, the rest of the world varies considerably in its statistical output. The weaker economies have weaker statistical services – many do not carry out a population census. In some countries there is only an estimate of the population.

2 The reliability of the data. Data may have been massaged by governments to prove a particular point or to gain funds from world bodies. Again the data may be time-lagged or even old and therefore may have limited bearing on the status quo.

3 The source of the data will inevitably reflect local/national conditions and may be meaningless to outsiders. Even something as straightforward as pensions both in terms of retirement age and size of payment show considerable differences between for example the UK and France.

4   Comparability across markets is difficult. The terms car owner, small business, householder, youth, health, engineer, family, leisure etc. mean different things in each country. The term middle-class is a good example. We know what it means in the UK cultural terms of reference (but each of us would find it difficult to explain precisely) – but in India it generally means adults with an annual income of £2,000 plus. A considerable difference, but one with broadly speaking similar purchasing powers within each country context.

5   Availability of sources either private or public varies enormously. The international major corporation such as A. C. Nielsen (the world's No. 1 researcher) is operating only in 28 countries. It and others are totally absent in more than half the countries in the world. Trade associations, chambers of commerce, all are equally variable in their existence and indeed in their output for they too mean different things country by country. In France, chambers of commerce are very powerful organizations, but what information might you expect from Burkina Faso?

Sources of secondary information

The UK and European Union has a rich source of secondary information covering everywhere in the world. We in the UK are awash with information and data sources. Although at first sight the gathering of information seems a daunting task, if set about logically and with diligence it is no more difficult than obtaining domestic data. The method is to accept that 'everything we need to know' is unlikely to be forthcoming but applying Pareto's 80:20 rule will unearth most of the key facts with the remainder to be discovered either via primary research (in sophisticated markets) or by using skilled executive judgement and testing in markets where such information may be less accessible. Set out below is a list of desk research sources. It is not a complete list but gives guidance – for much of the information sought will be industry-specific.

- Specialist trade press
- Quality press, journals and magazines
- Trade associations
- Directories, e.g. Kompass and Euromonitor
- Major university business schools
- Public libraries and specific business libraries
- Chamber of Commerce
- Your bankers
- International consultancies
- Electronic media, e.g. Internet
- Syndicated or published research
- Competitors' published information
- Export houses and freight forwarders
- Embassies, both UK ones overseas and foreign embassies in the UK

But for the majority of UK companies the first port of call for information on overseas markets will be the Department of Trade & Industry (DTI). With its vast database and many years of experience the DTI provides a wide-ranging and excellent service, and even if it does not have the answers can provide new leads. Reasonably priced, its services are invaluable and the staff helpful and accessible by phone/fax or personal visit to Victoria Street, London SW1.

Primary research – acquiring it and problems with it

In dealing with primary research we are discussing the everyday research technique utilized in our domestic market to unearth usage and attitude information concerning our company's customers, their choices and preferences, the stimuli that motivates them to behave positively to our products, prices, promotional practices, etc. By the time primary research is to be employed the organization will have narrowed down its choice of potential markets to a few. The complexity and cost of generating new, first-hand information is formidable. For example, a national usage and attitude survey in the UK might cost upwards of £80 000. Imagine replicating this across Europe.

We are not going to discuss the techniques of primary research, which should be familiar to readers. Instead we highlight the problems involved in carrying it out overseas.

Problems with primary research

Countries are different, people are different and respond differently. This makes uniformity of information a potential and often real nightmare from a research standpoint as self-reference criteria (SRC) are imposed. Let us examine some of the more obvious ones:

1 *Costs* Conducting primary research varies. The UK is one of the least expensive, Japan one of the most expensive.
2 *Language* In which language should the survey be conducted? Singapore with a population of about 3 million has four official languages requiring four translations and four different ethnic interviewers:
   - Interpretation of languages (translation) is frequently misleading and even back-translation into the author's language can be flawed. What is required is not translation but transposition of the questionnaire into the respondent's cultural framework. This is very sophisticated and difficult.
   - Literacy: pictorials are not easy to understand or interpret. Technical literacy is also a frequent problem, i.e. the non-comprehension of things abstract, etc., time or concepts such as health, leisure, etc.
3 *Sample* in a non-urban or low urbanized country where will you find AB respondents? They may be scattered far and wide. In Muslim countries who do you interview, buyer (male) or the user (female)? Interviewing the latter is rare.
4 *Geography* Where do you conduct the survey? For example, in Nigeria, the north is desert, the south Equatorial. Responses in one area may have no relevance in another. Similarly, tribal differences in a country will elicit different responses.
5 *Non Response* The Japanese always like to please and invariably say 'Yes'. Then they really mean they don't like your product. 'I will consider it very carefully' is Japanese for *no*. In other societies being interviewed has connotations of 'agents of the state' or, worse, tax inspectors.
6 *Social Organization* In some societies even business-to-business and industrial markets are affected. Unlike the West, companies are often family owned where openness is frowned upon and secrecy is important. Furthermore, Western terminology may have little direct relevance (e.g. cash flow, stock turnover are not everyday terminologies).
7 *Terminology* The point has already been made concerning the interpretation of language as it is bounded by SRC. What do we mean by holidays, well off, health food, live alone, family, youth, middle aged? In the USA researchers have divided the country into 62 separate classes according to wealth, education, mobility, location, ethnic background etc. Among the new classes are Urban Gold Coasters, Young Literati and Scrubbed Piners (Figure 5.3). Consider also the article in Figure 5.4 which appeared in connection with a survey about attitudes to drink-driving and attempt to explain the categories of offenders to anyone other than to a UK citizen. Come to think of it, explain the concept of drink-driving itself . . . .

In conclusion, it is certain that some cultural bias will exist in all primary research activities as SRC are applied depending on the cultural context of the host nation, for example Germany, Austria and Switzerland are described as having a low cultural context, i.e.

A member of the Scrubber class

MARKETING experts have divided the country into 62 separate classes according to wealth and education, mobility, location and ethnic and racial background. Among the new classes are Urban Gold Coasters, Young Literati and Scrubbed Piners.
Washington Post

Yuck, it must be health food

OVERHEARD in a Manhattan health food store as a mother coaxed her son into trying fruit-candy: 'It doesn't taste good,' he complained. 'Of course not,' she replied. 'It's health food.'
New York Times

Figure 5.3 (*Source: The Guardian*, 21 December 1994)

Persistent middle-aged offender image 'a myth'

THE IMAGE of the persistent drink-drive offender as middle-class, middle-aged and likely to drink twice the legal limit is dismissed as a myth by a new study, *writes Rebecca Smithers*.

The study, carried out by the Portman Group (a drinks industry initiative against alcohol misuse) in association with the Department of Transport, identified five main types of drink-drive offender; from the 'persisters' likely to have previous convictions and often unemployed, through to the 'young irresponsibles' who new their driving was impaired by drinking but who still took the risk.

The Portman Group says the problem of drinking and driving extends downwards into the teenage years and upwards into the mid-30s. High risk offenders tend to be slightly older – their peak age is 29 compared to 24 for all offenders. But it concludes there is 'little evidence of a significant problem among drivers in the 40s in the higher socio-economic groups'.

The problem of drink driving is still largely a male one; in 1992, only 7 per cent of drink-related fatal accidents involved a woman driver over the legal limit. Last year, only around 12 per cent of those who failed a breath test after an injury accident were women.

Altogether, drink-drive fatalities have fallen from 1550 in 1982 to 550 last year.

The five main types of drink-drive offender are:

☐ Persisters: 23 per cent of sample, aged 25 to 44, typically drinking beer (81 per cent) or strong beer (16 per cent) in pubs or at home before offending. Often unemployed, C2DE men with previous convictions for drink-driving and other crimes.

☐ Refuters: 22 per cent of sample, aged 25 to 54, typically drinking beer (80 per cent) or strong beer (13 per cent) in pubs before offending. They are C2DEs, deny drink-driving is wrong, and feel chances of being stopped are remote. Think they are good drivers, unaffected by drinking.

☐ Devastated professionals: 19 per cent of sample, aged 25 to 44, 72 per cent drinking beer, 16 per cent wine, 16 per cent spirits either in pubs or at home before offending. Predominantly middle-aged, ABs of C1s. Shocked at being treated as criminals. Felt they were able to drive after drinking.

☐ Young irresponsibles: 17 per cent of sample, aged 20 to 35, typically drinking strong beer at home or at friends' homes before offending. C1s and C2s with a carefree attitude to life, easily influenced in a group, and inexperienced drivers. Knew their driving was impaired but still took the risk.

☐ One-offs: 7 per cent of sample, aged 35 to 54, C1C2DEs, typicaly drinking beer at friends' or relatives' homes before offending. Unusual circumstances such as celebration, argument or depression led to offence. Severely affected by conviction, claimed to be reformed as a result.

Figure 5.4   (*Source: The Guardian*, 21 December 1994)

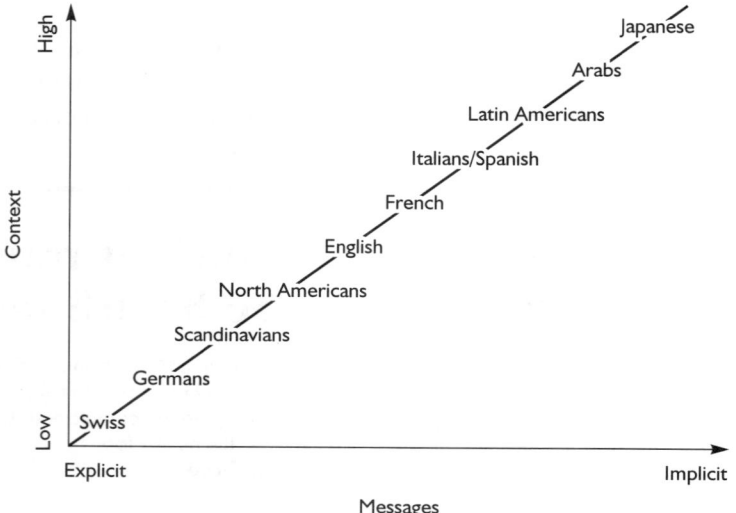

Figure 5.5   The contextual continuum of differing cultures. (From Usunier, adapted from Edward T. Hall)

responses to questions are straightforward. Japan, on the other hand is at the other extreme where the subtly of the response is important, i.e. the manner in which the question is answered is at least as important as the response itself. Figure 5.5 illustrates the contextual continuum of differing cultures. Most will be surprised to see the English and the French so close together. To paraphrase the research, Edward Hall found that some cultures, 'low context cultures', rely much more than others, 'high context cultures', on the actual words used in communication. Communication is complicated in high context cultures by the need to understand more aspects of the context surrounding the message, e.g. social setting, status etc. Usunier devised a contextual continuum of differing cultures, in which in the UK and the US are found to be similar in terms of the importance of context to the understanding of communication. It is also evident that SRC will exist between the client company and the organization(s) conducting the research if they are from different cultures.

Attempts are being made to make order out of cross-country research by using structured questionnaires, telephone interviews and postal surveys, but again infrastructure variables and cultural differences interfere. For example, some countries have a less than perfect postal service and telephone ownership is restricted to the elite. Furthermore such techniques are applicable only to certain areas.

Finally, the key to minimizing the variable response in primary research is superior research design, transposition of words and concepts in its cultural reference, an understanding (by the researcher) of the problem involved and the skill in interpretation of data into information and knowledge. With close to 50 per cent of the world's primary research being conducted in Europe there is clearly a long way to go.

Planning and organizing for international market research

We are going to focus on the medium to large firm as it is apparent that small firms will have too many restrictions to engage in multi-country primary research and will rely on gathering secondary data. Additionally, they will rely on channel intermediaries for their information.

The extent to which medium to large firms will engage in international market research will similarly be guided by the nature of the market and its customers, company resources, its marketing expertise and the scale of the task. A major consideration is whether to conduct the research in-house or to appoint external agencies. An industrial scenario might be handled in-house (there being few customers and each being identifiable) whereas a consumer goods scenario lends itself to the use of external research agencies.

In choosing an agency Doole, Lowe and Phillips suggest six options:

- An agency local to the chosen market
- A domestic agency with overseas subsidiaries
- A domestic agency with overseas associates
- A domestic agency with subcontracted fieldwork
- A domestic agency with competent foreign staff
- A global agency

The choice will depend on the variables in the market(s), the desired strategic level of marketing involvement on the part of the client company and the scale of the marketing task to be undertaken eventually. Further consideration includes:

- Language issues
- The level of 'specialist knowledge of the market'
- The budget
- The level of interpretation post-research

This suggests that there is no one solution and that companies select agencies appropriate to the task. It is vital to brief the agency(ies) carefully and to maintain a close relationship throughout. Piloting the research may be essential if comparative data are required. Care in analysis and interpretation of the data is equally important. The management role in organizing and coordinating international marketing research is not to be underestimated, especially if the findings are to be disseminated from one country to another in assisting marketing planning decisions.

• Identify the factors that would influence the choice of a market research agency the carry out a multi-country survey. Examine the rationale for carrying out research in the countries surrounding the Mediterranean from a base in Cyprus (June 1994, Question 7).

• Explain the process and problems of commissioning a marketing research survey in several different countries in which the comparability of results is a key issue (June 1993, Question 10).

(**See** Exam answers at the end of this unit.)

Summary

All too frequently organizations fall back on one of two strategies when dealing with information issues on the international front. Self-reference criteria i.e. foreigners are just like us and if we licked the problem 'here' we can do it overseas or, alternatively, use guesswork. Both approaches invariably result in grief. It is clear that if information = knowledge = power then it is even more important that we have the facts in dealing with environments beyond our normal range of experience. Knowing where to start and how to go about gathering information on overseas nations and customers must be the fundamental benchwork that underpins all our thinking.

Questions

• As the international marketing for Coca-Cola how would you monitor reactions around the world to a major competitor such as Pepsi?

• Identify the advantages and disadvantages of both secondary and primary data in international marketing.

• Why is it so difficult to assess demand for a product in multi-country research?

• Explain how screening can be used to prioritize international markets. Illustrate your answer by the use of models.

• Select a product category (e.g. Shampoo). What criteria might you apply to evaluate information internationally?

• Identify a major international firm in your locality. Establish what kinds of help in terms of marketing information assistance are available in the UK.

• Contact the DTI (or the equivalent bureau in your country) with a view to obtaining marketing information for a specific country.

For additional supporting information read:

International Marketing, V. Terpstra and R. Sarathy, The Dryden Press, 1997, Chapter 7.

International Marketing Strategy, I. Doole, R. Lowe and C. Phillips, Routledge, 1997, Chapter 4.

International Marketing, S. Paliwoda and M. Thomas, Butterworth-Heinemann, 1998.

Global Marketing Strategies, J.-P. Jeannet and H. D. Hennessey, Houghton Mifflin, 1998, Chapter 6.

June 1995, Question 3   This is not a question that requires one to discuss in depth the problems associated with international market research. Rather the issue is more macro orientated than micro, although it is important to recognize at the outset that to be successful information is required that covers both the SLEPT factors internationally and the important local aspects of Customers, Currency and Competitors (quote Kenichi Ohmae). With around 200 countries to aim for, it is obvious that some system of organizing the search is necessary. The information stream should broadly consider the following:

Where to go

- Assessment of global demand
- Ranking of potential by country
- Local competition
- Political rolee

How to get there

- Size of market/segment
- Barriers to entry
- Transport and logistics
- Government requirements

What shall we market?

- Government regulations
- Customer needs/wants/sophistication
- Competitive stance

How do we persuade them to buy it?

- Buyer behaviour
- Competitive practice
- Distribution channels
- Media and other promotional channels
- Company expertise

The methodology

In approaching this information stream and packaging it into manageable proportions the company should, in its initial stage of investigation, scan markets for attraction and prioritization. The search may be extremely wide, covering many countries, and three criteria lend themselves to this exercise:

1 *Accessibility* – Can we get there? What is preventing us? Trade barriers, government regulations, etc.
2 *Profitability* – Can customers afford our product(s)? Is competition too entrenched? Is the market ready? What is likely pay-back? Time scale? Will we get paid? etc.
3 *Market size and trend* – Both present and future trends.

Gilligan and Hird created a model for scanning purposes using a matrix. (**Note**: here you could sketch out the matrix we have produced above as Figure 5.1, p. 53).
Other methods of scanning countries include:

- *Analogy estimation* – i.e. using a cross-section comparison of economic and social indicators.
- *Regression analysis* – a more sophisticated version of the above using time factors and assuming linear development (frequently wrong).
- *BERI* – Business Environment Risk Index, assessing countries on 15 SLEPT factors and rating each on a four-point scale.

Finally, the aim of the company is to effect a 'match' between country attractiveness and the company's compatibility with each country. Harrel and Kiefer's model illustrates how this works. The major methodology is to classify clusters of market in terms of primary, secondary and tertiary opportunities. (**Note**: this is the business portfolio matrix we have produced as Figure 5.2, p. 55. A sketched version appears below in the answer to the following question.)

December 1995, Question 9

The major thrust of this question concerns international segmentation. Segmentation domestically tends to be concerned with consumers/customer behaviour set against a home background.

Internationally the company seeks segments of market attractiveness across market/country boundaries linking market attractiveness with company compatibility with the market.

The model to apply is Harrell and Keifer, which students should know. A full description appears on p. 55 with Figure 5.2 and a sketch version is offered in the answer to Question 6, December 1994, p. 67 below.

Key factors might include:

- Political and economic risk
- Infrastructure and support of product
- Accessibility to country and onwards to the customer
- Size of market and other qualifying criteria, e.g. number of refrigerators
- Level of competition
- Micro segments – the consumer segments – the use of market research defining these, e.g. using Euromosaic in defining elite suburbs, luxury flats etc.

June 1997 Major questions in international marketing revolve around two categories.

(a) Market and competitive decisions.
(b) Product and marketing mix decisions.

(a) The firm should concern itself with:
  - Identifying barriers to attractive markets and how to overcome them.
  - Understanding how customers rate it versus competitors.
  - On what basis will it compete or cooperate with competition.
(b) The important issues are:
  - What products to introduce.
  - Which distribution channels to use.
  - How to advertise and promote itself/products.

Market research is the mechanism to guide firms in their decision on the above.
  Characteristics of emerging markets/countries include:

- Lack of hard database, or even basic statistics.
- Absence of secondary data. If present may be inaccurate, old or irrelevant.
- Problems of gathering primary data (many). Students should elaborate by example.
- Management issues relating to collecting, analysing, interpreting data, e.g. lack of infrastructure.
- Lack of trained interviewers or even market research agencies.
- Difficulties in drawing management conclusions.

Against this background firms must rely on other techniques.

- Analysis of demand patterns – for primary and secondary industry sectors, e.g. food, textiles, motor cars.
- Multiple factors including – marketing potential indirectly using proxy variables, e.g. literacy levels, percentage of urbanization, number of households.

Estimates by analogy:

1 Cross-section comparisons relating data in one country to another with similar characteristics.
2 Time series approach – estimating demand in the emerging country by assumption linked with time lag.
  - Regression analysis – further refinement of estimates by analogy.
  - Cluster analysis – useful for developing a shortlist of priorities (a much favoured technique).

There should be a conclusion that relates to the introduction and covering the point that none of the above solutions is satisfactory but that in emerging markets 'near enough is good enough'. In information-gathering and executive judgement, observation and international experience are very important, as is learning by doing.

December 1994, Question 6 This is not as it might appear at first sight a question dealing with the implementation at a tactical level of international market research. It is a strategic level question and must be approached from a global perspective rather than a local/country viewpoint.

Secondly, candidates should address this question both in terms of identifying and justifying an approach.

The major thought therefore concerns scanning international markets in terms of:

- accessibility
- profitability
- market size/potential

Having identified these three broad areas, the next stage is to access markets in terms of market opportunities. Here, three types present themselves:

- existing markets, i.e. those served by existing companies where intensive competition would occur should you decide to enter;
- latent markets, i.e. potential exists but no one is yet fulfilling latent need;
- incipient markets, i.e. markets which do not yet exist but conditions can be identified that indicate future demand.

It is worth recording that other methods may be employed satisfactorily, e.g. demand pattern analysis, multiple factor indices, regression techniques, risk evaluation or BERI (Business Environment Risk Index). (**Note**: Candidates would be well advised to appraise themselves of these techniques.)

In terms of justification, the Existing, Latent, Incipient approach would seem to be a most appropriate method as it enables a large number of countries/markets to be accessed quickly within affordable costs.

The purpose of this scanning exercise is to narrow down the choice from many markets to a more manageable list: i.e. to prioritize the selection process. Following this, the company's compatability with the country, the international company will need to segment markets on the basis of matching country attractiveness and the company's compatibility with the country. Here the Harrell and Kiefer model can be employed.

Country attractiveness

	High	Medium	Low
High	P	S	T
Medium	S	T	
Low	T		

Company's compatibility with each country

P = primary opportunity
S = secondary opportunity
T = tertiary opportunity

Justification should be based on the fact that secondary market research can be employed (speed and cost benefits) before further reducing the scale of the task to a few specific countries for further research, employing both primary and secondary methodology. Once key markets/countries have been identified the normal research methods of qualitative and quantitative techniques would be applied to pinpoint further the opportunity – consumer motivation, buyer behaviour etc.

December 1997 Again candidates who write in general terms on the subject of international information-gathering will not be rewarded with a pass grade. Too often in the past answers to this type of question have revolved around the problems of gathering secondary and primary information. This question deals specifically with assessing potential in underdeveloped countries. It can be taken as read that there will be problems in gathering information on a formalized basis. Therefore the key information requirements might be:

1 Accessibility. Can we get there, what is preventing entry, barriers, government factors of all kinds?
2 Profitability. Can countries afford our products? What is the competition? Is the market ready? What is the likely payback period? Will we get paid?
3 Market size and trend. Present and future.

The principal methods in assessing underdeveloped countries include:

1 The Gilligan and Hird model as referred to on p. 53, which identifies markets in terms of Existing, Latent and Incipient. Good candidates might well be expected to draw the model.
2 Analogy estimation, i.e. using a cross-section comparison of economic and social indicators which again can only provide a rough guideline as no two country markets are identical.
3 Regression analysis – a more sophisticated version of (2) assuming linear development and which is frequently wrong.
4 BERI – Business Environment Risk Index.
5 Cluster analysis – making improvised assumptions.

The second part of the question requires suggestions on how the information might be used to prioritize countries. The obvious method is the Harrell and Keifer model which pulls together country attractiveness and the company's compatibility with each country. This is referred to on p. 55 above.

Top quality answers will explain the model and possibly relate some criteria for country attractiveness back to the original comment on accessibility, profitability, market size/potential etc. and add in other relevant factors such as language, psychological/geographic proximity etc.

June 1994, Question 7 Major factors likely to influence choice of agency include the following.

Agency has experience in product market and country surveys of this type. Many forms of international marketing research require an understanding of both markets and countries to be carried out intelligently and cost efficiently.

Further, the agency must have resources to coordinate and carry out the survey. This involves not only field-work management but also the cross-country and agency–client liaison necessary. Such resources include not only the usual market research facilities, but staff conversant with the peculiarities, in terms of the PEST factors for each country, that could affect the results and responses to the survey.

Following on from the above point, the agency must be adaptable. It is unlikely that an identical market research plan can be operated across all the relevant markets. The ability to adapt the survey methodology to each market as required is important.

At the analysis stage, the agency should be able to demonstrate an understanding of the different responses and methodologies used, to ensure compatible and comparable results emerge from the studies.

The agency will likely demonstrate its familiarity with the relevant countries by having relevant offices or associates in such markets. Normally it is preferable for personnel to be familiar with a market when carrying out research.

Ability to deal in the necessary language for the survey, including translation and interpretation of both questions and findings, is essential.

Choice of Cyprus as a base for Mediterranean survey

Geographically, Cyprus is well located for the area. The division of the island into Turkish and Greek Cypriot areas may cause concern as to the political stability of the centre. However, it is unlikely that such stability would deteriorate without significant warning and a survey would not be a long-term operation.

The Mediterranean is a mixture of cultures – Christian, Islamic, Judaic being the main influencing cultures – and covers highly developed Western economies such as France in the west to underdeveloped North African and Middle Eastern countries. It is unlikely that any one country as a base could affect the problem of coping with such diversity in a multi-country survey.

One major asset to Cyprus is its political neutrality – in the sense that it does not engage in power politics (e.g. Israel, Libya) and hence any survey emanating from the island would not have political undertones likely to cause reaction from the relevant country.

Being a relatively developed country, and with a long established tourism industry, good physical and electronic communications exist between Cyprus and the rest of the world, enabling easy co-ordination of the survey in its various countries.

The Cypriots are generally well educated and could well form a local workforce to assist in data preparation and analysis together with other clerical activities.

Being located at a 'crossing' point between European, Middle Eastern and North African markets, it is more likely that people with the relevant language skills will be found in the area than if (say) the study were located in mainland Europe.

June 1993, Question 10 In order to commission marketing research, the client has to have a fairly clear idea of what the marketing problem is in order that they can agree their information requirements. A brief can be prepared for an agency setting down all the basics of what needs to be established, from whom, by when and in what format. Conducted across several countries the process becomes more complicated.

The first step is to decide how the work will be handled. Assuming that the work will be commissioned from external marketing research houses rather than in-house, the choices are:

(a) use a local marketing agency in each country
(b) use a UK agency to handle the whole project
(c) use a non-UK agency to handle the whole project.

In order to achieve comparable results it is likely that options (b) or (c) will be selected unless the client company has substantial international marketing research expertise in-house. The choice of agency will be determined by appropriate country coverage, product expertise and MR techniques expertise. The price quoted will be an important factor in agency selection.

The issues of comparability will need to be handled by the marketing research agency at each stage of the MR process.

The selected research technique must be appropriate for each country. The sampling method must give similar levels of statistical accuracy. Respondents must give replies that are capable of consistent analysis from each country. The final analysis and presentation of results must give the client the opportunity to make assessments that are not biased because of unreliable marketing research findings.

Looking at some of the issues in more depth, the problem of language is likely to arise. Inevitably questionnaires will need to be translated. However, the meaning implicit in each question needs to be consistently reproduced in each language, rather than just the words used in the master questionnaire. The back translation method, using nationals with special knowledge of the market, is a good way to avoid translation errors.

The languages used between the marketing research agencies operating in each country and the client is another source of error. These errors will be minimized by using one lead agency to coordinate the agencies handling the field work in each country.

There are variations in the extent to which various data collection methods can be used. In less well developed countries the infrastructure of post and telephone systems is usually less than perfect. In some countries, even with widespread and reliable post and telephone systems, there might be cultural inhibitions to answering, for example, the telephone in response to an unintroduced marketing research interviewer. In some countries interviewing women (e.g. the Middle East) can be very difficult.

In some countries there are few complete and reliable lists that can be used to construct reliable sampling frames. This might result in adjustments to sampling methods to obtain comparable results.

Overall the problem of obtaining reliable comparable marketing research information is considerable. Providing the client and the marketing research agency understand the difficulties, useful comparable studies can be carried out for the benefit of improved quality in international marketing decision making.

Senior examiner's comments

This answer concentrated upon the commissioning of a marketing research survey. Some answers to this question placed far too much emphasis upon secondary data and the associated issues of data comparability. The answer above could have included a *brief* coverage of secondary data issues. The justification for this is that this is the usual process in marketing research. The use of all appropriate available information will aid the process of problem definition. However, the answer to Question 10 must, as in the answer above, be based upon primary data collection.

International market planning

This unit is concerned with the ways in which the firm can exploit defined marketing opportunities in international markets and how best it can organize itself. In studying the unit you will:

- Understand the concepts of international marketing strategy
- Come to terms with the importance of planning
- Review the key planning models and match marketing variables to strategic international decisions
- Understand the basics of an international marketing plan
- Recognize that control systems are even more important internationally than domestically
- Identify the key organizational issues that concern international development.

Having completed the unit you will be able to:

- Cross-reference planning with strategic issues
- Evaluate the suitability of specific marketing strategies
- Identify the elements of an international marketing plan
- List the stages of the control process and establish key principles of a control system
- Explain the different methods a firm might employ in creating and developing its international organization
- Explain the variables that affect organizational structure
- Evaluate the roles and conflicts of HQ versus local management structures.

This unit is concerned with planning in an international environment. Students must familiarize themselves with the planning process before addressing this unit. Therefore you must first have read one of the recognized texts (e.g. *The Strategic Marketing Management* workbook in this series) which will inform you on additional reading. Most students are unfamiliar with international planning and therefore it is especially important you read the texts in the Extending knowledge section at the end of the unit.

Strategic planning and control

It is not the intention to cover Planning and Control issues in depth as the benefits of Planning and the models we employed in the planning process are dealt with fully in the *Strategic Marketing Management* workbook in this series, authored by Fifield and Gilligan. The models of strategies are equally applicable internationally as they are in the domestic marketplace. However, it is important to recognize that planning and control are inescapably linked. The former is a structure (or series of structures) devised to develop a strategy and utilizing the capabilities of the organization against the background of the environment. Control is the process of monitoring and evaluating the implementation of the chosen strategy so that it can be developed to meet changes in the environment.

Issues in international planning

In marketing domestically the marketeer can readily apply his or her SRC, confident in meeting customer desires. Internationally this is rarely possible as customers, their culture and the environment changes by degree. Table 6.1 shows the issues involved in domestic versus international planning.

The difficulties of planning internationally are further identified by Brandt, Hulbert and Richers and are shown in Table 6.2.

The international planning process

Despite difficulties, planning remains an essential activity if the organization is to succeed. Moreover, planning demands structure and this becomes even more important unless one is dealing with a variety of markets/countries. As stated previously, we are not reviewing the

Table 6.1 Domestic versus international planning factors

Domestic planning	*International planning*
1 Single language and nationality	1 Multilingual/multinational/multicultural factors
2 Relatively homogeneous market	2 Fragmented and diverse markets
3 Data available, usually accurate, and collection easy	3 Data collection a formidable task, requiring significantly higher budgets and personnel allocation
4 Political factors relatively unimportant	4 Political factors frequently vital
5 Relative freedom from government interference	5 Involvement in national economic plans; government influences affect business decisions
6 Individual corporation has little effect on environment	6 'Gravitational' distortion by large companies
7 Chauvinism helps	7 Chauvinism hinders
8 Relatively stable business environment	8 Multiple environments, many of which are highly unstable (but may be highly profitable)
9 Uniform financial climate	9 Variety of financial climates ranging from overconservative to wildly inflationary
10 Single currency	10 Currencies differing in stability and real value
11 Business 'rules of the game' mature and understood	11 Rules diverse, changeable, and unclear
12 Management generally accustomed to sharing resonsibilities and using financial controls	12 Management frequently autonomous and unfamiliar with budgets and controls

Source: William W. Cain, 'International planning: mission impossible?' *Columbia Journal of World Business*, July–August 1970, p. 58. Reprinted by permission

Table 6.2 International planning problems

Headquarters	Overseas subsidiary
Management	*Management*
Unclear allocation of responsibilities and authority	Resistance to planning
Lack of multinational orientation	Lack of qualified personnel
Unrealistic expectations	Inadequate abilities
Lack of awareness of foreign markets	Misinterpretation of information
Unclear guidelines	Misunderstanding requirements and objectives
Insensitivity to local decisions	Resentment of HQ involvement
Insufficient provision of useful information	Lack of strategic thinking
	Lack of marketing expertise
Processes	*Processes*
Lack of standardized bases for evaluation	Lack of control by HQ
Poor IT systems and support	Incomplete or outdated internal and market information
Poor feedback and control systems	Poorly developed procedures
Excessive bureaucratic control procedures	Too little communication with HQ
Excessive marketing and financial constraints	Inaccurate data returns
Insufficient participation of subsidiaries in process	Insufficient use of multinational marketing expertise
	Excessive financial and marketing constraints

Source: Brandt, Hulbert and Richers (1980)

models of portfolio analysis but we remind students that the most widely applied methods are:

1 Boston Consulting Group (BCCG)
2 General Electric/McKinsey (GE)
3 Profit Impact of Market Strategy (PIMS)
4 Arthur D. Little
5 Scenario Planning
6 Michael Porter's work is also extremely important

Students are expected to be knowledgeable in the constructs of the models, their application, relevance and shortcomings. Once again, cross reference can be made with the *Strategic Marketing Management* workbook.

Examine the problems of using product portfolio analysis in international marketing (June 1994, Question 8).
(**See** Exam answers at the end of this unit.)

EXAM QUESTION

At the strategic level the organization has six key corporate decisions to take when moving into the international arena, beginning with the question 'Should we go?' and ending with 'What organization structure should we adopt?' Against these six key decisions they need to apply the marketing planning variables. Table 6.3 shows the interface between marketing planning and the key corporate decision to form the basis for strategic market planning.

Table 6.3 Strategic options and marketing planning: marketing planning variables

Key International Decisions	Marketing Environment and Scale of Marketing	Competitors	Objectives	Marketing Mix Variables	Marketing Budgets	Expected Outcomes
Should we go international?						
Where should we go?						
How should we get there?						
What should we sell?						
How should we market it?						
How do we organize?						

ACTIVITY 6.1

Go through Table 6.3 in depth. Select some product categories and then apply what you might consider to be the planning variables. In other words, get some simulated experience of marketing planning in action.

EXAM HINT

The matrix in Table 6.3 could be invaluable in examination terms. It allows you to get to the heart of planning immediately, saving you several pages of writing which means saving time. The marketing plan for any situation will follow the basic principles underpinning all marketing planning:

1 Who are we?
2 Where are we now?
3 Where do we want to be?
4 How might we get there?
5 How do we ensure we get there?

Following on from this the individual country plan should consider the following stages:

1 An evaluation of shareholder/stockholder expectations, together with ambition and resolve of key implementers
2 An audit of the firm's capabilities
3 An assessment of the environment – present and future
4 A statement of vision, mission, corporate objectives
5 An evaluation of strategic alternatives/options
6 An assessment of market/competitor responses
7 The selection and justification of a strategy
8 Effective implementation
9 Monitoring and control procedures
10 Development of organizational systems to ensure effective international co-ordination.

Control

The wider the range of international penetration, the greater will be the need and requirement for control. The establishment of an effective control system is interrelated to the organizational systems (people and procedures). The purpose of control is so that the business (not just marketing) activities can be measured. Measurement can only be achieved and proper assessment made if the plan contains clear objecives. No plan goes totally smoothly and deviations from expectations always occur, but without effective monitoring corrective action cannot be implemented. Control is the basic building block of management – not an afterthought. Future plans depend on control, for control is information and information is power. The issues that affect control are:

1 The scale of the task, the size of the firm
2 The diversity of markets, the number and range of markets/countries
3 The method of entry – which may vary by country
4 The availability and accuracy of data and information
5 The distance from the home market and the sophistication of communication, qualitative and quantitative.

Key factors in controlling international markets

The starting point is the marketing plan itself and the objectives it sets out to achieve. In basic terms the key control mechanisms are:

1 Establishing standards
2 Measuring performance against the standards
3 Correcting deviation.

Many methods apply in addressing the first of these two points, not least the establishment of common benchmarks and values across multi-markets. The task is extremely complicated and it is only the largest and most sophisticated organization that can consider a complex intermarket comparison of standards. But all firms can determine standards for individual markets and take the necessary action (see also Unit 14).

Organizing for international and global marketing

Managers are the company's scarcest resource and therefore their most valuable. It seems odd therefore that practically all the accepted textbooks on international marketing place the chapter on organizing for success at the end. People are very much a key resource and

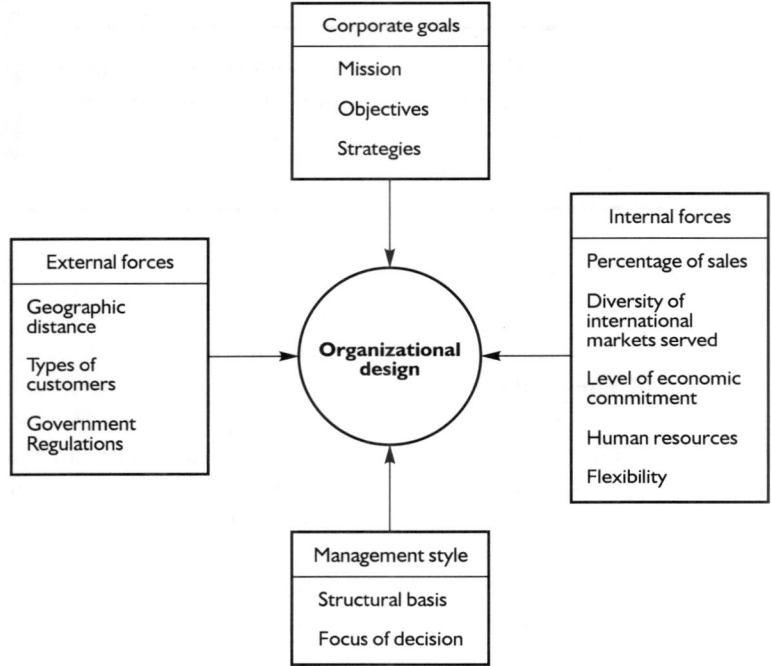

Figure 6.1 Factors affecting organizational design. (*Source*: Jeannet and Hennessey, 1994)

the model in Figure 6.1 places Company Objectives and Resources at the top of the linear sequence. Furthermore, planning for international expansion cannot take place in a vacuum, it needs the full consideration of the management of the company.

How an organization can structure itself to exploit overseas opportunities is a matter of considerable debate. As in the case of a 'plan' there is no one correct way. If there is a balance to be struck it should be as follows:

1   The organization should be structured in a way that best meets the task of servicing the customers' needs.
2   The structure must take full account of the environment, domestic and international, and the skills and resources of the organization.

For companies to be successful it is necessary to arrive at the appropriate balance.

It is not easy, for tensions exist simultaneously between the need for diversity and decentralization in terms of servicing customers in different markets and the corporate requirement of evaluation and control. The ideal organization structure should incorporate both – a goal rarely realized.

We must also recognize that as customers, markets and environments are dynamic, ever changing and never static so the organization and its structural interface with the customer/market must also change. Some companies are already anticipating the shape and nature of global competition and planning for it. Most are reactive to the changing situation.

ACTIVITY 6.2

Review past editions of the quality press, (e.g. *The Economist* or the *Financial Times*). See what information you can discover on firms reorganizing themselves to adapt to changing times. Are they reactive or proactive?

At all times the focus of the organization should be to develop a structure that provides the framework to 'optimize' the relationship between planning, strategy and control. Terpstra and Sarathy (1997) identify some of the variables in this process:

- Size of the business
- Number of markets
- Level of strategic involvement in the markets
- Corporate objectives
- The level of international experience
- The nature of the product category(ies)
- The scale of the marketing task

Types of international organizations

Domestic-led companies

In Unit 9 we see that it is possible for domestically orientated companies to operate in overseas markets receiving enquiries from overseas buyers. Domestic staff will respond as if they were home-based customers – which some may well be. Such companies will have few or no additional costs but they will gain relatively little from the exercise – lacking expertise or scale to profit greatly.

Domestic company with an export department

As the overseas opportunity grows companies begin to employ international specialists and create an export department. This brings advantages in expertise, faster response and the beginnings of a proactive international policy with the export department exploring new country opportunities. But the scale of search for overseas services will be relatively low-key and restricted largely to pockets of opportunity. Furthermore, the tendency will be to market unmodified products thus failing to optimize the potential even where the product is sold. Generally, sales per country will be modest.

Developing the international division

Jeannet and Hennessey suggest that companies should move to this phase when international business represents 15 per cent or so of the company's total. At this scale it is necessary to increase the level of involvement in overseas markets – paying close attention to consumer needs, attacking competition, modifying product and the marketing mix to create business proactively. This requires the development of an international division reporting at a senior level and capable of coordinating the business functions across country boundaries.

In terms of considering the appropriate stages of internationalization Doole, Lowe and Phillips have identified four stages through which the international strategies of most companies evolve:

- Developing the core strategy, usually for the home country first, on the basis of an identified sustainable competitive advantage.
- Internationalizing the core strategy through an international market extension strategy.
- Integrating the specific country strategies into a world-wide strategy on a multi-domestic basis.
- Rationalizing the integrated strategies to develop a regional or global strategy.

ACTIVITY 6.3

Stop at this point and see if you can think of any examples of how organizations simulate themselves internationally.

Worldwide organizational structure

Companies recognize the need to coordinate the operation spread geographically to cover large areas of the world. There are five recognized approaches:

1   *Country and regional centres*   This structure allows companies to delve even deeper into the dynamics of consumer behaviour and the environment within a country or region. The difference is essentially a matter of size. On reaching a certain size a market (country or region) will require management – staff located within it to maximize the business opportunity and creating a physical presence in the market, possibly for political as well as business reasons. It is very likely that production may be based within the market. Apart from the limits of economies of scale it allows greater sensitivity in building consumer relationships and understanding the culture, responding faster, being more flexible than operations centralized around HQs. Presently, many organizations are creating European centres to coordinate business functions such as R&D, production, distribution, marketing and finance. This regionalization in attitude is being rewarded with the creation of Eurobrands. For example, Unilever have created a European organization, Lever Europe, eliminating diverse brand names such as Cif, Viss and calling them Jif. Likewise, we have seen the demise of Marathon chocolate bars – renamed Snickers!

2   *Functional operation*   This structure is best suited to companies with a narrow product base with relatively homogenous customers around the world. Thus organizing worldwide on a functional basis is an option open only to a few companies. The structure itself is simple with senior executives having worldwide responsibility for their specialized function be it finance, R&D, marketing, production etc.

3   *Product structuring*   This is most common among companies with a portfolio of seemingly unrelated product lines where each product group may have its own international division. A difficulty with this structure is that conflicts will emerge between product groupings and therefore management problems arise with clashes of culture usually at the source. Similarly, a lack of coordination or of cross-fertilization of ideas often occurs. In an attempt to minimize the conflict, companies may provide functional coordination for customer-related activities such as marketing communication and after-sales service.

4   *Matrix structuring*   Very popular in the late 1970s but less so nowadays, this organizational structure appeared to offer solutions to the one-dimensional approach of the three previous methods. Matrices are created by combining two (or more) dimensions of equal importance in the decision-making process. Thus an organization has a dual chain of command. The two most popular dimensions are product and market (country/region). Despite appearing to resolve conflicts and giving greater control and flexibility (responsiveness), the matrix system has largely fallen by the wayside – a victim of its complexity as each axis of the matrix attempts to consolidate or indeed optimize its position within the organizational hierarchy. Sadly, matrix structures show up the weakness and fallibilities of human relationships creating power struggles. Matrices can and will work only when organizations can admit to conflict and are capable of resolving conflict positively by adopting an influence system rather than an authoritarian system of management. Philips was in the vanguard of introducing a matrix structure in the mid-1970s but has abandoned it in favour of global product divisions.

EXAM HINT

Create a file of examples of each type of organizational structure. Top marks are awarded to candidates who can demonstrate practical knowledge alongside theory.

5   *Strategic Business Units* (SBUs)   These are currently in vogue and consist of dividing the global organization into defined businesses, each addressing an identified customer base either by country/region or even on a worldwide basis. The advantages are corporate flexibility in disposing of an SBU or, alternatively, the company can refocus the overall business more easily. The integration of new acquisitions is easier and from

a financial and operational control perspective SBUs make for good sense. However, the downside is that the company is not optimizing its economies of scale in world markets and it makes acquisition of the company itself by predators easier, so the unwanted SBUs can be disposed of more readily.

Examine the organizational implications for a company moving from modest exporting to an aggressive international marketing approach (December 1993, Question 4).

What are the stages companies go through in moving from a domestic to a global operation? What management issues are involved at each stage? (June 1997, Question 3)

(**See** Exam answers at the end of this unit.)

EXAM QUESTION

Majaro (1991) developed the scenario in Figure 6.2 identifying three basic formats for large international/worldwide organizations calling them macropyramid, umbrella and interglomerate structures:

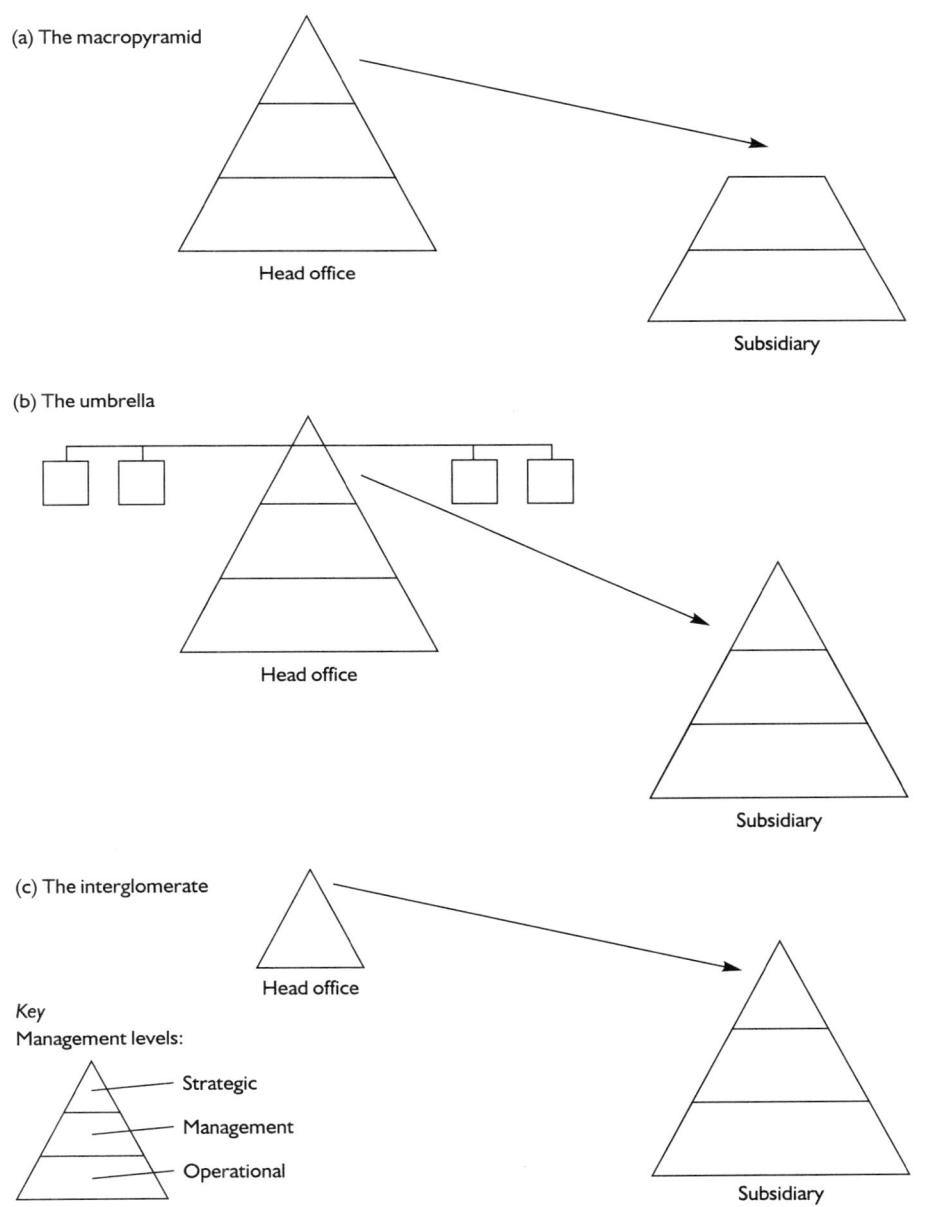

Figure 6.2 Organizational structures and the head office–subsidiary relationship (Majaro, 1991)

- *Macropyramid* Power is concentrated at the centre – taking strategic decisions concerning marketing along with the standardization of production and R&D. The weakness is self-evident; lack of motivation in the subsidiary, little or no local creativity or flexibility, with communication being largely one-way and the subsidiary being measured usually on monthly financial performance.
- *Umbrella* This is the opposite approach, with the company creating a clone of itself in each market, decentralizing decision making to the local level and allowing flexibility in product and market mix variables. Although having advantages at the local level there is little global benefit as a plethora of products/brand names erupt with overduplication and little coordination, resulting in the erosion of potential economies of scale. Procter & Gamble and Unilever pioneered this structure though both have moved away from it in recent years.
- *Interglomerate* The centre is run on strict financial criteria allowing the SBUs total autonomy. Such companies are driven by acquisition and break-ups. Hanson is a typical interglomerate.

Trends in global organizations

With more firms moving into the international arena and with the growing importance and power of the mega corporations, it is inevitable that cultural differences need to be considered carefully in creating the 'optimum' organizational framework. There are a number of alternative philosophical positions a multinational/transnational may adopt. The one chosen will reflect the strategic predisposition of the firm which will be guided by the value, long-term objectives and the extent of its 'globalization'.

- *Ethnocentric* – This positioning is when the strategic position and the key managers in the majority of the overseas subsidiaries are from the home country. In other words, headquarters personnel and culture dominates and pervades internationally.
- *Polycentric* – Here the culture of the subsidiary countries take the lead. Headquarters set the agenda in terms of return on investment etc. leaving local managers to devise appropriate strategies and implementation.
- *Regiocentric* – A mid point – so to speak, attempting to coordinate a geographic region, e.g. EU, or perhaps more appropriately utilizing a country such as Singapore as a regional hub. Managers tend to come from the region and strategic decisions are taken to develop pan-regional marketing and production. A good case is the appointment of an Indian national to lead Nestlé's South East Asian region. He was previously General Manager of Nestlé Indonesia.
- *Geocentric* – Simply the attempt to manage and integrate strategy globally. Managers are appointed on the best person for the job basis. An Indian national is the head of Mckinsey's, the leading management constancy; Tony O'Reilly (Irish) heads up Heinz world-wide, Alex Trottman (Scottish) heads the Ford Motor Company.

It is worth noting that no one method is the correct one – the one that reflects the strategic intent matched to the objectives is the most appropriate.

It is abundantly clear that the management issues surrounding international organizations are extremely complex. There are a number of trends to add to the already lengthy discussion:

1 Organizational structures are becoming 'flatter' with individual managers having wider responsibility and more subordinates.
2 Correspondingly, responsibility and authority are being pushed closer to the relevant point of contact with the customer.

3   The trend will therefore be towards the macropyramid format with the centre deciding the global corporate decisions relating to the direction the company should take but the marketing decisions will be made increasingly with the subsidiaries.

4   Transnational organizations – the latest thinking in international management is that being global is not enough. Kenichi Ohmae, a disciple of globalization curiously argues against rigidity, believing that as the world increasingly develops around the Triad economies the global company must be equidistant from each of the three major trading blocs yet simultaneously position itself as an insider within each. This renaissance corporation should exploit whatever economies of scale, technology or branding it has within the Triad. Ohmae's argument is that while tastes may vary, the broad motivations among consumers are similar.

- How would a transnational company differ in its marketing approach to a multi-national enterprise (MNE) (June 1993, Question 4).
- Examine the arguments for using a multidomestic (polycentric) strategy in preference to a global strategy (June 1995, Question 6).
(**See** Exam answers at the end of this unit.)

Bartlett and Ghoshal (1992) broadly confirm the view that renaissance companies must be composed of specialist managers who network across countries/regions. They explain the management implications as:

- Global managers need to be multi-disciplined providing leadership and innovation.
- The country manager is a pivotal character, being closest to the customer and understanding the finesse required in building customer relationships.
- Global product group managers have the responsibility for quality control and efficiency and driving down costs. Additionally, they will be the architects for worldwide resourcing.

Return to Unit 3 briefly and see how the points made here match the challenges outlined. There should be a direct correlation. No aspect of international planning/organization acts independently of its environment.

5   Shared vision.   The task of moulding an organization to the needs of an ever-changing world marketplace involves building a shared vision and developing human resources. For example, Coca-Cola's vision is simple – 'To put Coca-Cola within arm's reach of everyone in the world'.

    To succeed, the company must employ all its talents and avoid the pitfalls of adopting the narrow vision of ethnocentric management employing both a polycentric style yet recognizing the importance of the regiocentric and geocentric contributions.

- In the role of the director responsible for international marketing of a blue-chip company, explain how you would identify and justify the resource requirements for a global marketing plan (June 1993, Question 9).
- Briefly explain the different forms of organizational structure used in international marketing. For each organizational type, indicate the roles of management at different levels and in different locations in the determination of international marketing plans (December 1994, Question 7).
- Identify and critically comment upon the probable marketing differences between organizations that divide markets between the 'domestic' market and the 'rest of the world' and organizations that take a more geographically neutral approach (December 1993, Question 8).

(**See** Exam answers at the end of this unit.)

Summary

This unit has covered two strategic aspects of international marketing: first, the line of marketing planning and second the organizational implications. Both involved a high degree of personnel issues. The unit discussed briefly the importance of models in developing strategy and also considered the marketing planning variables set against the key international decision areas. This particular matrix is of considerable help in defining quickly your options (from the perspective of the examination) and the issues revolving around control.

Likewise, the manner in which the company organizes itself to best deal with its international development establishes the level of involvement and the intensity of its competitive impact. There is a wide variety of choice. Finally, the unit discussed developments that will shape the competitive challenges in the future.

Questions

- In creating an international plan what basic elements might you consider important?
- What are the difficulties in adapting headquarters' broad plan to local countries?
- What impact should competition play in affecting international marketing planning?
- What are the benefits of choosing region, product or function as the basis for organizing the firm on an international basis?
- Headquarters hinder local market development. Discuss.
- What control elements do you consider appropriate in multi-country marketing planning?
- What is the purpose of control systems? What distinguishes a good one?
- What is a marketing audit and what are its strengths and weaknesses in developing international markets?
- What is the relevance of the BCG model in planning for international markets?
- What decisions are best left to local managers?
- Is a transnational approach to strategy the best way forward for a global cooperation? Indicate circumstance where it might or might not be appropriate.
- Itemize and justify six characteristics you consider necessary for an organization to compete successfully in a global market.

International Marketing Strategy, I. Doole, R. Lowe and C. Phillips, Routledge, 1997, Chapters 5 and 6.

International Marketing, S. Paliwoda and M. Thomas, Butterworth-Heinemann, 1998.

Global Marketing Strategies, J.-P. Jeannet and H. D. Hennessey, Houghton Mifflin, 1998, Chapter 16 and 17.

International Marketing, V. Terpstra and R. Sarathy, The Dryden Press, 1997, Chapter 17.

June 1994, Question 8 **Product portfolio analysis** is normally used to evaluate Strategic Business Units (SBUs) along several dimensions on a comparative basis. Thus in the Boston Consulting Group model, SBUs are located in a two – dimensional map with market share and market growth as the axes. Many different evaluation models exist. The SBUs may be one-product divisions operating in a number of countries, or a geographic SBU (e.g. European division) with possibly a wide range of products and services.

In either case we have several problems of concern to the international marketer.

First, the choice of appropriate measures of performance that are relevant to all the markets concerned. Generally, the dimension evaluating the SBU's performance is related to the objectives for that market. In situations where there are diverse objectives for each market and where the operations are involved in different stages of the product life cycle, it becomes difficult to select appropriate measures.

Secondly, portfolio analysis usually involves comparison with the growth of the market in which the SBU is operating. Different countries may not only have different growth rates but, depending on the size of the market and the stage of development of the country, the necessary market research data regarding size, growth, competition and other relevant market data may be difficult to collect.

Thirdly, portfolio analysis is used to decide the allocation of limited resources to particular SBUs. The decision to divest, harvest, hold or build a particular SBU may not be totally decided by the performance of the SBU. Other factors involving political, cultural, economic, social, legal and infrastructural/technological issues may be involved, acting as constraints on the decision. In such cases the analysis may be regarded as rather limited in an international marketing context, involving as it does the usual economic criteria only.

A final criticism of 'uncritical use' of portfolio analysis in international marketing has to be the move towards a more integrated and regional approach to markets. Thus, not only does the evaluation of countries in isolation become questionable, but the interdependence of operations between countries makes isolated evaluations difficult.

Having said the above, it is likely that similar criticisms could be raised on any method of evaluation across markets. The application of portfolio analysis is not, therefore, to be ignored, but the results must be carefully interpreted rather than uncritically accepted.

June 1994, Question 4 The international marketer has to consider a number of issues when examining how to enter countries with different cultures. Basically one is looking for a fit (Porter) between the company and its environment. This involves carefully selecting countries with whom the company is capable of dealing and adapting the company's marketing plans to fit in with the restrictions demanded in the market place.

The company will largely be modifying and adapting the classical four Ps – Price, Product, Promotion and Place – and the market will be demanding suitable adaptation to the PEST factors – Political/legal, Social/cultural, Economic and Technological influences. Adaptation is normally expensive, and hence not only should the company be considering the differences between countries and the need to adapt the mix, but also the similarities and the possibility of common elements in the mix being used.

A diagrammatic representation of this process is shown on the next page.

To illustrate the complexity of the process, Vietnam and the Czech Republic will be compared.

Market entry and distribution

Vietnam has recently lowered trade restrictions with the outside world. The Czech Republic, on the other hand, has always, even under Comecon membership, acted as a gateway to Western goods. Whilst good distributive systems exist almost everywhere in

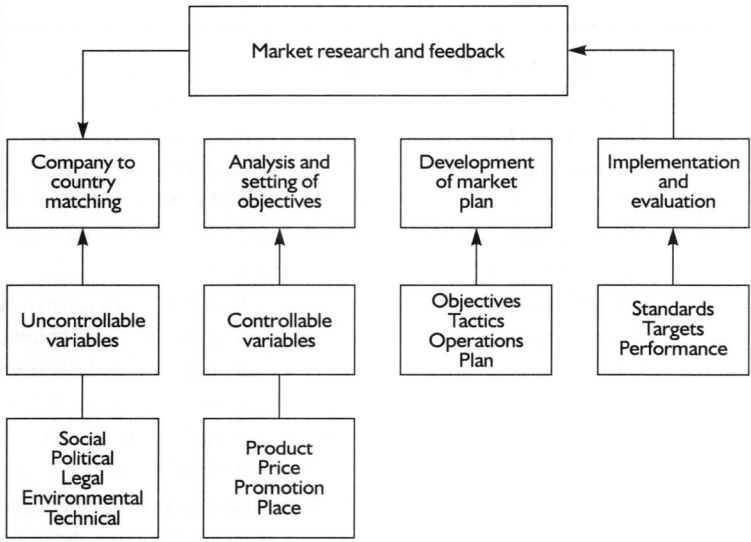

the Czech republic, with good communications infrastructure, this tends to be limited to urban areas in Vietnam. Thus any plans for Vietnam would probably confine their geographic scope to the major cities. In terms of method of entry, the unstable nature of the whole area in political terms would make significant inward investment (overseas manufacture of one type or another) unwise. In contrast, the Czech Republic is considered sufficiently economically and politically stable for such investment to be considered if suitable.

Product

Local legislation and technical infrastructure will normally have to be coped with and the product modified accordingly in both cases. However, the Czech Republic is generally more advanced educationally than Vietnam and would likely be capable of dealing with more complex products than Vietnam. Economic levels would also suggest that the Far East market would require cheaper products than the European comparison.

Promotion

Apart from legislation relating to promotion and restrictions on promotion, the availability of media, the coverage and literacy of audience would be crucial. In both cases it is likely radio is the most significant media, and even in the Czech Republic the opportunities for commercial TV will be limited. Cultural differences will make messages significantly different, although where the products are 'culturally neutral' it is likely that the same platform for promotion can be used. Both economic and educational factors suggest that published media are more likely to play a role in the Czech Republic, with personal selling via retailers and posters important in Vietnam.

Price

The linking of the Czech economy to the Comecon market has led to a significant period of adjustment and inflation as a true parity on the world currency market is established. Thus in the Czech Republic we have a situation of stagflation, with a highly educated but poor population. In Vietnam, the aftermath of civil war and the high expenditure of GNP on defence has created a similar situation with the urban, educated Vietnamese. Such similarities would lead to similar pricing strategies by a company operating in both markets.

The above illustrate clearly the process of creating a fit between a company and its markets and the need to adopt a flexible approach in such markets.

December 1995, Question 8

Stages of internationalization
This is a straightforward question and the structure can be found in depth in the Phillips, Doole and Lowe text featured throughout this book (Doole, Lowe and Phillips, 1994, pp. 27, 28).

1   What are the stages?
    – No interest
    – Fulfils unsolicited order
    – Explores the feasibility of exporting
    – The firm gains experience and confidence and exports to a number of overseas markets
    – Exporting becomes a significant proportion of turnover
    – Development of long-term strategy (true international marketing)
2   A good answer must discuss how a company develops an international management perspective. (See TZ Pipes mini-case study in Unit 15 for additional guidance). The management issues should be dealt with, maybe with comments on organizational impact and time scales. This unit covers strategic organizational issues in depth.

June 1995, Question 8   The question stipulates a three-year planning horizon yet it is equally apparent that the plan must contain both one-year and two-year objectives, strategies and implemented programmes of a reasonably tactical nature that will, among other things, provide the framework for bench-marking against projected forecasts and provide the evaluation and control process that is essential if the three-year plan is to be successful.

A checklist of *essential* elements of an international marketing plan might include the majority of the following points:

1   Assumptions about the world economy, world trading patterns and shift in regions/markets, etc.
2   Details of the company's historical performance highlighting achievements and failures – sales, costs, profit etc.
3   A forecast of future potential based on an interpretation of points 1 and 2 and extrapolating scenarios, e.g. growth in Chinese manufacturing.
4   Identified opportunities and threats with the emphasis on the positive, i.e. the opportunities and how specific threats might prevent the firm capturing them. Country analysis is an important consideration here.
5   Analysis of the company's strengths in relation to the opportunities and a clear evaluation of weaknesses that must be addressed if opportunities are to be captured.
6   A clear vision, clearly stated objectives over the long term at least three years, preferably five.
7   A clear statement of the strategies that will be followed in order to reach the objectives – again thinking long term.
8   One-year and two-year objectives and tactics (cascading down from the strategies), e.g. budgets, brand objectives and human resource developments.
9   Detailed country by country forecasts and targets (years one, two and three).
10   Detailed country by country plans (years one, two and three) in terms of production, R&D and marketing.
11   A clear explanation (plan) how country plans for all marketing activities might be co-ordinated and integrated to maximize synergy and facilitate international commercialization of new product development.
12   A summary of the critical factors for success.

13 A control process for feedback, evaluation and taking corrective action (years one, two and three).

14 The development of a contingency planning framework or process.

In itself, the above is little more than a list, but it contains the framework for international planning. It is apparent that in following through the process, great attention must be paid to factors relating to organizational issues, as is the way (style of management) in which the business is run. Above all else, it is critical that companies adopt a planning culture where:

- planning becomes part of the continuous process of management rather than an annual 'event';
- strategic thinking becomes the responsibility of every manager, rather than being the province of a separate strategic planning department;
- the planning process becomes standardized with a format which allows contribution from all parts of the company (not just the marketing department);
- the plan becomes a working document, regularly updated, against which performance evaluations are measured;
- the planning process itself is reviewed regularly to improve its relevance and performance.

December 1993, Question 4 The organization will have to change fundamentally. The range of tasks and markets will expand. More resources will be required to allow the development of international markets. The 'aggressive' approach will be reflected in corporate and international marketing objectives. These objectives will show large increases and will be difficult to achieve.

The existing organizational structure could be illustrated in the following:

In this organization the export manager is subordinate to the domestic marketing director. To enable a more significant top level management focus on international marketing, the organization would need to change.

Stage 1 – organizational change

At the stage one level, international markets are given board level representation. This will allow more attention and resources to be used internationally. It should give a more balanced view of activities between the domestic and international markets. The use of a dedicated marketing research manager will allow the systematic collection and analysis of data on which the international expansion can be built.

The influence of domestic business might be powerful, particularly if the managing director is more experienced in the domestic market. A further move to focus international markets can be seen in the next stage, stage two.

Stage 2 – organizational change

```
                    ┌─────────────────┐
                    │ Managing director│
                    └─────────────────┘
          ┌──────────────┬──────────────┐
   ┌──────────┐    ┌──────────┐   ┌──────────────┐
   │ Director │    │ Director │   │   Director    │
   │  Europe  │    │   Asia   │   │ North America │
   └──────────┘    └──────────┘   └──────────────┘
          ┌──────────────┬──────────────┐
   ┌──────────┐    ┌──────────┐   ┌──────────┐
   │ Marketing│    │Production│   │  Finance │
   └──────────┘    └──────────┘   └──────────┘
```

The stage two approach uses the international division organizational approach. The domestic market loses much of its influence because it is contained within one of the major international divisions. The domestic market will only receive resources if it can logically demonstrate the need for those resources, in competition with counter claims from other parts of the world. The international focus of the company will be encouraged by divisions being located in their own particular region. In this way, for example, the faster growth rates being achieved in China and South East Asia would result in the director for Asia being able to respond much more quickly and decisively than would be the case in the two earlier organizational structures.

Summary

The changes required to become internationally marketing orientated rather than domestically marketing orientated are large and they are fundamental. To be successful, commitment is required at the highest managerial level. However aggressive the aims of the company are, changes of the magnitude contained in this question will take many years to achieve.

Senior Examiner's comments

There are a number of different organizational approaches that could be adopted to answer this question. Organizational specialization could be developed through a matrix in which functional and geographic specializations are overlaid. The answer given is to a very good pass standard. It could have been developed by considering the cultural change that would be necessary in moving from an exporting approach to an international **marketing** approach. The need to gain knowledge of customer buying behaviour from many countries, to have the expertise to understand the marketing research data and to enable international marketing plans to be developed requires careful personnel selection, development and training in international marketing.

June 1997, Question 3   The question has two basic components.

(a)   The process of internationalization. A diagram of the various stages is required. A model can be taken from any key textbook (see p. ix above). A description of the model is required.

Evidence must be shown of an understanding of what is involved and why companies shift their emphasis into deepening involvement in internationalization, e.g. geographic spreading, economies of scale, diversification of risk, technological pressures, customer demand, advances in communication etc. A clear portrayal of these key trigger mechanisms is important.

Good quality students will be capable of condensing the range of international market entry methods to three basic phases.

1. Initial international market entry; signified by lack of experience/familiarity, e.g. indirect and direct marketing.
2. Local market expansion; where the strategic thrust is centred on fuelling growth in each market, e.g. overseas production.
3. Regional and global rationalization; where the orientation of the firm focuses on improving the efficiency of all its operations worldwide and develops mechanisms for improved transnational co-ordination and integration of strategy across countries.

(b) Taking the three basic phases, each should be examined from the management perspective, e.g:

Phase 1   Initial entry – key factors include:
- which country/countries to enter
- timing of entry
- how operations might be conducted

Critical issues include learning curve, gaining beachhead, risks (of all kinds), size of markets, level of resources, degree of adaptation, and recognition of constraints.

Phase 2   Local market expansion – key factors include:
- organizational structure, hire of local management
- leveraging of proprietary assets, e.g. brand names
- sharing of physical assets, e.g. production and distribution
- greater costs, risks etc. balanced against scale of opportunity and profitability

Phase 3   Global rationalization – key factors include:
- search for synergies across all business functions; rapid transfer of success
- optimization of efficiencies
- global development guides strategy
- allocation of resources to be global

June 1993, Question 4   A transnational company identifies *global* marketing opportunities, anticipates changes in customer requirements, whilst aiming to satisfy customers' needs and wants profitably. On the other hand, the multinational enterprise, whilst often as large or larger than transnational companies, views the world as a series of separate country markets treated as domestic markets.

The difference in approach is seen in the company's view or orientation. The transnational adopts a geocentric view of the world. It seeks to increase standardization in marketing planning internationally. It seeks to view competition from a world perspective. It might mean adopting a global brand strategy whereby one range of product offerings is marketed using the same strategies worldwide. Or it might mean a strategically coordinated approach in which certain adaptations are used to exploit significant differences in customer requirements or market conditions.

The MNE view of the world is polycentric. Often the result of investments in a number of country markets is a series of well-entrenched organizations in different countries. Each organization is tuned to its country market and thus tends to emphasize the difference between its market and other country markets. This approach tends to limit the advantages of scale and standardization. It also tends to neglect international competitors, except in a narrower country by country approach.

It is difficult to find perfect examples of transnational companies. The ideal is very demanding. It presupposes that the company is staffed with high quality international managers operating with the 'equidistant' perspective preached by Kenichi Ohmae in *The Borderless World*. An example of a transnational company is Coca-Cola. The company strives to standardize its approach where it is profitable, but it does adapt where it is necessary. Like a number of other US companies, Coca-Cola uses the American theme to back a number of its global marketing communications.

Both the transnational and the MNE are likely to have manufacturing in more than two different countries. However, both are most unlikely to produce in every country in which they sell. Both, therefore, will be involved in international marketing in its broad sense of exporting, manufacturing and using a variety of market entry methods.

The differences in approach between the transnational and the MNE are best seen in their respective planning approaches and their organizational structures. The transnational aims towards a geocentric approach whereas the MNE is multidomestic.

The more outwardly visible signs of a developing transnational approach are moves to minimize the number of different brand and company names for similar products; moves to standardize company trade marks and logos; attempts to produce similar company literature and advertising; and attempts to standardize research and development and new product development.

In a world of increasingly tough international competition many MNEs are attempting to adopt a geocentric view of world markets and of their competitors. Cost levels are a major factor in survival and success. The transnational approach, by seeking similarities across the globe, searches for economies through scale and standardization and aims to reach new lower cost levels whilst at the same time satisfying customers around the world. It should be noted, however, that the transition from a polycentric view to a geocentric view is neither easy nor quick.

Senior Examiner's comments
This answer was to an excellent standard. Candidates divided into two groups: one group understood the term transnational and, in general, produced very good answers; the other group guessed the meaning of transnational and failed to reach the pass standard.

June 1995, Question 6 Managers are the company's scarcest resource and therefore their most valuable. It stands to reason, therefore, that organizing the company to best achieve international/global success is of paramount importance. Problems (of all kinds) multiply with distance. Control is the cornerstone of planning – planning the essential key to success. None of this is possible without a management organization that best matches the customer with the company and its objectives.

In organizing for international markets there is a balance to be struck:

1   The organization should be structured in a way that best meets the task of servicing the customer's needs.
2   The structure must take full account of the environment, domestic and international, and the skills and resources of the organization.

This is difficult as tensions exist simultaneously between the need for diversity and decentralization in terms of serving customers in different markets and the corporate requirement of evaluation and control. The Jeannet and Hennessey model illustrates the complexity of international organization design. (**Note**: We have produced this model as Figure 6.1, p. 76.)

In formalizing the international organization a variety of structural approaches has been designed. Organizations can be Country, Function, Product or Matrix structured. Majaro suggests a macro pyramid, umbrella or interglomerate approach, whilst others focus on being ethnocentric, polycentric, regiocentric or global. The question concerns a comparison between multidomestic (polycentric) versus global in terms of marketing strategy.

A **polycentric organization** is essentially one that is involved in widespread international marketing but operates via considerable adaption to local markets. The management will be local/domestic and will be best placed to understand and manipulate the local customer nuances. Production may or may not be local but the overall management approach from headquarters is one of portfolio development, with each country having its own profit and loss responsibility. The argument for such an approach is straightforward. Country by country the company is maximizing potential. However, there is a downside. Because no one is considering the global position it is perfectly feasible for a major global competitor to utilize its corporate brand strength to aggressively attack what is essentially a local product. Kenichi Ohmae observes that when this happens no matter the size of the individual market/country, the management time and resources necessary to overcome this problem are about the same, i.e. the company (internationally) will need to send the best production engineer, best financial accountant, best labour negotiator, best marketing specialist and so on to the country concerned. The result is that management at the centre (headquarters) is drained of its energy and its driving force. This, of course, is one of the central arguments for globalization – although in my view it is a rather supply-led not customer-focused viewpoint.

A **global marketing organization** is one where the company coordinates worldwide production, research, finance and marketing as well as business strategy. In doing so it treats the world (or large parts of it) as a single market – a lofty ambition that few ever achieve. But that should not prevent companies striving for globalized marketing. Kenichi Ohmae makes an interesting comment that future successful globalized corporations will bring together a shared global vision/production/R&D and human resources whilst employing locals on a country by country basis – a globalized polycentric approach that he terms 'insideration'.

June 1993, Question 9

From: Director of International Marketing
To: Budget Review Committee
Subject: Global Marketing Plan (first draft)

Background

In this paper I will outline the current thinking with regard to producing a detailed global marketing plan for the financial year 1994/95 and beyond.

As we are all aware, our current planning process has been based on achieving the HQ determined rate of return on capital employed in each major region of our international business. For our major markets of the United States and the United Kingdom this has been shown by country; in other parts of the world we have aggregated our country plans into relevant groups. Changes in competition and different growth rates and opportunities around the world, along with moves by other companies to plan on a global basis, have prompted the decision to produce a global marketing plan.

Identification of opportunities

We will use our new international marketing information system to scan for opportunities. We will develop a priority ranked programme based on our corporate strategy of using clearly differentiated approaches through which we can add value.

A key factor in our global plan will be the coordination of our approach. We will develop opportunities to a clear plan. Major opportunities will have a substantial and interlinked implementation. More limited opportunities will be progressed only if above average returns are possible.

It is proposed that we concentrate our activities in those parts of the world which have a faster than average growth in the GNP. This will be modified to make allowance for market attractiveness by country and by world region; for example, the European Community.

Resource requirements

The appropriate headings under this item seem to be employees (both numbers and payroll cost); marketing budgets for new product development; marketing research and MIS, and marketing communications; the use of external agencies, particularly for advertising, public relations and marketing research.

We propose to continue our current blend of direct investment in key markets and joint ventures and alliances in markets of greater uncertainty (for example, the former Comecon bloc).

There is a need to develop more managers with a good understanding of operating in an international setting; at a very senior level we need a multi-cultural management team to ensure that global opportunities are thoroughly analysed and that appropriate plans are developed and implemented.

Control

To achieve a global approach we need to take an overall view which must take account of trading off between various country and regional plans. The main marketing controls will be market share against specified objectives, both in absolute terms and against identified major world competitors. In addition, we would expect to use the company standard measures of sales, profit contribution and return on capital employed. However, a balancing figure must be used to adjust for each area's contribution towards, or received benefit from, the overall global plan.

Senior Examiner's comments

As in the answer above, a good pass standard requires an application of marketing planning to the very difficult, complex task of global planning. The achievement of a global plan requires substantial adjustments to be made. The behavioural approach within the organization to find agreement will be lengthy and often acrimonious. The scarce resources of even the largest of organizations need to be used in the most profitable ways. The international manager will need to make a strong case, otherwise the claims of other areas of the organization – for example, production or finance – might prevent sufficient resources flowing to support the global marketing plan.

December 1994, Question 7 This is a rather more complex question than it appears at first sight. Candidates are advised to explain the different forms of organizational structure. This in itself is straightforward. Of a rather more complex nature is the second part of the question dealing with the roles of management at different levels (not over-difficult actually), but also in different locations (a rather more difficult task). Great care has to be taken in planning the answer so as to avoid over-answering the question, thus using up valuable time.

Organizational structure

Candidates might begin by outlining the more obvious forms of international organization structure:

- product
- geographic
- function
  etc.

In doing so, the answer should focus on the separation of responsibilities between domestic and international divisions.

Candidates might next employ Majaro's structures as examples of how larger and more complex businesses might organize themselves. The benefits of using Majaro's structures are that in each case he isolates the management role in terms of three levels:

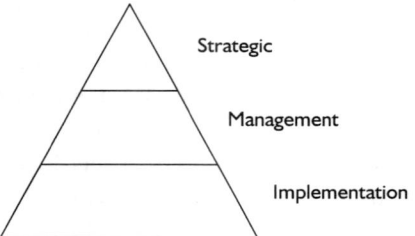

Candidates would be expected to construct Majaro's three basic structures of Macro pyramid, Umbrella and Interglomerate. (**Note**: see Figure 6.2.)

Having completed the three structures the answer should move on to discuss the functions/roles of management at different levels.

Functions of different management levels

Strategic

- identify stakeholders' requirements
- define corporate objectives
- evaluate global opportunities
- organize the business structure
- control the corporate performance

Management

- set the SBU objectives and allocate resources
- control the SBU programme
- organize opportunity analysis and research
- control international marketing planning

Implementation

- set and achieve budgets
- manage the functions (marketing, R&D, probation etc.)
- carry out marketing campaigns and manage distribution

Finally, the answer should comment on the role/function of management at different locations, e.g.:

Country manager: concerned with creating profit from local needs
Functional manager: the business environment scanner and champion of cross-fertilization of ideas
Global manager: providing global leadership, the developer of other levels of management

To gain a top grade, a candidate's answer should comment on the growing trend towards transnational corporations and the management issues involved; namely, highly specialized networks of global business managers, country and functional managers, all working together in a multinational organization which has no traditional country/functional boundaries.

December 1993, Question 8 Most companies are more inclined to develop their marketing approaches around their own domestic market. The majority of companies grow within a country before they embark on exporting and international marketing.

The EPRG orientations approach can be used to show the differences caused by each of the four orientations – ethnocentric, polycentric, regiocentric and geocentric. In the question the two different positions exclude polycentric and regiocentric orientation. Polycentric orientation relates to those organizations that adapt to the host country and is particularly related to multinational enterprise 'multi-local' marketing approaches. Regiocentric orientation relates to those organizations that relate particularly to a world region or a trading bloc.

The organizations that divide markets between domestic and the rest of the world (ROW) might be following an ethnocentric orientation. The home market is known best and takes a disproportionate amount of company resources. The company is likely to be unduly influenced by managers whose marketing planning is affected by the self-reference criterion. Without a significant amount of marketing knowledge about each of the markets contained within the all-embracing group of the ROW and with cultural misunderstandings resulting from a lack of cultural perception and cross-analysis, this company will produce weak marketing plans for the ROW.

Marketing planning for the ROW is likely to include marketing mix variations that are not part of a well thought through planning process. If the ethnocentric view is strong, the product part of the marketing mix will be sold to the ROW and will only be adapted when it is absolutely necessary; for example, to comply with different electrical or other power supply requirements. The other elements of the marketing mix will show considerable adaptation bounded by the different requirements of various distribution channels, price and marketing communications.

Organizations that take a more geographically neutral stance will try to concentrate on identifying the best opportunities on which to focus their marketing efforts. It will mean that the organization will move away from an ethnocentric orientation in its attempt to avoid overemphasizing its reference to its home domestic market. Companies with an ambitious view of their international reach will attempt to become geocentric in their orientation. In their attempt to achieve a global coverage, in which resources are allocated according to the profit opportunities, companies will need to develop good quality marketing research and an international marketing information system. The company will need to develop marketing managers with the ability to manage many country markets.

Companies can take a variety of approaches to develop their international markets. Companies that rely too heavily on their home market will often miss out on marketing opportunities in other markets. Some companies can benefit from a strong 'country of origin' influence; for example, a French company marketing perfume. However, if they lump all other country markets into one ROW group, necessary marketing standardization or adaptation will not take place in a systematic way. Companies attempting to take a more geographically neutral approach face a particularly hard task to develop sufficiently unbiased approaches.

Senior Examiner's comments
This question demands an answer that is based upon the EPRG orientations approach. An attempt which is based merely upon the PEST/SLEPT environmental analysis will not give a sufficiently strong organizational focus. PEST and EPRG are linked because the differences in the country environment will influence market sizes and trends and the responses of buyers to marketing plans. The responsiveness of the organization to these differences will relate to the predominant EPRG orientation.

Globalization

Globalization as a strategic option open to the international organization has been a major topic of discussion since Theodore Levitt wrote his mould-breaking article in 1983 (*Harvard Business Review*). Globalization, in essence, is about treating the world as one market both for marketing and for production purposes. In this unit you will:

- Understand what globalization means
- Consider the factors which drive an organization towards a globalized strategy
- Understand the factors which may affect or inhibit a drive towards globalization
- Be aware of when a globalized strategy is appropriate for an organization and when it is not.

Having completed this unit you will be able to:

- Consider the viability or otherwise of globalization as a strategy for the international organization
- Understand the implications of a globalization strategy upon the organization, its marketing, its production and organizational structure
- Understand the effects of a globalization strategy upon the international marketing mix.

This unit is important to an overall understanding of international marketing strategy. Although globalization represents only a very small part of the syllabus (5%), the effects of following a globalization strategy will be felt throughout the entire operation and implementation of the international marketing mix. Decisions taken at this level will also affect how activities are evaluated and controlled in the international marketplace.

Globalization as a strategy offers significant potential savings through economies of scale but is also clearly an inappropriate strategy in certain situations. The key to understanding globalization is being able to differentiate the times and occasions when it is a suitable strategy for the organization and when it should be avoided in favour of other, more local, approaches to markets.

As you work through this unit remember that good strategy must be thought out carefully. The international market, as always, must be the inspiration for good marketing and when local needs are so divergent in their nature as to make a standardized (globalized) approach inappropriate the international marketer needs to be able to direct strategy accordingly.

What is globalization?

Globalization as an issue came to the fore in 1983 with the publication of Theodore Levitt's article in the *Harvard Business Review*. Levitt's initial article on globalization put forward the view that there was simply no such thing as local markets, that all markets tended towards a universal standard and that organizations indulging themselves in producing many variants in overseas markets were simply wasting resources on a grand scale. He suggested that organizations would be much more efficient and effective if they were to standardize their marketing approaches to overseas markets. They should not only market themselves and their products on a global basis but also consider production and service on a globalized basis. Since Levitt's first article a number of articles have appeared by various authors both for and against this basic premise. Indeed, Levitt himself joined the fray a few years later, saying that wasn't exactly what he meant and that in some instances 'think global, act local' was the right and proper policy for international markets.

> Global marketing can be defined as 'the process of focusing an organization's resources on the selection and exploitation of global market opportunities consistent with and supportive of its short- and long-term strategic objectives and goals' (Source: Toyne and Walters, 1989).

It is relatively easy to see Levitt's original inspiration for the globalization concept. If we consider the North American market, although it is called 'domestic' by US companies, it is far less homogeneous than most other domestic/national markets with which the organization has to deal. While in the domestic marketing situation most US companies will look for similarities among quite often varied market needs, as soon as these same organizations consider overseas markets they start by looking at differences rather than similarities. While there is obviously much fluency in the globalization argument it is equally difficult to understand how it will be universally applicable to all organizations in all situations.

International or Global?

Definitions in textbooks abound to describe the different types of international operations. A simple checklist is:

Domestic marketing

Marketing directed at the domestic or home market only.

Export marketing

Making the product or service in the home markets and selling it in international markets.

International marketing

Moving beyond exporting, the organization often still makes the product or service in the home market but has it own representation for sales, marketing and distribution in the foreign market(s).

Multinational marketing

The next stage of growth and involvement. The organization has a greater proportion of its assets in markets other than its domestic base. The domestic market is now one of many markets all approached mainly on an individual basis. Sometimes called a multidomestic strategy, the organization puts local market considerations first.

Multiregional marketing

In an attempt to find economies of scale in their operations, the organization has started to standardize its international marketing strategies around regional groupings of markets.

Global marketing

The organization defines a single strategy for a product, service or company that can be followed in all markets in which the organization operates. Typically, senior management will set general strategic guidelines and local offices will develop these at local market levels.

Examine the ways in which a major international company, operating in many countries around the world, can use new product development and commercialization to enhance its ambitions to become a global company (December 1994).

(**See** Exam answers at the end of this unit.)

As it is described above, global marketing can be seen as the latest stage in the development of the organization into international markets. Clearly globalization is not appropriate to all organizations, nor does an organization necessarily have to go through all the stages described above to get to globalization. The best way to understand globalization and its applicability for any given organization is to understand the factors which drive globalization and those which may inhibit its implementation in an organization's marketing strategy.

Factors driving to globalization

There are a number of factors in today's modern world which may drive an organization toward a global marketing strategy. Some of the most important are:

1   *The international flow of information*   Predictions of the 'global village' were being made 10 and 15 years ago and they are now starting to come true. The flow of information across national boundaries is becoming both faster and greater in quantity. People also are much more able and willing to travel than a decade ago. This increased flow of international information and customer awareness means that consumers and suppliers nowadays are much more aware of products and services that are available in often very distant markets. With this increased flow of information and awareness comes demand, and markets for products and services grow on a global scale.

2   *The international spread of technology*   As with information, technology is now flowing much more freely across national boundaries and frontiers. With the international spread of technology the ability to design, develop, manufacture and market products and services of all descriptions is available on a much more global scale than 10 or 20 years ago.

3   *Size of investment required*   Driven by the spread of international information and technology, the minimum production batch size is starting to decrease as enabling technology spreads. Consequently, the size of financial and human investment required in developing new products or services has grown. In a number of markets, for example motor cars, military hardware and pharmaceuticals, the absolute size of the investment required to develop the next generation of new products has outstripped the ability of any one single market or company to pay back on the investment. In these industries (among others) investment has to be based on the likely future demand in more than one market, if possible for global application, in order to make such investments financially viable. So we see that developments such as the Ford world car (Mondeo) and the European fighter aircraft are now developed by and for more than one marketplace.

4   *Reduction of trade barriers*   As the world develops into a smaller number of larger economic and political regions (EU, LAFTA, NAFTA) so the number of small, independent markets with their own regulations and legislations requiring adapted or specialized products reduces. As trade barriers and restrictions fall away so the marketplace opens up for much more standardized products and services and makes a globalized international marketing strategy more viable for many organizations.

Examine the similarities and differences between global branding and global marketing. Are they the same? Under what conditions would each be likely to succeed? (December 1993)

(**See** Exam answers at the end of this unit.)

Factors inhibiting globalization

As well as the easily identifiable factors which encourage organizations to take a more globalized international marketing strategy, there are a number of factors which can be identified that may make such a strategy inappropriate or impractical. Some of the more common factors are as follows:

1   *Customer tastes*   The key concept upon which globalization is based is that of a broadly standardized approach to international markets. Before any form of standardization can be applied it requires that customers' tastes in various markets are also standardized. In many cases this is simply not the case. If customers actually want or need or require different products or services from a neighbouring or other foreign market and if competition is such that their needs can be met, they will not buy the standardized (globalized) products or service. Even where tastes converge, many organizations have found that other elements of the product or marketing mix may need to be varied on a local basis in order to gain acceptability. For example, many American adverts on TV might be visually acceptable but may be have to be dubbed in to the local language – including English!

The debate between total globalization and adaptation to local market needs continues to be waged in the pages of marketing journals. You should be aware of the arguments on both sides. You should have an opinion and be prepared to justify it.

2   *Culture*   As we have already seen from Unit 4, culture is a major force in determining customer and buyer behaviour. In the same way, culture can be a major barrier to globalization strategies. Culture is a major factor in everybody's life and people (and organizations) will seek out products and services which enable them to reinforce their sense of belonging to a given culture and will avoid those products and services that are seen as transgressing particular cultural rules. Certain products and services are evidently the product of an identifiable culture. For example, McDonald's, Coca-Cola and Harley-Davidson are seen as products of US culture. In these cases, they will still be purchased as people wish to sample that culture as well as consume the product. In other cases such as Phileas Fogg snacks, the organization may find that while the concept behind the snacks is valid on a worldwide basis the actual products required to deliver the company's promise differ from culture to culture and need to be modified accordingly.

Select a company that is generally thought of as being a global operator. (McDonald's, Coca-Cola, Pepsi, Ford, International Harvester, Compaq, etc.). What degree of standardization are they actually able to achieve? What adaptation in the marketing mix can you identify?

3   *Local market conditions* As well as the strictly cultural variables at play when considering globalization strategy, there are a number of other variables that also need to be taken into account. These will vary from organization to organization and from product to product but may include issues such as the local market's need for particular national or regional identity, the role of individualism in the target market and the degree of nationalism inherent in local purchase behaviour. In these instances a degree of globalization may be possible but also some degree of adaptation to local requirements may be required.

Global marketing strategy

If, depending on the organization, its competition and its target customers' needs, globalization is deemed a valid international strategy, then there will be many consequences for the organization and its marketing. Globalized organizations need to develop and refine the ability to consider business, markets and competition all over the world and to distil this (often conflicting) data into a practical marketing plan. Global marketing strategy is not the same as domestic marketing strategy applied all over the world. The skills and management required to develop and implement global strategies are different.

Think Global, Act Local requires a constant knowledge of where the line lies that divides globalization from multinational marketing. Striking the balance between Standardization and Adaptation is difficult. Setting central, global strategic guidelines for local, tactical, implementation requires precise strategic skills. The ability to think above the detail is rare. All elements of the international marketing mix will be influenced by the global strategy. Balancing local requirements against the wider global benefits may not always be popular in local operating units.

Policing (monitoring and controlling) products, services and global brands in diverse markets needs tact, diplomacy and interpersonal skills native to the international marketer.

The Diploma examinations are strategic. Examiners are looking for evidence of candidates' ability to think for themselves about issues that really matter. Globalization, too, has its critics. One, Sir James Goldsmith, was decidedly anti-free trade. He said:

'The doctrine of free trade, if applied globally, will be a disaster.'
'Economies should not be self-serving structures, but directed at promoting the stability and contentment of the societies within which they operate.'
'Europe faces a future of unemployment, poverty and social instability.'
'Britain will become the Mexico of Europe.'
'A reason for this is our quasi-religious belief in free trade. A moral dogma which was born when Britain was the manufacturing centre of the world.'

He suggested the future should be based on:

'Country preference.'
'A world of fenced-off regions with economies that reflect local conditions, cultures and needs.'

You can read more – and make up your own mind – *The Trap*, J. Goldsmith, Macmillan, 1994

Examine the factors by which country markets can be grouped in order to develop standardized multi-country marketing plans (December 1994).

Kenichi Ohmae writes of the need to 'think global, act local'. What are the organizational issues for a company in achieving this and how might they reconcile the conflicting pressures? (June 1997, Question 7)

(**See** Exam answers at the end of this unit.)

Conclusions

Any discussion on globalization cannot take place in a vacuum. As you consider this concept of a standardized international approach to marketing and production you need also to bear in mind the customers (Unit 3), the infrastructure within which international trade is carried out (Unit 2) as well as the implications for product policy (Unit 9). It is probably fair to say that, given their choice, most organizations would prefer that they provided a completely standardized global product and marketing programme and would ideally have only one major worldwide centre for production. The financial and human resource economies that such an approach would produce are undeniable. However, the international marketer needs to realize that the world simply is not like this. Apart from a few companies who have truly global markets, most organizations have to come to grips with the fact that the world is still not homogeneous and needs to be catered for on a local basis. Obviously, it is a question of balance. To what extent can we standardize our approaches to overseas markets and to what extent do we have to make modifications in order to achieve customer acceptance and acceptable sales levels in overseas markets? Significant economies can come from standardization but if the standardized product or service is too far from local requirements, sales volumes and revenues may suffer as a result.

In any event, the importance of conducting careful market research (see Unit 4) into the needs and requirements of overseas markets cannot be overemphasized.

Summary

In this unit we have seen that globalization is a major force in international marketing strategy. The benefits from a globalized marketing approach are significant and offer major economies from a standardized approach to foreign markets.

There are a number of reasons globalization is coming to the fore and many international marketing variables are stimulating interest in this area. There are also a number of factors which may stand in the way of an organization successfully globalizing its operations, and most of these are concerned with local tastes, requirements and perceptions.

In any event, the organization considering globalization should:

1 Not to be dazzled by the rare instances of successful pure globalization
2 Carefully research and understand overseas markets before moving to globalization
3 Look for similarities as well as differences in overseas markets before planning
4 Carefully evaluate the savings to be made from a globalized/standardized approach against the likely loss of sales from not fully meeting local market requirements.

Questions

As a check on your understanding of what has been covered in this unit, consider the following questions:

- What is meant by 'globalization'?
- How practical is a strategy of pure globalization?
- What factors actively promote globalization?
- What factors will inhibit a globalization strategy?
- How close to a true global strategy can an organization plan?

For a more detailed analysis and explanation of globalization, read:

International Marketing, S. Paliwoda and M. Thomas, Butterworth-Heinemann, 1998.

International Marketing Strategy, I. Doole, R. Lowe and C. Phillips, Routledge, 1997.

December 1994 **Notes to candidates**: The question revolves around a major multinational organization and candidates should therefore avoid discussing companies that merely export. The major thrust should be concerning international, i.e. multi-country, expansion of new product introduction with a view to being global.

New product development

It is increasingly apparent that companies need to have a dynamic and proactive policy for developing new products. The nature of world trade, the growth of global consumers with broadly similar needs and wants is forcing the pace. Multinationals are nowadays focusing their policies on standardization and market spreading and/or market concentration in an ever-shrinking time frame. The time from idea generation through to commercialization is decreasing.

In its simplest form, product development follows a similar process for international to that in domestic markets:

- idea generation
- initial testing
- business analysis
- development
- market testing
- commercialization – launch

Where the process differs in international markets is in the level of analysis, coordination and communication when assessing the suitability of the product for multi-country exploitation.

Of paramount importance is the quality of the information system since it is essential the launch is successful and the product is correctly positioned and aligned to the target market.

Methods of achieving this internationally include:

- Idea generation must include worldwide monitoring to avoid duplication.
- Initial screening. Here the screening criteria need to be wider than for a single/domestic market to take account that 'some' adaptation might be necessary for separate markets. Obviously the less the adaptation the closer the positioning.
- Business analysis. The criteria for success may vary across markets.
- Product development. Great consideration must be given as to where research and development (R&D) take place. Should it be centralized or located in lead markets. This is a most important debate nowadays for most multinational/global corporations. The trend is towards centralization or, at the very least, towards pan-regional research centre location.
- Market testing. Careful steps need to be taken to ensure the test market is sufficiently representative of multi-country markets. Allowances need to be built into the control mechanisms to measure the likely impact of the launch in other

markets. Considerations such as buyer behaviour, competitive responses, distribution networks etc.

- The launch/commercialization. The roll-out from the test market needs careful attention. It must be planned sequentially and the common technique nowadays is to identify lead markets where there are greater similarities and to launch in these first. Secondary markets follow later as experience is gained.

In today's competitive world it is recognized that roll-out is faster than of old. Competitors scour the world for new products to copy or imitate. Many products cannot be patented. Companies with global ambitions need to balance rapid commercialization against that of risk analysis. The Japanese method is to take the risk and commercialize rapidly. If the product fails they withdraw equally rapidly and return with a more appropriate version.

December 1993

Global brand
There are very few true global brands. These are brands that are identifiable throughout the world with a standardized brand name and trade mark and consistent packaging. Sony, Kodak and Coca-Cola are examples of global brands.

Global marketing
This type of international marketing is concerned with analysing opportunities around the world and in developing appropriate and coordinated international marketing plans on a worldwide basis.

It can be seen from the definitions of global branding and global marketing that they are not the same. It should be noted that in certain circumstances the two approaches can be similar. If a global marketing approach identifies that an opportunity exists for a standardized brand approach based on considerable demand similarity around the world, then the global marketing solution would be to develop a global brand.

It is very difficult to find situations in which customer needs are similar in a number of different countries. In many markets customer demands are varied and the various elements of the marketing mix need to be adapted to work effectively in each country market. To succeed in global branding, companies need to find markets where there are few cultural barriers to acceptance of the product or service. There needs to be a lack of government or country barriers. Barriers such as technical standards or health and safety legislation can cause products to be adapted extensively. Products and services in which the customer is mobile internationally can develop global brands; for example, British Airways in air travel, Hilton in hotels and Hertz in car hire.

Global marketing needs to be undertaken by companies with substantial resources. They need to have the ability to analyse many markets. It is likely that global marketing will exist if the company is coordinating its marketing approach across the main markets of the world. The 'triad' markets of Japan, US and Europe represent, for most markets, over 75% of the total world demand in that market. Global marketing cannot, therefore, be marketing that is restricted to one or two continents or to just a number of markets. The conditions under which global marketing can exist are more varied than for global branding. In global marketing extensive adaptations for market differences can be made. Different brand names and different marketing mix approaches can be used. However, the relentless drive to find lower cost positions will tend to encourage some companies to move towards standardization rather than adaptation.

Summary
Both global branding and global marketing will require substantial resources. The global brand requires substantial efforts to gain worldwide awareness and a favourable brand image. It requires attention to the legal protection of its trade mark. To succeed the global brand requires a convergence of customer need and an absence of strong

cultural or country barriers. The global marketing approach requires a worldwide vision and a corporate ability to orchestrate its activities around the world.

Senior Examiner's comments
The global brand approach places a strong emphasis on visual standardization. The trade mark becomes a very important property. Packaging will show adaptation for language requirements but the dominant features of the brand logo and the trade mark, with the appropriate colours, will remain as a constant feature around the world. The global marketing approach is a strategic blend of standardization and adaptation. A particular difficulty in global marketing is developing international marketing managers with a sufficiently geocentric view to be able to operate the highly demanding global marketing approach.

December 1994 **Note to candidates**: This is something of a 'catch all' question in that candidates can approach this from the general viewpoint of international marketing.

Unquestionably there is a strong trend towards standardization in international markets. Whilst globalization might be the ultimate goal to some organizations, others are pursuing a pan-regional multi-country approach. Both are different points on the continuum towards standardization.

General factors underpinning standardization
These might include:

- Technology creating new world markets, e.g. Microsoft Windows.
- Multinationals creating worldwide systems and products
- Multinationals with intra-company purchasing
- The development of a one-world youth culture: Reebok, Niké and Timberland in the footwear market – and there are many more examples.
- Shrinking communications: nothing and nowhere is far away. Increasingly we all live in a global village. This is particularly true of developed nations.
- Global capital. $1 trillion cross national boundaries daily. Money truly exists in a borderless world.
- Information technology is becoming universal. Business managers everywhere have access to the latest inventions and increasingly plan and operate processing systems globally.

Again, the opening section could be expanded by the better candidate.
Factors relating to multi-country marketing plans might be:

- The development of regionalism, i.e. the trend towards countries cooperating to create a large internal market, e.g. European Union, where regional standards on product formulation, packaging, harmony of pricing, legislation etc. is creating a convergence towards standardization. This is not an instant transformation but is likely to happen over time.
- Product life cycle similarities, e.g. First World countries adopting state of the art technology in order to cooperate. Less developed countries being catered for by older products.
- Culture. Loosely based around customer clusters exhibiting similarities.
- Geographic proximity. If a product is relatively homogenous or ubiquitous, e.g. chewing gum, then multi-country marketing is relatively easy.
- Standard of living equating to ability to pay.

The critical and distinguishing feature ultimately must be buyer similarities in terms of needs and wants. There is a clear paradox emerging in international business. Whilst some markets are definitely converging towards standardized marketing, e.g. Coca-cola,

Benetton, McDonald's, Fuji, BMW, Marlboro – the list is quite long – other markets are becoming more 'individual' or ethnic in their identified niches. Both are likely to prosper as we as customers seek convergence (convenience) and diversity (self-expression and self-actualization).

The argument will continue to rage and a good candidate will, I am sure, expand on this guideline. Consideration could be given to an analysis of similarities under the SLEPT headings and then developing an approach to standardization using the four Ps. This is perfectly acceptable.

June 1997, Question 7 'Think global, act local' has become the international battle cry of the 1990s. Traditionally seen as the prerogative of multinationals, today it applies equally to small firms, i.e. those who market via electronic communications (Internet).

Trends are to exert leverage across corporate capabilities so the whole is greater than the sum of the parts.

Globalization is based on the belief that the world is becoming more homogeneous. Forces underpinning this include the global consumer, convergent needs, affluence, income levels, communication and technology.

By concentrating on fewer basic solutions marketers can cater to a universal need at the lowest cost. But, at the same time, marketers have to remain responsive to differences between national and regional markets. Respecting differences is critical not only in terms of customer preferences but also internally within the company itself.

Note: Candidates will not be rewarded simply on the basis of a list of factors influencing adaptations to markets. It is accepted they know these. Additionally, the question does not seek answers in terms of international organizational structures – macro, umbrella, pyramid or whatever.

Global markets are frequently characterized by a limited number of players who confront each other in different markets.

The critical organizational issues are:

1 Degree of control
   Globalization usually dictates a high leverage of control across all the business functions but marketing has the tendency to be a local/micro activity dealing as it does with customers as individuals. So control needs to be balanced against local intuition.
2 Global strategic motivation
   The pressure to go global within a company may subordinate national/regional motivation.

Organizational implications are:

Develop synergies in the following:
- Manufacturing know-how.
- Manufacturing location.
- Marketing know-how.
- Marketing co-ordination of key values.
- Development and transfer of management expertise.
- Co-ordination of R&D resources.
- Production and operational personnel.
- Distribution and logistic co-ordination, i.e. channel management.
- Management uncertainties (retaining a degree of flexibility in an ever more uncertain world).
- Responding to competitive pressures however/whenever/wherever they arise.

Market entry methods

The purpose of this unit is to consider the alternative routes through which the firm might enter foreign markets. Having already taken the decision to market overseas, i.e. where we should go, the key decision becomes what the best way is of entering the chosen markets. We review the major routes and markets and criteria for selecting them. In this unit you will:

- Understand the range of options available.
- See that size (or lack of) is no barrier to exporting or foreign production.
- Discuss the criteria for chosing each entry strategy.
- Understand the importance of the level of involvement and the management issues that accompany it.

Having completed the unit you will be able to:

- Grasp the importance of choosing the right method of entry and realize that decisions must be taken with the utmost care
- Understand the implications of your choice from a marketing perspective
- Recognize that each entry method has management implications
- See that there is no one right route. Markets vary, and so we must choose the appropriate route to customers. Flexibility, learning and gaining experience are necessary stages of developing entry strategies.

Step by step you will discover the different methods of proceeding into overseas markets. The stages increase in complexity and have management implications. From the crucial and often hesitant initial stage the picture builds to a conclusion that is concerned not so much with entry methods but with how to exploit opportunities within the context of a multi-country scenario.

No ideal strategy exists – one firm may choose a variety of methods, appropriate to each country/market situation. In the same way, entry methods change over time. But underpinning the decision is the firms objectives, attitudes and commitment to successful exploitation of overseas opportunities. The level of involvement referred to in the text (and also in the introduction to the Workbook) is the key factor in determining the correct strategy.

International market entry strategies

Having previously identified where we wish to go in developing overseas business and having addressed our basic marketing strategies, the next step is deciding how we might get there – the market entry strategy. This is of critical importance for it sets the agenda for future battles. It signals to competitors the scale of our intention and, with it, our commitment.

There is no one ideal way of entering an overseas market. There are options to suit all sizes of firms and all situations. There are no barriers preventing the smallest firm from taking the first tentative steps overseas, for international marketing is not the exclusive preserve of large companies. Indeed, large companies do not pursue a rigid policy in exploiting opportunities but often seek to take the most appropriate route for each market judged as an entity. Du Pont operates with wholly owned or joint-venture operations in 40 countries, with marketing subsidiaries in 20 and with distributors in 60. McDonald's has a mixture of wholly owned or franchised operations. No route is the correct one.

However, the chosen entry method requires the greatest of care. Once selected and resourced, it may not be easy to change or withdraw from the market. (Exit strategies are also important, especially in high-risk markets.) Similarly, the extent to which the company's marketing strategy can be employed is also dependent upon the decision. So the alternatives must be weighed most carefully and should be viewed by the international marketer over the longer- rather than the shorter-term horizons. A straightforward exports orientated company can take a short-term tactical approach but international marketing involves dialogue with consumers, understanding their needs and wants, creating appropriate satisfactions and managing the relationship between the company, its intermediaries and its consumers.

Entry strategy alternatives

- If international marketing is about relationships with overseas customers/consumers then the starting point in considering market entry alternatives is a strategic not a tactical one and revolves around the question of 'level of involvement', or, putting it simpler 'how close do I need to be to the consumer in order to succeed?' As in all markets, closeness to the consumer is the discriminator of success. Refer here to the International Business Process model in the section 'What is international marketing?' for guidance and reinforcement of the point.

Level of involvement

This is dictated by the following:

- Corporate objectives/ambition/resources. These will shape the market entry strategy in terms of narrowing the options but will not necessarily constrain the organization to a single-entry choice.
- Nature of the markets/product category/competition. The scale of the market, the number of markets, the nature of the product category and the level of competition will influence market entry strategy.
- Nature of consumer culture. What customers buy, where they buy, why they buy and how often will certainly focus thinking.
- Coverage of the market – breadth, depth and quality. Again, this is largely dictated by consumer needs. The product has to be available where the customer expects to find it. The basic choice of market entry strategy is influenced by the required penetration demands.
- Speed of entry. The nature of the product, where it is on the product life cycle, the rate of new product innovation diffusion and the pace of market development will have a profound bearing on our choice.
- Level of control. What feedback is required? What research information do we need on customer purchasing to assist future planning and to effect current and future controls?
- Marketing costs and commitment. Consumer demands and competitive pressure will influence this. Clearly, the greater the marketing cost, the higher will be the level of involvement.
- Profit payback. This is related to corporate aims and objectives but varying by company and by country. The general rule is that paybacks are longer overseas. Sony, when

entering the UK market, took a corporate decision not to take profit for the first 10 years, but to invest it in the development of its market share. At the other extreme, a leading question might be 'Can I get my money out?'. This, too, will colour the approach to market entry.

- Investment costs. The deeper the involvement, the higher the costs; inventory, finance, credit, management, etc.
- Administrative requirements. Documentation, detailed knowledge of legal requirements, foreign taxation.
- Personnel. This obviously increases with greater involvement; management, training, language, cultural assimilation are all factors to consider.
- Flexibility. Learning from doing; testing the situation before heavy involvement, political risk, multi-market entry are just some of the factors to take into account in planning the entry strategy.

ACTIVITY 8.1

What does level of involvement mean? Take a small firm and compare it with a major multinational. See how this equates with cost.

EXAM HINT

Practically every examination paper has questions on entry methods either in the mini case or in the Section B part of the examination. It is extremely rare that the subject is not included in the paper. Therefore it is essential you have a very thorough grasp of the subject.

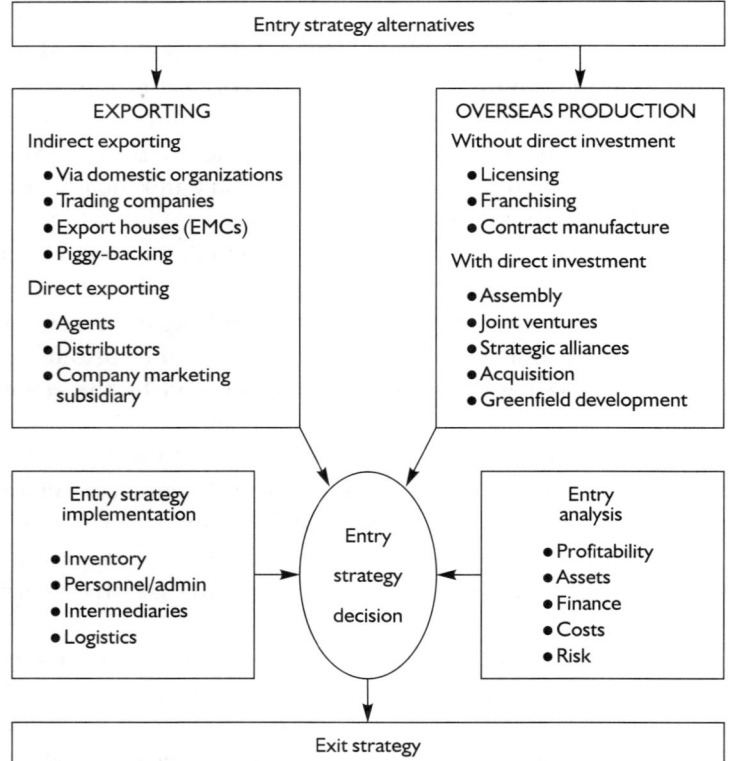

Figure 8.1 Market entry alternatives

With entry strategy alternatives two basic routes present themselves:

1 Exporting – defined as 'Making it here, selling it there'.
2 Overseas Production – 'Making it there and selling it there' (not necessarily the same country)

Figure 8.1 sets out the strategic alternatives under both headings. The choice is extensive and we propose to comment briefly on all of them. But before doing so it is important to recognize that the level of involvement increases in descending order and that overseas production requires greater involvement than exporting.

Exporting

Indirect exporting

This deals with exports as if they were domestic sales. No specific overseas knowledge is required as the work is done by others. New opportunities can be opened up but control is limited and profitability generally low (others are taking the risk, doing the work). Various methods exist:

- *Overseas organizations with buyers in domestic markets* Major retailers have UK buyers (e.g. Macy's in New York has buying offices in 30 countries). The Body Shop procures products from obscure sources (e.g. the Kayapo Indians deep within the Brazilian rainforest).
- *Multinationals' procurement offices* The major multinationals source widely.

Study some trade magazines in more than one industry (e.g. fashion, electrical equipment, etc.). What avenues and approaches are there for small firms to export?

ACTIVITY 8.2

- *International trading companies* With their roots in the colonial era and consequently of fading importance, nevertheless ITCs are important in gaining access to many Third World countries. United Africa Company, a Unilever subsidiary, is the largest trader in Africa. The Japanese Sogo Shosha, as their ITCs are known, are major international players embracing Mitsui and Mitsubishi. The Sogo Shosha handle the majority of Japanese imports today. Their advantages are wide market coverage and fast, easy access to markets. However, they will carry a wide portfolio of products, often competitors, and therefore there will be a dilution of effort. Additionally, a feeling of resentment may persist in some countries due to the historical legacy of colonialism. Burma and Egypt have nationalized ITCs to rid themselves of foreign influence. In summary, sales are less stable but there is little company control.
- *Export houses (Export Management Companies – EMCs in American textbooks)* This is by far the most important method of exporting (numerically) with around 800 operating in the UK. Ranging from generalist to specialist (by industry and country), they provide the performance of an export department without direct involvement and generally allow the company some (if small) degree of cooperation and control. Most suitable for the small to medium firm. The *CIM Quarterly Review* (Autumn 1987) suggested that 63 per cent of small/medium firms involved in exporting used export houses.

Further advantages include: instant market contact and knowledge (particularly local purchasing practices and government regulations). They are paid on commission and therefore are motivated to develop the business (ensuring that the product is attractive to sell). Additionally they offer freight savings by consolidating shipments and, if selling complementary products, can enhance the representation. Disadvantages include: the country coverage by the export house may not coincide with the company's objectives, and they may carry too many products (including competitive ones) thus diluting the effort.

Therefore care must be taken in choosing the appropriate export house. The company's trade association is often a helpful source of advice.

Contact a trade association, see if you can obtain a list of export houses or alternatively via a trade telephone directory contact an export house direct. See what they offer small firms.

- *Piggy-backing* This is essentially a form of cooperation in exporting where one company uses its facilities to sell another's product. It is more common between US multinationals and exporters than in Europe. Generally, piggy-backing involves longer-term involvement and it is certain that partner choice requires great care. The advantages are introductions to new markets via an organization established and respected in the country together with savings in infrastructure costs covering warehousing marketing and sales. *Note:* Piggy-backing is often included under direct exporting as this utilizes the resources of an intermediary based in overseas countries.

Direct exporting

This is exporting using intermediaries located in foreign markets. In doing so the exporter is becoming more involved and committed to the new marketplace, adding investment, time and management expertise. The benefits of greater involvement are more influence, greater strategic leverage (variable) control (also variable) and, of course, profit. The step from indirect to direct exporting should not be taken lightly as the costs and expertise levels rise sharply and therefore the company must be sure it has the capabilities of managing this significantly higher workload and knowledge requirement. Mahon and Vachini (1992) suggest that a 'beach-head' strategy be employed initially, thereby testing overseas markets (small countries or niche markets) prior to a full-scale abandonment of indirect exporting.

Factors for success

- Top management commitment
- Confidence
- International marketing skills
- Detailed planning
- Commitment to quality
- Research and development
- Reliability/relationship building

Factors for failure

- Failure to research the market
- Inadequate funds/financial backing
- Failure of commitment/perseverance
- Under representation in the market
- Failure to understand cultural reference
- Inexperienced management and personnel

Once individual countries have been selected the first decision is how the company will be represented. The size of the market, the nature of the product category, the level of involvement and contact with the consumer pre- and post-purchase will influence the degree of contact between the company and the market (e.g. a full-time staff in residence at one end of the spectrum to a home-based export sales manager liaising with intermediaries or, alternatively, simply communicating by telephone and fax at the other end).

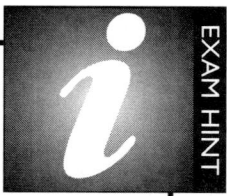

Throughout the book we stress the importance of using examples. However, don't just quote ours – think of ones of your own. Originality will be rewarded in the examination.

Agents

These represent the lowest level of direct involvement in exporting. Their distinguishing feature is that they are country/territory bound (be sure your contact states this to avoid parallel exporting/importing). Paid on commission for orders obtained they, as a norm, represent non-competing manufacturers with sole rights. The critical fact to keep in mind is that agents do not take title to the goods (although there are exceptions). Their advantage lies in that they are paid by results, there is limited risk involved, they can tap into existing contacts, they have a cultural and linguistic affinity. Furthermore start-up costs are low. Their disadvantages stem from quality of service, coverage of the market, conflict of interest (dilution factor), lack of control over them. They are difficult to fire due to legal complexities, stretched resources, communication (both inward and outward), motivation, distribution and their financial competence, i.e. you getting paid! Great care needs to be taken in drafting the agreement and agents are usually chosen when high-price, low-volume goods are ordered – business-to-business or industrial products.

Distributors

These differ considerably from agents in both the level of involvement and the relationship. Distributors represent the major (most popular) form of international distribution numerically. They are used by small and large firms alike for entering markets where a marketing as well as a sales presence is required. This marketing input accounts largely for the deeper level of involvement. Distributors differ from agents also by buying the goods themselves and selling them on – usually at their own determined price (although company considerations and cooperation in pricing the product is important). In other words, distributors 'take title to the goods'.

It is apparent that success in the market is largely dependent on the performance of the chosen distributor (the selection process is critical). The challenge then becomes 'how to motivate the distributor'. The key is through building intercompany relationships; by continually rewarding the distributor to do as well, treating them as if they were in your own organization. Recognizing such perfection is unlikely, the company should take all necessary steps to create distributor loyalty, e.g. ensuring an adequate payment structure, developing training programmes, determining agreed targets and other performance standards; and evaluating those performance levels regularly at the same time as maintaining an efficient communication system.

The distributor is not your employee but your business partner and your sole representation in a country. Treat the arrangement on a mutually (equally) beneficial one, for an unhappy or disgruntled distributor can inflict great damage. Gaining success breeds confidence and greater cooperation. Finally, the advantages and disadvantage of distribution broadly coincide with those for agents.

ACTIVITY 8.4

Examine the question 'When exporting, you are only as good as your distributor'. Draw up a plan for forging a positive relationship.

Other direct export methods

These include management contracts and usually relate to large-scale undertakings, e.g. the running of international hotels, turnkey projects, etc. Also included is the growing field of direct marketing via 0800 numbers and/or direct mail brought about by advances in information technology and converges in consumer lifestyles.

Operating through an overseas sales/marketing subsidiary

This subject is examined in Unit 11 dealing with international promotion. However, it is often the case that companies set up overseas sales/marketing subsidiaries either to operate within the market via expatriates or to manage a local sales force. Additionally, an overseas subsidiary might provide technical back-up in terms of after-sales service to distributors contract manufacturers or licensees.

The advantages of an overseas presence are closer contact, specialized know-how and faster/more efficient control. The disadvantages include higher initial costs and a time-lag in becoming estabished, no initial local contacts, cultural disharmony and a risk to company reputation if failure is the result. Re-establishing the company's presence in the marketplace may not be straightforward re-entry.

Do some digging. Identify firms, by example, who are involved in each of the identified methods of entry. This will serve you well in examination terms.

Questions occur frequently on indirect and direct market entry. Look back at some past question papers. Be absolutely certain you understand the differences between, for example, agents and distributors. Often candidates mix these two alternatives in terms of description using such phrases as 'appointing agents or distributors'. This is a fatal error – they are patently not similar.

Overseas production

This is the starting point for serious involvement – making the product overseas. For most companies the determining factor in manufacturing overseas is the size of the market and the profit potential. The greater the opportunity, the more is the likelihood of production overseas. However, before discussing the alternatives it is important to point out that overseeing production in foreign markets is a vast step upwards in terms of company commitment and involvement from the previous entry strategies. Although labour and buildings may be cheaper, the additional costs involved in transferring technological know-how, quality control and the management of the operation together with the finance involved should not be underestimated. Usually the additional 'pressure' is placed on the domestic production and operational staff who are transferred overseas to supervise the new start-up, often with regressive performance on domestic quality and supply. Reasons for producing overseas include:

- Size of market and profitability
- Tariff barriers reduce competitiveness in the chosen market
- Government regulations (e.g. India, Egypt) demand production be located there for some categories of product
- A major client company moves into overseas production. Japanese sub-contractors moved into the USA when Honda set up production
- Government contacts and support to inward investment
- Regionalization – being an 'insider' within the EU is important and, as a result, Toyota and Nissan have opened plants in the UK
- Speed of response, delivery, feedback and after-sales service.

Having decided to become involved in overseas production it is possible to hedge the limit of that involvement from licensing at one extreme to building a manufacturing plant on a greenfield site at the other.

Examine the steps taken by a firm moving from a domestic business to an international business (December 1992, Question 7).
(**See** Exam answers at the end of this unit.)

Foreign manufacture without direct investment

Licensing

This requires a low level of direct investment. It confers the right to utilize a company-specific patent, trademark, copyright, product or process for an agreed fee, in a given country, over a prescribed timespan. The benefits to the licensor i.e. the company giving the licence are:

- No capital outlay, considerable cost savings
- Attractive to small and large firms alike
- Multi-market penetration quickly, especially important when dealing with 'products' with a short life-cycle (e.g. *Jurassic Park* merchandising, Power Rangers, Ninja Turtles, computer games. etc.)
- Access to local distribution
- Payment by results

It is easy to see how licensing has emerged as one of the frontrunners in penetrating global markets speedily. Furthermore, licensing is attractive where markets are politically sensitive, the risk is high, the tariff barriers are prohibitive or government regulations forbid company control in the market. The disadvantages are:

- Limitations on control of licensee
- May be establishing competition at end of the agreement
- Limited returns – the licensee is doing the work and will seek the major reward. Licensing fees can vary from 2–3 per cent for industrial products to 30 per cent for faster-moving short life-span products e.g. Computer games.
- Quality control and assurance. Given these circumstances, it is hardly surprising that the company's home standards or quality levels may have limited relevance.

Managing the licensing agreements

With these pitfalls in mind:

- Careful selection of the licensee is essential, especially in the area of quality control.
- Careful drafting of the agreement is necessary (domestic language and legal systems whenever possible).

- Retain control of key component/formulation. Coca-Cola is a licensing operation worldwide. The essence is produced in Atlanta, shipped everywhere to which 99 per cent local product is added (i.e. water!).
- Don't license latest state-of-the-art technology – license yesterday's technology (dependent, of course, on the market).
- Limit the geographic area of the licence.
- Register all trademarks, patents, copyrights, etc. in licensor's name.
- Finally, make the agreement attractive to retain.

Franchising

This has similarities with licensing but is more complex and involves greater management commitment and expertise as the franchiser makes a total production, operational and marketing programme available. Usually the franchise includes the full process of overseas operations and all the factors involved are prescribed.

Generally, franchises involve a service element and well-known international franchises include The Body Shop and McDonald's. Franchising, too, is expanding rapidly. It is a fast track to internationalization for many organizations. As the franchisee pays into the franchise the capital outlay is reduced and the financial risk lies mainly with the franchisee. McDonald's has recently announced that it is opening 1200 new outlets every year until the end of the century. It already has 14 000 outlets in 70 countries and is planning to expand this to 20 000 by opening up more outlets in Eastern Europe and launching in India. The vast majority of McDonald's outlets are franchises – although it is customary for the company initially to enter a country with its wholly owned outlets to establish standards of service and to train franchisees. For the record, in the UK McDonald's can open a restaurant for around £400 000 in 30 days. Most of this outlay (i.e. £250 000 +) will be put up by the franchisee.

For the franchisee the arrangement enables small, independent, entrepreneurial individual(s) to enjoy the benefits of belonging to a large organization with all its power of economies of scale and marketing expertise.

Franchising is very fast-growing but not without its problems which centre on standards of efficiency and service levels and reflect cultural expectations. Even McDonald's has bowed to cultural values, and Kentucky Fried Chicken (KFC) in Japan has succeeded (after initial failure) by adapting to Japanese cultural values and expectation of what a US product should feel like. Similarly, The Body Shop sets its overriding corporate standards but the management and the delivery of the 'product offer' are left to locally determined values.

Contract manufacture

This is manufacturing by proxy, with a third party producing the product under contract. Besides obviating the need for investment and therefore entailing less risk, it avoids labour problems but enables the company to advertise 'local made'. Differing from licensing in that the end product is usually turned over to the company for distribution, sales, marketing, etc., contract manufacture is usually undertaken where political risk is high, the country is economically unstable, sales volumes are relatively low or tariffs are high.

In seeking contract manufacturers the company should give consideration to quality control issues and not produce where there is only one manufacturer, seeking to offset alternative producers. Finally, proxy manufacturing should take place where the marketing effort is of crucial importance to the success.

EXAM HINT

In the same way as candidates mix up agents and distributors, they do the same when considering licensing and franchising. Make sure you know the differences. Return to the text and check this point now.

Foreign manufacture with direct investment

In moving toward direct investment the company is again increasing its level of involvement.

Assembly

This typically involves the last stages of manufacture and usually depends on the ready supply of components shipped from another overseas country(ies). The key figures in this practice are the world's major car manufacturers who have created integrated component supply and assembly from CKD (Completely Knocked Down) operations, often referred to as 'screwdriver plants' to extensive deconstruction arrangements with specialized components, gearboxes, engines, etc. being made in highly automated plants and then shipped to a common assembly point – usually within a region (e.g. the EU).

Often local governments force manufacturers into assembly operations by banning the import of fully made-up vehicles. BMW, Mercedes and others are assembled in Thailand and Malaysia. The success of Proton cars, the indigenous Malaysian producer, partly reflects barriers and taxes on imported vehicles.

Other reasons for establishing foreign production include:

- *To defend existing business* Fearing US government intervention against Japanese imported vehicles, Honda started the move to produce within the USA. Other Japanese vehicle producers have followed this trend.
- *Moving with established customer* Once Honda moved to producing cars in the USA its Japanese suppliers soon followed to maintain the relationship and partnership bonding at the same time preventing US suppliers from cutting in on 'their market'. Suppliers here include banking and financial services and not just vehicle component suppliers.
- *To cut costs* With total quality management (TQM) becoming increasingly global manufacturers no longer feel so insecure about moving production overseas to benefit from lower labour costs, fewer restrictions or less taxes. The massive inward investment in China, India and Indonesia reflects this move and it will further accelerate.

Joint ventures

In joint ventures two companies decide to get together and form a third company that is co-owned (not necessarily equally). The third company then is an entity in itself and the proceeds (and pitfalls) are jointly shared according to the proportion of ownership. Generally, the two parties contribute complementary expertise of resources to the joint company. Joint ventures differ from licensing in that an equity stake exists in the newly formed company.

Increasingly, joint ventures are an attractive option for international companies. Factors accounting for this include:

- Technological development is prohibitively expensive but necessary to achieve break-throughs. Companies increasingly compete on this front.
- Rapid internationalization of many markets is beyond the resources of many major companies. Cooperation on production, distribution and marketing have brought benefits.
- Complementary management or skills and especially finance deals have led to new companies being jointly formed.
- Many countries restrict foreign ownership. China, India and South Korea are among those who insist on a form of joint venture.

Many hi-tech companies are now forging joint venture links to cut the costs of development and speed up market development. Those companies moving into Russia or Eastern Europe are nearly all doing so via this route. In 1990 Russia saw 150 joint venture deals signed, McDonald's and Pepsi among them. Obviously, partner choice is important. McDonald's and Pepsi chose the city of Moscow as its partner; Procter & Gamble's chosen partner in Russia is the University of St Petersburg. All three partners are preferred to the normal commercial arrangement partly because none of any substance or reputation exists.

On a negative note there is always the possibility of joint venture divorce. Some points for consideration before entering into the arrangement are:

- The venture must develop its own culture
- Venture partners must be prepared to share the problems, not try to blame the other party
- The venture managers must have access to top management of both parties
- The venture should receive sufficient capital and finance to develop
- The venture should not be overcontrolled by central bureaucracy

Strategic alliances

A strategic alliance has no precise definition but is different from a joint venture in that there is often no equity involvement, no separate organization is created. Loosely described, a strategic alliance is a 'swap shop' between two or more organizations who agree to cooperate strategically to the mutual benefit of both or all parties to the arrangement.

The development of strategic alliances is continuing apace. Hardly a month elapses without one or more being announced. May 1996 saw Disney and McDonalds cooperating for a ten year period to exploit Disney characters worldwide. The forces underpinning the creation of strategic alliances include:

- High R&D costs
- Pace of innovation and market diffusion
- Concentration of firms in mature industries
- Insufficient resources to exploit new technological breakthroughs
- Government cooperation
- Regionalization
- The fast-developing global consumer – the fundamental and most important reason
- Self-protection against predators
- Access to otherwise difficult markets.

Like joint ventures, strategic alliances need to be considered carefully before entering into the agreement. They should either be seen as a short-term, stop-gap arrangement or as a long-term partnership. Divorce is always messy and reneging on strategic alliances often brings repercussions at a later date. British Aerospace's cavalier abandonment of a 15-year partnership with Honda will hardly have gone unnoticed in Japan Inc. with a potentially long-term impact on future development of this kind between UK and Japanese firms.

ACTIVITY 8.6

Read the quality press, cut out examples/articles of joint ventures and strategic alliances – they are happening weekly. Create a file. Build your knowledge. It could be vital in the examination.

Wholly owned overseas production

One hundred per cent ownership representing the maximum level of commitment, complete management control and maximum profitability optimizes international integration – but is exposed to foreign problems and could face higher risk. Two main routes present themselves:

1 Acquisition
2 Development of facilities from a 'greenfield' situation

Acquisition is the quick way in, direct in approach with a clear picture of what is being bought – trained labour, management, sales, market share, distribution and an immediate return on the investment. However, many come to grief due to existing management leaving and clashes in cultural approach with management. Firms buy in haste but repent at leisure for, in buying an overseas firm, the company may be taking on board everything that is culturally at odds with the home way of doing things. Selecting the right company to acquire is difficult. It is easy to buy up a weak or 'poor firm' but turning it into a high-performance competitor is difficult. Volkswagen has struggled for years to come to terms with Seat (its Spanish subsidiary's inability to match Volkswagen standards of output and quality. Good-quality firms are not always available for purchase and are difficult to acquire – often requiring paying 'over the odds'. When Nestlé acquired Rowntrees in 1984 for £1.4 billion (at the time this was 30 per cent of the projected cost for constructing the Channel Tunnel) *The Economist* remarked: 'What price for 2 ft, (60 cm), of Supermarket Shelfspace – £1.4 billion!'. Nestlé were not just buying technology, factories, management – they were paying £1.4 billion for Brands, primarily Kit Kat, the UK brand leader in chocolate snack bars, and in doing so were eliminating uncertainty and risk in their market growth and search for pan-European brands and the development of a world brand.

With greenfield development, of course Nestlé could have chosen the option of building its own factories, developing its own brand over time. But time is a premium in today's marketplace and success in new product introduction is often ephemeral – few achieve it. Cadbury's spent years and a fortune in creating and developing Wispa (a chocolate bar) – a success but nowhere near on the scale of Kit-Kat.

Having said that the benefits of greenfield developments are also significant. Nissan and Toyota deliberately located their new plants in locations away from exposure and experience in motor car construction so as to inculcate new employees with modern Japanese work patterns. (Acquiring firms means that you acquire their bad habits as well as their good ones.)

In summary, the pendulum has swung towards acquisition, particularly in the world of modern developments such as information, technology, multimedia and other communications (e.g. satellite stations and entertainment industries). In 1994 Viacom (ever heard of them?) acquired Paramount Communications for $8.4 billion and it is rumoured that CBS will shortly be the subject of a bid. The worlds largest communications company was created in 1995 as Time-Warner and Turner News.

Who's merging or taking over whom? Again study the quality press – something big is happening regularly. Create a file of examples. Additionally, consider the benefits accruing from each example you discover.

Why is there such a variation in market entry approaches? Using specific examples, show how a company uses different market entry methods in different country markets (December 1994, Question 8).
(**See** Exam answers at the end of this unit.)

Entry strategy implementation
This aspect of the model has been covered comprehensively in the section dealing with channel distribution and logistics.

Entry analysis
A simple method of examining the options can be found in Terpstra and Sarathy; and also in Cateora. It is brief but does give the reader insight into some of the variables of choice (Table 8.1).

Jeannet and Hennessey have assembled a more complex model analysing the data required to assist the company in selecting its entry mode (Figure 8.2). It is complex for the variables are many. Getting it right is important. There must be a clear relationship between the benefits accruing from the method chosen and the implication for the firm.

Table 8.1 Matrix for comparing alternative methods of market entry

Evaluation criteria	Entry methods						
	Indirect export	Direct export	Marketing subsidiary	Marketing subsidiary– local assembly	Licensing	Joint venture	Wholly owned operation
1 Number of markets							
2 Market penentration							
3 Market feedback							
4 International Marketing Learning							
5 Control							
6 Marketing costs							
7 Profits							
8 Investment							
9 Administration							
10 Foreign problems							
11 Flexibility							
12 Risk							

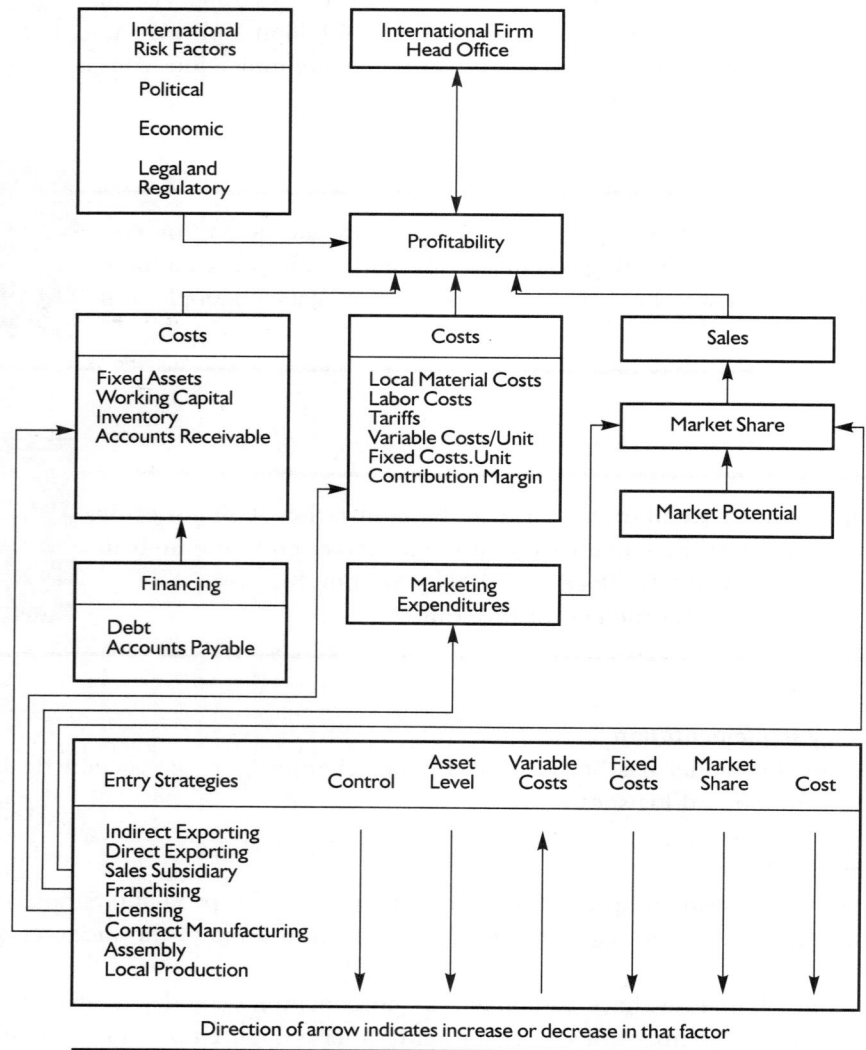

Figure 8.2 Considerations for market entry decisions (*source*: Jeannett and Hennessey)

- Identify the main market entry methods used in international marketing. For two market entry methods of your choice explain the financial implications of this implementation (December 1995, Question 3).
- Licensing, joint ventures and strategic alliances are becoming increasingly more important in terms of market entry strategies for multinational companies. Briefly describe each entry strategy and explain why it is becoming more popular with multinationals. What are the control and strategic management issues on each method? (December 1996, Question 5)

Selecting the market entry strategy is the key decision many companies have to take in expanding into overseas markets. Explain why this decision is so critical and identify the criteria that should be used in choosing between the alternatives. (December 1997, Question 2)

Exit strategy

Painful as it may be, companies are sometimes forced to leave a market(s). The conclusion is that with foresight firms may dispose of their assets profitably (occasionally) and consideration should always be given to evacuating a lost-cause position 'before' taking the plunge and entering a market.

Political reasons

Changing political situations sometimes force companies to exit markets. Expropriation is often a risk in some countries and companies are advised to plan their exit strategies accordingly. Coca-Cola departed the Indian market rather than sell its controlling interest to local investors as required by local laws. Now it is re-entering the market after an absence of almost a decade.

Business failure

Before entering any market, consideration should be given to the cost of failure. Peugeot, Renault and others have left the US market with their fingers burned. Volvo similarly pulled out (at the last minute) of a strategic alliance with Renault. Lancia have withdrawn from the UK car market. Abandonment of a market, especially a major one such as the US is very expensive and can be damaging to the reputation of the organization.

Summary

Choosing the appropriate entry strategy is probably the most perplexing decision that companies have to make. A survey among CEOs of American companies suggested that they spent more time deliberating this question than any other in international business. Once the decision is taken it determines the rest of your strategy – financial, managerial as well as marketing. Moreover, it establishes the terms of engagement on the war for sales in a chosen marketplace. Such decisions are not taken lightly. But success in the future is not for the slow or the timid. Companies are going to have to become more ambitious and radical in their approach to the question – joint ventures, strategic alliances, complex partnerships between firms and governments are becoming the order of the day. The pace of advancement, customer demand and technology are forcing developments. Yet exit strategies are also important considerations. So the final thought is that flexibility will prevail over rigidity in the future.

EXTENDING KNOWLEDGE

International Marketing, S. Paliwoda and M. Thomas, Butterworth-Heinemann, 1998.
International Marketing Strategy, I. Doole, R. Lowe and C. Phillips, Routledge, 1997.
International Marketing, V. Terpstra and R. Sarathy, The Dryden Press, 1997.
Global Marketing Strategies, J.-P. Jeannet and H. D. Hennessey, Houghton-Mifflin, 1998.

Questions

- Identify the ways in which a domestic organization might obtain foreign sales without having any knowledge of overseas markets.
- Outline what might be some of the goals that a company might set itself in individual country markets.
- Consider for each of the market entry options the control elements the firm might wish to apply.
- What is meant by control? What are the difficulties in implementing control in international marketing?
- What procedures should a firm consider in appointing an agent, distributor, licensee?
- When might contract manufacturing be the 'right' method of entry?
- What criteria would you attach to appointing a franchisee?
- Acquisition, the easy route: greenfield development, the tough one. Discuss the pros and cons of each.
- Strategic alliances often fail. Can you explain why?

EXAM ANSWERS

December 1992, Question 3 In all markets, domestic or international, the marketing manager needs to determine the balance between improving customer service levels and control of costs in marketing strategy. Although this is to some extent true of all the elements of the marketing mix, it is particularly true of the distribution (or place) element of the mix. But why is there a trade-off between service levels and cost, particularly in the place element of the mix, and how can any potential conflicts be resolved?

There is no doubt that improving customer service levels in international markets is a potentially very powerful competitive tool in achieving increased sales and market share. In order to understand this we need to consider some of the key components of customer service levels in international markets. A company can offer improved customer service in the following:

- Speed of delivery (delivering more quickly)
- Consistency of delivery (delivering more reliably)
- Ability to deal with special orders, small orders, etc. (flexibility of delivery)
- Packaging and protection (fewer damaged products)
- After-sales service (maintenance, spare parts, etc.)

We can see from this list why improved customer service levels might be welcomed by customers who, in turn, might be more tempted to purchase from the supplier who is prepared to offer improved service. In the same way, research has consistently shown that one of the major reasons why United Kingdom exporters have lost sales in world markets in the past has been a reputation for poor delivery – a key element of service.

So, by offering improved customer service levels, the export marketer would hope to generate increased revenue. However, balanced against this potential for increased revenue are the increased costs which improving levels of customer service invariably incur. Put simply, even small improvements in customer service can involve substantial cost for the marketer.

For example, improving delivery performance can involve investment in new warehouses, a company's fleet of vehicles and even new computer systems. Of course, not all improvements necessarily involve these sorts of outlay, but there are nearly always costs involved. What is important therefore is that the potentially higher costs of improved customer service levels are carefully compared with the potential revenue generating capacity of these improvements. Put simply, the cost should not exceed the revenue. However, when determining levels of customer service it is important to start with the needs of customers.

Customer needs should be researched to determine what service elements they require and to what level. Service levels should not be increased beyond what the customer requires and will pay for. Having determined these requirements for customer service elements and levels, the exporter can then set about designing the service provision systems to provide these predetermined levels of service at minimum cost.

If approached in this way the exporter is able to reap the full marketing potential of improved levels of customer service in a cost-effective manner and with little or no conflict.

December 1993, Question 3   A multinational enterprise is an organization with marketing activities in more than one country. It will have direct investment in at least one other country in addition to the home country. These direct investments would include sales and distribution facilities and might include production plants. The Japanese car manufacturers Nissan and Toyota have invested in the UK to set up the manufacture of cars. The multinational enterprise (MNE) will gain its profits and sales from more than one country. It will gain profits and sales from a variety of sources. Product sales, remittance of profits from subsidiary companies and licensing revenues are three possible sources. The MNE will have a level of experience in international business which is usually in excess of smaller companies whose experience of international marketing is limited to the physical movement of goods across country boundaries (exporting).

The factors that influence an MNE to export can be divided into internal and external factors.

Internal factors

The MNE may wish to concentrate production in certain countries for cost and logistics reasons. In their case it will export product to the countries in which it is not producing.

Lower costs are generally obtainable through economies of scale and through the experience curve effects. The concentration of production in a limited number of countries will encourage standardization and the associated lowering of unit production costs. In the past the tendency for multinational enterprises to operate with a polycentric orientation encouraged a multi-location approach in which adaptation to country markets became the norm. If this extent of adaptation occurred it would reduce partially or completely the benefits of the increased scale of production.

Logistics reasons would encourage the export of goods to countries that are physically close or to those countries where established modes of transport allow the efficient movement of products.

In addition to cost and logistics, the MNE is concerned with risk management. It is risky to invest in certain countries. For these countries the mode of market entry is safer through exporting. If things go wrong the MNE loses its products but does not suffer the much greater costs of losing its investment in sales and distribution or production facilities.

Senior Examiner's comments

The answer shows a range of factors that influence MNEs. MNEs are large companies but they will be involved in export activities for some countries. The amount of exporting will be influenced by a number of corporate decisions related to production cost and risk management. The decisions on standardization/adaptation and the type of organizational culture (for example, geocentric or polycentric) will have an influence on the number of production plants around the world and will influence the extent to which exporting rather than host country marketing will be used by the MNE.

December 1992, Question 7   Moving from being a purely domestic business to an international one can be both a lengthy and painful process for the organization involved. Rarely, if ever, is this transformation achieved 'overnight'. More often the process is one of a gradual evolution through a number of distinct stages or steps.

(a) *Purely domestic*
    The first stage is where a company operates only in domestic markets and hence requires no skills, staff or procedures to investigate and explore international opportunities. No doubt many companies have been and will continue to be

content to operate on a purely domestic basis. However, even the smallest company these days can no longer afford to ignore the international aspects of production and trade, and the opportunities and threats which are presented by these aspects. In particular, the company that wishes to expand and grow beyond a certain size will almost certainly have to become international.

(b) *Experimental/'passive' involvement in exporting*

Most frequently the purely domestic marketer starts on the process to becoming an international marketer through experimental and/or 'passive' involvement in exporting. Very often this is as a result of, say, a casual enquiry from a potential overseas customer or possibly due to, say, an overseas agent spotting an opportunity after attendance at a trade fair. Whatever the impetus to become involved at this stage, commitment and involvement on the part of the exporter are likely to be low. Much of the 'marketing' will be passive and/or left to intermediaries. Time horizons will tend to be short, with little or no systematic market selection – other than perhaps on the grounds of physical proximity – and with the dominant objective of immediate sales. Very few, if any, changes will be made to the planning process and/or structure of the organization.

(c) *Active involvement/exporting*

If the results of being involved in exporting are perceived to be beneficial the emphasis may then switch to a more active involvement in export markets. At this stage commitment to export markets begins to grow. As a result more resources will begin to be devoted to this area of the firm's activity together with a more formal approach to planning. The company will now begin to become more systematic in country/market selection. Specialist staff might be employed and the company will begin to explore how to secure more control over its exporting activities.

At this stage, the company has moved beyond being a purely passive exporter. The company may well have a specialist export marketing function and/or some sort of overseas investment in one or more markets. However, even at this stage international markets and marketing are still viewed as being of secondary importance to domestic ones.

(d) *Total involvement/international marketing*

Although often subtle in difference and hence difficult to spot compared to the previous stage, in fact the international marketer has evolved to look at international markets and marketing as being central to the company's future and growth. Put another way, at this stage of development there is total commitment to the development of international markets in company strategy. Planning horizons now become long run. There is systematic selection of target markets and entry modes. Resource commitment and organizational structures are focused on international market opportunities. Perhaps the most important and telling feature of the truly international company can be found in the attitudes and outlook of its management, and particularly its most senior personnel. In a company which is truly international, opportunities are examined and acted upon in an international context with little or no distinction between these and purely domestic opportunities. The company that has reached this stage is probably ready to take the final step in the process of evolution by becoming 'global' in outlook.

December 1994, Question 8 It is quite clear that the starting point in answering this question should be a model showing the wide range of market entry methods. All the acknowledged texts contain such models ranging from domestic purchasing to acquisition/greenfield site development. It is important that candidates display their knowledge of the full range of market entry options. It is not necessary to produce a drawing of a model here as every candidate must be familiar with the mechanics and the strengths and weaknesses of each method of entry.

The crux of the question is twofold:

1 An explanation of why there is such a wide variation in choice
2 Illustrate why a company (*one*) might use three different market entry methods in different country markets. Examples are of critical importance.

(**Examination tip**: Although one cannot predict future questions, it is sensible for candidates to prepare in advance examples of companies using different market entry approaches; it avoids the problem of having to think of examples under the stress of examination conditions.)

Explanation of the wide variation
Factors to consider are:

- strategic level of involvement, usually directed by the nature of the consumer demand
- issues of risk (political and financial)
- size of the market/country
- financial resources of the company
- level of company experience in the market/country
- the importance of the market/country
- availability of distribution channels
- cultural influences
- company objectives and expectations
- competition in the market
- the product life cycle expectancy
- the need for flexibility
- the speed of entry; fast or slow, dependent on market circumstances
- government taxes/other barriers in a given market

Actually, the list could be continued but there is enough here to illustrate the point.
Take *one* company to illustrate how it might:

(a) invest in a greenfield site in a major secure long-term market with its own production/marketing operation
(b) appoint a distributor in a different market
(c) assemble important components in a third market

An example from my own (Keith Lewis) personal business experience is the Mentholatum Company, a US multinational manufacturing 'over-the-counter' (OTC) medicines:

- in the UK the company manufactured and marketed products;
- in Europe, the Middle East and much of West Africa, it operated distributors – managed from a UK base;
- in Nigeria, a large market in its own right, the company assembled components that were in part shipped from the UK and added to packaging which was produced locally. There the company had its own production and sales subsidiary reporting to the UK.
- Overall, the UK (European, Middle East and Africa HQ) reported to the US parent.

December 1995, Question 3   There is no ideal way of entering an overseas market. There are options to suit all sizes of firms and situations. There are no barriers preventing even the smallest firm, for international marketing is not the preserve of large companies. Even large companies seek different routes to markets, depending on individual situations.

With such a wide choice of market entry routes, the decision to be taken is: 'How best can I make my goods/services available for purchase?'

Before describing the alternatives, the first question to consider is the 'strategic level of involvement'. This is determined by a number of considerations, not least of which is financial – and this will be discussed later. But if marketing is essentially about servicing customers, then it is ultimately the customer who determines the focus, in terms of the strategic level of involvement.

Strategic level of involvement is dictated by:

- corporate objectives, ambition and resources (financial, operational and managerial)
- nature of the market/product category/competitors
- nature of the customer culture – who buys what/where/how
- market coverage – breadth, depth, quality
- speed of market entry – product life cycle implication and innovation diffusion
- marketing costs
- profit payback
- level of control
- and, most importantly, level of risk!

Method of entry

Time precludes a discussion of the various methods. However, the following diagram indicates the range of options:

Market Planning

Market Segmentation

Marketing Communications Research

Media Planning

Marketing Testing

Monitoring

In answering the second part of the question i.e. financial implications, I have selected the following two entry methods. (Note to candidates – the two methods selected are simply to show the differences in financial implications.)

Financial implications

Licensing

The advantages include a quick route to markets with no capital outlay and considerable cost savings, as there is virtually no direct financial involvement. Additionally payment received is often on a 'by results' basis (dependent on the agreement).

The negative side is that the returns may be limited – the licensee is doing the work and will seek the major reward. Typically, licensing fees can vary from 2–3% for some product categories to 30% plus for fast-moving short-lifespan products, e.g. computer games and film merchandising (*Jurassic Park* etc.).

There is also the consideration of financial exposure to foreign exchange – but this will be dependent on the nature of the agreement. The licensee will naturally want to be paid in his/her local currency, whilst the licenser will require payment in home currency i.e. both will wish to limit their exposure.

Acquisition

Whilst this is a quick way to market, direct in approach with a clear picture of what is being purchased – trained labour, sales, market share, distribution etc., it is in financial terms a considerable risk.

First there is the purchase price – which may be extremely high, dependent on the nature of the business. The price paid will reflect several considerations:

- the historical profit record
- the brand values
- the future prospects in terms of growth/profitability
- the management expertise/skills

The problems arise in buying a good firm and giving due consideration for what one is buying. The risk is that management might leave – remember you are not just buying the firm and its products, you are taking over its entire culture, with important ramifications from a financial perspective. The risks of outright purchase are very considerable. And, remember companies have to pay 'above the odds' for a good firm, i.e. maybe 22 times earnings! Getting it wrong can be expensive.

On the positive side, buying a known quantity has very powerful advantages – market share, brand values and a strong cash flow. Nestlé paid £1.4 bn in 1984 for Rowntrees – a high price at the time but a superb investment in brand values. In doing so, they were eliminating uncertainty and risk in the development of a pan-European and long-term global brand.

December 1996, Question 5   **Note:** The following are guidelines only.

Potentially a long question, so there is opportunity to expand views. Good structure and especially examples will improve the marks awarded.

Licensing

- Brief description.
- Benefits include: low level investment, little capital, attractions to companies of all sizes, rapid multimarket penetration (essential for 'fashion' products, e.g. films, computer games), good access to local distribution, payment by results.
- Control – careful partner selection, quality issues vital, careful agreement from legal viewpoint, retain control of key component (Coca-Cola), restrict geographic coverage, register all patents/trademark.

Joint venture (J.V.)

- Description.
- Benefits include: sharing development costs, rapid internationalization, complementary management skills, entry to 'closed' markets.
- Control – share problems, don't blame others, J.V. develops its own culture, open access to both managements, avoid bureaucracy, be entrepreneurial.

Strategic alliances

- Description – note very fast growing (examples abound)
- Benefits – mostly similar to J.V., particularly in development terms and complementary resources/skills, e.g. products – distribution, but also pace of innovation diffusion, regionalism, self-protection, access to different markets.

Control

- Largely same as J.V. – and based on stability, clear-cut objectives shared by parties involved.

December 1997, Question 2 The answer should recognize the importance of the market entry choice. Specifically:

- It establishes the rules of engagement in the battleground for sales.
- It sets the parameters for the company's marketing activities.
- It establishes the boundaries in terms of the company's objectives, marketing and other business functions.
- It signals to the local competition the scale of the company's ambition and it enables them to create an appropriate level of response.

These introductory remarks are very important in terms of marks awarded. Getting the appropriate market entry strategy correctly formulated ranks high among the critical success factors.

The answer should very briefly outline the range of options. Figure 8.1 on page 106 does this succinctly.

Criteria to consider include:

- Strategic level of involvement, i.e. having a clear picture of how close the company has to be to the consumer in order to deliver the appropriate level of satisfaction.
- Corporate objectives, ambition, resources available to the company.
- Nature of the market, product category.
- Competition, both scale and positioning.
- Nature of consumer culture.
- Coverage of the market, breadth/depth/quality.
- Speed of entry.
- Level of control.
- Costs including marketing, operational and finance.
- Pay-back period.
- Administration costs.
- Human resource, both external and internal.
- Flexibility, i.e. Risk.

What is required is a recognition of the importance, the range of options, and between eight and ten criteria balanced in a logical answer.

Product policy

Product policy and product management are key to any successful international or domestic marketing strategy. International marketing, like domestic marketing, ultimately depends upon satisfying customer needs. In order to do this the customers have to be presented with the right product or service which is capable of meeting their needs as they perceive them. This unit will consider both physical products and intangible services and will extend understanding to areas of product tangibles and product intangibles including packaging and after-sales service as well as branding and imagery. In this unit you will:

* Review the forces at work which will enable the international marketer to standardize a product offering across foreign markets
* Understand the factors which inhibit or restrain standardization
* Consider the relationship between product and promotion in international marketing scenarios
* Review the application of portfolio analysis to international product management
* Consider the factors affecting international branding and product positioning
* Consider the factors affecting choice of packaging for products and/or services in foreign markets.

Having completed this unit you will be able to:

* Evaluate the factors which influence the implementation of product policy in foreign markets
* Identify the scope for standardization and globalization of product policy in international marketing
* Evaluate the optimum product range through international portfolio analysis.

Product policy and product management are key to successful development and implementation of international marketing strategy. Although product policy as a separate item takes up only a fairly small part of the syllabus in International Marketing Strategy (5%), the correct selection of the product–market match is essential for the development of any strategy and resulting marketing mix.

This unit cannot be studied alone and needs to be reviewed in conjunction with other major sections of this work book including globalization (Unit 7), customer needs (Unit 4) and the other major elements of the international marketing mix (Units 11–14).

International product policy will be critical to many of your examination answer strategies (part 1) and questions (part 2). But it must not be the starting point for your answers. In marketing the customer is the starting point and the product follows from that. Study of this unit is important but cannot be understood out of context.

As you work through this unit remember that product is far more than just the physical product, the technology or the functional features offered to the customer. You will see from Figure 9.2 that the product needs to be considered in deeper terms than just that. The packaging and support services component of physical products and of services are becoming much more important in the competitive environment of the 1990s.

In addition, it has been argued in many papers that the intangible aspects of physical products as well as services are crucial to competitive success. As technology becomes more widespread and cheaper for many organizations to harness, a certain degree of standardization becomes inevitable. If you consider for a moment the case of motor cars, computers, washing machines or bedroom furniture there is little nowadays to choose among the actual functuality of various products. However, the difference perceived by customers in areas such as status, brand, design and styling are key features which lead to the ultimate choice of product or service.

Developing the international product policy

During the discussions of product policy in this unit we will be considering both physical (manufactured) product as well as services. Services differ from physical products in a number of ways. Most importantly:

- Intangibility – we are unable to see, touch, smell or feel services.
- Perishability – services cannot be stored and these left unsold today cannot be sold tomorrow.
- Heterogeneity – services are very rarely identical from one delivery to the next.
- Inseparability – the consumption of the service normally takes place at the same point at which it is created, therefore being inseparable from the source of that service.

(For a more detailed explanation of the nature of services and services marketing consider *International Marketing Strategy* by Doole, Lowe and Phillips, or *The Marketing of Services* by Donald Cowell, Butterworth-Heinemann.)

There are five key areas of analysis in international product management. They include the question of standardization/adaptation – to what extent can or should the international product be standardized for overseas markets? Second is product–promotion mix – how do standardized or adapted products blend with standardized or adapted promotional practices? Third, we will consider the question of image, branding and positioning of products in foreign markets. Fourth, we will describe the special factors influencing packaging decisions in foreign markets. Finally, we will consider the application of portfolio analysis to international product range decisions.

Refer back to Unit 7 and the different types of marketing strategy that were described there. In each case can you explain the effects that these will have on international product policy?

Product standardization and adaptation

As we have also seen from our study of Unit 7 (Globalization) the advantages to be gained from a standardized product range marketed throughout the countries of the world are significant. In today's highly competitive environment, savings that can be made in areas of production, research and development and marketing could be a valuable source of competitive advantage to the international organization. On the other hand, there are a number of reasons why a standardized approach to all overseas markets is unlikely to be feasible for all organizations. From Table 9.1 we can see a résumé of the arguments made in Unit 7 which illustrate the various factors that can be identified as either driving or restraining the organization from a significant move towards a standardized approach to product policy.

In Figure 9.1 we attempt to identify the situation which faces most organizations operating internationally in the 1990s. Although conditions will vary from one organization to another and from industry to industry, generally the current situation for markets, supply and competition are as follows.

Markets

Most markets generally are between either the national level market or the regional level (i.e., EU, LAFTA, NAFTA, etc.). Driven by tastes, available distribution channel, prices and predominant trade barriers, the majority of markets (especially consumer) exist either on a national scale or a regional scale. There is also a marked tendency for polarization here. Some markets by their nature are becoming more national and even sub-national as people

Table 9.1 Product standardization

'Drivers'	'Restrainers'
• Economies of scale in production • Economies of scale in R&D • Economies of scale in marketing • Consumer mobility • The 'French'/'American' image • Spread of technology • Flow of technology • Flow in information • Cost of investment • Reducing trade barriers	• Differing use conditions • Government factors • Culture and language • Local market needs • Local tastes • Company history and operations

	Markets	Supply	Competition
National			
Regional			
Global			
Critical issues	Tastes Channels Prices Trade barriers	Trade costs Technology Scale Investment	Cash flows Cross-subsidies Brands Positioning

Figure 9.1 Factors influencing standardization adaptation

search for products and services which reinforce their own local identity. Other markets, meanwhile, are becoming more regional than national in their nature as consumers respond to the significant economies of scale that are available from a standardized product. Examples of these two forms of polarization would include motor cars tending towards the regional market size while snack foods are tending to polarize more towards the national and local market.

Supply

Supply conditions generally tend towards the regional. This is driven by technology, by economies of scale and by the increasing costs of investment. We see also from Figure 9.1 that the supply is being drawn both towards the global for reasons of scale and ever-increasing investment costs and towards the local in order to satisfy increasingly individualistic/nationalistic needs.

For your organization (or an organization of your choice) can you identify the major trends in markets, supply and competition? What implications does this have for your marketing strategy?

ACTIVITY 9.2

Competition

Competition faced by most organizations is predominantly regional in nature. The larger international and multinational organizations operating globally or in regions such as Europe, North America or the Pacific Rim are the driving force behind most competition in the 1990s. However, there are also signs here of polarization towards competition of a much more local nature as markets driven by a sense of fierce individualism as well as global competition in those industries and industry sectors which are driven by scale and investment decisions.

From this discussion it would seem that the world appears to be facing a polarization of most economic variables. This should not necessarily surprise us and if we consider the international trading environment we can see the two trends being equally successful. The global trend to production of standardized products for worldwide consumption at highly competitive prices is meeting a section of the market's needs. At the same time, organizations and consumers are feeling an increased need to demonstrate their own local or national identity and sense of individuality. As both these trends accelerate, often within the same individual or organization, purchase patterns will continue to polarize.

Product adaptation

Where globalization or standardization of product is not possible, knowing why to adapt products and how products need to be adapted to meet local market requirements is often the key to international marketing success. Before we consider the nature of product adaptation it is worth reminding ourselves of the constituent parts which go to make up the 'product'.

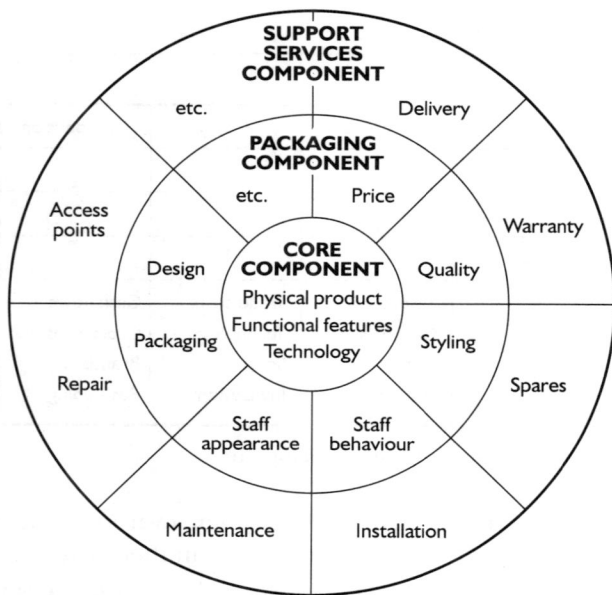

Figure 9.2 Product components

From Figure 9.2 we can see the classical approach to product components. From the customer's point of view the product or service which they eventually decide to purchase is much more than simply the physical product or functional features which go to make up a product or service. Customer choice revolves around the packaging and support service elements of a product offer as much as (if not more than) the actual core component itself. For example, the ultimate choice between two competing brands of washing machine or machine tool can equally be made upon the question of guarantees and after-sales service as they can upon the actual product features inherent within the core product component.

Examine the conflicts between improving customer service levels and controlling costs in export marketing (December 1992).

(**See** Exam answers at the end of this unit.)

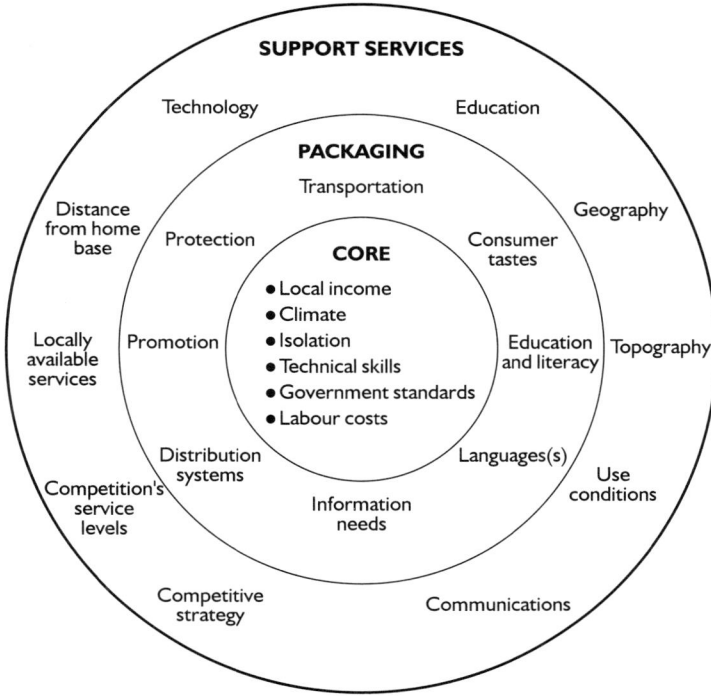

Figure 9.3 Product adaptation

The question of adapting products or services for overseas markets can logically be extended from this understanding of product components (see Figure 9.3). This diagram builds on the previous Figure (9.2) and attempts to identify a number of the characteristics in foreign markets which might possibly drive the producing organization to adapt or modify its total product offer in some way.

To explain the diagram in slightly more detail: a company considering marketing, for example bicycles in a foreign market, might look at the local pressures in the core component and consider that lower local income and isolation from points of service would drive it to 'de-engineer' the basic bicycle marketed in the home market in favour of one which had both less parts to go wrong and also was cheaper to produce. A cosmetics company might look at the packaging component and consider that transportation and distribution networks in the foreign market linked to differences in consumer tastes would drive it to a completely different form of packaging and presentation of the product than they would use to present the products in, for example, Selfridges perfume department. When considering questions such as adaptation within the context of the CIM examination this diagram produces a useful checklist which can highlight areas of market differences that demand changes or modifications in the basic (domestic) product or service offer.

The product–promotion mix

Having decided upon the optimum standardization/adaptation route for the product or service which the organization markets, the next most important, (and culturally sensitive) factor to be considered is that of international promotion. Product and promotion go hand in hand in foreign markets and together are able to create or destroy markets in very short order. We have considered above the factors which may drive an organization to standardize or adapt its product range for foreign markets. Equally important is the promotion or the performance promises which the organization makes for its product or service in the target market. As with product decisions, promotion can be either standardized or adapted for foreign markets. Figure 9.4 demonstrates the options available to the organization when it considers blending its product and promotional mix.

We can see from Figure 9.4 that there are four options open to the organization. The top left-hand position is that of standard product and standard promotion to overseas markets producing the global approach (Pepsi-Cola). The top right-hand box will be an appropriate strategy for organizations which find they need to adapt or modify the product in order to deliver the same perceived benefits on a market, national or cultural basis. A good example of this approach would be Phileas Fogg snacks or 'After Eight' mints.

Product

	Standard	Adapt
Standard	Global	Product extension
Adapt	Promotion extension	Dual adaption

Promotion (left side label)

Figure 9.4 Product–promotion matrix

ACTIVITY 9.3

Choose a product or a product class that you know or use. Try to identify the particular product–promotion mix strategies that are used in various markets. (A good holiday hobby!)

The bottom left-hand box in Figure 9.4 demonstrates the strategy appropriate to an organization that will produce a standardized product for overseas markets but requires an adapted promotions approach, often to support a different position in different foreign markets. An example of this strategy would be that used by bicycle and four-wheel drive vehicle manufacturers. A broadly similar product may be perceived as a transportation or utility item in some markets and a leisure product in others. The final box is that of dual adaptation, where both the product and the promotional approaches are also varied on a market-by-market basis. Many food items fall into this category with products such as sausages, soup and confectionery items being both different physical products and occupying different positions in the customers' perception.

Product positioning

The question of image, branding and positioning is culturally a highly sensitive area and it is true to say that real global brands are still surprisingly rare. Product and company positioning, we should remember, is not something we do to a product – it is something we have to do to the prospect's mind.

EXTENDING KNOWLEDGE

For a more detailed explanation of product positioning and differentiation see the companion workbook: *Strategic Marketing Management 1998–99* (Unit 4) by Fifield and Gilligan (Butterworth-Heinemann).

Product positioning is a key element to the successful marketing of any organization in any market. The product or company which does not have a clear position in the customer's mind consequently stands for nothing and is rarely able to command more than a simple commodity or utility price. Premium pricing and competitive advantage is largely dependent upon the customer's perception that the product or service on offer is markedly different in some important and relevant way from competitive offers. How can we achieve a credible market position in international markets?

The standardization/adaptation argument raises its head yet again. Depending on the nature of the product it may be possible to achieve a standardized market position in all or most of the international markets in which the company operates. On the other hand, the market characteristics and, most importantly, customer needs and values may be so different as to make a standardized position impossible. Examples of reasonably standardized market positions do exist (for example, Nescafé instant coffee) where the organization attempts to create and maintain a standardized position in all the markets in which it operates. To do this does not necessarily mean that the product itself is standardized. (In fact Nescafé offers a range of blends and roasts in order to achieve a standardized market position.) In other markets this standardized position is just not available. For example, the leading Japanese car maker in the North American market is perceived as Honda. If they were able to achieve a standardized position in all markets then one would expect them also to hold the number-one car position in the Japanese market – where, in fact, they are number four. What is the reason for this difference? Quite simply if you ask an American what Honda means he or she will respond with the word 'automobile'. If you ask a Japanese the same question the reply will be 'motorbike'.

Of course, existing, and possibly different, positions in various international markets does not mean that the organization cannot reposition in one or more of its markets to achieve a standardized international position. If this is deemed to be a profitable route for the organization to take then classical strategies on repositioning are appropriate in all international markets.

Branding

Closely linked to market positioning is the question of brands and product image. Brands are the names and personas which we give to our products and services and anything which involves language is liable to cause problems for the international marketer. There are a number of branding strategies and the four most commonly used are:

1 Corporate umbrella branding
2 Family umbrella names
3 Range branding
4 Individual brand names

(See Doole, Lowe and Phillips)

We meet the question of standardization/adaptation again in the area of international product and service branding. Should brand names be internationalized to the extent that they can be used everywhere that the company operates? To what extent is such standardization possible or even desirable? As with the discussion about products and the standardization approach, there are many benefits to be achieved from maintaining standard brands across a number of markets. On the other hand, there are a number of reasons why organizations have tried and found this a difficult route to follow. The principal reasons why international standardized branding is difficult resides in the area of cultural and linguistic differences between markets. Many brands, brand names, brand marks or brand concepts simply do not travel well and need to be modified in order to gain local market acceptance.

Branding is a major strategic issue and needs to be understood. There is a lengthy debate about how to build in the obvious value of brands on to an organization's balance sheet to give a true representation of the organization's worth. Internationally the issue is accentuated. When Nestlé pays so much money for Rowntree that only 15% of the purchase price is covered by balance sheet assets, we have to ask about the remaining 85% of the purchase price. Major brands like Kit-Kat are obviously the answer. It is estimated that the biggest global brand (Coca-Cola) is worth in the region of US$ 39 billion, and that the total value of 'brand equity' globally is US$ 1 trillion – all of it off the balance sheet!. Brands have also been described as the world's number one intellectual property.

Much of the debate about brand equity centres around how brands are and should be valued. There are a number of methods. The Interbrand method is one of the most popular and attempts to measure a number of dimensions, both hard and soft. Common to all methods, though, is the importance given to what the Interbrand method calls 'reach' or degree of internationalization within the brand. In other words, the more global the brand the greater its value – I think the message is clear. (See also *Strategic Marketing Management 1998–99* workbook, Fifield and Gilligan, 1998).

Packaging

Packaging for international markets also creates a standardization debate and to what extent adaptation will be required. As well as the obvious communications and presentation/promotional aspect of packaging which may or may not be standardizable for foreign markets, packaging also needs to consider any transportation and logistics problems. The decisions relating to international packaging might be dependent upon aspects such as:

EXAM QUESTION

In what ways do the demands of international marketing influence packaging decisions? Use examples to illustrate your answer (December 1992).

Facing an increasingly competitive international environment, how might companies speed up their new product development process? (June 1997, Question 5)

(**See** Exam answers at the end of this unit.)

- *Local distribution considerations* How are products or services distributed within the marketplace? Are there understood and well-configured channels of distribution? Are there middlemen or intermediaries in the channel and what are their requirements? If retail distribution is an important feature, are they served or self-service outlets?
- *Climate* Is the local market subject to extremes or climatic swings? Will there be extremes of heat, cold or humidity which the packaging must withstand?
- *Geographical* How far will products or services have to travel? What is the logistics pattern that must be followed?

ACTIVITY 9.4

Choose two imported products in your home market. Can you identify those elements of the packaging that have been driven by your local market requirements? What factors in your market have made the changes necessary?

- *Economic* What is the predominant economic structure of the target market? To what extent will packaging be used after the primary product has been consumed? (Metal and plastic containers may be put to other, secondary, uses after purchase.)

Portfolio analysis

Standard portfolio analysis has been used by a number of international and multinational organizations to help them to identify priorities in their international marketing operations. The four most commonly used methods are the Boston Consulting Group approach, the GEC/McKinsey approach, the Arthur D. Little approach and Product Life Cycle Analysis.

Students will be aware of the current discussion surrounding the use of portfolio analysis and some of the limitations which relate to its application. The same arguments apply to portfolio analysis within the international context as within the domestic marketing situation. Portfolio analyses of various sorts have been used over the past 20 years to consider options for both products and for markets that the organization might address. In international marketing the problems associated with portfolio analysis are probably even greater than in domestic marketing due primarily to the complexity of the data and the analysis required to produce a sensible result. If the evaluation of a portfolio within a single market produces problems then comparing the potential of portfolios across a range of markets becomes even more difficult.

As in domestic marketing, portfolio analysis is a good way of dealing with the product market match in conceptual terms – its use as a mathematical model must be viewed as suspect.

Summary

In this unit we have seen that the primary question in international product policy is that of product standardization. The argument over standardization–adaptation is a very important one because:

- The economies of scale which can be obtained through a standardized approach to international markets are considerable.
- The reasons for an organization to adapt or modify its product/service offering to each separate international market are also compelling. At the end of the day, the primary consideration must be for long-term profitability and the candidate will be required to assess this objective against any situations presented in the questions or the case study. Remember also that profitability is not the same thing as sales maximization, nor is it driven out by economies of scale on their own. A balance needs to be struck between the needs of the organization and those of the marketplace.

Product policy is a key area in international marketing and decisions here will affect the entire marketing mix which follows. Customer considerations must always be top of mind for the marketer – domestic or international, and the role of market research in uncovering market needs cannot be overestimated in the international market situation.

Questions

As a check on your understanding of what has been covered in this unit, consider the following questions:

- What are the basic 'components' of the product? How will this understanding help your development of international product policy?
- What are the special aspects of services?
- What are the five key aspects of international product policy?
- What are the observed trends in markets, supply and competition?
- What are the benefits arising from a standardized product approach to international markets?
- What are the factors which might drive the company to adapt its product offerings to different markets?
- Explain the meaning and importance of the 'product–promotion' mix.
- How are products 'positioned' in international markets?
- How are brands managed in international markets?
- Can a company develop and maintain a global brand?
- What affects a company's international packaging decisions?
- Can portfolio analysis be applied in international product policy? What are the limitations on its use?

For a more detailed analysis and explanation of international product policy, read:

International Marketing, S. Paliwoda and M. Thomas, Butterworth-Heinemann, 1998.
International Marketing Strategy, I. Doole, R. Lowe and C. Phillips, Routledge, 1997.

December 1992 In all markets, domestic or international, the marketing manager needs to determine the balance between improving customer service levels and control of costs in marketing strategy. Although this is to some extent true of all the elements of the marketing mix, it is particularly true of the distribution (or place) element of the mix. But why is there a trade-off between service levels and cost, particularly in the place element of the mix and how can any potential conflicts be resolved?

There is no doubt that improving customer service levels in international markets is a potentially very powerful competitive tool in achieving increased sales and market share. In order to understand this we need to consider some of the key components of customer service levels in international markets. A company can offer improved customer service in the following:

- Speed of delivery (delivering more quickly)
- Consistency of delivery (delivering more reliably)
- Ability to deal with special orders, small orders etc. (flexibility of delivery)
- Packaging and protection (fewer damaged products)
- After-sales service (maintenance, spare parts etc.)

We can see from this list why improved customer service levels might be welcomed by customers who, in turn, might be more tempted to purchase from the supplier who is prepared to offer improved service. In the same way, research has consistently shown that one of the major reasons why United Kingdom exporters have lost sales in world markets in the past has been a reputation for poor delivery – a key element of service.

So, by offering improved customer service levels, the export marketer would hope to generate increased revenue. However, balanced against this potential for increased revenue are the increased costs which improving levels of customer service invariably incur. Put simply, even small improvements in customer service can involve substantial cost for the marketer.

For example, improving delivery performance can involve investment in new warehouses, a company's fleet of vehicles and even new computer systems. Of course, not all improvements necessarily involve these sorts of outlay, but there are nearly always costs involved. What is important therefore is that the potentially higher costs of improved customer service levels are carefully compared with the potential revenue generating capacity of these improvements. Put simply, the cost should not exceed the revenue. However, when determining levels of customer service, it is important to start with the needs of customers.

Customer needs should be researched to determine what service elements they require and to what level. Service levels should not be increased beyond what the customer requires and will pay for. Having determined these requirements for customer service elements and levels, the exporter can then set about designing the service provision systems to provide these predetermined levels of service at minimum cost.

If approached in this way, the exporter is able to reap the full marketing potential of improved levels of customer service in a cost-effective manner and with little or no conflict.

December 1992 The term 'packaging' involves a number of different facets and considerations for the marketer which are greatly influenced by the demand of international marketing. 'Packaging' here is interpreted as meaning anything which surrounds the product itself as a means of protecting, promoting or even using the product. So, for example, 'packaging' could mean the tin in which, say, a food product is packed. It could also mean the labels which are attached to these tins and which, say, identify the contents. Finally, packaging could mean the type of containers in which hundreds of these tins are transported across seas and continents. In other words, a very broad view of the term 'packaging' is used here to discuss the influence of the demands of international marketing.

Perhaps one of the best ways of illustrating how the demands of international marketing influence packaging decisions is to examine the range of considerations which a would-be first time exporter would need to assess regarding the appropriateness, or otherwise, of his current packaging:

- *Differences in climate*
  Differences in climate can give rise to different packaging requirements; for example, if one were marketing salt, a hot humid climate may require the marketer to provide a very different package than if the climate were cool and dry.
- *Distances involved*
  Invariably international marketing involves products being carried greater distances than those involved in purely domestic marketing. Because of this, packaging for protection may need to be much more substantial.
- *Different modes of transport*
  Possibly because of distance and/or crossing oceans etc., products intended for international markets may require particular types of packaging in order to facilitate handling, e.g. goods intended for shipment by container.
- *Differences in regulations/legislation*
  Products intended for distribution and sale in other countries may need to be packaged differently due to legislation. For example, in some countries chemicals need to be in stipulated types of containers. Similarly, in many markets spray type packaging needs to be free of CFCs. Differences in regulation/legislation may also give rise to differences in the labelling aspects of packaging.
- *Differences in customer tastes/culture*
  Customers may demand different types of packaging due to differences in tastes and/or culture. For example, colours are interpreted in different ways in different cultures.
- *Differences in levels of income*
  Packaging which may be appropriate/affordable in, say, a developed economy may be less so in a less developed one. For example, fewer customers in less developed economies may be willing and/or able to pay for expensive, but cosmetic, packaging.
- *Differences in channels of distribution*
  The distribution channel environment may give rise to differences in packaging in international markets. For example, exporting to a country with a well-developed system of retail outlets such as, say, supermarkets, may require a very different type of packaging from, say, a country with few supermarket outlets.

These are just some of the ways in which the demands of international marketing affect packaging decisions. We can see that the implications for packaging design and development are substantial. It is important therefore to ensure that these implications are fully researched and understood by the marketer before making packaging decisions.

June 1997, Question 5 Any answer must recognize the changing nature of international business and the changing bases of competition, with innovation and communications creating greater and more intensive competition. Understanding the forces that underpin this is the foundation of the answer, e.g. globalization, multinationals, shrinking communications, the development of the global village, greater liberalization of trade and wider awareness of global issues.

The majority of companies have no choice – innovate or die. Students should make this clear.

As to how companies might speed up their innovation orientation process, the answers are varied. Critical ones include:

- Development of an international innovation orientation. Coming from the CEO (Chief Executive Officer) a recognition that innovation might be the only competitive advantage.
- Be totally committed to NPD (New Product Development).
- Build in obsolescence from the beginning. Restructure the product life-cycle to a time frame. Force continued development.
- Organize for multi-country R&D (if appropriate). Decentralize the function to the key market, e.g. Japanese cars in USA. Note: this point is debatable as some companies centralize their R&D successfully.
- Invest heavily in R&D.
- Organize for rapid transference of any breakthrough from country to country.
- Track competitors religiously. Create an efficient MIS (Management Information System) and CIS (Competitor Information System) structure.
- Take risks. Test by doing on a modest scale.
- Spread the risk geographically.
- Spread the R&D cost geographically.
- Create reward systems in the R&D process.
- Build in flexibility in R&D so that the process can be speeded up or teams can be mobilized where and when necessary.
- Harness external resources. Outsource key technical activities to experts, e.g. universities.
- Cooperate on research via strategic alliances.
- Use database techniques to anticipate changes in customer preferences.
- Seek clusters of customer similarities where product modifications are minimized.
- Use electronic communication (Internet) to search for innovation.

This is not a checklist, where one or two marks will be awarded for each point made, but the quality of the answer and the degree of sophistication would be assessed taking the above into consideration.

Financial implications of international marketing

The financial implications of international marketing are too often ignored or are placed in a less important role by modern marketers. Finance and marketing are inextricably linked. Marketing is the primary source of revenue to any organization (interfacing as it does with the customer). Whether revenue produces profits, the lifeblood of the organization, depends on the ability of marketing and finance to work together. In this unit you will:

- Review the role of capital in international marketing operations
- Understand and be able to assess the risk involved in international operations
- Consider how profits are repatriated to the home organization.
  Having completed this unit you will be able to:
- Understand the financial implications of different international marketing strategies
- Evaluate suitable marketing strategies from any financial viewpoint.

The role of finance in marketing and international marketing strategy are relatively recent additions to the syllabus but are nevertheless essential for marketing management. The ultimate success of any marketing strategy must be judged on the profitability of the organization following the proposed strategy.

It is not always guaranteed that a question on the paper will be directed exclusively at the role of finance and financial implications of international marketing, However, it is clear from recent examiners' reports that answers to the mini case study which do not offer a clear perspective on the financial implications of proposed strategy will now be considered incomplete.

Prudent financial management is essential to the profitability and success of any organization, domestic or international. The major unique difference of an international organization is that the fund flows occur in a variety of currencies and in a variety of nations having distinct legal, political, social and cultural characteristics. These currency and national differences, in turn, create risks unique to international business. Additionally, a number of specialized international institutions and arrangements have developed because of these currency and national differences.

Who is responsible for international financial controls in your organization? How is responsibility split between finance and marketing? How is international marketing strategy affected by international financial considerations?

There are three principal aspects to the question of financial and international marketing strategy. This unit will consider these elements in order.

International capital

The organization embarking on international marketing must deal with a number of issues about its need for capital. Strategically the organization's capital requirements will depend largely upon the preferred method of market entry. In simple terms there are two forms of capital that will be needed:

- *Start-up or investment capital* is required to set-up the production, research and analysis, marketing, distribution and access processes before the sales process itself has started.
- *Working capital* is that cash required to finance the working transactions on a day-to-day basis. Working capital typically includes stock held and financing the debtor period between delivery and payment of invoice.

The international marketing organization's need for capital will be directly linked to its chosen method of market entry and level of involvement in international markets. For example, the organization exporting through agents or distributors will have fairly low capital requirements since it often has to produce few variations in product and only has to finance one or two deliveries at a time. If dealing through distributors, they will often take title to the goods and pay before they themselves have sold the goods on to the final users.

If an organization, for its own strategic reasons, has decided to enter a market through its own sales and marketing subsidiary, or even local manufacturing, it will require more capital to set up and establish the venture as well as additional levels of working capital to finance local stocks and wider product or service distribution in the target market.

Obviously, financial requirements may prohibit smaller organizations from taking on levels of involvement that are beyond them. Larger organizations may consider that their capital may be more profitably employed in other markets and will evaluate different market opportunities accordingly.

According to the finance textbooks the financial management of any organization, domestic or international, can be considered as having four separate tasks:

1 The acquisition of funds
2 The investing of funds in economically productive assets
3 The managing of those assets
4 The eventual reconversion of some (or all) of the productive assets into funds to return to the original investors, creditors, suppliers, employees and other interest groups.

International capital requirements will probably be higher (in relation to total business) than is normally acceptable in the home market. International business will likely involve the organization in travel costs, shipping costs, duties, start-up costs, higher inventories produced by delivery time lags and smaller fragmented markets, as well as trade and export credit facilities.

International financial risk

There are two types of financial risk unique to international business:

- Foreign exchange risk
- Political risk

Foreign exchange risk

Foreign exchange risks arise from the need to operate in more than one currency. When an organization has assets or liabilities denominated in a foreign currency, or is doing business in a foreign currency, profitability will be influenced by changes in the value of that currency relative to the home or reported currency.

How do fluctuations in foreign exchange markets influence the pricing decisions of export marketing managers and how can they minimize the problems raised by such fluctuations? (December 1993).

(**See** Exam answers at the end of this unit.)

The most important foreign exchange risk is 'transaction exposure' which refers to gains and losses that arise from the settlement of transactions whose terms are stated in a foreign currency. Transaction exposure can be avoided, at a cost, by entering into forward contracts (this is a contract to buy or sell a given currency at an agreed price at an agreed future date). Some organizations simply ignore transaction exposure – and pay the price. Others, like the very large tour operators, have turned it into a separate business and actively manage their transaction operations as a distinct profit centre.

Take a market of your choice, or one that is particularly important to your organization.

- What is the history of currency movement over the past 12/24 months?
- What is the future prediction for movement?
- What are the prices of forward contracts being offered?

Political risk

Political risk is the term used to cover those risks arising from an array of legal, political, social and cultural differences in the target foreign market. Such risk normally produces losses where there is conflict between the goals of the organization and those of the host government.

The government controls the nation's financial rules and structure as well as a variety of non-financial instruments designed to help achieve society's economic, political, social, cultural and ideological goals. Also, since the relative importance of the foreign government's goals is likely to vary from time to time the organization may find itself unprepared and therefore paying extra taxes and able to repatriate fewer funds than previously. The organization may also find itself employing more local managers or paying higher wages to its labour force.

International financial risk is an integral part of carrying out business in the international arena. It therefore cannot be completely avoided but its effects can be lessened by careful planning and prediction of likely future events.

EXAM QUESTION

- Review the different approaches that a company can take to minimize the currency risks that relate to international trade (December 1994).
- A survey of Chief Executive Officers in the USA indicated that a major concern for multinationals is political risk. What are the main methods of assessing the level of this risk and how might a multinational corporation adapt the management of its business in a country identified as having a high political risk? (December 1996, Question 4)
- 'Going international' involves increased financial risk. Identify the major types of international financial risk facing international business and how companies might plan to manage this risk. (December 1997, Question 5)

(**See** Exam answers at the end of this unit.)

Repatriation of profits

In financial terms any project, including the decision to move into an international market, can be financially assessed according to the amount of investment required and the estimated funds which flow from the project. Internationally, of course, the organization will only take into account the funds which can be successfully repatriated from the foreign market in its assessment of the project.

Although the same theoretical financial framework applies to international as well as domestic projects, the calculation of returns is made more complex due to the special factors which influence international marketing. These factors include differing tax systems and legislation which affect the repatriated flows as well as differential inflation rates which can change competitive positions and so cash flows over time. Nevertheless, in the long run the international investment project must be judged on repatriated cash flows.

The organizations employing discounted cash flow methods of analysis (DCF) can assess competing domestic and international projects by building an additional amount into the discount factor to allow for the increased level of uncertainty in dealing in foreign markets.

ACTIVITY 10.3

Do you understand DCF methodology? Does your organization use DCF? What discount factors does it use for:

- Domestic operations?
- International operations?

How are these discount factors made up?

Conclusions

An understanding of the financial implications of any proposed international marketing strategy is essential for the international marketer if he or she hopes to get their project into the organization's list of priorities. Any organization exists to make a profit through satisfying its customers. International operations also need to be net providers of profit to the organization (see Table 10.1).

Having said that, there may also be non-financial reasons for the organization approaching certain international markets. Such reasons might include competitive defence of a major market through involvement in a minor foreign market, use of a particular foreign market

Table 10.1 Financial implications of international marketing

---

1 Capital requirements
  - Investment capital
  - Working capital

2 Financial risk
  - Exchange risk
  - Political risk

3 Repatriation of profits
  - Taxation
  - Political factors

---

as a test-bed for new product development or image and positioning reasons on a broader international basis

This unit on financial implications needs to be read and understood alongside Unit 13 – Pricing in international markets.

Summary

In this unit we have seen that every marketing strategy activity in foreign markets has financial implication for the organization. The international marketer must understand the financial implications of any proposed strategy and given a choice between alternative strategic choices the marketer should be able to bring an understanding of financial implications to bear on the eventual recommendations.

Financial implications of marketing to foreign markets comes under three separate headings:

- Capital requirement
- International financial risks
- The repatriation of profits

Remember, business upon which we make no profit or for which we cannot repatriate the funds to the home office is business we can easily find in the domestic market!

Questions

As a check on your understanding of what has been covered in this unit, consider the following questions:

- What is the role of financial management in international operations?
- What are the three principal financial aspects to international marketing strategy?
- What are the two types of international capital that may be required?
- What are the two types of international financial risk?
- How can transaction exposure be avoided?
- How can political risk be reduced?
- What are the key problems associated with profit repatriation?

For a more detailed analysis and explanation of the financial aspects of international marketing strategy, read:

International Marketing, S. Paliwoda and M. Thomas, Butterworth-Heinemann, 1998.
International Marketing Strategy, I. Doole, R. Lowe and C. Phillips, Routledge, 1997.

EXTENDING KNOWLEDGE

December 1993

Pricing decisions

Pricing decisions are influenced by costs, demand and competition. In export marketing, a number of elements influence the total amount of cost. Extra distribution logistics costs, extra administration of the export order and extra distribution channel margins are normal features of exporting. Foreign exchange fluctuations are another factor that will influence costs.

Companies may wish to set low prices – penetration pricing – in order to gain extra market share. Other pricing options are 'follow the market' pricing and price skimming. The unpredictability of foreign exchange rates means that it is a cost factor that can seriously disrupt attempts to develop a specific pricing policy.

Fluctuations in foreign exchange markets can be very large. For example, the £ Sterling has exchanged at rates varying from US $2.40 to as low as almost $1 to the £. The Japanese yen has appreciated considerably against most other world currencies.

Very dramatic foreign exchange fluctuations are difficult to predict. These fluctuations are often related to speculative influences rather than imbalances in trading patterns between countries; although, of course, deficits in trade balances will be one of the factors influencing speculative pressures.

In many cases, fluctuations in foreign exchange rates will be greater than the profit margin earned by the company. In the highly competitive markets around the world it is most unlikely that companies can allow, as a cost factor, a margin of, say, 10% for possible exchange fluctuations and still make its target profit return.

If prices are allowed to fluctuate according to foreign exchange influences, it will prevent the logical development of a pricing approach based upon customer demand and competitive forces. In frequently purchased items, the customer will be unwilling to cope with uncertain and changing prices. The force of appreciating currency in a domestic market will make products more expensive in other countries. The reverse will be true when the currency is depreciating. This will give the company the opportunity to sell its products at lower prices in other people's currencies.

Minimization of foreign exchange problems

Better foreign exchange protection can be achieved by:

1 Spreading risks by dealing within the company in a number of countries. In this way the amount of currency exchange can be minimized by trading products and services within the company. Only the balances need be subject to foreign exchange conversion. This approach is particularly appropriate to the large MNEs.

2 Engaging in counter-trade. In this way foreign exchange influence is reduced.

3 Buying currency forward. In this way the 'price' of the currency is known. However, if currency movements continue over a number of months or years, the forward buying protection will eventually run out. The company will then need to make price and cost readjustments.

Summary

Foreign exchange fluctuations are an important factor in influencing the price of goods and services in international markets. Some companies will attempt to minimize fluctuations by adjusting their profit levels. A stabilizing effect can be achieved, but in the long term major foreign exchange movements will be too great to stabilize. Large companies will work to minimize foreign exchange influences by developing an interlinking spread of worldwide business. Other companies will need to assess their international marketing priorities as prices become too expensive in some markets, and yet in others they can achieve bigger profits or lower prices.

The answer to this question has to balance pricing decisions and the influences of foreign exchange fluctuations. Most companies will undertake some management of their exposure to foreign exchange risk. Activities such as buying forward have to be paid for; they represent an extra cost in exporting. Very large companies will attempt to spread their foreign exchange risks by deliberately changing the balance of their activities to minimize the exchange of foreign currencies. In addition, they will move their activities to take the best advantages out of appreciating and depreciating currencies.

December 1994 **Note**: Essentially, this is a 'technical' question and there is nearly always one of this nature in the examination. Those actively involved in exporting should have no difficulty in answering it, but for others it might prove a little difficult. The suggested approach is as follows.

Currency fluctuations

The fact that most countries use different currencies means that international trade involves the need to exchange currencies. Foreign currency (FOREX) transactions increase the risks involved in cross-border marketing. The prices charged in different markets are influenced by the exchange rate of the currencies involved. This has a knock-on impact on the profit (and more importantly loss) resulting from the sales in non-domestic markets.

Dealing with the problems of changing exchange rates has always been a problem in exporting and international marketing. The parties involved need to manage the process. Kenichi Ohmae states: 'When a sudden fluctuation in trade policy or exchange rates can turn an otherwise brilliant strategy into a seemingly irreparable haemorrhage of cash, making arrangements to deal with such fluctuations must lie at the very heart of strategy, not an afterthought to a strategy defined by other considerations.'

Managing currency fluctuations

For the major international corporation operating in many countries, the solution generally lies in balancing or spreading the risk in the major world markets. Money/currency operates without borders. The major world corporations use experts to manage the risks of moving money from one currency to another irrespective of whether this money is connected directly with goods or services.

For the smaller firm the issues are more piercing, for fluctuation cannot be managed so easily and money is tied directly to goods/services bought or sold between trading nations. One specific problem is that of differential inflation.

Exporters have the option of quoting in either the domestic or local currency (although in general terms it is the buyer who has the upper hand in deciding). Quoting in domestic currency is simpler, with the risk being borne by the customer, the reverse being true of quoting in foreign currency.

Tactics employed to adapt to currency fluctuations depend on whether the domestic currency is weak or strong.

Domestic currency weak

- Compete on a price platform (this is at the heart of the current UK boom in exports)
- Introduce new products with additional features
- Source and manufacture in home country
- Fully exploit export opportunities (via market spreading)
- Obtain payment in cash
- Minimize overseas borrowing
- Invoice in home/domestic currency

Domestic currency strong

- Compete on non-price factors (quality, delivery, service). The German economy and the Japanese also have pursued this strategy successfully for the Past 20 years. German products are expensive yet are in demand
- Improve productivity and cut costs. The Germans lead the field in this too. Labour costs are the highest in the world but the productivity of that labour ranks equally high due to investment in machinery etc.
- Prioritize strong currency countries for exports
- Use counter trade for weak currency countries
- Reduce profit margins – maintain share in foreign markets. The Japanese nearly always follow this route, pursuing long-term goals at the expense of short-term profits
- Maximize expenditure in the foreign currency
- Buy augmented product services in local/foreign currency
- Borrow money for expansion in local currency
- Invoice foreign customers in their own currency

Finally, the frequent exporter should set up an information system to monitor currency fluctuations, generally speaking via their own bank, which today is computer-linked to the latest changes. Doing it oneself is a high risk activity and it is better left to specialists like banks.

Additionally, the exporter can set dates for payment with penalties in-built and finally the exporter might dispatch goods in controlled quantities, limiting the company's exposure.

December 1996, Question 4 **Note:** The following guidelines have been deliberately broadened to indicate the potential for candidates to express their knowledge.

Surveys in the USA indicate political risk assessment to be the most prominent challenge to international managers, i.e. defined as the possibility of any government action affecting their operation.

The political risk indicators are:

Economic	**Political**	**Social**
Level of GDP	Relationship with neighbours	Urbanism
Inflation	Degree of authorization	Religious fundamentalism
Capital flight	Legitimacy of government	Ethnic tension
Foreign debt	Staleness of government	Complexity of culture
Food output	Military control	
Commodity dependence	Foreign conflict	

Management of business in high-risk scenarios

- Low physical presence – capital, HR and everything
- Deal via third parties
- Deal at high levels of authority
- Monitor everything carefully
- Get paid in stable currency
- Have contingency
- Be flexible in entry strategy
- Buy insurance

December 1997, Question 5 Begin by acknowledging that international expansion involves risk.

1 *The major risk* is associated with the strategic level of involvement undertaken. Doole, Lowe and Phillips illustrate this in their 'Risk vs control in market entry model'. It plots the options from domestic purchasing through to wholly owned manufacturing plant overseas.

Having discussed this model candidates might then move on to the important subject area of international capital requirement, dividing it into:

- Start up/Investment capital.
- Working capital.

This needs to be related to the market entry decision and the answer developed in some depth, i.e. even the relatively low level of involvement might include heavy working capital in travel costs, shipping costs, duties, start up costs, higher inventories and delayed payments. The importance of planning carefully to manage this exposure related to the entry strategy should be explained.

2 *The second aspect of financial risk* includes:

- Foreign exchange risk.
- Political risk.

Candidates should show an awareness of the issues surrounding exchange risks and the impact on profitability. The standard methods include forward buying etc. Also important is payment in a third currency, usually dollars, yen or Deutschmarks. Counter trade is yet another option. Political factors also have a financial calculation, e.g. the potential of expropriation. This aspect might be linked back to a company's market entry method and additionally candidates might mention how companies might access political risk, e.g. BERI.

3 *Repatriation of profit, the third area of risk*
These risks relate to:

- Taxation – both at the host and the home country end of the trading relationships.
- Government – policies influencing the host economy.
- Differential inflation.

Quality answers will cover all three major considerations but will add that having an understanding of all the principal factors is essential. Whilst customers may be the only source of profit, management of the international operation is the key to delivering net profit.

Marketing communications

Communicating in a multi-country setting is particularly difficult. The process involves dealing with language, culture, political and social constraints and local regulations. Customers differ, so how we address them needs careful consideration. Customers rarely buy features, they buy perceived benefits that reflect on their needs, motivations and behaviour. Applying a domestic SRC is of little use in international marketing. The subject of international marketing communication is a challenge. In this unit you will:

- Study the barriers to communication
- Appreciate the need to adapt the basic strategy to fit country/market needs
- Consider the implications of establishing a local sales force, mounting PR compaigns and using other Marcom tools
- See that sales promotion and advertising are particularly sensitive areas of communication
- Review briefly the problems of coordination and control in international communications.

Having completed the unit you will be able to:

- Understand that differences in macro and micro environments (markets and customers) affect how and why companies need to adapt their communication strategies
- Appreciate how marketing communications is driven by local needs
- Apply the tools of marketing communication to a given set of circumstances.
- Discuss the global versus local debate on branding and marketing
- Address issues concerning the international organization of marketing communication.

At the outset it is worth noting that students of this subject should also be familiar with the unit on international marketing communication in the *Marketing Communications Strategy* workbook. Will candidates please note that examination questions relating to International Marketing Communications appear frequently in the Marketing Communications Strategy paper.

The global versus local issue is one that is in constant debate. Here we set out the mechanics of marketing communications in dealing with the central issue of creating awareness, persuading and motivating customers from a rich, varied and diverse background to buy. This unit should therefore be considered alongside Unit 4 of this book, as it deals with customers and the international environment.

The management of international marketing communications (Marcom)

Marketing communications (Marcom) is the most culturally sensitive area of international marketing. Cultural barriers abound and the SRC must be avoided.

In Unit 4 we discussed in depth the issues of culture. Perhaps we can redefine it in simple terms: 'It's the way we do things round here.' Failure to recognize the difference and plan to take account of this will invite disaster. Remember, customers do not buy products but the benefits that accrue from them. These benefits are often mostly intangible. Marcom must ensure that all aspects of communication is compatible with the expectation and desires of the customer. Figure 11.1 indicates the potential 'break' in the flow of communication that can occur due to the cultural environment being different.

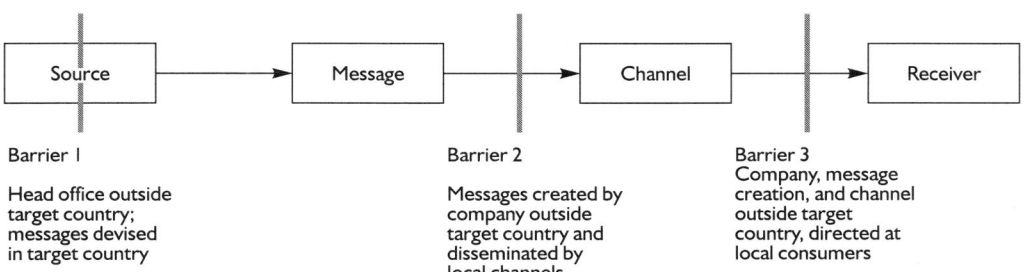

Figure 11.1 Barriers in the multi-country communications process (Jeannet and Hennessey, 1994)

The danger, of course, when faced with cultural barriers is to fall back on one's own SRC not just at the tactical level but at the strategic and management decision level. The textbooks abound with examples and case studies of companies who have failed to accommodate cultural differences in their Marcom planning and execution.

It is quoted that convergence and modernity is minimizing cultural differences and as such fosters the spread of globalization. But even such global giants as Marlborough, Coca-Cola, McDonald's, Sony and others take great care and fine tune their Marcom to meet local requirements. In purist terminology there is no such thing as a global brand, i.e. one that communicates with 'one sight, one sound, one sell'. All companies have some adaptation in their mix.

The international promotional mix

It is assumed that the reader is familiar with the tools of Marcom and their roles in persuading customers to buy. As markets differ, so must strategies. The first strategic consideration is whether to adapt a push versus a pull strategy. Figure 11.2 indicates how the tools of Marcom relate to their strategic decision.

Push strategy is less familiar in Westernized countries and is usually employed when:

1 The consumer culture is less Westernized
2 Wages are low and it is cheaper to employ sales-people than advertise

Figure 11.2 International and global promotion strategies (Jeannet and Hennessey, 1994)

3 A variety of languages, ethnic and racial groupings are present
4 Limited media availability
5 Channels are short and direct
6 The culture dictates its use (e.g. business etiquette)
7 The market is varied, i.e. split between urban and rural.

Pull strategy is familiar to the UK audience and is used when:

1 Advertising has great leverage in the consumer culture
2 Wide media choice together with the wide availability of other Marcom tools
3 Marcom budgets are high
4 Self-service predominates, i.e. supermarket culture
5 The trade is influenced by advertising.

Having decided the appropriate Marcom strategy, push or pull, the next decision is which Marcom tools are appropriate to the task and what difficulties arise in the international sphere.

Personal selling

This generally forms the major thrust in international Marcom when:

- *Wages are low* Mitsubishi's Thailand subsidiary selling mainly air-conditioning units has 80 sales people in Bangkok. Philip Morris in Venezuela employs 300 sales people and assistants.
- *Linguistic pluralism exists* (multi-language) There are two points to be made, contradictory in essence. The first is that there is a trend to spoken English in business-to-business markets. The second and more important point is that knowledge and understanding of the local language is essential. Never forget, it is the buyer who chooses the language, not the seller. In situations where linguistic pluralization exists (e.g. India) it is essential that personal selling plays a major role in Marcom – particularly when it is also the case that literacy is low and alternative Marcom tools are not relevant in the situation.
- *Business etiquette* Success in selling can only be achieved if there is a relationship between buyer and seller. Few products are so unique that there are no alternatives or substitutes. Understanding and relating to the buyer's culture is a prerequisite of making the sale. Consider some examples. Lateness is inexcusable in Hong Kong – but expected in India; the performance of business introductions in Japan with the elaborate ritual of exchanging business cards; the banquets and frequent toasts in China; the lengthy process of familiarization between buyer and seller in Japan. These and many other examples make it clear that Western etiquette is at odds with many cultures. Even in Europe business etiquette varies considerably, e.g. meetings start early morning in northern Europe, not so in southern Europe. Incidentally, whoever invented breakfast meetings?

Negotiations strategies

Following on, it is apparent that negotiations and bargaining varies by culture. The Americans prefer confrontation with short exchanges and early decisions on the big issues leaving the details to later or to less senior management. The Japanese and the Chinese take the opposite view: great attention to detail, consensus within the group, long protracted negotiations. Before entering negotiations it is essential to understand the mindset of the other party. Being unprepared is a guarantee of failure. Other considerations are also important. For example:

- Location and space – where are the negotiations being held, how big is the room/office, seating arrangements (too close or not close enough)?
- Friendship – is it important to know your customer in terms of their family details?
- Agreements – are these rigid or flexible? (The Americans prefer rigid agreements, the Greek ones that are open to some interpretation and flexibility.)

Staffing the sales force

Increasingly, the trend is towards using local employees as opposed to expatriates. They are closer to the customers in culture and behaviour. They allow the company to position itself as an 'insider', reducing the risk of conveying a feeling of cultural imperialism. They subvert local restrictions on employing non-nationals. However, there are occasions when 'the person from HQ' syndrome still has a value.

Training or deployment of expatriates

Besides basic training in the PEST factors relating to a particular country it is sensible for the individual to acquire at least a basic understanding of the language. Having done that, an 'immersion' in the local culture prior to taking up a post is equally important. Toyne and Walters (1993) outline a programme shown in Table 11.1.

Table 11.1 Approaches to implementation

Initial training	
Length of training	Less than one week
Main objectives	Knowledge of key country facts and key cultural differences. Some words of the (main) country language
Training activities	Area briefings. Cultural briefings, Distance-learning kits of books, video and audio tapes. Survival language training
Location and timing	Before departure to assigned country
Follow-up training	
Length of training	One to four weeks
Main objectives	Development of a more sophisticated knowledge of culture and language. Attitudes and beliefs need to be considered and perhaps adjusted
Training activities	Cultural assimilation training. Role playing. Handling critical incidents. Case studies. Stress-reduction training. Moderate language training
Location and timing	Preferably before departure to the assigned country
Immersion training	
Length of training	More than one month
Main objectives	To develop appropriate competencies to manage in a culturally sensitive way and be functionally efficient and effective
Training activities	Assessment centre Field experiences Simulations Sensitivity training Extensive language training
Location and timing	In the assigned country during the work assignment, preferably front-load the activities

Source: Toyne and Walters (1993)

There is often the knock-on effect of how to deploy the expatriate sales person after the period of overseas activity and re-integrating him or her back into the company. Additionally, the cost of sending an expatriate overseas is increasingly expensive. Dependent on the 'attractiveness' of the location and the 'local' cost of living, it costs upwards of three times domestic salary to deploy someone overseas. The 'total' cost of employing a salesperson within the UK is currently put at around £60,000. Transferring the person overseas could easily exceed £150 000 p.a. and in some cases exceed £250 000 p.a.

Recruitment, training, motivation – control of local sales force

The employment of a local sales force implies a single country and maybe even a single culture sales force. Briefly, the critical issues are:

- *Recruitment* Finding suitable sales representatives may be problematical, e.g. where qualified candidates are in short supply or because of the low status associated with selling. Selling may conflict with the culture. Local requirements may favour certain ethnic groups (not suited to selling characteristics). Tribal differences may forbid cross-cultural selling.

- *Training* Once trained loyalty may diminish if the culture is entrepreneurial or, alternatively staff may be 'head-hunted'. Who does the training? Are the trainers acculturalized with both company culture and local culture? Training of this nature is expensive in time and money.
- *Motivation*   This may be more of a challenge than in the domestic market where money is the appropriate method. Titles, overseas trips, the size of office, entertainment allowances may all improve self-image which may be more important than monetary rewards, especially where selling is not held in high esteem.
- Control and evaluation   Utilizing the commission method of reward control is easier than using straight salary. But the conventional rules of sales territory, call frequencies, quotas and strict reporting procedures may have little effect in some situations. Freedom to negotiate (failure means loss of face) may be paramount. Comparison among the sales team may also be culturally negative. So the conventional methods may well require modification although those basic principles should apply.

EXAM QUESTIONS

?

Analyse the appropriateness of using head office home-based, expatriates and nationals to develop an international sales force to cover a wide variety of country markets (December 1994, Question 2).

What training and familiarization procedures would you propose for sales people, experienced and successful in the UK, to enable them to be effective in sales negotiations in a foreign country with a different culture and language (June 1993, Question 6).

(**See** Exam answers at the end of this unit.)

Personal selling through intermediaries

Many companies sell indirect, via their distributors or licensees. Success increases if they think of the distributor's sales force as their own, keeping them motivated, abreast of domestic/global developments within the organization, mailing them regularly with information, involving them in the company, making them feel part of a far bigger organization, rewarding them as part of the organization. Run a sales conference for them. Invite successful sales persons to a pan-distributors conference. Make them feel important – they *are* important!

Government sponsored trade missions

The DTI regularly sponsors trade missions for which there is financial support as well as technical and other advisory services. This is a vitally important avenue for selling overseas and is particularly relevant to the smaller firms. The DTI publishes a monthly update on what is available and when. It is worth recording that in 1994 the UK government supported export promotion to the tune of 25 cents for every $1000 of GDP (Source: US Department of Commerce). France came second with approximately 18 cents. Japan spent over 12 cents while the US spent less then 3 cents. What is more, over 20% of UK diplomats abroad are engaged in full time commercial work.

International trade fairs

These can be generalized or industry-specific and over 1500 international trade fairs occur annually. They play an important role in bringing buyers and sellers together in a way that would normally not be feasible – particularly for the 'missionary' firm wishing to enter a sub-continent or a region. The Hanover Fair, held annually, attracts 5000 exhibitors from around the world. Its origins were to make the link between East and West Europe but its scope and attractiveness is now global.

Trade fairs have many advantages:

- There is the interface between buyers and sellers
- Potential licensees or joint-venture partners may be discovered

- Products can be tested for interest
- Competitors' activities can be assessed
- They may be the only point of contact between buyers and sellers especially with former Communist bloc countries
- They are ideal for business-to-business organizations who often concentrate their Marcom budget around trade fairs
- Sometimes government assistance is available to fund the exercise. Contact the DTI for advice
- As such, trade fairs require careful planning, specialist advice and involvement, especially in language interpretation.

Contact the trade association for a major industry. Get some information on the scale of an international trade fair – they often are very much bigger than anything on the domestic front.

ACTIVITY 11.1

Consortium selling

This is usually associated with large-scale projects (airports, hospitals, hydroelectric plants, etc.). Partner selection is the crucial point here as is good to excellent relations with the host government.

Sales promotion

This is more common ground and most of us have familiarity with this area of Marcom. But beware, it is very culturally loaded. Sales promotions have a local focus both in terms of the offer and also from a legal perspective:

- *The offer* Airmiles are a great success in the UK but may have no relevance in most of Africa. Prosperity statuettes are popular in Chinese culture but would they work in the UK?

Table 11.2 Does you does or does you don't . . . ?

	UK	IRL	Spa	Ger	F	Den	Bel	NL	POL	Ita	Gre	Lux	Aus	Fin	Nor	Swe	Swi	Rus	Hun	Cz
On-pack price cut	Y	Y	Y	Y	Y	Y	Y	Y	Y	Y	Y	Y	Y	Y	Y	Y	Y	Y	Y	Y
Branded offers	Y	Y	Y	?	Y	?	N	Y	Y	Y	Y	N	?	?	?	?	N	Y	Y	Y
In-pack premiums	Y	Y	Y	?	?	?	Y	?	Y	Y	Y	N	?	Y	N	?	N	Y	Y	Y
Multi-buy offers	Y	Y	Y	?	Y	?	?	Y	Y	Y	Y	N	?	?	Y	?	N	?	Y	Y
Extra product	Y	Y	Y	?	Y	Y	?	?	Y	Y	Y	Y	?	Y	?	?	?	Y	Y	Y
Free product	Y	Y	Y	Y	Y	Y	?	Y	Y	Y	Y	Y	Y	Y	Y	Y	Y	Y	Y	Y
Re-use product	Y	Y	Y	Y	Y	Y	Y	Y	Y	Y	Y	Y	?	Y	Y	Y	Y	Y	Y	Y
Free mail-ins	Y	Y	Y	N	Y	?	Y	Y	Y	Y	Y	?	N	Y	Y	N	N	Y	Y	Y
With-purchase	Y	Y	Y	?	Y	?	?	?	Y	Y	N	N	?	Y	?	?	N	Y	Y	Y
X-product offers	Y	Y	Y	?	Y	?	N	?	Y	Y	N	N	?	?	N	?	N	Y	Y	Y
Collector devices	Y	Y	Y	?	?	?	?	?	Y	Y	Y	?	?	Y	?	Y	Y	Y	Y	Y
Competitions	Y	Y	Y	?	?	?	Y	?	Y	Y	Y	N	Y	Y	Y	Y	N	Y	Y	Y
Self-liquidators	Y	Y	Y	Y	Y	Y	Y	?	Y	Y	Y	N	N	Y	N	N	N	Y	?	Y
Free draws	Y	Y	Y	N	Y	N	N	N	Y	Y	Y	N	N	?	?	N	N	Y	Y	Y
Share-outs	Y	Y	Y	N	?	N	N	N	Y	?	Y	N	?	Y	N	N	N	Y	?	?
Sweep/lottery	Y	?	?	?	?	N	?	?	?	?	?	N	?	Y	?	N	?	N	Y	?
Cash-off vouchers	Y	Y	Y	N	Y	?	Y	Y	Y	?	Y	?	?	?	N	?	N	Y	Y	Y
Cash-off purchase	Y	Y	Y	N	Y	N	Y	Y	Y	?	Y	N	N	?	N	N	N	Y	Y	Y
Cash back	Y	Y	Y	?	Y	Y	Y	Y	Y	N	Y	N	?	?	?	Y	N	Y	Y	Y
In-store demos	Y	Y	Y	Y	Y	Y	Y	Y	Y	Y	Y	Y	Y	Y	Y	Y	Y	Y	?	Y

Y permitted, N not permitted, ? may be permitted with certain conditions
Source: Institute of Sales Promotion

- *Cooperation from intermediaries* Retailers may be adept at processing coupons, handling oddly shaped premiums, creating displays, etc. – or they may not. Assuming that a French pharmacist is the same as a UK chemist would be a mistake. A country with small retailers may be difficult to contact (no phone, poor or non-existent postal service) and difficult to control.
- *Regulations* Laws relating to sales promotion differ virtually everywhere. The UK and the USA, for example, have few restrictions, other countries (e.g. Germany, Sweden, Japan) have many. What you can offer, where, when, how depends on the laws of each country. As of this moment there is no agreement within the 15 members of the EU. Table 11.2 shows current practice in Europe.
- *Bribery* Again a cultural reference – the way we do things round here! It is difficult and presumptuous to comment on practices in a specific country, simply to say corporate hospitality is an important customer motivator in the UK!

Getting it wrong on the international sales promotion front can have implications more severe than the Hoover debâcle of the early 1990s in the UK, when several executives lost their jobs in a miscalculated promotion. Pepsi-Cola mounted a lottery promotion in the Philippines but it announced a wrong winning number resulting in 800,000 families demanding the $40,000 prize – that's a 32 thousand million dollar pay out! In trying to back out Pepsi found its offices fire-bombed and the executives escorted to safety to the USA accompanied to the airport by an armoured guard.

Sponsorship

This is growing in importance on the international front as global sports events proliferate. Coca-Cola, Mars, Gillette, Niké and other transnational organizations are busy building international awareness and identities via events such as the Olympic Games, World Cup Football, world tennis and golf, etc. Global media and communication will greatly expand and accelerate this trend – but it is only for the few companies that are capable of capturing mass-market international customers.

Barter – counter-trade

Although, strictly speaking, outside the scope of Marcom, one of the biggest motivators in terms of purchase is counter-trade. Multinationals are extensively involved supported by and even initiating government involvement. Until recently it was the preferred method of exchange between East European countries and the West. Counter-trade and barter involves an exchange of goods or services. Its advantages are no currency risk, no trade barriers or taxes. In some cases the alternative to barter is no-deal. The disadvantages are numerous. To begin with, you might not want the counter-traded goods – having to dispose of them is wasteful of time and management resources. The quality of the goods you receive might well be variable, further handicapping your sale of them. However, it is thought that counter-trade and barter is on the increase, and as such, firms entering it must possess the required management expertise.

ACTIVITY 11.2

Track back through some quality press. Seek out examples of counter-trading – often with government support.

Direct marketing

This is well established in Western cultures and growing in importance. It is also expanding in countries like Hong Kong and Singapore – but has made, as yet, little impact in Eastern Europe and South America, most of Asia or Africa. It is culturally bound and limited by the dynamics of communication and distribution. Additionally, it is constrained by legislation playing a low key role in Germany, for example.

Telemarketing, like direct marketing is booming in the USA, growing in the UK but constrained for similar reasons elsewhere, particularly those of infrastructure. Having said that, 0800 marketing looks like being one of the major Marcom tools of the 1990s. Colleagues of mine regularly phone the USA to order computer equipment, pay by credit card and get delivery within 2 weeks. Dell computers have their pan-European help-line based in Ireland contacted by 0800 local rate calls and ICL's equivalent is in Delhi.

Door-to-door marketing is again dependent on the cultural reference. The concept is not well received everywhere and Amway and Tupper Ware are hardly household names in every country. However, it is well received in Japan where even stocks and shares are sold door to door – and incidentally the technique has a place in the selling of motor cars. It was suggested that one of the reasons the Japanese stock market bounced back from a major fall in 1987 was the confidence gained from door-to-door sales persons exhorting customers to 'buy now, shares are cheap'!

Direct mail again is growing. It is increasingly sophisticated in its targeting and its creative delivery but again is limited in its development by cultural inhibitions and infrastructure. Recently Fiat had to apologize publicly in Spain for offence caused by a direct mail letter sent to females implying a romantic affair. It was to launch a new car but many were offended by its flirtatious tone.

ACTIVITY 11.3

Can you think of any instance of receiving any direct marketing communication from overseas? Will a fair proportion of the material you receive be postmarked Amsterdam? Can you explain why?

Public relations

Strictly speaking, the remit of PR extends beyond the scope of marketing to embrace corporate issues. Positioning the company within the host country is a corporate task. Being seen as an 'insider' is regarded as increasingly important – political links, employee relations and communicating with the wide spectrum of target markets such as the media, influencers, the general public, financial markets, local community, etc. The list is extensive. Foreign firms have a particularly sensitive role to consider in portraying themselves. We do not propose to cover the range of PR tactics but simply state the importance of PR in marketing the organization in overseas markets.

On a more tactical level (i.e. product level marketing) PR can be important where the market is both sophisticated or the opposite. In sophisticated Western markets PR agencies are employed in familiar terms of reference. In the case of developing markets PR is most important in spreading the message by word of mouth. Travelling exhibitions visiting small towns and villages, staging plays, sponsored by company X are frequently employed. In such an environment word-of-mouth communication has high believability.

EXAM QUESTION

Using an example of an organization opening internationally show how public relations could be used to address a variety of different specified audiences (June 1994, Question 5).

(**See** Exam answers at the end of this unit.)

The development and management of international advertising

This is by far the most culturally sensitive of Marcom tools. Correspondingly no other aspect of international Marcom has been examined so critically. The textbooks abound with examples of international advertising misinterpreted and misused.

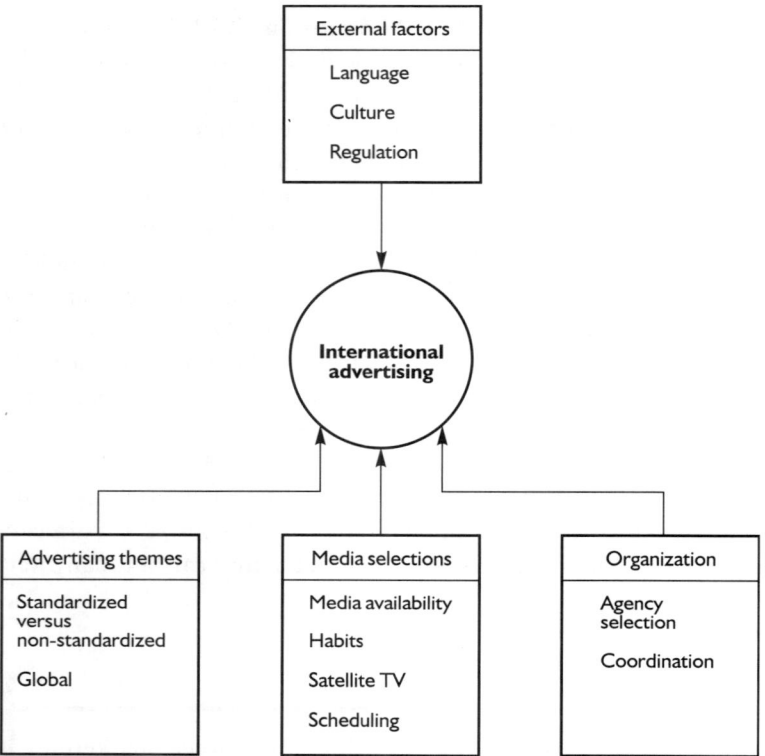

Figure 11.3 International and global advertising (Jeannet and Hennessey, 1994)

International advertising

Putting it simply, any advertisement is 'a message sent in code'. It is encoded by the sender and decoded by the receiver. Some messages are easy to decode (e.g. 'Harrod's Sale Starts Friday'!). Others are complex. But each message is designed to appeal to a targeted group and is invariably surrounded by its cultural reference. Since culture differs by country (and frequently within countries), decoding the message internationally becomes more difficult, is wrongly decoded or is irrelevant. Try explaining a Silk Cut cigarette advertisement to anyone who isn't British. So it is hardly surprising that sometimes controversy rages over international advertising. Perhaps Benetton is a good example here. It has variously offended cultural, ethnic and racial norms in several countries – occasionally its advertisements have been 'pulled' from a market. However, it is Benetton's aim to shock and to challenge accepted wisdom – and in this they have succeeded. Their message is probably 'if you're a non-traditionalist and a mould breaker by nature then Benetton reflects your mood'. Awareness of the campaign and the company is extremely high in all the countries it operates and, to date, sales appear to have benefited from the campaign. Other companies have not been so lucky.

So the three central issues in developing international advertising are:

- *Message*   What do we need to change in our advertising (from our domestic campaign) in order that foreign customers can decode the message? Alternatively, do we need to construct a totally different message?
- *Media*   Having solved that specific question we have then to decide what is the appropriate medium to communicate the message.
- *Control*   Finally, will we coordinate the various activities across countries?

Skim through some popular magazines and identify advertisements that you think are international (i.e. apart from language translation, they are used in a variety of markets).

154

Influence of external factors (culture, language and regulation)

Culture

It is apparent to all that culture is the most difficult aspect to master. Unit 4 addresses 'What is culture?' in depth and the pitfalls that surround it. Recently Moscow television screened some UK advertisements. Russian viewers understood the product-led features' dominant claims (but did not necessarily believe them). However, they seemed baffled by campaigns set in beautiful green countryside – the Timotei lady walking through Elysian fields. Only peasants live in the countryside was a typical reaction – what is she doing there? Similarly, although they liked the Andrex commercials with the lovable puppy they could make no connection between the advertisement and the product and thought it a waste of time.

Ronald McDonald's is not liked in Japan. His 'white' face is synonymous with death – white being the funereal colour in most of the Far East.

Perhaps the major *faux pas* of 1995 was the deal between Mohammed Azharuddin, India's captain of cricket, and Reebok sports shoes. Muslim leaders considered it blasphemous that his signature should appear on such a humble object, for 'Mohammed' is the name of the prophet Allah and 'Azhar' is one of Allah's 99 names.

International advertising is full of anecdotal examples. Collect as many as you can and use them on the day!

EXAM HINT

Language

Pepsi-Cola's campaign of 'Come alive with Pepsi' translated into 'Pepsi will bring your relatives back from the grave' is only one of many *faux-pas*. The critical factor here is to transpose the language, not simply translate it. The textbooks abound with examples. The slogan 'Hertz puts you in the driving seat' can mean you are a chauffeur rather than a go-ahead business person.

Regulation

Each country has its own rules, laws and codes of practice. The Marlboro cowboy cannot run in the UK. There is a ban on cigarette advertising in France. What you can say, when you can say it, where you can say it and how you can say it varies across national boundaries. Muslim countries forbid campaigns showing scantily clad females or consumption of alcohol (although this varies by country). Advertising to children is another culturally sensitive area. Some countries do not allow commercials concerned with 'violent' toys and Power Rangers have been banished from Swedish television. Others forbid the use of children in commercials; others permit their employment but restrict them to certain categories of products. The list is formidable. Even now the EU has no harmonization proposals in place.

The role of advertising in society

Although a sub-sector of culture, governments occasionally take a standpoint on this issue. Recently Singapore and Malaysia have declared their opposition to advertising campaigns that are not consistent with the culture of the country – banning campaigns they consider excessively detrimental to the development of 'good behaviour characteristics' particularly among the young and adolescent. Good behaviour is defined as respectful to parents, religious values and authority.

Frequently the tone of voice of advertising reflects the culture of the society. German advertising is far more matter of fact and informative than its UK equivalent which relies more on humour. For the record, the most 'subtle' campaigns come from Japan, where talking about the product is considered bad taste. (For further elaboration on this point you should refer to textbooks commenting on low-context and high-context cultures.)

Advertising themes (standard versus non-standard)

The advantage of a standardized theme is obvious. It gives economies of scale and allows the creation of pan-regional or even global brands. But such campaigns are rare. The first requirement is a standardized product (or virtually standardized) with a standardized name. Such do exist (Kodak, Fuji, BMW). But the facts are that these are exceptions, not the rule, and there are few examples of successful standardized themes on the contextual content of the advertisement. The actors, their clothes, the situation in which the advertisement is set are all culturally loaded and open to different decoding. One successful campaign is for 7-Up, a soft drink which utilizes a certain character Fido-Dido. The product is always pronounced in English and the character remains unchanged – appealing to the 'one-world youth culture'. Campaigns for major international brands invariably differ by country/region (e.g. Levi have adjusted its 'Launderette' and 'Refrigerator' advertisement to meet the cultural requirement). However, what is important is that the theme of youth remains constant – it is the interpretation of it that varies (i.e. decoding of the message is unchanged). The danger of going down the route of a standardized campaign, creating advertising that has 'some' meaning in every country, is that it motivates no-one anywhere. Euro advertising campaigns occasionally appear on UK television mainly to the annoyance of all. At the very least, they appear irrelevant. See if you can identify some.

EXAM HINT

Create examples of global advertising. You will find this of invaluable assistance when you're in the examination room. Examples of practical knowledge are always rewarded. But do think beyond Coca-Cola, please – the examiner is easily bored.

There is very little global advertising, although global positioning is on the increase. Coca-Cola's approach is to make a 'batch' of commercials which portray a similar positioning of the brand image and then discuss with country managers which commercials are most appropriate to their culture and environment. McDonald's adopt a broadly similar approach, taking a global position. Within Europe, Nescafé is positioned as the premier instant coffee with 'best beans, best blend, best taste' and uses as its icon the red mug. The transposition of 'best, best, best' is left to local marketers as coffee and instant coffee specifically has vastly different perceptions across the European marketplace.

Summarizing, standardized advertising requires similar consumers, with similar lifestyles and aspirations seeking similar rewards. Such clusters exist e.g. business travellers, senior business executives etc. and it often seems that the inhabitants of Upper East Side, Manhattan have more in common with their counterparts in Kensington, London than they do with their neighbours a block away. How else would you explain the success of Hugo Boss suits, Rolex watches and other designer type products, Armani, Versace, etc?

EXAM QUESTION

Examine the similarities and differences between global branding and global marketing. Are they the same? Under what conditions would each be likely to succeed? (December 1993, Question 7)
(**See** Exam answers at the end of this unit.)

Media selection (media availability, satellite TV, scheduling)

Media availability

Setting aside regulations on advertising themes the choice of media to carry messages varies enormously. The UK has abundant choice in newsprint with six or seven national newspapers. Nowhere else has this breadth of choice. Newsprint in most European countries is largely regional, although Germany has the Continent's biggest circulation paper with *Bild Zeitung*, selling about 5 million copies per day. Circulation for the No. 2 newspaper *FAZ* is little more than 500 000. France is dominated by a regional press, with *Ouest France*'s circulation being double that of *Le Figaro* or *Le Monde*.

It is impossible to cover the subject of media availability in depth: it is sufficient to acknowledge its wide variability in terms of type of media – and the degree of penetration and influence in the marketplace.

For the record, media consists of television, newspapers and magazines, outdoor, cinema and radio.

It would be useful if students obtained a copy of the *European Market and Media Fact Book* if they are serious about international (in their case European) media.

Satellite TV

This is a recent development but one that will grow into enormous proportions by the end of the decade. Europe and the Far East are in the forefront of its current development phase with the creation of Sky Channel and CNN. Satellite, with its multi-country footprints, is becoming more prominent. Besides the language difficulties (i.e. transmitting in multi-languages) the beneficiaries of satellite are likely to be the major pan-regional advertisers. Satellite transmissions are being focused on by national governments as they frequently breach country regulations. Singapore and Malaysia have recently banned Star TV to protect their population from 'foreign values'. In the Far East, Star TV, a Hong Kong-based satellite company, owned by Richard Murdoch's corporation, overtook CNN as India's favourite foreign programme. It and others' growth potential in the Far East is colossal. Satellite will be a huge communication medium in the next century as technology advances.

Scheduling media

The timing of the delivery of the message is decided by the demand of the audience. Most products have a cyclical sales demand peaking seasonally or in line with religious festivals and national holidays. Obviously, these differ by country/region (the Southern Hemisphere's Christmas is in their Summer). But holidays are also key purchasing moments and since holidays vary, media must be scheduled accordingly. In France most of the country closes down in July–August. The Germans stagger their summer holidays by *landes* (their equivalent of counties). In some Muslim countries advertising is restricted, or banned, during Ramadan. Winters and summers vary in duration and intensity across the globe. Thus seasonal products such as de-icing equipment or air-conditioning units will be advertised at different times. The international marketing company needs to take account of differences in scheduling (and budgets).

- What implications does the variability of media in different countries have for the strategy, implementation and control of advertising for the international manager (June 1994, Question 9).
- Examine the implications of variations in media availability, media cost and audience coverage on a company wishing to develop a standardized media approach to its many international markets (June 1993, Question 5).
- Select an economic region, e.g. EU or ASEAN (or another). Identify the advantages and disadvantages of pan-regional advertising. Taking the element of control, show how you might manage a pan-regional campaign for a product/ service of your choice (December 1996, Question 2).
- Marketing communications is frequently the most difficult part of the international marketing mix to plan and control. Making reference to examples, show why this is so and how a marketing communications programme might best be managed strategically. (December 1997, Question 2)

(**See** Exam answers at the end of this unit.)

Give serious thought to collecting examples of companies who utilize all the tools of marketing communications internationally. It might be useful to select a major multinational (not a UK company) and examine its Marcom plans in the UK. IBM is just such an organization. American, yet deeply entrenched in the UK. What are its advertising, PR, sales promotion, direct marketing and sales programmes?

Organizing and coordinating the advertising effort

Time and effort spent organizing and coordinating the advertizing effort is at least as important as time spent crafting the message and the media. The basic choices facing the multi-country international advertiser are:

1 *Domestic agency*   It is most common that advertisers use their domestic agencies when first expanding overseas, for reasons of familiarity, relationship, trust and knowledge of their business (all the normal reasons for choosing an agency in the first place). But many smaller domestic agencies have no international experience themselves but form a liaison and association with similar-sized agencies overseas and service the advertiser's account by proxy. This generally is a stage-one operation.

2 *Appointing local agencies*   This is generally a step taken by advertisers who recognize the need for a differentiated campaign. Local agencies understand local cultures, have the relevant contacts among the media and can create or adopt campaigns to meet the local requirements. Jaguar found, to its cost, when advertising in the Middle East that Arab headwear differed in detail from country to country. Locals easily spotted the difference and ridiculed the campaign, which was attempting to appeal to all suitably wealthy males. Nestlé adopt a roster approach, appointing from an approved shortlist of advertising agencies, thus getting benefits of acculturalization by market and minimizing the degree of control to a few agencies.

3 *Centralizing the effort*   The 1980s in particular saw the spread of major agencies into the global arena. Many of the US majors were already established servicing global clients such as Esso, Coca-Cola, etc. But it was Saatchi & Saatchi who really began the trend towards global advertising, exploiting the theories of Levitt regarding globalization and persuaded major multinational corporations to develop world advertising (e.g. British Airways and Mars). It was Saatchi who coined, or at least popularized, the phrase 'one

sight, one sound, one sell' – global communication. The advantages of such a campaign are apparent and have been discussed extensively in the textbooks. Similarly, the advantages of central creativity and global servicing through a single agency are equally obvious. However, although global agencies are still a growing trend they have been shown to have limitations in that the global advertisement has been elusive. To many it is seen as a shimmering oasis that appears wonderful but impossibly difficult to grasp or achieve. Having said that, IBM in 1994 has placed all its Marcom through Ogilvy & Mather in an attempt to speak to all its customers with one corporate voice. It remains to be seen whether customers will respond to this positively. For decades McCann-Erickson (an Inter-public group agency) played the role of guardian of the universal brand values for Esso ensuring consistency of corporate logo and brand communication. Until recently another Inter-public group agency fulfilled the same task for Coca-Cola.

Who are the major advertising agencies in the UK? How many of them are international? Get a feel for what the structure of the advertising industry is like. How many international agencies have international clients?

ACTIVITY 11.4

Coordination

Whatever the strategic choice, domestic, local or central, international advertising has to be controlled both in terms of the message and in budgetary terms. This requires management expertise at the marketing headquarters (usually at the domestic base). While decentralization has its distinct advantages – the locals are closer to the customers – the danger is fragmentation, with country managers pursuing their own agendas frequently to the overall detriment to international brand values – imperceptibly at first but, over time, shifting consumer recognition and understanding away from the corporate goals. Decentralization requires very careful handling and control in terms of guidelines relating to advertising claims, tone of voice, logo, colours, etc. and in terms of scale of the budget and scheduling of the campaign. Conversely, heavy-handed centralized control can be equally destructive, stifling creativity if overprescribed. Creative personnel – with the talent for differentiating your product offer from competition – dislike working within rigid guidelines. Essentially, the way (the style) through which international advertising is administered is at least as important as the company procedures employed.

Summary

Marketing communication is probably the most discussed area of international marketing. Not only is it rarely out of the news (it invites controversy) but the majority of us have exposure to it. What makes it so interesting is that it is culturally loaded. Everyone has a view. The challenge for the future is increasingly to internationalize the communicative mix. World consumers, world competitors, world advertising agencies lead to a consolidation in strategic terms of the marketing effort. Yet the paradox exists. Consumers though seeking global benefits remain doggedly local in their outlook. While strategy can take the global view, marketing must balance the benefits of 'one sight, one sound, one sell' with local needs. Issues such as cost, coordination and control also require careful consideration before any decisions are taken.

Questions
- Explain the greater importance often attached to personal selling in overseas markets.
- What are the problems and difficulties in establishing a local sales force?

- Specify some of the issues involved with sales promotions overseas. How might the deployment of a local rather than a domestic sales promotions agency assist in overcoming problems?
- What factors influence the development of push or pull strategies in international marketing communications?
- Specify the conditions under which a company might employ a local versus a home-based sales effort.
- What patterns do you reserve in the use of sales promotion across Europe?
- What type of companies sponsor Formula 1 motor racing (apart from the oil giants)? What benefits do you think they gain?
- Is global advertising for the few, or do you see it developing as a major force?
- How should the advertising industry respond to the new technological trends in mass media communication (e.g. cable, satellite, Internet etc.)?
- Why are some global advertising campaigns successful while others fail?
  Illustrate your answer by examples.

Global Marketing Strategies, J.-P. Jeannet and H. D. Hennessey, Houghton-Mifflin, 1998.

International Marketing, S. Paliwoda and M. Thomas, Butterworth-Heinemann, 1998.

International Marketing Strategy, I. Doole, R. Lowe and C. Phillips, Routledge, 1997.

International Marketing, V. Terpstra and R. Sarathy, The Dryden Press, 1997.

Marketing Communication Strategy 1998–99, T. Yeshin, Butterworth-Heinemann, 1998.

December 1994, Question 2 The question divides into three distinct headings. Answers should therefore be structured around them. Additionally, the issues to be dealt with are international sales and not international marketing. Thirdly, the question asks you to deal with a wide variety of markets – not one single foreign market. So the approach might be:

1 *Head office home-based sales force*

- best suited to large capital projects where high profits can be made and need to be made to cover potential high costs
- detailed high level knowledge is essential (a good example of the kind of industry we are talking about is aircraft engines)
- high level contacts are required both at company level (home and host companies) and frequently inter-government support is necessary

2 *Expatriate sales force*

- best suited where knowledge of the home company and its systems is essential in selling the product in a multi-country environment with a compensatory advantage in less training being required and avoidance of issues relating to recruitment of overseas sales staff
- the ability to adapt both linguistically and culturally is important
- high value, technology-led industries lend themselves to this method

- the trend is inexorably in this direction
- apart from lower costs (than expatriates), the sales person has far greater cultural assimilation and in a way that no expatriate could imitate
- the key issues relate to recruitment, training and motivation
- control and feedback are additional factors to be considered

Having identified the critical factors concerning the deployment of the three types of sales force organization, candidates should then go on to discuss:

1 the relative cost, e.g. if a UK domestic sales person costs an average total cost of £40,000–£50,000 per annum, the cost of an expatriate is believed to be $2\frac{1}{2}$–4 times that amount, depending on the country involved;
2 the relative efficiencies of each method; and then
3 draw their own conclusions in the form of a summary.

June 1993, Question 6   The training and familiarization procedures fall into three main categories:

(a) Enabling the sales person to become aware of their own self-reference criterion so that they can identify and act to minimize the impact of their own cultural biases when preparing for and undertaking sales negotiations in a foreign country.
(b) Enabling the sales person to understand their customers and the environmental and cultural reference framework that they will bring to the negotiations.
(c) Teaching the sales person the practical skills necessary to allow them to function in a foreign country.

Sales negotiations can vary considerably in different countries. The Western approach with a probe, confirm, match and close type of approach is much less appropriate in high context cultures. Not only is the spoken language often different, but the silent languages, which communicate considerable meaning, are usually significantly different. The time taken to negotiate is often much longer, with different demands placed on information collection and processing. The decision-making process and the roles and level of importance of the participants in that process are usually different.

It is important to recognize that sales people who have been successful in the UK are not always successful abroad unless they are the right type of people. Away from the UK and the company headquarters, sales people are isolated to a considerable extent. Confidence and resilience are important to sustain performance in an unfamiliar setting.

The training programme could be divided into cultural issues related to the country in general, cultural issues related to business and the particular product market in question, language and specific details connected with a company; for example, pricing, distribution and documentation.

Issues connected with general culture related to a country can be communicated through seminars/lectures (preferably by an expert local business person), through country guides (for example, from the DTI's export service) and through various books and articles. A really detailed appreciation of culture will not be achieved, but the main issues can be covered. The aim should be to avoid making major mistakes because of a lack of understanding of cultural differences.

Business-specific cultural issues need to be understood. The importance and variety of timing, the use of various 'incentives' to gain the order and the significance of technical performance and technical standards need to be employed to succeed.

Language training should be used to cover the basic social vocabulary. In some countries, with major world languages and culture – for example, France – it is usually expected that sales people are fluent in the language. In this case, sales people need to be selected with an existing significant level of language skill. Learning a language from the beginning is a difficult and very time-consuming process. It is most unlikely that fluency can be achieved significantly quickly, although intensive immersion language courses can be used. Language teaching should incorporate cultural appreciation and should include business vocabulary.

Familiarization can be encouraged through role play, preferably with a person native to the country concerned.

In some companies there are people in the organization working in the country. These people can be used to accompany the sales person on initial country visits to form a bridge between the training and experiencing the country with its full cultural complexity.

To conclude, the training and familiarization should cover the important commercial and international differences in order that the sales people can become effective in the new country.

Senior Examiner's comments

To be successful in sales negotiations is challenging. To be able to do so in a different cultural setting (or a number of different settings) is particularly difficult. The above answer reaches a good standard in showing an applied knowledge of culture when related to selling.

The answer could be improved to gain higher marks by taking a more objective view of the training and familiarization requirements. By identifying the differences between the UK and the foreign country in question, the precise nature of the cultural differences and the product market differences can be isolated. In this way detailed training and familiarization programmes can be developed. The programme should be timescaled and have clear objectives.

June 1994, Question 5

Introduction

The multinational used in this answer is a diversified medical products organization involved in pharmaceutical, diagnostic and surgical products. The range of markets covered is diverse, including rich advanced economies with significant public and private health care markets and underdeveloped countries with embryonic health services coping with significant health problems.

Such companies involved with both government and private customers have a wide range of publics who can influence the degree of success that the organization will achieve in any market place. Governments are both regulators and significant customers. Medical practitioners and medical staff are often the most significant influencing factor in the consumer DMU. Patients are the ultimate consumers.

Relations with governments

Health care issues are one of the most controversial areas of government expenditure. Many governments are trying to contain health care costs in the face of rising public expectations as to health care provisions.

Many products and services provided in the health care market require extensive R&D prior to launch, and thus significant markets to ensure adequate payback on the investment. The attitude of public health services in prioritizing the use of a particular treatment may be critical to the viability of a particular product.

At the governmental level, the lobbying of parliamentary influencers – ministers, interested MPs, advisers etc. – ensures that the issues are kept well to the fore. This may involve visits and trips to view schemes in other countries and meet users, enabling such influencers to form an opinion.

A second use of PR in this context is the provision of articles in the medical press which are aimed both at the medical profession and the governmental bodies. In this context a particular threat to major medical suppliers has been the proposal to use generic (BP designated) products rather than branded original products which involve significant research. Both in the UK and the USA, the PR campaign emphasizing the significant cost of drug development and the loss of profits to fund future research has for the time being been successful.

In a more international context, the acceptance by significant governmental bodies in one country (e.g. US Federal Drug Administration) is often taken as a signal of acceptability by other governments worldwide.

The medical profession

The use of international conferences and seminars greatly aids the transfer across markets of knowledge about leading edge methods and practices. In this context the endorsement by acknowledged world experts of a particular drug or treatment is a key to acceptance in other markets.

Such seminars are backed up by appropriate media articles in local markets, where appropriate, and the use of sales promotion and personal selling activities tied in with the PR programme as an integrated 'roll-out' into a market.

In the area of R&D the use of PR in transmitting the results of key clinical trials sends signals to investors and the financial media worldwide as to the future flow of products and services, and thus encourages shareholders and investors to support the company. It also enhances the image of the company concerned as a significant actor at the leading edge of medical technology – giving confidence to the medical profession in the advice issued by the company in a particular treatment.

An additional use of trial evidence is the advanced information to potential users in the medical profession who, through seminars, conferences, articles, participation in the trials and other activities, are informed in advance of new products being developed for the market place.

One area of great difficulty in the PR context is that of minimizing the damage when, very occasionally, a treatment exhibits long-term side-effects, such as the Thalidomide disaster. This may create significant dissonance with governments, medical professionals and shareholders – and can spread across markets, creating not just local but worldwide problems.

It is the job of PR in this context to act as the interface between the company and its publics and attempt, via information flows, to keep favourable attitudes whilst exhibiting a caring face.

Patients and the general public

Depending on the country, access to the general public varies. In the UK, for example, it is only 'non prescription' items that may be sold or promoted to the public and then only under strict codes of practice and legislation. In other countries contact with the general public is more open.

The use of PR in this context is to ensure that more 'popular' features and articles are placed in appropriate media to inform and advise the public what treatments are open to them – if only to ask their GP as to the efficacy and appropriateness.

A particular area of PR activity which often acts as a cross-national flow of influence and information is cooperation with particular patient organizations – such as the British Diabetic Association for example – in developing and endorsing home medical kits (in this case simple home blood sugar testing equipment). Again, endorsement in respected institutions in one country will often be taken as a signal of acceptability by institutions in other countries, enabling the product to enter wider and diverse international markets.

In-company relations

With a diverse health care products company spread over many countries, a major use of PR is the creation of a corporate identity amongst employees, and to emphasize corporate values and goals. The use of newsletters, team briefings, staff exchanges etc. actually assists in creating a cohesive employee base, despite different and disparate locations and cultures.

December 1993, Question 7 Please refer to unit 7 page 97 for the answer to this question.

June 1994, Question 9 Probably the most significant factor affecting the advertising strategy in a particular country will be the PEST constraints and the objectives for that market, which will not necessarily be the same over all markets. Media differences are more likely to have an effect at the implementation and control level of the plan.

Major factors that are likely to vary the attractiveness of various media from country to country include:

1 The availability of the media – both to the public and the advertiser. In the first case, this will affect the size of the audience and in the second case, the restrictions placed on advertisers as to how much, what and when they may be allowed to advertise. In most countries there are severe restrictions on the promotion of alcohol, drugs and tobacco, and variations in media availability not only depend on the medium but also on the country – with outright advertising bans on some media to relatively liberal attitudes in other countries.

2 The use of anti-trust legislation – in many countries (including the UK) this has often been used to limit the amount of advertising that a company may carry out. In some special cases (often varying from country to country) specific limits may be stipulated on the promotional budget.

3 The quality of the media – again two factors are involved. First, the reach of a particular media vehicle to the target audience, and secondly, the suitability of a particular media vehicle to carry and portray the company message. Advertisements are seen in a context and the image generated is not solely generated by the advertisement but also by the context in which it is received.

4 Unless the advertising industry is well developed in a particular country, it may actually be difficult to identify and evaluate different media. The lack of data on audience, socio-economic profile of audience, circulation/coverage etc. may mean that cross-media comparisons are almost impossible; whereas in major developed countries the availability of such data allows sophisticated media selection and analysis to be carried out, allowing reach, opportunity to see etc. to be calculated for a particular campaign.

5 The issue of media coverage and integration can also be problematical. The UK is almost unique in having national media which have a high audience almost over the whole nation. However, the expansion of local media – TV, radio, press especially – is leading to fragmented coverage. Countries like Italy, with a proliferation of TV and radio stations, make it difficult to identify and plan a cohesive publicity campaign with any confidence.

6 In selecting a particular set of media, cost related to market coverage will always be an issue – the cost per thousand criterion and the relative cost of media from country to country, as well as the absolute cost, may vary significantly. Thus the traditional assumption that TV is expensive and posters inexpensive with other media in between may not hold, and media buyers have to suspend their belief in looking at different markets.

7 Finally, we need to consider the consumer/customer attitude to the media we are considering. For example, in the UK direct mail and telemarketing are considered by a significant number to be intrusive and the efficacy of such media vehicles becomes questionable. In other countries (for example, France) the use of electronic based promotional systems (e.g. Minitel/TV usage) is widely accepted, but not generally available elsewhere.

As a result of the above, it is unlikely that a standardized media approach can be used, even if conditions allow a standardized message. Thus some degree of adaptation of the media selected, and hence knowledge of suitability of media, will be required.

The need for adaptation will have implications on resources. First, the normal way of budget allocation – percentage of sales – will not be the same over all markets because of cost/response structures. Secondly, the cost of achieving particular objectives will differ from market to market.

Finally, the need to adapt will put pressure on those – in-house or agency-based – responsible for coordinating and rolling out a campaign across several markets.

June 1993, Question 5 Companies have been encouraged to standardize their advertising messages and the delivery of those messages because economies can be made. In addition, the increasing mobility of consumers encourages consistent marketing communications across country boundaries.

Obstacles to standardization

Media markets are becoming more fragmented and diverse, reflecting the consumer markets to which they are closely linked. Furthermore, there are many differences between countries.

Media availability

An advertiser may not be allowed to advertise the product on television. Some products are banned; for example, cigarettes in the UK and United States. In some countries there is no commercial television and, therefore, no medium for TV commercials.

In less developed countries, the ownership of television sets may be limited. Literacy levels may also be low, which means that press advertising has only limited value because of modest readership levels.

Lack of international media

There are very few true international media. Pan-European TV satellite channels, for example, are seen in many countries but have limited reach within each country. They might be suitable for special target groups but not for mass market approaches. In the business to business market, publications like *The Economist* can, for some markets, give good multi-country coverage.

Media cost

The cost of advertising varies a great deal between countries, partly as a function of each country's economic development, the development and degree of competition in the media and partly as a function of supply and demand between the media and advertisers.

Media cost will vary in absolute amount and relatively when compared on cost per thousand basis between, say, Canada and India.

Audience coverage

The same target audience may be reached in different ways within different countries. Housewives in one country may be more efficiently covered using TV, in other countries using outdoor advertising with posters and in other markets through cinema advertising.

Conclusion

The variations in media between different countries make it very difficult to implement a completely standard approach.

Considerations of language and culture, which affect the creative treatment of advertising, have not been mentioned here, but make the problem even more complex.

Senior Examiner's comments

The extent to which standardization of international advertising can be achieved to good effect provokes a lively debate amongst advertising and marketing managers. This question concentrated upon media standardization rather than message standardization. Good answers established the links between the media and message, but maintained a strong emphasis on media issues.

Excellent answers contained a number of specific examples to illustrate each of the main sections of the answer. In addition, they demonstrated an understanding of the need for accurate marketing research of the audiences/readership for the main media vehicles country by country. Good quality international media planning and media buying would be required to implement a good quality standardized media approach to its many international markets.

December 1996, Question 2   Candidates should apply the principles rather than simply write advantages/disadvantages from a textbook perspective. Examples will be rewarded.

For reference terms the European Union is taken as a model here.

Advantages

- Cost savings (maybe) and economies of scale
- Positioning
- Brand building – creating Eurobrands
  – creating customer and financial added value

It is important to note that such examples are rare and depend to a large degree on standardized (or near) product and a pan-Euro customer acceptance. Also, whilst pan-Euro positioning is on the increase, genuine pan-Euro communication is not. This does not deter companies from pursuing the goal, e.g. Nescafe.

Disadvantages

These are many and mainly cultural. Candidates should refer to the components of culture (Terpstra and Sarathy) and apply with examples where relevant. Also, candidates might use the Jeannet and Hennessy model.

Control

Coordination is perhaps a better word. This is an important, difficult task that perplexes many companies:

- Agency choice; domestic, local, region/global
- Degree of flexibility/centralization of creating and media execution
- Depth of management expertise

December 1997, Question 2   Answers should display familiarity with the subject area of Marketing Communications, as it features in the Diploma syllabus. Also, there are frequently in the Marketing Communications diploma paper questions of an international dimension. It is also important to recognize that international marketing communication is a topic of weekly debate in the quality journals, *Marketing, Marketing Week, Campaign, The Economist, Financial Times* etc.

The question is *not* about writing in general terms but asks specifically about the planning and control functions. However, the answer should begin by reference to the importance of culture in international marketing and that failure on the part of the company to recognize this invites disaster. (*Note*: Culture is loosely defined as 'the way we do things around here'.) Additionally, answers that do not address the specifics of the question will not be awarded a pass grade.

What is required is a recognition that all aspects of the communication process must be compatible with the expectations and desires of the customer. Even in a world of convergence, global village etc. the multinationals take great care to fine tune their marketing communications to meet local requirements. Examples include: Marlborough, Coca-Cola, Sony, McDonald's. Showing how this is implemented will be rewarded, while exploring rather more out of the ordinary examples will gain even higher marks.

In the *planning process* the key issues include:

- The balance between standardization and adaptation.
- The emphasis between pull vs push strategies.
- The appropriateness of the various tools of marketing communications and their availability.
- The legal, political and other formal differences that might be addressed.
- The management issues relating to multi-country marketing communications activities (depending on the degree of standardization required).

- The choice between central vs. decentralization in terms of the marketing/marcom implementation.
- The availability and choice of professional collaborators, i.e. agencies etc. Particularly their selection/appointment/evaluation.

Control issues revolve around:

- Establishing objectives.
- Establishing standards, particularly in message delivery, i.e. the creative execution and the performance of the relevant media.
- Management issues relating to monitoring and controlling international Marcom and multi-country agencies.

What is ultimately required is evidence of a sound grasp of the strategic issues influencing management decisions as covered in this unit. (See also Doole, Lowe and Phillips, 1997: chapter 9.)

Distribution and logistics

OBJECTIVES

Distribution and logistics are fast becoming critical factors in international marketing. Speed or time is increasingly the critical differential linked to costs. Getting the product or service delivered to the customer when it is needed and responding flexibly to marketplace demands has now assumed paramount importance. Federal Express is the world's sixth largest airline, succeeding by fast delivery worldwide. Customerization and groupage are again logistic advances. In the field of distribution things are equally dynamic with technology and modernity changing old-established routes to the customer (e.g. garage forecourts have become a major competitor in grocery retailing terms in the past 5 years). In this unit you will:

- Study the factors important in developing distribution strategies
- Recognize the *cost* implications of logistics
- Be aware that service levels are a very important marketing tool
- Consider the management aspects of distribution
- Study new trends for the future.

On completing the unit you will be able to:

- Explain the basis of a distribution strategy
- Identify the step-by-step approach and the impact each step might have on the overall delivery
- Review the impact of cost versus service and the management implication emanating from service-level decisions
- Evaluate the changing patterns in distribution and predict trends in what is happening (or likely to happen) in the future.

STUDY GUIDE

This unit sets out to guide the reader through the balance of satisfying customers and making profits. Both are essential to commercial success. No business succeeds by totally putting one at the forefront.

International distribution and logistics is fast becoming the difference between success and failure. Customers will no longer wait on your terms. Your organization has to match their requirements or face the consequences.

The management of distribution and logistics

Getting the goods ready and available for purchase by foreign customers is an integral part of the marketing mix. It is not the remit of this text to cover the transport of goods via Incoterms such as Free On Board (FOB), Carriage Insurance Freight (CIF) etc. These are essential tactical issues of export implementation and important though they are, are not essentially a strategic issue and therefore outside the scope of this text. However, all students and practitioners of international marketing must be aware of Incoterms. Both the business environment and the cultural frame of reference vary by country – so therefore must the distribution and logistics underpinning it. The number of retail outlets per population varies enormously, as do the range and variety of intermediaries. The degree of government control over them also varies. What they sell, how they sell it and everything that goes along with effective 'delivery' of the offer is ultimately dependent upon one thing – the consumer. What we offer has to be available on terms that are compatible with the customers' needs and wants and match or exceed competitors' performance.

If this is so, then the company's distribution strategy is one part of the marketing mix and it needs to be consistent with other aspects of the marketing strategy namely product, price and communications. Furthermore, Stern and El-Ansary (1982) make the point that the marketing channel (distribution) is a continuation of interdependent organizations in the process of making the product available for use or consumption. As such, the distribution channel is different in that it is largely managed rather than controlled. The management of channel within the chosen market is a combination of:

1 The culture, business environment and customer expectation
2 The objectives of the company, its resources, the availability of suitable channels and the ability of the company to service the channel appropriately.

Factors in developing the distribution strategy

Jeannet and Hennessey highlight four distribution decisions within the marketing mix, making the connection that distribution must be consistent with the rest of the mix (Figure 12.1).

The four decision points are:

1 *Distribution density* What is the ideal number of sales outlets required in order to service the customer? Remember, to be successful we need to be available where the customer expects it, so the critical factor is the consumer's shopping/buying behaviour. In general, fast-moving consumer goods are expected to be in extensive distribution and if that means every 'Mom and Pop' store then so be it. If the culture is to sell the

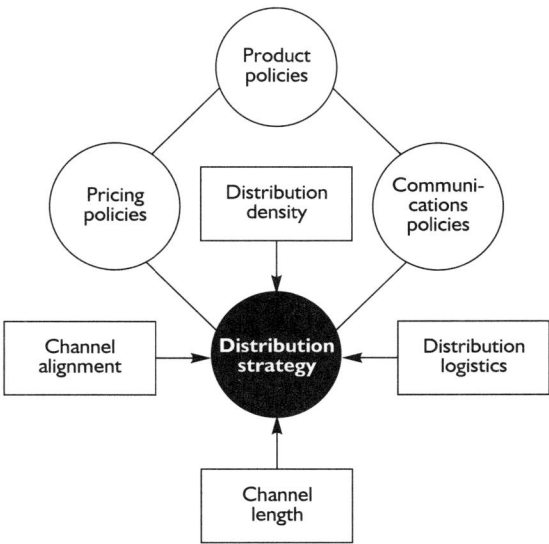

Figure 12.1 Distribution policies

product in single units (e.g. one cigarette or one sweet via street hawkers) then the company has to respond. The opposite is true in selling speciality and up-market branded goods where exclusive distribution may be required. Similarly, the purchase of industrial or business-to-business goods varies by country, from selling direct to end users, on the one hand, to recognized government suppliers/intermediaries, on the other. But throughout it is the buyer/customer who decides.

2 *Channel length* Put simply, this is the number of intermediaries involved in connecting the company, its product and the end buyer/user. Again, this is mainly determined culturally and varies by country. Japan, the leading high-tech country, has an exceedingly low-tech distribution system with many intermediaries connected via *Keiretsu* agreements. This makes distribution slow, wearisome and very expensive as each intermediary takes their 'cut'. Few Western companies have broken this internal mechanism and sell direct to customers. Toys'R'Us is such an exception but it took US government pressure to succeed – opening in direct competition with over 600 small traditional toy-sellers. *Note:* the successful innovations in creating different routes have been exclusively the major international brands/retailers who have had the financial muscle and government corporation (Coca-Cola, Nestlé, Niké, etc.).

Increasingly, in Western societies channel length is shrinking, making it at once easier and more difficult to break into a market. The UK grocery is dominated by five major multiples and, at a glance, it is easy to see how national distribution can be achieved. But failure to gain 'listing' means failure in the marketplace. France is undergoing remarkable change, leaping from a nation of village storekeepers to supermarket giants. For example, Mammouth, Leclerc and Casino have achieved national prominence in less than a decade, so don't assume a linear programme from small to large – it happens overnight, driven by technology and satisfied customers.

3 *Channel alignment* This concerns the effective management of the various inter-mediaries in its distribution chain. For a company with no direct involvement in a foreign market this is a most difficult task. Distance seriously hampers coordination. Generally, one of the participants in the distribution chain stands out as the dominant member – major retailers in the UK; wholesalers in the USA; distributors (often the only importers) in emerging countries. The company has to recognize the dominant channel member country by country and align itself accordingly. Relationships are crucial, for the channel intermediaries are not and never will be in the control of the company. The skill is in managing the relationship.

4 *Distribution logistics* Physical distribution management (PDM) is described by Kotler as concerning the planning, implementation and control of physical flows of materials and final goods from points of origin to points of use in order to meet customers' requirements. However, in this context we will limit ourselves to the logistical aspect, i.e. to view the process from the perspective of the customer and to work our way backwards towards the factory. We recognize, in passing, the very important point of cost, for it is the balancing between customer needs and costs that is the basis for profit. Drucker, some while ago, dwelt on the balance between efficiency (doing things right) and effectiveness (doing the right things). A combination of the two is the ideal – but the realities of international distribution logistics mean there is always a trade-off.

ACTIVITY 12.1

Select any industry in your domestic market. Specify the separate stages in the distribution process dealing with each outlet type separately (e.g. food/grocery retailing). Then try to second-guess some of the additional factors that might affect servicing the same industry/market overseas.

High costs in international logistics

Moving goods from country to country is expensive. Up to 35 per cent of the cost of goods can be accounted for by distribution (varying by distance and other visible/invisible barriers). Additional impediments include:

- Delivery scheduling
- Just-in-Time (JIT)
- Inventory holding levels
- Zero defect delivery
- Emergency need systems.

Intermediaries

Customers the world over are becoming increasingly demanding – the field of distribution logistics increasingly competitive, internationalised and dominated by major players. As mentioned earlier Federal Express has the sixth largest fleet of aircraft in the world, yet flies no passengers – dealing only with the shipment of goods. The following table puts this into perspective:

Table 12.1 Top scheduled freight carriers, 1994

	'000 tonnes
Federal Express	3,198
Lufthansa	909
Japan Airlines	778
Northwest Airlines	754
Korean Airlines	751
Air France	647
American Airlines	638
KLM	564
Singapore Airlines	534
United Airlines	523

Taking the same industry, determine what are the changes taking place that affect logistics (e.g. windows of delivery, development of new outlet types such as Garages). See if you can plot the dynamics of distribution and logistics.

ACTIVITY 12.2

The total distribution cost approach

Doole, Lowe and Phillips (1997) explain how and why international logistics not only incurs additional costs but is more complicated. The formula they propose is:

$$D = T + W + I + O + P + S$$

D = total distribution costs, T = transport cost, W = warehousing, I = inventory costs, O = order processing and documentation, P = packaging, and S = total cost of lost sales resulting in failure to meet customers' performance standards.

The extra costs in international logistics

1 Distance from customers means increased:
- Transport time
- Inventory
- Cashflow
- Insurance.

2 Additional variables include:
- transport   – sea
  - – air
  - – land
- Documentation
- Robust packaging (resistant to damage/pilfering)

3   Greater complexity
    • The dimension of culture
    • Language
    • More documentation
    • The management of additional transport modes.

ACTIVITY 12.3

In Unit 3 we identified macro factors influencing world trade. Can you relate some of these to the micro environment of distribution (e.g. the impact of urbanization)? Furthermore, examine the material towards the end of the unit dealing with global trends. Try bringing it all together.

Service levels

A few years ago successful businesses would have identified Information Technology (IT) as being the competitive differential. Today having IT means you can 'take part in the game', i.e. it is an essential prerequisite. The focus of competitive advantage has shifted to service.

Costs accelerate rapidly in response to increase in customer demands for availability and delivery. Near-perfect service (customer defined not company defined) is becoming the critical differentiator in the world marketplace as products become increasingly similar and it is difficult to distinguish one from another. Christopher (1987) identified the key discrimination as:

• Delivery response time to order
• Consistency and reliability of delivery
• Inventory availability
• Flexibility
• Ordering convenience
• Simplification of documentation
• Claims procedures
• Condition of goods on arrival
• Order status updates
• After-sales support.

These factors are difficult enough to deal with effectively on home territory. Problems magnify with physical and cultural differences. But remember, service standards will not be the same everywhere and the company, in order to succeed (profitably), must adjust its logistic to the needs of the customer and the marketplace. For example, in the UK, The Body Shop dictates a 2-hour delivery window on a designated date. Failure to comply means that its trucking company gets paid only certifiable costs and therefore delivers for free. Such demanding service levels are not universal, therefore why attempt to meet them? Deliver when the customer demands.

The subject of logistics is extremely complex. The international manager needs to be fully abreast of development in this field. However, the remit of this text is to remain strategic.

EXAM HINT

i

Under market entry strategies we highlighted the importance of making the right choice. Can you make the important linkage between entry strategy (see Unit 8) and implementation activities in the market? There is a direct relationship. In other words, follow through your thinking to make the link with the customer – getting close to customers is one of the basic rules of marketing.

Managing, selecting and controlling the distribution channel

Outside of setting up the firm's own distribution channel the organization is in part, or wholly, in the hands of intermediaries. Managing rather than controlling the channel(s) is critical to success in the marketplace. Here the dangers of SRC become apparent. Doole, Lowe and Phillips express this diagrammatically in Figure 12.2.

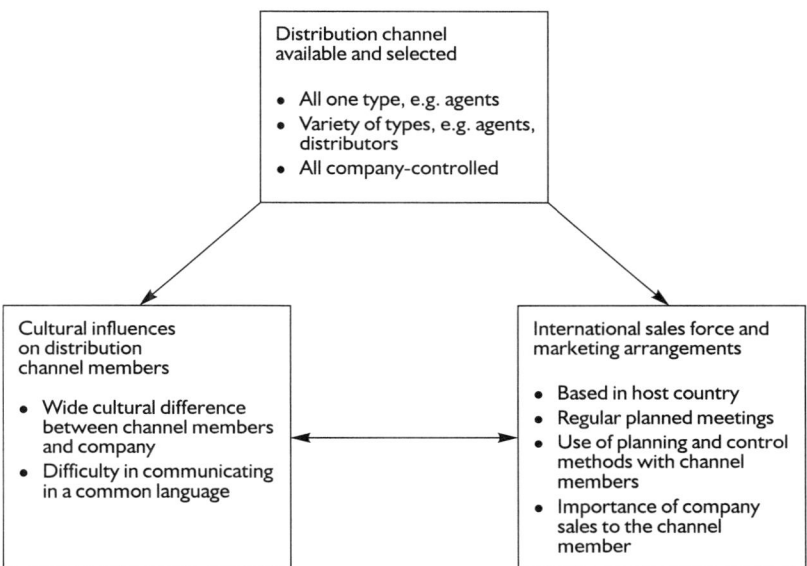

Figure 12.2 Distribution channels, cultural influences and their management. *Source*: Doole, Lowe and Phillips (1997)

The management and control aspect of distribution will inevitably be influenced by the channels selected and the number of intermediaries employed. The methods of selection have been distilled by various authors to a number of 'Cs' (Table 12.2). The factors that combine to deliver the critical balance between efficiency and effectiveness become immediately apparent. The first six in both lists are essentially concerned with Efficiency, the remainder Effectiveness. If there is to be a trade-off then Effectiveness must dominate and Efficiency is judged subjectively by the Customer, Culture and Competition in the marketplace.

Table 12.2 Different C methods for selecting distribution channels

Cateora	Czinkota and Ronkainen	Usunier	
Cost	Cost	Cost	
Capital	Capital	Capital	
Control	Control	Control	Efficiency
Coverage	Coverage	Coverage	
Character	Character	Character	
Continuity	Continuity	Continuity	
	PLUS	PLUS	
	Customer characteristics*	Customers and	
	Culture*	their characteristics*	
	Competition*	Culture*	Effectiveness
	Company objectives	Competition	
	Communication		

* External factors

Study your own organization, even if it is a domestic-only one. Examine the balance between the efficiency factor versus the effective ones. Be critical. My guess is that 80 per cent of your company's effort is not behind being effective (from the customer's viewpoint). If you can't do it in your domestic base, what chance overseas?

Selecting the intermediaries

These may be self-selecting where there is little alternative on offer. Where choice is available selection might be based on:

- Compatibility with customer requirements
- Sales potential
- Geographic coverage
- Breadth of coverage – present and future (always think ahead)
- Financial strength
- Managerial competence
- Service-mindedness, self-motivation
- Synergy with company goals and management.

Occasionally quite different intermediaries might be necessary within a single country – dependent upon ethnic and racial differences, and the urban–rural split.

Motivation of intermediaries

Cateora (1993) identifies five key categories:

- Financial rewards
- Psychological rewards
- Communications
- Company support
- Corporate rapport

Money is not always the right reward mechanism, although it is a powerful motivator everywhere. In the USA individual rewards work best, likewise in south-east Asia. In many countries, e.g. India, the ethics of non-confrontation clearly clashes with performance-led reviews. An additional point worth remembering is a product with poor sales potential is hardly likely to enthuse intermediaries.

A feeling of belonging, participating in success, partnership bonding all go a long way to bring the company and its intermediaries closer. Relationship building through communication, support and feeling a part of the company add the value that brings success, especially if the product is only a small part of the intermediary's wider portfolio.

Control

This is generally reduced or limited when dealing with intermediaries and sometimes objective performance cannot be implemented. However, a contractual agreement may be arrived at although this may not be binding, more a statement of intent. The Western practice is to create written legal agreements – the Eastern practice often takes the form of obligation and working together. Care needs to be employed in introducing the Western SRC of formalizing control via mechanistic methodology.

Finally, the termination of an agreement may not be simple or straightforward. Exit distribution strategies can be extremely costly in some parts of the world where agents can demand up to five times the annual gross profit, plus other penalties to account for goodwill, the cost of laying off employees, etc.

How do the differences in distribution channel arrangements adversely influence international logistics? Examine how customer service levels can be managed to reduce the impact of these differences (December 1994, Question 4).

The arrival of the global village has had a major impact on companies' distribution methods. Identify four major factors involved and explain how each has influenced distribution. (December 1997, Question 4)

(**See** Exam answers at the end of this unit.)

Global trends in distribution

Jeannet and Hennessey identify six major shifts in world distribution patterns:

1 *The internationalization of retailing* IKEA, Pizza Hut, Marks & Spencer, KFC, Toys'R'Us, McDonald's, The Body Shop, Benetton and others have all migrated around the world. It has recently been announced that Marks & Spencer are to open up in Shanghai as a first step in its planned expansion into China. It believes that there is potential to expand to 50 stores in the near future. This view is based on the company's successful foray into Hong Kong where it has eight stores, with many customers coming from the mainland.

   McDonald's, the world's largest fast food chain, is expanding its UK outlets by a further 50 in 1995 increasing its total to 630. A similar expansion programme is under way in many countries. With 14 000 outlets in 70 countries already, the group believes there is capacity for 20,000 by expanding into Eastern Europe and India. They bring with them world standards and systems, suppliers and financing and in doing so simplify the marketing environment.

2 *Large-scale retailing* This is a corollary of the above – the inevitable trend is towards large-scale retailers. The small retailer is in decline everywhere – even in developing countries as consumer mobility increases. There are serious implications for employment and dislocation to traditional cultural patterns of shopping.

3 *Direct marketing* This is restricted to countries with sophisticated infrastructure, nonetheless this field of distribution is expected to grow rapidly. Changing life-styles, the growth of women in employment, mobile phones and home PCs will fuel this growth.

4 *Discounting* Lower distribution costs bring suppliers, distributors and customers closer, forcing down prices worldwide; just about everybody now lives in a 'deal culture' with few wanting to pay top price. A direct result of points 1–3 has generated international competition with a driving down of prices. A further factor is the growth of regionalism, the removal of barriers, the ease and speed of distribution within the region – all serving to direct customers to bargain deals.

5 *Information technology* Suppliers source the world and so do distribution chains. The development of Just-in-Time inventory management means that products are delivered from all over the world, in a matter of days in some cases, broadening customer choice. In doing so they will simultaneously impair local customs and culture yet at the same time create world niche markets for products that otherwise might be restricted to a tiny corner of the world. An interesting paradox.

6 *Growth of own-label brands and development of retailer Eurobrands* Everywhere in the developed world manufactured brands are under challenge. The growth of major retailers has limited the power of the manufacturers to both develop and maintain their brands (e.g. Coca-Cola is under threat from Sainsbury's Classic Cola in the UK). As Sainsbury's and others internationalize (by acquisition or natural growth) so will the retailers' power place increasing pressure on manufacturers' brands. Whether this will

be of long-term benefit to customers remains an open question. That it will happen is not in doubt. Eventually there may be greater overlap and vertical integration between manufacturers and retailers globally.

EXAM QUESTIONS

- Evaluate the marketing factors that influence the attempts by retailers to become more international (June 1995, Question 5).
- What are the factors that influence the typical differences between retailers in developing and developed countries? Use examples to illustrate your answer (December 1995, Question 10).
- Moving goods from country to country is expensive. Up to 35% of the total cost of a product is accounted for by logistics and distribution. What are the main influences impacting on logistics and distribution strategy for international companies? (December 1996, Question 7)

ACTIVITY 12.5

See what linkage you can establish between the points made concerning the changing dynamics of distribution and the main factors under-pinning world trade in Unit 2 and Unit 3. There is a direct relationship.

Summary

Distribution and logistics is the fastest-changing area in international marketing. It is essential that companies monitor trends in international trade. Yesterday's methods can and are being outdated virtually overnight. Think how companies such as Direct Line have revolutionized the marketing of motor insurance in the UK and are now moving on to household insurance and mortgages.

Ideally, firms would like to deal direct with customers. It may happen in the UK but in overseas markets it may not be feasible. Political and other numerous factors prevent this. The firm would also like to use a similar distribution chain to its home market. Again it is extremely rare that distribution and logistical systems in one country is replicated elsewhere. There are too many variables. Whatever route(s) is chosen, care must be taken to plan and control the effort. Inefficiencies have to be minimized in order to succeed.

Questions

- Outline the key factors in developing distribution strategy.
- Put in charge of exporting JCB constructional equipment, what issues do you need to consider in entering the Kuwait market following the termination of the Gulf War?
- Having considered the dynamics of fashion retailing, what distribution strategies would you recommend for a worldwide manufacture of designer footwear (e.g. the Timberland range of shoes)?
- In what way might the element of an international logistics system be different from a domestic one?
- As the marketing manager of a range of car polishes and equipment sold to car owners you have been asked to consider an appropriate distribution system. As an export organization what steps might you take before implementing any distribution system? What logistical concern do you have and what control mechanisms might you apply?

International Marketing Strategy, I. Doole, R. Lowe and C. Phillips, Routledge, 1997.

International Marketing, S. Paliwoda and M. Thomas, Butterworth-Heinemann, 1998.

International Marketing, V. Terpstra and R. Sarathy, The Dryden Press, 1997.

Global Marketing Strategies, J.-P. Jeannet and H. D. Hennessey, Houghton-Mifflin, 1998.

Because of the complex detail involved in fully comprehending distribution and logistics the following reference text is included as recommended reading:

Elements of Export Marketing & Management, Branch, Chapman & Hall, 1990.

With the introduction of Syllabus '94 the emphasis of the examination paper has shifted away from the tactical aspects of marketing (e.g. export documentation) to a wider appreciation of distribution and logistics. There has only been one question set on this specific topic to date. Expect more in the future.

December 1994, Question 4 This question has a certain overlap and similarities with the mini-case (World Freight Services, see Unit 15, p. 232). This subject is in the forefront of international marketing. Candidates should take note of the observations made in the mini-case study guideline answer. As ever, structure is the key to a successful answer, which should contain the following:

1 Definition and description of the main distribution channels, e.g. for a consumer goods company.
2 Definition of logistics, i.e. logistics are concerned with considering the customer and working back to the factory (Kotler).

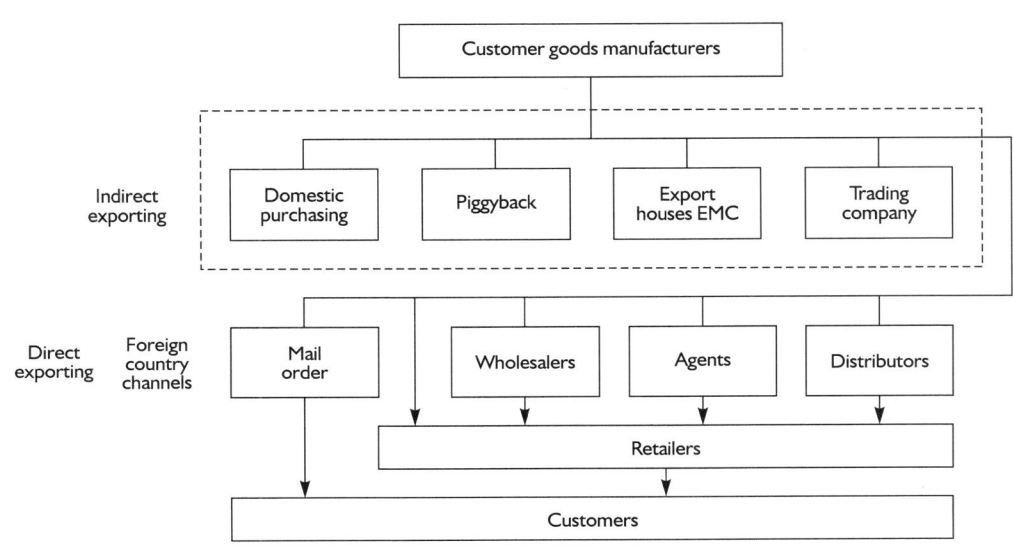

3   An understanding of the make-up of customer service levels, e.g. Christopher has identified that effective service levels revolve around:

- delivery on time
- consistency/reliability of delivery
- inventory availability
- order, size constraints
- ordering convenience
- delivery time/flexibility
- condition of goods
- relationship with sales person
- after sales support
  etc.

4   Following on from this, an understanding of the total distribution concept would need to be shown. One such method might be expressed in the following formula:

$$D = T + W + I + O + P + S$$

where
D = distribution
T = transport cost
W = warehouse cost
I = inventory cost
O = order processing
P = packaging cost
S = total cost of lost sales from not meeting performance standards

5   How can service levels be managed etc? The issues are:

- cost versus profitability
- the specific needs of its market (markets differ, therefore customer needs differ and so must service levels: the key is to match the service level appropriateness of the customers)
- competition, both domestic and international
- cultural interactions
- success in this area comes from matching strategic planning with detailed tactical implementation

December 1997, Question 4   Answering this question allows candidates a fair degree of flexibility as the factors influencing the global village are numerous. Unit 2 above identifies the following points, but the list could continue.

- Population explosion.
- Increasing affluence.
- One world youth culture.
- Global consumers.
- Multinationals.
- Shrinking communications (of all sorts).
- Information revolution.
- Time! the competitive differential.
- Global product standardization.
- Global competition.
- World brands.
- Urbanization.

- Global interconnection of capital.
- Globalization of management and marketing skills.
- Development of world technology.
- Strategic and international cooperation.
- Regionalization and trade blocks.

All of the factors interconnect and create the global village.

The question asks that four of these factors be related to the distribution function of the international marketing mix. Purely for indication purposes I have selected only two.

1 Multinationals
   With 500 or so companies controlling (directly and indirectly) up to 30% of global product; up to 70% of world trade and around 80% of international investment, their impact on distribution cannot be underestimated. Everywhere multinationals are coordinating their logistical/distribution function.

   - They are cutting costs by reducing inventory.
   - Production sharing is essential to success.
   - They are standardizing both components and finished goods.
   - They are focusing on being world class producers of goods – forming strategic alliances (partnerships) with world class distribution companies, e.g. Hewlett Packard and Federal Express. The former ships (by air) its entire worldwide production to Singapore where it is then moved onwards to customers – on demand and within 24 hours. Fed-Ex has the expertise to accomplish this.

   Answers should be expressed along the lines of the strategic issues just highlighted.

2 Time: the competitive differential
   Federal Express is the sixth largest airline in the world, yet flies no passengers. Companies, their suppliers and their customers are all increasingly interlinked and everyone nowadays demands near perfect service. With increasing similarity of products, delivery and service is increasingly the competitive differential. The key discriminators have been identified as:

   - Delivery response time to order, i.e. flexibility.
   - Consistency of delivery.
   - Reliability of delivery.
   - Inventory availability.
   - Flexibility.
   - Ordering convenience.
   - After sales support.

Top quality answers must contain one solid example in every case; really good candidates will have read extensively in this subject area. The quality press does contain relevant examples. (See also Doole, Lowe and Phillips, 1997, chapter 10.)

June 1995, Question 5 As one travels the world today, it is increasingly common to find not only the same products in different countries but even the same retailers – although it must be stated clearly that for the vast majority of organizations, international retailing is very much in its infancy and is today largely ethnocentric. Take a good close look at your high street – how many shops have international parents or subsidiaries? But returning to the first point, set out below is a short list of retailers who are already internationalizing their operations.

- Benetton (Italy)
- Body Shop (UK)
- McDonald's (USA)
- Pizza Hut (USA)
- KFC (USA)
- Toys 'R' Us (USA)
- Ikea (Sweden)
- C&A (Holland)
- Marks & Spencer (UK)

Of course, there are many others.

Factors influencing the internationalizing of retailing are many. They include:

- The development of global consumers with broadly similar requirements.
- The recent creation of the one-world youth culture; where teenagers everywhere project worldwide cultural icons – Niké, Benetton.
- Increasing affluence – people everywhere are getting richer with more disposable income, with personal transport, etc.
- The information revolution; technology has made logistics simpler and has transformed the transference of news, fashion trends, etc.
- Shrinking communications – nowhere is far away, customers are converging.
- The development of world brands – a recent global survey showed that McDonald's Golden Arches is now the world's number one reconizable symbol (Coca-Cola being the number one brand).

There are, of course, other reasons, not least of which is the growing social trend towards urbanization, which in marketing terms means that customers can more easily converge to a single retail site, e.g. supermarket, whereas previously they could only shop in their immediate locality. This factor probably is the most single influence in the development of modern retailing.

However, as stated earlier, although there is a strong trend towards retailing becoming more international, there are many reasons why this development should not proceed as quickly as international product development:

1 Customers often remain rooted in their ethnocentricity with product manu-facturers adapting to local distribution networks.
2 Government regulations often restrict the growth of large scale retailing, e.g. Japan has a law, Daiten Ho, which gives existing retailers a veto over the establishment of any new large scale retailers. It took government to government intervention for Toys 'R' Us to gain entry into the Japanese market.
3 Developing countries often have a dual economy, with capital cities being modern whilst 20 km away the population exists in a large rural society served by village shops. Only prosperity and personal mobility (motor bikes/ cars) can break down the pattern. But it probably will come.

Note: This is a guideline answer. There are many influences on international retailing not covered above, e.g. saturation of home market, i.e. several major UK food retailers are moving on to continental Europe. It is a 'catch all' question designed to test candidates' awareness of international marketing/business. The answers to this type of question are to be found in the quality press/journals.

December 1995, Question 10 **Note:** This was the third question on this paper that dealt with culture. It is a question that demands examples and would be answered easily by those candidates who have engaged in the wider reading in the subject area via the quality press and journals.

It is true that in recent years we have witnessed a growth in the internationalization of retailing, with firms such as Body Shop, Benetton, McDonalds, Pizza Hut and others becoming world/global organizations. But despite this trend, the fact remains that retailing is essentially an ethnocentric industry, reflecting local values, different levels of economic development and local culture variations.

For example, the cultural importance in some countries – notably Italy – provides opportunities for small specialist food shops to thrive. But in the UK and the USA, the trend is towards out-of-town superstores and shopping malls. This has important implications for manufacturers, for to receive a 'no' decision from a few retailers on stocking a product in Italy does not have a major impact on sales, but in the UK a 'no' from Sainsbury, Tesco and Asda means losing over 50% of sterling distribution, virtually consigning a product to a non-runner in branded goods category markets.

In comparing developing with developed countries, we can consider the following factors that influence the differences:

Retailing issues	Urban and rural retailers in developing countries	Retailers in developed countries
Concentration of retailer power	Low	High (frequency)
Site selection and location	Limited in scale and immediate locality	Vital – huge investment to obtain optimum location between urban centres
Size of outlet	Small	Very large/superstores
Capital employed	Limited	Very large, wide range of stock with multi-brand/own label etc.
Corporate identity/retail concept	Very low	Essential – Tesco, Toys'R'Us etc.
Promotional expenditure	Low/rare	Vital in branding/offers etc.
Use of technology	Low; counter service	Very important, self-selection, EPOS, Just-in-Time

It is clear from the above table that the differences can be profound – this is not to say that large cities in developing countries are dominated by 'moma & papa' stores, for they are not. Urbanization creates a purchasing dynamic, with married couples both working, shopping weekly, buying in bulk and having branded goods with convenience values such as chilled complete meals/refrigerated and microwave-ready products.

December 1996, Question 7 The following are guidelines only.

This is a contemporary question, as logistics and distribution are rapidly becoming a competitive advantage. Top-quality answers will draw the links between a shrinking world, developments of world market – global customers with business-to-business customer segments and the key role of logistics. The key to the answer is the customer – meeting and satisfying the needs of whom is the only requirement of business. In this regard the following are essential requirements and increasingly essential just to 'remain in the game':

- Delivery scheduling
- JIT
- Zero defect
- Flexibility
- Inventory holding
- Simplifying of procedure
- After-sales support and service levels

Really good answers incorporate current trends – developments in distribution/logistics of the moment, which include:

- International retailing
- Global brands
- International direct marketing and electronic marketing worldwide (IT)

Dull answers will focus just around the total distribution cost of

$$D = T + W + I + O + P + S$$

A further description of the key components of the answer appear in this unit (p. 171).

International pricing policy

Pricing policy generally is one of the most important yet often least recognized of all the elements of the marketing mix. If we stop to think about it, all the other elements of the marketing mix (both domestic and international) are costs. The only source of profit to the organization comes from revenue, which is in turn dictated by pricing policy. Internationally as well, the way in which an organization fixes and regulates prices in its foreign markets will have a direct affect on profits and profitability. In this unit you will:

- Evaluate the factors which influence the implementation of pricing policy in international markets
- Review the objectives behind pricing policy
- Understand how prices are set
- Consider how export prices are set
- Consider internal transfer pricing and methods of non-cash payment
- Review alternative pricing strategies for international markets.

Having completed this unit you will be able to:

- Appreciate the factors which affect pricing policy
- Understand how to respond to these factors and set market-based pricing strategies
- Integrate pricing policy into the other elements of the international marketing mix.

As already stated, the appreciation of pricing policy is essential to the long-term profitability and growth of any organization. Although often integrated into other aspects and questions such as marketing mix analyses, pricing forms a major plank between the organization and its customer base. Consequently, this unit on pricing policy needs to be studied in conjunction with many of the other units in this book, specifically Unit 9 (Product policy), Unit 10 (Financial implications) and Unit 14 (Evaluation and control methods).

As you proceed through this unit you should also bear in mind that international markets, like domestic markets, are driven not by cost but by value. While very few customers, both industrial and consumer, will automatically buy the cheapest product or service on offer they will constantly search for the offer which they believe offers them greatest value for money given their needs and aspirations.

Questions on international pricing have also appeared in a number of the major cases (Analysis and Decision) with, it must be said, disappointing results. Pricing policy is simply too important to ignore; the successful marketer cannot progress while ignoring anything to do with numbers.

International pricing policy

Establishing the right price for international markets is no easy matter. There are a number of factors involved in the decision process and a number of stages which it may be worth reviewing before the organization sets its price or establishes any precedents in a foreign marketplace. Figure 13.1 shows a logical flow process through the eight major questions which confront the international marketer considering pricing policy. The rest of this unit will consider these steps one by one and the major issues involved in setting the right price.

Figure 13.1   Setting the right price

How are prices determined in your organization:

- For the domestic market?
- For international markets?

Are they the same or different methods? Why?

Pricing objectives

Before we can decide what price or prices the organization should be charging for its products and services in an overseas market or markets we need to understand clearly the objectives behind the pricing policy that will meet the organization's needs. Some of the objectives which may be relevant to the organization are as follows:

- *Rate of return*   Often useful for setting minimum price levels. What is the required internal rate of return that the organization needs to justify the investment in the overseas market in the first instance?
- *Market stabilisation*   Keeping prices relatively constant and secure over the long term against competition so as not to provoke retaliation.
- *Demand-led pricing*   Where prices are adjusted to meet changes in customer demand. These may be caused by seasonality or other market changes.

- *Competition-led pricing*   Where prices are kept closely tagged to the competition and thereby maximize profit and profitability for all players.
- *Product differentiation*   Pricing the product or service on offer differently to add to the sense and imagery surrounding the differentiated nature of the product.
- *Market skimming*   Pricing to attract the very top end of any market at premium price levels, thereby also controlling distribution and sales and stocking levels.
- *Market penetration*   The opposite of market skimming whereby the organization prices to maximize sales and normally operates at relatively low margins.

Why should a UK supplier invoice export goods in a foreign currency? Examine the advantages and disadvantages of foreign currency invoicing (December 1992).

(**See** Exam answers at the end of this unit.)

- *Early cash recovery*   If the organization, for whatever reasons, requires fast recovery and cash in its balances to price the product or service accordingly to generate a fast response from the marketplace.
- *To prevent competitive entry*   Often a lower price is used as a barrier to prevent other organizations from entering into a market by making it unprofitable to do so.

Factors affecting prices

The second stage in the pricing process is to identify all those factors that are likely to affect the price that the organization sets. Factors affecting pricing can be broken down into three broad areas as follows:

- *Company and product factors*   Would include corporate and marketing objectives as well as the market position held by the organization and the product. The product or service being priced also has a position in the product range and on the life-cycle and faces certain types of competition from the market in which it is to be placed. Cost structures within the organization as well as inventory and transportation costs will be major factors which will influence the final price level.

What is the relative importance of company/market/environment factors in the pricing policy in your organization? Do you think this is the right balance?

- *Market factors*   Primarily centred around customers and their expectations and perceptions of the product or service which the organization is offering, exactly what price level is the market willing to pay? The local market situation in terms of distribution channels and accepted practice in discounting procedures as well as market growth and elasticity of demand will also affect the price potential. The extent to which the organization has had to adapt or modify the product or service and the level to which the market requires service around the core product will also affect cost and will have some influence on pricing.
- *Environmental factors*   Factors beyond the customer that will affect the prices charged will include competition (their objectives, strategies and relative strengths) as well as government and legislative influences (currency fluctuations, recession, business cycle stage, inflation, etc.).

All these factors will need to be analysed and assessed on a market-by-market basis to produce a pricing policy that is both profitable and acceptable to the local marketplace. At the same time, the international marketer must balance the local requirements and interests against the organization's aspirations on a broader international/global basis. While factors may push price levels in one direction for a given market, a close or neighbouring market may be influenced differently. Although, as we will see later, standardization of prices is not necessarily an objective that the organization should follow, neither should prices in neighbouring or comparative markets be too far out of line.

EXAM QUESTION

What measures can a company take to minimize the impact of parallel importing? (December 1994)

(**See** Exam answers at the end of this unit.)

Setting prices

There are a number of ways in which the organization might decide to fix its prices in its international markets. These are briefly described as follows:

- *Cost based* The process by which prices are based on costs of production (and may include costs of distribution too) and then are normally marked up by a predetermined margin level. The cost-based approach to pricing is likely to produce price levels that appear inconsistent from a customer or market point of view. At the same time, this approach can be useful in order to stimulate a fast return of cash from the marketplace and/or inhibit the entry of the competition into that marketplace.
- *Market based pricing* The customers' willingness to pay. This approach needs to be based on market research or a good understanding of the competition's pricing approach and can be a useful method of extracting the maximum profitability from the marketplace.
- *Competition based pricing* Involves using the competition as a benchmark for fixing prices. Competition either in direct or substitutional form allows the organization to position its product or service relative to the competition in the customers' eyes and to establish a differentiated offer in the competitive range. This method can also be used as a way of creating barriers to entry with low prices preventing competitive entry to particular international markets.

Export pricing

When marketing internationally through exports (from domestic production) there is the question of what price to set relative to the domestic price. Generally, costs are slightly higher for export than for domestic operations because markets are often smaller and transportation costs tend to be higher. Prices could be higher to cover these additional costs but, at the same time, if they are too high they are likely to encourage parallel importing. Another question to consider in export pricing is the currency of quotation. Some organizations quote export prices in domestic currency and some in foreign currency. One of the two parties, the buyer or the seller, will eventually need to carry the transaction risk associated with currency fluctuations in international markets. The longer the period between quotation and invoice payment, the greater that transaction risk will be.

A final point in terms of export pricing, typically of interest to smaller organizations, is the possibility for export credit or payment guarantees offered by many governments throughout the world. Under this method (which in the UK is run by the ECGD), subject to certain conditions, the governments, in order to promote export sales, offers insurance against non-payment of export orders.

- What is dumping? Identify three different types of dumping. Taking one type of dumping, explain why evidence of dumping might be difficult to establish (December 1992)
- Explain the factors companies need to take into account in establishing an international pricing strategy (December 1996, Question 6).

(**See** Exam answers at the end of this unit.)

Transfer pricing (internal)

Another pricing question which affects many international and multinational organizations is how to arrange the pricing between two subsidiaries of the same organization in different foreign markets. The three approaches open to the organization in this instance are as follows:

- *At cost*   The producing subsidiary supplies to the marketing subsidiary at cost. In this event the producing subsidiary is treated as a cost base and the profits are accumulated at the point-of-sale (the marketing subsidiary).
- *At cost plus*   Through this approach the profits are either shared between the two subsidiaries or, at the extreme, superprofits can be made at the producing subsidiary while losses can be incurred at the marketing subsidiary.
- *At arms length*   Under this approach the producing subsidiary treats the marketing subsidiary as it would any other customer and deals on a straight and strict commercial basis with the other part of the organization.

With transfer pricing international and multinational organizations have some degree of control about where profits are created in the organization as well as how funds might be moved among the various subsidiaries of the business. However, where profits are made is also where taxes are payable, and tax authorities on a worldwide basis are increasingly interested in how multinational organizations arrange pricing between subsidiaries. Penalties for misuse of the transfer pricing system are extremely high in many countries and the multinational organizations have only limited power to manipulate margins and the accumulation of profits on a global scale.

Questions on pricing and pricing strategy are regular in the examinations. Experience, however, has shown that candidates' grasp of the factors which influence pricing is shaky. Make sure you understand:

- The role of pricing in marketing strategy
- The special challenges in pricing for international markets.

Pricing strategies

When considering international pricing strategy international marketers have two broad extremes open to them. The organization can attempt to standardize its prices throughout all the markets in which it operates or it can opt to adapt them to local conditions on a market-by-market basis.

The arguments for standardization and for adaptation were well outlined in Unit 9 where we considered product policy. The same arguments apply in terms of pricing policy for international markets.

The optimum approach, as ever, will depend upon the market and the organization's characteristics. Generally, a balance between the two extremes will be the most profitable and most logical route for the organization to follow. Some degree of standardization or conformity on pricing is required, certainly among markets or groups of markets which are geographically close. On the other hand, the number of factors that drive prices are likely to vary to such an extent as to make standardized pricing an impractical proposition for most organizations.

Non-cash payment

In some international marketing situations the case may arise where payment is offered but not in normal cash terms. This is often the case with business from less developed countries (LDCs) and former Eastern bloc markets which may not have access to foreign currency or whose own local currency is not acceptable to the marketing organization. In these instances it is often wiser not simply to discard the transaction out of hand but to look at other still profitable ways of concluding the business. There are two broad areas in which such non-cash payments can be acceptable. These are:

- *Leasing* This can be used as an alternative to straight purchase in markets where currency or capital is simply not available to the purchasing organization. Leasing can be attractive to both the buyer since it enables use of a product or service which otherwise would not be available to them and to the seller since a sale is made and purchase price is staggered (possibly including full service and maintenance) over a longer period of time.
- *Counter-trade* This is a term used to cover a range of arrangements where some or all of the payment for the products or service is in the form of other products or services rather than in cash. Estimates vary as to the proportion of world trade which is covered by counter-trade measures but the proportion is significant. Arrangements included under the heading of counter-trade include items such as barter (a straight swap or transfer of goods) through to switch deals often including a third party which disposes of the bartered goods in exchange for currency through to buy-back arrangements whereby some or all of the cost of purchase is paid for through the production generated by the purchase items.

ACTIVITY 13.3

In your organization (or one that you know well), how important is non-cash payment? Have offers of non-cash payment been refused in the past? How might a western company be made aware of the potential for deals of this type?

Although Western marketers have a natural inclination to concentrate on arrangements which involve the transfer of cash, counter-trade should not be ignored. Not only does it open up markets which otherwise would remain closed for many years, it also, surprisingly enough, offers the opportunity for even greater profits than might be achievable through a straightforward cash transaction.

ACTIVITY 13.4

Have you heard of the 'Big Mac Index' as a method of assessing and comparing markets? Find out what it is and who might use it.

Summary

In this unit we have considered the array of factors which influence and should help the international marketer to determine international pricing policy. Pricing is probably one of the most complicated areas of international marketing strategy but has major impact upon the financial performance of the organization. Pricing also plays a major role in supporting product strategy (differentiation and positioning) as well as communication strategy where it has a major impact on perceived quality.

We have seen that in order to arrive at sensible prices the international marketer needs to understand the objectives behind the pricing approach as well as the factors which are often different from market to market. Standardized pricing approaches for international markets are not always necessary although some degree of coordination between markets may be desirable if only to stop the possibility of parallel importing.

Pricing is treated by many marketers as a tactical activity. In this unit you should have understood that pricing policy has a major strategic influence on the organization and should not be relegated to purely tactical decision making at a lower level.

Questions

As a check on your understanding of what has been covered in this unit, consider the following questions:

- How does pricing policy interact with other elements of the marketing mix?
- What might affect an organization's pricing objectives?
- What factors affect a final price?
- How might an organization go about setting the price for its product/service in an international market?
- How are the domestic and export prices linked?
- What are the three methods of transfer pricing?
- What is meant by 'non-cash payment'?
- Give examples of 'countertrade'.

For a more detailed analysis and explanation of international pricing policy read:

International Marketing, S. Paliwoda and M. Thomas, Butterworth-Heinemann, 1998.
International Marketing Strategy, I. Doole, R. Lowe and C. Phillips, Routledge, 1997.

December 1992 Setting foreign market prices is a critical task for the international marketer. However, setting the price level is only one, albeit important, facet of the international pricing decision. In addition, a decision must be made as to the currency in which export goods will be invoiced. There are four major alternatives for the international marketer, namely:

- invoicing in the seller's own (domestic) currency;
- invoicing in the buyer's (foreign) currency;
- invoicing in a 'third party' currency;
- invoicing in a common currency.

There is little doubt that the easiest and, in one sense, least risky of all of these alternatives is where the seller (exporter) quotes and invoices in his own (domestic) currency. Invoicing in this way is administratively simple for the seller and the risk of the exchange rate is carried by the customer. However, not surprisingly, invoicing in the seller's currency is not very customer-orientated – indeed, it is not customer-orientated at all. The risk, therefore, is that a potential customer may be lost to another supplier who is prepared to quote and invoice in the currency of the customer. The advantages to the customer of invoicing in his/her currency are as follows:

- Any exchange risks due to devaluation in the customer's currency are imposed on the exporter.
- It is simpler for the customer to understand and administer.

The main advantage to the seller of invoicing in the foreign currency is that because it is more marketing-orientated there is a greater chance of securing and retaining customers.

As so often in marketing, there is a trade-off between invoicing in either the customer's or the supplier's currency. So how should the trade-off be resolved, i.e. how can the marketer decide on the issue of currency of invoice? The following will tend to affect the choice between these two alternatives.

- Trade practices in the country and industry in question, i.e. in some countries/industries trade practices would mean that invoicing in the supplier's currency would not be acceptable.
- The bargaining power of the parties/extent of competition: in a buyer's market the exporters will be more anxious to clinch a sale. Consequently, the invoice will more likely be in the customer's currency. In a seller's market and/or where there is little competition, the supplier will be able to invoice in the domestic currency.

Since the early 1970s most major currencies have been floating, giving rise to considerable potential risk to both importers and exporters alike. Because of this, the supplier in particular may decide to try to cover the risk by covering forward in the exchange market. In fact, covering forward needs to be done with great care. Considerable profit can be achieved in this way, but so too can dramatic losses.

Sometimes, both seller and buyer may agree to pricing in a third party currency, particularly where this currency is widely available and reasonably stable.

Increasingly though, common currencies may be used for quoting and invoicing in the future between members of trading blocks. For example, many members of the European Common Market use the European currency unit (ECU) for cross-border invoicing purposes. Alternatively, another system is the use of the special drawing right (SDR) system to some of the risks associated with floating exchange rates and invoicing.

Overall great care needs to be taken when considering the issue of the currency of invoicing.

December 1994 **Notes to candidates**: A good approach might be to define parallel importing followed by a brief description of its causes with the measures to minimize it related directly to the causes, i.e. pose the problems – provide the solutions.

Parallel importing

Sometimes referred to as grey marketing, which involves the importing and selling of products through market distribution channels not authorized by the manufacturer. It tends to occur when there are significant differences in prices for the same product in different countries. With modern distribution systems driving down costs, parallel importing has spread from a practice that generally affected neighbouring countries, to become a worldwide problem. The key requirement for parallel importing is a significant end price to the consumer. This tends to happen when:

1 companies have different distribution mechanisms in different countries;
2 there is an agreed pricing structure in a given market with a key distributor;

3   companies practise price skimming strategies in some markets and penetration strategies in other, e.g. a skimming or high price strategy in a mature market, a penetration strategy in a newly entered market where buying share is important.

Other factors considered to be important are:

1   Products must be available internationally, i.e. desired by a wide consumer base – increasingly so as markets standardize or globalize.
2   Barriers to entry are low in terms of tariffs, legal restrictions (I have already mentioned transport/distribution).

A further very important factor is *currency fluctuations* which enable products to be bought in markets with weak currencies and sold where currencies are strong.

Measures/factors to be considered to minimize parallel importing

1   Better price planning on a pan-regional/worldwide basis.
2   Track/monitor abnormal purchases either from unusual sources or on unusually high orders from one of the company's named distributors in an overseas market.
3   Educate/replace weaker dealers.
4   Confront the grey marketer by tactical pricing. Let him know you will restrict his opportunity.
5   Take legal action if it is possible. In the UK the major cosmetic companies successfully sued Superdrug – a price discounter.
6   Be creative in marketing communications – build brand loyalties.
7   Acquire the grey marketer or reach a mutually satisfactory accommodation.
8   Develop good management information systems to identify the problem.

This answer could be expanded to discuss ethical issues such as: Is parallel importing such a bad thing? Should not the consumer be the one to benefit? The major drug/ pharmaceutical companies sometimes agree high prices with a country's government. The UK is a case in point where local health authorities cannot purchase certain drugs at below a specific price – even though they are theoretically available from other neighbouring markets.

December 1992   Put simply, 'dumping' is where an exporter has a deliberate policy of selling items abroad at prices which do not cover the total cost incurred in producing and marketing the items. Or put another way, it is a deliberate policy of selling products at a 'loss'. The definition and ensuing identification of dumping strategies is vitally important due to the fact that in most economies and trading blocs and agreements 'dumping' is not only frowned upon but is actually illegal. There are a number of reasons for this dim view of dumping, but essentially dumping is felt to be unfair trade leading to overall imbalances in the use of world resources. GATT, in particular, has been a leading advocate in the fight against the worst excesses of unfair dumping.

However, the seemingly simple and straightforward description of what constitutes dumping outlined at the start of this answer in fact masks the complexity of the dumping process. There are different types of dumping, and in practice, evidence of dumping – often needed as a prelude to taking action against it – can be difficult to establish.

The three principal different types of dumping are as follows:

(a)   *Sporadic*   This is usually a response to an excess production/stock situation. Rather than unload this surplus at reduced prices in the home market – which might destroy long-term demand – the surplus is 'dumped' into export markets.

(b) *Predatory* This type of dumping is part of a long-term strategy to undermine indigenous producers and marketers by undercutting their prices. In the long term it is hoped to buy market share and make it impossible for the local producers to survive. This strategy requires considerable financial resources and is often said to be supported by hidden government subsidies.

(c) *Persistent* This type of dumping is where products are consistently sold at prices lower than those in the home market for a long period of time. This might be done, for example, in order to obtain foreign currency and so can be politically – or at least governmentally – inspired.

All three types of dumping are illegal under most trade agreements. However, even though based on different approaches and reasons, all three types of dumping can be very difficult to 'prove' and hence act against. Remember that 'dumping' is selling at less than home produced cost; hence one might argue that the easiest way to 'prove' dumping is to compare prices in the exporter's home country with those being charged in export markets. Where export prices are lower, then one might argue there is evidence of dumping.

However, if we take the example of predatory dumping, the exporter might argue that costs, and hence prices, are lower than in domestic markets because of the improved economies of scale which access to export markets gives rise to. Alternatively, it might be argued that the costs of distribution and/or margins required by distributors are lower in export markets, giving rise to lower prices. Finally, with this form of dumping, prices in export markets may in fact not be lower than those in the exporter's domestic market simply because the exporter's government are in fact providing some sort of subsidy to the exporter, effectively allowing the products to be sold (dumped) at less than full cost. Needless to say, this sort of 'dumping' can be very difficult to prove, particularly where the subsidies are hidden.

In conclusion, dumping results in long-term distortion to international trade. It is also unfair. Because of this it will continue to be outlawed by most governments and/or trading blocs.

However, although seemingly simple to define and identify in principle, in practice dumping can be extremely difficult to identify and even more difficult to police and control.

December 1996, Question 6 This is an 'open' question – therefore there is a degree of largesse in the scope for answers. Some candidates (weaker ones) will focus on the tactical aspects, giving for example, the components of the development of a 'price' in an export-driven organization. Better candidates will grasp the more strategic aspects of the role of price in international marketing relating to corporate positioning and developing global strategies.

Factors influencing pricing

Company and product pricing

- Corporate and marketing objectives
- Company and product positioning – plus ethnocentric, polycentric, regiocentric, geocentric positioning
- Product range, life cycle, substitute, Unique Selling Proposition, etc.
- Cost structure, production, economies of scale, production sharing
- Marketing and new product development costs
- Inventory
- Distribution and logistics
- Working capital
- etc.

Market factors

- Customer perceptions, expectation, ability to pay
- Degree of adaptability of product to market
- Market servicing
- Market structure, distribution channels length and breadth
- Degree of discounting, margins
- Market growth, elasticity of demand
- Credit facilities – cost of money
- Competition; direct, indirect, substitute

Environmental factors

- Government influence and constraints
- Currency fluctuations
- Inflation
- Business cycle stage
- Use of non-money payment
- Leasing

Evaluation and control methods

Evaluation and control methods are key issues in international marketing strategy. Nothing the international marketing manager can do can remove risk completely from business decisions that are made, but careful and proper evaluation of strategy before implementation, coupled with rigorous control methods during implementation itself, can reduce these risks to levels more acceptable in highly competitive situations. In this unit you will learn how to evaluate international marketing strategy and control strategic implementation. More specifically, you will:

- Review the objectives set for international marketing strategy
- Evaluate strategy against the set objectives
- Review the planning processes appropriate with the international business strategy
- Understand the control systems necessary to ensure proper implementations of international marketing plans.

Having completed this unit you will be able to:

- Evaluate the suitability of specific international marketing strategies
- Develop control systems for the implementation of international marketing strategy.

STUDY GUIDE

It is an important fact in today's markets that no matter how elegant, sophisticated or quantified an international marketing plan might be, unless it is executed in an equally sophisticated manner it will remain simply a document on a manager's shelf. Implementation and control systems are now key features on all Diploma examination papers and you are urged to prepare this section fully and be able to explain various measures open to the organization in your examination answer. To underline the importance that the examiners place on this unit, they estimate that it should require 10% of notional hours taught. That is twice the amount of time dedicated to any of the components of the international marketing mix (Product, Price, Distribution or Promotion)!

In this section you should be able to work carefully to apply the knowledge you have acquired in domestic marketing strategy into the international marketing arena. The Planning and Control paper and the Analysis and Decision paper now cover this element of the syllabus in great detail.

After you have completed this unit you should also spend some time talking to managers in your organization as well as looking beyond your organization to other industries to discover the different criteria used and control systems which are employed in practice.

This unit should be studied in relation to other units in this workbook, notably Introduction, Unit 1 (Identifying international opportunities) and Unit 6 (International market planning). The activities in this unit are especially important. Evaluation and control methods are difficult to learn from a book and need to be seen in operation. Try hard to complete the activities before taking the examination.

Evaluating strategies

How do we evaluate international marketing strategy? Here the answer is relatively simple and straightforward. It is the extent to which the strategy is expected to or is seen to achieve the objectives set for the activity.

When looking at organizations' objectives for international marketing strategy we should refer back to the introduction section of this workbook and specifically Figure I.4. This diagram, which outlines the international business process, starts, quite properly, with two key inputs. These are: information on foreign market potential and the organization's objectives. A clear, concise and understandable definition of the organization's objectives is crucial to the development of any robust and practical international marketing strategy.

EXAM HINT

Examination questions on evaluation and control are rare. However, a number of questions contain an evaluation or control element. The mini-case study is an area where control systems are important. The major case study (Analysis and Decision) paper has taken to making evaluation and control of international operations a major element to the questions!

Set against the background of a clear, concise and understandable objective for the organization, the evaluation of the marketing strategy becomes a relatively straightforward operation. As we can see from Figure 14.1, the strategic process as followed by all papers in the Diploma set of examinations essentially follows four steps. Stage 1 involves an audit of the organization's current situation, Stage 2 involves setting clear, concise objectives for the future development of the organization, Stage 3 involves strategic options and Stage 4 involves choice and control systems. For the international organization, having proceeded from Stage 1 through to 2 the next question is what are the various routes by which the organization might achieve its international objectives. Stage 4 (the section with which we are concerned in this unit) is about how we choose among the alternative strategic options and how we control implementation.

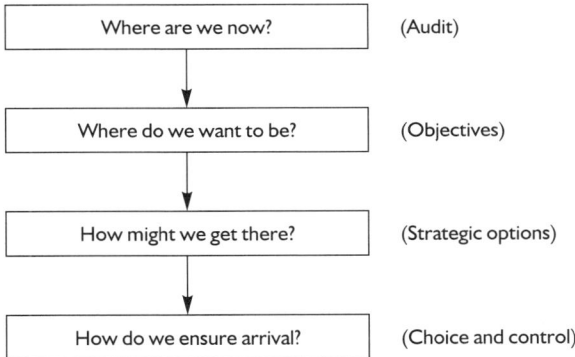

Figure 14.1

Evaluation of strategic options is never simple since nothing in the commercial world is guaranteed. We are never sure which strategic options are likely to work within the competitive environment and which ones, although looking very good, will not produce the results required.

How is international marketing strategy evaluated in your organization? Comparing the method to the ideas contained in this workbook, what changes, if any, would you recommend?

Typically, evaluation of strategic options falls under a number of concise categories. These are as follows:

Short versus long term

Strategy is about marshalling the gross resources of the organization to match the needs of the marketplaces and achieve the business objective, so this cannot be a short-term activity. Marketing, like other areas of management is full of managers who are driven solely by the short term. Not only is such short-termism inefficient, it can also be dangerous for the organization. Strategic decisions, like a General choosing his battleground, will have long-term implications and momentum has to be built up over a planned period of time.

On the other hand, like people who cannot exist for ever on a promise of 'jam tomorrow', so organizations need a constant flow of business, profits and cash to survive today so that they may live to see tomorrow! What is 'short term' and what is 'long term' will of course vary with the industry and the nature (and perceptions) of the target international markets. Like much in marketing, there is no 'right' answer. The Western financial markets, especially the USA and Great Britain, are often criticized for forcing organizations to concentrate on the shorter rather than the longer term. However, the recent collapse of the Asian markets has shown that having a 50-year view is no protection against a shortfall in today's profits!

Financial measures

The typical financial measures used in the evaluation of international marketing strategy will include:

- Profit
- Profitability
- Shareholder return
- Cash flow/liquidity
- Share price
- Earnings per share
- Return on net assets
- Return on sales

These are measures which will apply to any strategy for an organization in any situation, including international. The special aspect of international is that the strategy will normally be evaluated on repatriated cash flows in home rather than foreign currencies.

How are financial and non-financial measures of evaluation and control balanced in your organization? Do non-financial measures add an extra dimension to your organization's ability to control its international activity?

Non-financial measures

The non-financial measures of performance tend to measure external rather than internal performance of an organization and such measures may include:

- Market share
- Growth
- Competitive advantage
- Competitive position
- Sales volume
- Market penetration levels
- New product development
- Customer satisfaction
- Customer brand franchise
- Market image and awareness levels

These measures, naturally, will vary from market to market in the international area and will need to be measured on a market and a global/international basis for the organization's international activities.

For a discussion of the use of financial versus non-financial measures and using multiple criteria, see the *Strategic Marketing Management 1998–99* workbook (Fifield and Gilligan, 1998).

It is important that the student of international marketing strategy be aware, first and foremost, of the primary measures of marketing strategy in a domestic situation. For further understanding of the measures of performance and evaluating strategies, the student is directed towards the readings on the area within domestic marketing strategy such as:

Strategic Marketing Management, R. M. S. Wilson and C. Gilligan, Butterworth-Heinemann (1997).
Strategic Marketing Management 1998–99, P. Fifield and C. Gilligan, Butterworth-Heinemann (1998).

Evaluating international business planning

In international marketing, as with domestic marketing, the use of models in planning is a way of evaluating strategic options. A number of models have been used in international marketing that were developed primarily for domestic marketing purposes. These include the Boston Consulting Group matrix, the GEC/McKinsey approach and the Arthur D. Little method.

Although there has been much in the recent literature criticizing the use of models such as these, they are still a valid mechanism to test the *conceptual approach* to international marketing strategy. These models have been described in detail in the recommended texts so they will not be repeated here. The use of models such as these and others can be a helpful way of discriminating between likely strategic options and the results that they will bring in the market place when implemented.

Barriers to implementation

There are many barriers that stand in the way of successful implementation of international marketing strategy – some evident, some less so. The barriers fall broadly into three separate categories:

- Environmental barriers.
- Organizational barriers.
- Marketing department barriers.

Environmental or external barriers are focused around the 'SLEPT' methodology which we discussed in Unit 4. There are a number of factors under each of these headings which will work against the organization looking to develop or even start its international business. For example:

- Government restrictions on exports.
- Product, communication or other laws.
- Levels of economic activity in overseas markets etc.

Organizational barriers are inherent in areas such as Leadership, Organizational Culture, Organizational Design, Resources and Control Measures. For example:

- Top management sees itself as running a successful domestic company.
- Senior management has experience in developing and satisfying domestic customer needs only.
- Organization is designed for the efficient running of a domestic business and international operations are 'fit into' the existing system.
- There is little or no specific international expertise.
- There is little or no understanding of the special nature of international business.
- Resources for international operations are dedicated only after domestic operations have been satisfied – the 'what is left' method.
- Resources for international operations are considered 'high risk'.
- Top and senior management are measured and rewarded according to domestic success only.

Marketing department barriers are often the most difficult to spot. If the marketing department is domestic market- and product- or sales-focused, there is little hope for internationalization.

For more background on barriers to strategic implementation, see the *Strategic Marketing Management 1998–99* workbook (Fifield and Gilligan, 1998).

Control systems

If planning is defined as 'deciding what to do' then control can be defined as 'ensuring that the desired results are obtained'. Planning without control is a purely intellectual exercise. Control systems are essential to make sure that an organization drives through the content of its international marketing plans and achieves its organization's objectives in the marketplace. Control systems are varied and selecting the right method of control will depend upon the nature of the international markets that the organization is addressing, the particular goals and objectives which the organization has set itself as well as the environments within which the organization has to operate internationally. In simple terms, a control process can be described as in Figure 14.2.

Control systems, then, are a matter of balancing four primary issues:

1 Standard setting
2 Performance measurement
3 Performance diagnosis
4 Taking corrective action (if required)

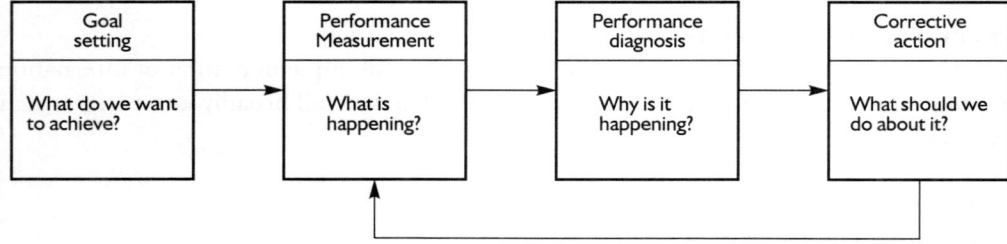

Figure 14.2 The control process

What control mechanisms are used in your organization? How, if at all, would you improve on your organization's control systems?

Setting standards

This is the role of the planning element of the process and the goals and objectives to which the organization's international marketing activity is directed. These activities are then translated into standards which, if met, will produce successful implementation of the international marketing strategy.

Performance standards tend to be measured in simple terms such as:

- *Quantity* How much was achieved? How much should have been achieved?
- *Quality* How good was that which was achieved? How good was it meant to be?
- *Cost* How much did the achievement cost? How much was it planned to cost?

Performance measurement

Typically, divergence from pre-set standards is normally picked up in the organization through a process of:

- *Regular auditing* of the organization's finance and marketing activities or
- *Budgets* – developing and identifying divergence from budgeted inflows and outflows or
- *Variance analysis* – falling out of the budgeting process, the detailed analysis of the variance (difference between actual and expected results) that arises from the organization's activities.

Performance diagnosis

Once the control system has been established and during the implementation phase of the international marketing plan, differences or deviations from the estimated (targeted) results can be highlighted. The international marketer's role is then to decide whether corrective action is required in one or more of the foreign markets and, if so, how to implement this action to bring the plan back on to target. The selection of corrective action depends to a large extent on the reasons behind the divergence from the planned results, and it is essential that the international marketer understands the reason for variances before simply setting off pre-planned contingency activities.

In the role of the director responsible for international marketing of a major blue-chip company, explain how you would identify and justify the resource requirements for a global marketing plan (June 1993).

(**See** Exam answers at the end of this unit.)

Factors affecting international controls

There are a number of factors which affect the degree and effectiveness of a control system for international marketing strategy. Some of the most important are:

For an organization other than your own can you:

- Identify an occasion where problems in the international control system caused inappropriate marketing action to be taken
- Identify an occasion where control systems resulted in proper action being taken in an international market.

- *Communications* Control systems rely on effective communications (two-way) for their accuracy. The opportunities for breakdown of communication systems in the international organization are varied and the problems of both timely and accurate communications between head office and subsidiaries and/or agents and distributors have been well documented. Before any corrective action is taken it is important that the marketer understands the reasons for discrepancies against planned outcomes and the role that communications or miscommunications may have played in the process.

- *Data* The accuracy and flow of international data has always been a problem in international marketing situations. As international activity moves beyond the developed Western markets the availability and accuracy of international market/product/industry data becomes increasingly less reliable. It is important to understand that control systems start off with data that may not be as reliable as in domestic marketing situations. In these instances greater degrees of latitude should be allowed in the control process before contingency plans are activated.

- *Environmental change* The diversity of environments within which the organization must operate internationally will undoubtedly affect control systems and the data used for their calculation. Currency values, legal structures, political systems, public holidays and the inevitable cultural factors will all influence the development and control of marketing strategy. The issue of diversity of local environments must be reflected in the control system.

- *Organizational culture* The organization's culture and management philosophy about issues such as centralization or decentralization, internationalization or globalization will affect development of any control system. A highly centralized/global organization will likely require a control system that is detailed and all encompassing. Organizations where authority and decision making is devolved to the local unit level are likely to require a much less mechanistic approach to control systems.

- *Size of international operations* Depending on the nature of the international operation, the organization and the relative importance that international earnings play on the organization's balance sheet, the control system may be fundamental to the organization's reported profit levels. In the organization where international business is a very small part of its day-to-day operations, control systems will be less rigorously applied and divergences from plan will be less closely scrutinized.

- *Faulty estimating* It may also be apparent from an analysis of the variances that the problem does not lie in the market nor in the organization's ability to deliver to a market's need but the original estimates set against which the plan was going to be judged. In this case the organization and the international marketer needs to re-estimate the rate at which the organization will achieve its strategic objectives.

EXAM HINT

Faulty estimating is rarely cited as a problem in control systems – managers tend to believe figures. The mini-cases and the major case (analysis and decision) may contain suspect data – use your intuitive skills to assess whether the given targets are right in the first place.

Summary

In this unit we have looked at the important stages of strategic evaluation and the control of implementation. First, we considered the problem of evaluating alternative strategies for international operations and deciding which strategic option offered the best chance of achieving the organization's objectives. Evaluation will be driven largely by the organization's objectives but can be measured both internally (financial measures), externally (non-financial measures) or, ideally, a combination of the two.

Second, we considered the control mechanisms that are necessary to ensure that the strategic plan is implemented in the foreign markets and the organization's objectives are achieved. We considered the range of analysis and control mechanisms which are used in different organizations including auditing, budgeting and variance analysis.

Finally, we considered the nature of the corrective action that can be taken by the marketer and the variables which affect the control mechanisms and the results that these give.

Questions

As a check on your understanding of what has been covered in this unit, consider the following questions:

- What is the role of the control system in international marketing strategy?
- What are the two categories by which strategy can be evaluated?
- What are the types of measure that are included under the heading of 'financial measures'?
- What are the types of measure that are included under the heading of 'non-financial measures'?
- How can strategic models be used in evaluating international strategy?
- What is a 'control system'? Give examples.
- What are the four key issues in any control system?
- By what methods can divergence from standards be picked up?
- What are the special factors that affect the efficiency and effectiveness of control systems in international operations?

For a more detailed analysis and explanation of evaluation and control methods for international marketing strategy, read:

International Marketing', S. Paliwoda and M. Thomas, Butterworth-Heinemann, 1998.
International Marketing Strategy, I. Doole, R. Lowe and C. Phillips, Routledge, 1997.

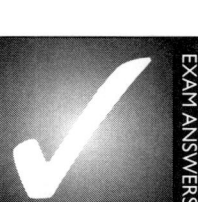

June 1993

From: Director of International Marketing

To: Budget Review Committee

Subject: Global Marketing Plan (first draft)

Background

In this paper I will outline the current thinking with regard to producing a detailed global marketing plan for the financial year 1994/95 and beyond.

As we are all aware, our current planning process has been based on achieving the HQ-determined rate of return on capital employed in each major region of our international business. For our major markets of the United States and the United Kingdom this has been shown by country; in other parts of the world we have aggregated our country plans into relevant groups. Changes in competition and different growth rates and opportunities around the world, along with moves by other companies to plan on a global basis, have prompted the decision to produce a global marketing plan.

Identification of opportunities

We will use our new international marketing information system to scan for opportunities. We will develop a priority ranked programme based on our corporate strategy of using clearly differentiated approaches through which we can add value.

A key factor in our global plan will be the coordination of our approach. We will develop opportunities to a clear plan. Major opportunities will have a substantial and interlinked implementation. More limited opportunities will be progressed only if above average returns are possible.

It is proposed that we concentrate our activities in those parts of the world which have a faster than average growth in the GNP. This will be modified to make allowance for market attractiveness by country and by world region; for example, the European Community.

Resource requirements

The appropriate headings under this item seem to be employees (both numbers and payroll cost); marketing budgets for new product development; marketing research and MIS, and marketing communications; the use of external agencies, particularly for advertising, public relations and marketing research.

We propose to continue our current blend of direct investment in key markets and joint ventures and alliances in markets of greater uncertainty (for example, the former Comecon bloc).

There is a need to develop more managers with a good understanding of operating in an international setting; at a very senior level we need a multi-cultural management team to ensure that global opportunities are thoroughly analysed and that appropriate plans are developed and implemented.

Control

To achieve a global approach we need to take an overall view which must take account of trading off between various country and regional plans. The main marketing controls will be market share against specified objectives, both in absolute terms and against identified major world competitors. In addition, we would expect to use the company standard measures of sales, profit contribution and return on capital employed. However, a balancing figure must be used to adjust for each area's contribution towards, or received benefit from, the overall global plan.

Senior Examiner's comments

As in the answer above, a good pass standard requires an application of marketing planning to the very difficult, complex task of global planning. The achievement of a global plan requires substantial adjustments to be made. The behavioural approach within the organization to find agreement will often be lengthy and often acrimonious. The scarce resources of even the largest of organizations need to be used in the most profitable ways. The international manager will need to make a strong case, otherwise the claims of other areas of the organization – for example, production or finance – might prevent sufficient resources flowing to support the global marketing plan.

The mini-case study

A mini-case is a compulsory part of the examination and designed to provide you with an opportunity to apply your knowledge to a particular situation. The purpose of this unit is therefore:

- To help you understand how best to approach the mini-case study
- To highlight the sorts of mistakes that are commonly made
- To give you an opportunity to prepare a number of practice solutions

By the end of this unit, you will:

- Be familiar with the sorts of mini-case studies that have been used over the past few years
- Have an understanding of the issues that they raise
- Have gained some practice at approaching these cases.

Although with each of the previous units it has been a relatively straightforward exercise to identify how long you should spend working on the unit, it is far harder to do this with the mini-case. Instead, you should recognize that the more practice you get with the mini-case, the more likely it is that you will approach it in your examination with a degree of confidence and an understanding of what is required from you. You should, therefore, spend as much time as you can familiarizing yourself with the format of the mini-cases and the sorts of questions that are asked. Practise preparing solutions to the questions and then compare your answers with the solutions that we have included at the end of the unit.

It needs to be recognized that the type of short case (popularly called the mini-case) set in the examinations cannot be treated in exactly the same way as the extremely long case set for the subject of *Strategic Marketing: Analysis and Decision.*

However, far too many students adopt a maxi-case approach, using a detailed marketing audit outline which is largely inappropriate to a case consisting of just two or three pages. Others use SWOT analysis and simply rewrite the case under the four headings of strengths, weaknesses, opportunities and threats.

Some students even go so far as to ignore the specific questions set and present a standard maxi-case analysis, including environmental reviews and contingency plans. Others adopt a vague and far too superficial approach. In each case, students are penalized. You should recognize therefore that the mini-case is simply an *outline* of a given situation whose purpose is to test whether candidates can apply their knowledge of marketing operations to the environment described in the scenario. For example, answers advocating retail audits as part of the marketing information system for a small industrial goods manufacturer confirm that the examinee has learned a given MkIS outline by rote and simply regurgitated this with complete disregard of the scenario. Such an approach cannot be passed. A more appropriate approach to the scenario involves a mental review of the areas covered by the question and the selection by the candidate of those particular parts of knowledge or techniques which apply to the case. This implies a rejection of those parts of the student's knowledge which clearly do not apply to the scenario.

All scenarios are based upon real-world companies and situations and are written with a full knowledge of how that organization operates in its planning environments. Often, the organization described in the scenario will not be a giant fast-moving consumer goods manufacturing and marketing company but is instead an innovative, small or medium-sized firm faced with a particular problem or challenge. The cases are often, but not invariably, written from the viewpoint of a consultant and include an extract from a consultant's report.

The examination as a whole lasts for three hours. Including your reading time, you therefore have one-and-a-half hours for the mini-case.

The mistakes that candidates make

We have already touched upon some of the mistakes that candidates make in approaching the mini-case. We can, however, take these futher with the list of the ten most common errors that candidates make.

The ten most common mini-case errors

1. Ignoring the specific questions posed and providing instead a general treatment of the case.
2. Thinking that every mini-case study demands a SWOT analysis; it doesn't.
3. Not answering in the format asked for. You will normally be asked for a report, a memorandum or a marketing plan and should answer using one of these frameworks.
4. Making unrealistic assumptions about the extent to which organizations can change their working practices.
5. Assuming that unlimited financial resources will be available to you.
6. Failing to recognize the difficulties of implementation.
7. Introducing hypothetical data on costs.
8. Rewriting the case and ignoring the questions.
9. Failing to give full recognition to the implications of what is recommended.
10. Not spending sufficient time on the second of the two questions.

Note to candidates and CIM tutors

In preparing the following schematic answer schemes reference has been made to two essential text books:

- *International Marketing Strategy, 1998–1999* (Fifield and Lewis), Butterworth-Heinemann, 1998
- *International Marketing Strategy* (Doole, Lowe and Phillips), Routledge, 1997

To have any chance of doing well in this subject, candidates are advised to have studied both these texts. Top quality candidates must have read widely via accepted quality journals.

Another vital point here is that the writing of an an actual prescribed answer is often misleading. There is no single approach or answer that is correct (and which therefore makes all others wrong). At the Diploma level the CIM is seeking professional, logical solutions that are frequently underpinned by academic theories. It is therefore of more help and assistance to provide here guidelines and frameworks. We seek to communicate to you an 'approach' to each of the questions from the perspective of the examination, paying regard to the specific construct of each question.

McDonald's – A challenge to globalization (December 1997)

The golden arches of McDonald's rank first among the world's best known corporate symbols, assuring customers that their Big Mac will look and taste the same whether ordered in Manchester or Malaysia. That rigorous consistency has been a key factor in helping McDonald's build the biggest and most successful fast food brand in the world.

However, others envious of McDonald's success have started to carve their own niche in the burger market, some making inroads into what was McDonald's domain. This is the normal course of business, as successful innovation in any market will attract competition. The example that follows is one of several instances where McDonald's success has created an opportunity for the competition.

Jollibee Foods, a family owned chain in the Philippines, has borrowed every trick from McDonald's marketing know-how but instead of selling a generic burger acceptable to any market in the world, Jollibee caters to a local preference for sweet and spicy flavours. 'We've designed our products to suit the Filipino palate', says Mr Bibonia, Jollibee's vice president of marketing.

The secret of success – Rice and spice

The combination of first class service and matching and sometimes beating McDonald's in delivery of the product in-store, plus the creation of tailored menus, has resulted in Jollibee outperforming McDonalds in the Philippines. Indeed, according to the market researchers A.C. Neilsen, in 10 years Jollibee has grabbed 46% of the market versus McDonald's 16% based on the share of total number of visits. McDonald's have stabilized the number of stores as a result of a corporate decision taken when the Philippines was undergoing political change in the late 1980s and early 1990s, Jollibee has surged ahead and now has 177 outlets – roughly double McDonald's total of 90, with another 36 added in 1996/97. Jollibee's strategy in distribution has been to locate alongside McDonald's and with their superior store numbers, to 'surround McDonald's'. Additionally, the fact that Jollibee's prices are 5% lower on average than McDonald's is also an advantage.

The Jollibee burger isn't that different from a McDonald's; the basic product is broadly similar but the sauce (or spice if you like) is different. 'It's familiar to customers – it's the spice a Filipino mother would cook at home', says Tessa Puno, a consumer analyst. Besides the spicy sauces, Jollibee offers, rice and spaghetti as an alternative to French fries, though these are also available.

Local promotion

Just like McDonald's, Jollibee works hard to attract kids, with in-store play activities and a line of heavily advertised characters, including a hamburger-headed boxer called Champ and a spaghetti-haired girl named Hetty. Licensed toys, towels and other novelties promoting the characters are on sale in stores. Again, the characters have a local expression and a Filipino feel to them, as does the television advertising. Here again Jollibee feels it has the edge in communicating local values to local customers creating the position of being like McDonald's in broad terms, but being Filipino in the style and manner of delivery.

With sales of £170 million (US$250 m) in 1995, Jollibee is the second largest consumer goods company in the Philippines – but minuscule compared with McDonald's £20 billion (US$30 bn) world-wide sales. But it can see opportunities overseas in niche markets. Already is has pilot ventures in South East Asia alongside the Middle East, and plans to open a total of 40 restaurants there by the end of 1996. It has already opened in California and thinks Chicago, New York and Miami with their Asian and Hispanic population could be good prospects. The threat to McDonald's might just get serious.

McDonald's response

Jollibee's success has not gone unnoticed, although McDonald's subsidiary in Manila has not commented officially and corporate headquarters had little to say: 'We focus on our customers there just as anywhere else' has been the response. McDonald's may have been handicapped by the fact that government legislation has prohibited foreign companies from owning retail chains, restricting the company therefore to a franchise operation. But this constraint is in the process of being lifted, allowing McDonald's to operate its own stores. Furthermore money is no object. The company could pour in advertising and attempt to overwhelm Jollibee reminding other upstart burger-chains around the world of the might of the Golden Arches. Whatever the response, McDonald's is unlikely to resist retaliation for long and when it comes it will be serious.

Question 1: your task

You have been asked to head a task force at McDonald's headquarters in lllinois with the brief to plan, implement and control the company's response to Jollibee. No budget has been set and the time frame is 3 years from January 1998. Specifically the brief covers two critical areas:

(a) What investigations would be carried out prior to preparing your planned response?

(20 marks)

(b) Plan and implement your response over a 3-year period. In doing so your plan must include issues broader than just the 7 P's of marketing and must incorporate issues of control.

(30 marks)

Preliminary notes to candidates and CIM tutors diploma

What follows is an indicative scheme: it is deliberately not prescriptive as at the Diploma level the examiner seeks rewarding innovative solutions and expects quality candidates to think broadly and provide professional solutions. In particular those candidates who demonstrate the breadth and depth of marketing within the wider business context will be rewarded.

However there are some critical guidelines that underpin answers:

1 Answers will be judged against the specific tasks of each question. Broad sweeping generalizations are not really acceptable.
2 Candidates will be rewarded for evidence of professionalism, namely:
   • a proper structure and use of the correct format, e.g. report, marketing plan etc.;
   • presentation of a logical well-rounded argument;
   • brief introduction/scene setting and a conclusion;
   • identification and recognition of the key issues underpinning the mini-case together with critical success factors etc.;
   • the demonstration of a strategic perspective and an avoidance of tactical issues.

Additional note to examination candidates and CIM Diploma tutors

This is a real-life case. It is not constructed or written to be a teaching model with a clear-cut prescribed solution. As in real life there are several ways in which McDonald's might respond, from doing nothing to deciding to virtually eliminate Jollibee, even buying them. As such it is not feasible to write the definitive answer and each script will be considered on its individual merit, taking into account the quality of the answer, its realism, and its depth of understanding of what being a global corporation means. Weak answers will inevitably position McDonald's (Phillipines) as if it were a stand-alone business with no global interlinking. The essence of the case is one that is commonplace, how to remain global, focused on a global positioning with a global brand equity yet be perceived as having a degree of 'localness' in meeting consumer expectation. A case of 'glocalization' to use the jargon of today.

Question 1(a): indicative answer

Introduction
Perhaps candidates might begin with establishing:

Critical issues
1   McDonald's (McD) is the world's benchmark in fast foods. They created the world market by exporting their successful US formula.
2   As such McD is a world brand. Its golden arches symbol is the world's No. 1 symbol in terms of consumer recognition (Coca-Cola is the world's No. 1 recognized brand).
3   McD's brand equity must be its greatest asset. The physical products are easily imitated as are its service standards. However it is to the brand that consumers are attracted.
4   This brand equity must be global. Moreover it must be protected, nurtured and above all consistent and of course superior (different) to that of it's competitors.
5   A different set of brand values for different countries is totally unrealistic and unacceptable to a global corporation although the communication and interpretation of what local customers actually purchase may be different.
6   There is ample evidence from sources such as *The Economist, Financial Times* and *Asian Business,* the actual source of the case study, that McD have become F.L.C., i.e. Fat, Lazy and Complacent, in its established markets. Its success has arisen from geographic expansion of a largely (not exclusively) standard formula. A new McD outlet opens every 3 hours – a staggering performance. Nevertheless, in the USA, South Africa and as we see in South East Asia, McD is increasingly under threat.
7   It may be appropriate for McD's response in the Philippines to be a test bed for other countries.

Recommendations
McD must carry out extensive market research and analysis prior to formulating a **strategic** response.

Candidates should be capable of writing an outline market audit of a quantitative and qualitative nature. Figuratively:

- Who buys?
- Who buys what?
- Why do they buy?
- Benefits sought.
- Perceptions, expectations, actual performance in terms of the full range of the marketing mix. (It is anticipated that candidates will expand the answer across the 7 P's of the mix.)
- Additionally you should explore a comprehensive evaluation of all the above for McD vs. Jollibee and other competitors.
- An understanding of the key, core values of McD and how they compare with Jollibee etc.
- Identification of the critical differences that will enable McD to respond strategically.
- An ability of McD to relate the core values to the critical differences, i.e. where do the universal values of the brand equity begin and end and what are the important peripheral values identified by consumers?

Other important points for consideration are aspects of:

- Future political risk (ownership of properties).
- Location of properties.
- Investment risk vs. pay-off period.
- Evaluation of operational implications of changing the McD formula.

- Human resource implication, from both a management and operational perspective (recruitment motivation and training).

The above is not a complete audit and it is anticipated that candidates will explore the market research angle in depth, going on to discuss quantitative and qualitative research although this is not a requirement of the question. The key discriminator is the strategic perspective, not the tactical implications of market research.

Question 1(b): indicative answer

The question requires candidates to plan and implement a 3-year response taking into account the impact and implications across the main business functions. Control is also a critical issue.

Inevitably you will need to consider answering holistically, in terms of the degree of professionalism displayed. What must be established by good quality answers (B grade) is:

- A clear statement of objectives, for 3 years hence.
- Identification of a defined strategy with strong reference to the critical factors of global vs. local positioning.
- Consideration of the strategic level of involvement and its implication (in broad terms) across key business functions of finance, production, operation and human resources.

A reference is the international business process model in Figure I.4, p. xix.

What is critically important is that McDonalds USA must rethink its corporate strategy. Is it correct? Is the company too ethnocentric? The consensus is that McD needs to become more international in its outlook and needs to explore greater internationalization in its marketing while retaining a global perspective. It also needs to appoint new management with international expertise. Candidates who have read widely in international marketing will know that many McD executives who have been with the company for 20 years or more, in some cases occupying senior positions, have recently been ousted (Summer 1997).

Some candidates may choose to outline a realistic operational plan from a marketing perspective incorporating the 7 P's. I have deliberately avoided a detailed 7 P's approach here, concentrating instead on a holistic view dealing with strategic issues.

Year 1

- Reassertion of the global brand equity (the specialness of McD) using established Marcom tools.
- Upgrading of service and product delivery standards consolidating the core values.
- Testing of product modification to peripherals retaining the core products.
- Identification of new locations – purchase/leasing of appropriate properties – outflanking Jollibee.
- Increased training provision, employee motivation etc.
- Continuous tracking/monitoring.

Year 2

- Continued restatement of global brand equity.
- Relaunch of product portfolio to 'match' local needs while retaining core values.
- Begin repositioning McD as the premier Global Company in fast food retailing.
- Open new outlets.
- Continue tracking/monitoring.
- Maintain McD price superiority/premium and if possible increase it.
- Continue to seek new outlets.
- Constantly evaluate and review everything, product, service and importantly consumers and profitability.

Year 3

- Position McD as 'the' Global Company that is equally seen as the 'insider', to quote Ohmae.
- Continue to position McD as 'special', reinforcing the global brand equity.
- All aspects of the service delivery should reflect customer perception/expectation.
- Product and delivery should be continually evaluated.
- Continue to open new outlets.

King Carpets – Franchising in Europe (June 1997)

The background

Max King started his carpet business in Los Angeles, California in 1988 with a brainwave idea: Why do customers need to travel to out of town stores in order to buy their carpets – why doesn't the store come to them? So hiring a van equipped with samples, he travelled the city door-to-door selling carpets direct and contracting out the fitting to local carpet fitters. The venture 'took off' and soon he had more business than he could cope with. Not having the capital to expand himself, he hit on another brainwave – why not franchise the business? In return, King Carpets as the company was called would supply the training, the sales techniques and the samples. In less than 6 years over 500 franchises had been appointed in the USA and King Carpets is now established as one of the Top 100 privately owned businesses. Its slogan, 'The Carpet Store to your Door', had clearly taken the USA by storm.

Details of the offer

The key factors of the success of King Carpets are convenience, value and customer service. With a range of over 1,500 carpets and other floor coverings such as wood, vinyl and ceramic tiles, the customer choice is extremely comprehensive. But more than that, the range can be inspected under actual home conditions to enable customers to get a feel for what the product might look like against the background of their furniture, curtains and wallpaper. Even more persuasive is the unique 'King computers imaging system' whereby customers can see the room to be carpeted on a computer screen replicating exactly how it would appear after being fitted with the choice of each carpet under consideration.

With no retailer or middlemen, low staff overheads and no heavy stock to carry King Carpets can pass on much of the saving to the customer guaranteeing lower prices than carpet shops, whilst at the same time making higher profits.

Expansion into Europe

Having conquered America, Max King began to eye the overseas market. From his base in Los Angeles he decided that Europe would be his next stage of development. He called in his most successful Californian franchisees for a discussion and on discovering that Luis Pedraza, of Mexican parentage, could speak Spanish, appointed him as European Vice President – although Luis had never been to Europe. The meeting in Los Angeles concluded that Europe would be a good place to go. After all 'it is all one single market now, isn't it?' 'In any case', said Max, 'I've licked the problem in the USA and I'll do the same in Europe.' He didn't believe there were any differences between Americans and Europeans apart from the language and that would be overcome by appointing local franchisees. So it was agreed to launch into the 15 countries of the European Union in mid 1997.

Franchisees would be sought and appointed on the following basis:

- An up-front fee of £15 000 would be paid to King Carpets.
- Franchisees would need to lease a mid-sized van, e.g. Ford Transit, Toyota Hiace, Renault Trafic or local equivalent.
- Each franchisee would be given an exclusive operating territory of 15 000 households.
- King Carpets would hold training sessions in how to handle the computer software that generated the in-house simulation imagery in European capital cities.

Question 1

(a) As an international consultant, advise King Carpets on a research programme to underpin the successful launch in Europe. **(20 marks)**

(b) What strategic planning and control issues does the company need to address in undertaking the pan-European launch? **(30 marks)**

Question 1(a): indicative answer

It can be assumed King Carpets have the financial resources to conduct a full analysis of the European opportunity.

The case declares the decision to enter Europe has been taken, although good candidates might well (should) question the wisdom of this approach in their introduction.

It is accepted that candidates will produce a certain variety in their answer and marks will be awarded for creativity and the ability to relate specific recommendations to the case. What is set out below is a formal programme to international market research which can be applied. It is a framework that good candidates might adopt.

Aims and objectives
1   Scan EU markets to identify and analyse opportunities.
2   Carry out detail studies in order to:
    (a)   Input to the development of appropriate strategies.
    (b)   Test the feasibility of the market mix options.
3   Build a market information system to monitor trends.

1   Scanning marketing for:
- Accessibility (should not be a problem but there may be detailed import regulations).
- Profitability (currency, exchange rates etc.).
- Market size (the standard measures would apply).

Competitor information (paying attention to competitive stance).

The programme should next consider International Marketing Segmentation. Good students might consider the Harrell and Kiefer model to prioritize markets and even better ones refer to Kale and Sudharshan to define Strategically Equivalent Segments (SES), seeking clusters of similarities.

2   Customer segmentation
Once the prime markets are identified, the standard techniques would be used to segment individual markets on the basis of:

- demographic/economic factors;
- lifestyles – leading to product preference;
- buyer motivation;
- buyer behaviour;
- psychographic characteristics.

Quality answers will refer to pan-European segmentation, e.g. Euro mosaic identifying neighbourhood categories, although overseas students who may not be aware of this will not be discriminated against.

3   MIS
Although many of the considerations set out below would be built into the scanning programme it would be advisable that King Carpets build a MIS for monitoring and control purposes.

Candidates might employ the 12 Cs approach suggested by the Doole, Lowe and Phillips (1997).

Finally, a good answer will conclude with a statement referring to time, cost and any management problems relating to carrying out the total programme.

Question 1(b): indicative answer
1   The key components concern planning and control in a pan-European context.
2   The question will inevitably be approached from different perspectives but candidates should stay **strategic** in their approach.

The start point might be the International Business Process model identified in Fig. I.4 (p. xix).

Candidates can take for granted, the research, the commitment and the selection of countries. The level of involvement will be serious – dictated by the nature of the market(s) and consumer behaviour/motivation. What is required is an understanding of the strategic issues surrounding:

- The development of a lead market strategy i.e. prioritizing countries.
- The market mix.
- Finance.
- Operations.
- Organization/HR.

Answers should cover the strategic implications for each in terms of launching and operating a pan-European programme.

Strategic issues (Planning and Control) in the marketing mix will inevitably include:

- Setting marketing objectives (by country).
- Seeking Pan-European segmentation (by country, e.g. Southern Europe is likely to prefer tile or marble effect flooring).
- Identification of Target Markets (by country), pointing out potential differences, i.e. the cultural imperative.
- Development of a defined strategy.
- Strategic issues revolving around the 7 P's.
- Product policy (product portfolio).
- Pricing policy (finance and trading terms).
- Place policy (franchising considerations).
- Promotion policy (branding, particularly Pan-European).
- People policy (franchise selection, motivation, standards of delivery training etc.).
- Process policy (cultural issues relating to delivery levels).
- Physical evidence (cultural relevances).

Control issues will revolve around:

- Setting the objectives.
- Monitoring everything.
- Organizational issues (especially from a US perspective – managing up to 15 European countries).
- Budgets.
- Time scales for management.

Amway expands into China (December 1996)

Background

China is on the verge of surpassing all known growth records. To begin with, far from being a slowly emerging economic force it is already the world's third largest economy trailing only USA and Japan, but not for much longer. By the year 2000 it will be the world's largest. But of course size of economy does not equate to standard of living. Within China itself the major growth is taking place in the coastal regions where roughly one quarter of the population lives (a total of 300 million people); where income is set to grow at 11 per cent a year for the next ten years. To quote Lee Kuan Yew formerly Prime Minister of Singapore, "Never in human history have so many grown so rich so fast". China with 1.2 billion people (25 percent of the world's population) offers the greatest single opportunity and threat for Western products.

Guandong province neighbouring on Hong Kong with 60 million people is China's showpiece. Since barriers with Hong Kong ceased in 1978 its GDP has grown 13% per annum, and is generally proving to be the springboard for Western products entering the Chinese market. For example Guandong is Proctor and Gamble's second largest market world-wide for shampoos.

Entering the Chinese market

Patience is a virtue, creativity a must! More open than the Japanese market, nevertheless the careful cultivation of special relationships from influential people down to the everyday consumer is important in doing business. The word for this is Guanxi – Chinese for connections. Cultivating connections is part of the culture; word of mouth counting for more than most of the other forms of marketing communications. Whilst it is true that the market poses challenges to foreign investors many companies are discovering the key to success is to start at the local level, learn the market, develop trust with Chinese partners, let each experience make the relationship stronger. In other words the traditional Western approach of marketing as exemplified by the FMCG route requires serious modifications – besides which the normal tools of marketing communication i.e. advertising etc. are not greatly in evidence.

Amway takes the plunge

Amway the world's biggest direct marketing firm is gearing itself to enter the Chinese market, focusing on Guandong Province in the short-term. Amway operates world-wide via a system of personal sales people, each of whom has a number of sales people reporting to them. Much is made of door-to-door selling and what are known as 'party programmes' where groups of potential customers meet in a friend's home. It has already invested £60m in a new factory in the province. The factory produces products for the Pacific region, but these are standard products to meet consumer needs in Japan, Philippines, Taiwan, Singapore etc. This product range which includes detergents, washing liquids, household cleaners and even cosmetics and vitamins may not be appropriate for China. So whilst Amway has considerable experience in the Far East where sales have been extremely buoyant, the downside is that the Chinese market is not a mirror image of Taiwan, Philippines etc. where capitalist economies are well established. So, it has to start virtually from scratch in marketing the business in China.

Direct marketing has great potential in China. There is a history of trading stretching back hundreds of years, albeit briefly interrupted by Communist rule. The Chinese are natural entrepreneurs. With an underdeveloped retail structure i.e. few supermarkets – a culture of Guanxi networking already established and a population with rapidly expanding disposable income – the future is rosy. But pitfalls abound; the market is riddled with unscrupulous operators selling substandard goods with poor service, claiming to be legitimate direct marketers. The Chinese are naturally apprehensive – and they ask questions. Door-to-door cold calling is not part of the culture. But the overall portents are good. Avon, a rival direct marketer has been in China for five years and has racked up impressive sales growth projecting sales of £40m in 1995. Avon has taken the route of following the culture rather than imposing itself via heavy advertising and price promotion. Indeed price promotion is virtually unheard of as are discount operators.

PART A

Question 1

    (a) Identify what you consider to be the strategic corporate concerns facing Amway in the development of its Chinese business. **(20 marks)**

    (b) Using the 7 Ps, specify the issues Amway must address in developing its marketing plan and state how it might address them. **(30 marks)**

                    (50 marks total)

Question 1(a): answer

Background

Amway is a global corporation. The company has experience in international business development and it can be assumed that financial resources, together with the organisational ambitions, are available. For Amway to maintain its position dominance it must address the Chinese potential – the largest untapped single market in the world. But in developing the Chinese potential, Amway must proceed with caution and will engage a strategic outlook planning over a long-term horizon i.e. 5 to 10 years. It will do this before considering the details of the marketing plan.

Identification of the strategic concerns

Perhaps the basis of the development of the international business procession the Fifield and Lewis model (Figure 15.1) expressed as follows:

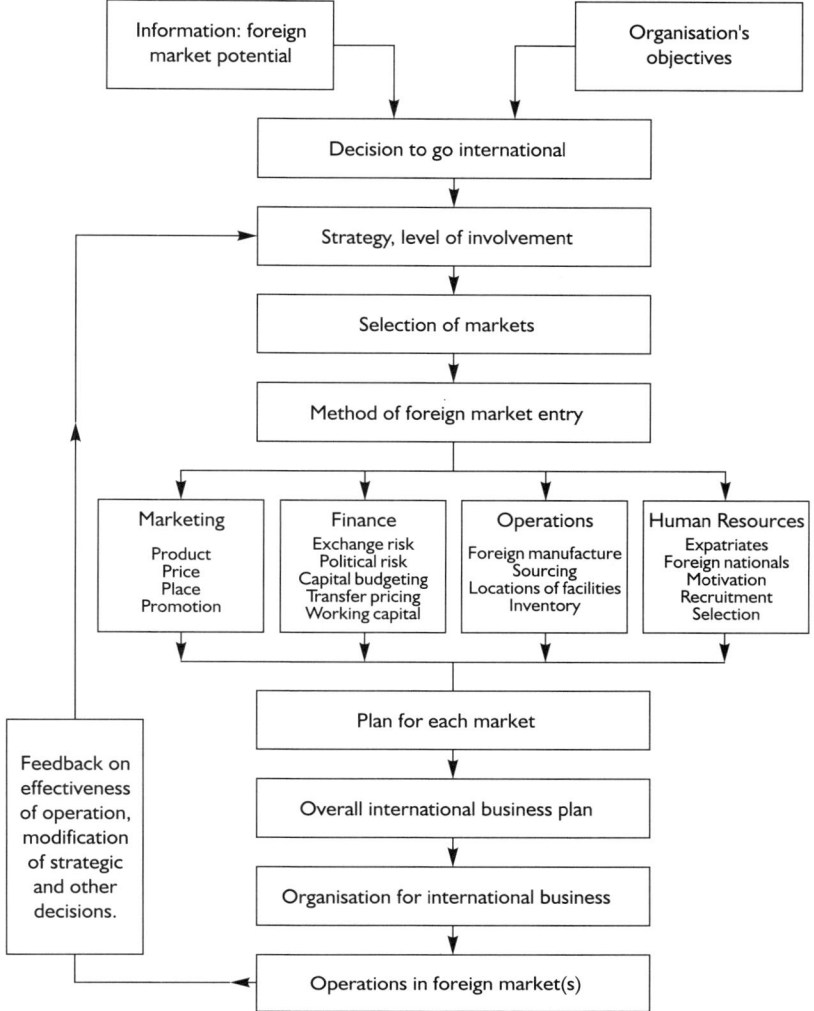

Figure 15.1 The international business process (*Source:* Fifield & Lewis)

Without recourse to a detailed explanation of the model it is sufficient to state categorically that Amway has the vision and commitment embodied in its corporate objectives and it has sufficient basic information to enable the 'decision to go' to have been taken. The key decision is the **Strategic level of involvement.** This decision commits the organisation to a chosen long-term path. It imposes the level of marketing, finance, operational and human resource commitment. It is the consumer that ultimately decides the strategic level of involvement together with a balance of other strategic considerations. These are described by Doole, Lowe and Phillips in the 12 C's (Figure 15.2).

Taking each in turn (briefly):

1 *Country*

   Amway will need to consider the scale of the country, the political, economic, social economic and other relevant factors.

   China geographically is a huge country and tackling it in one all-embracing move is unlikely. It is most feasible to focus on the key conurbation's, firstly in the coastal littoral together with Beijing.

   Consideration must be given to whether China will exist as a single country 10 years hence, given its vastness and its cultural diversity. (Co-incidentally as the answers are being written news of the death of Deng Xiao-ping was announced triggering political comment regarding the economic and political future for China – nothing is certain in today's world).

2 *Consumption*

   The level of consumer demand would need to be determined: the Gilligan and Hird model could be used to assess latent demand. Whilst this could be assured in major

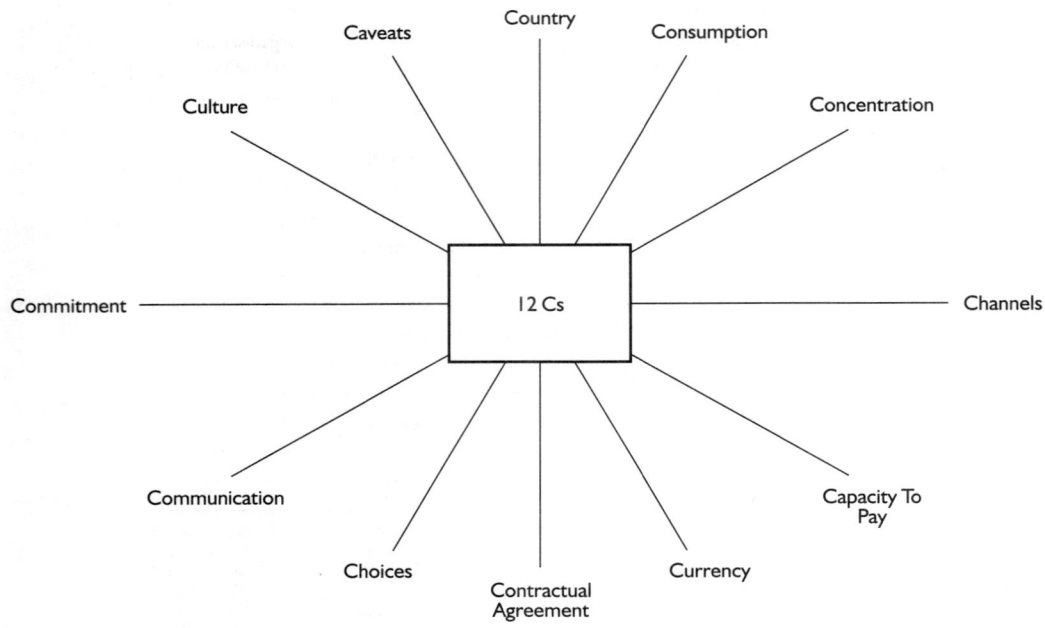

Figure 15.2 The 12 C's (*Source:* Doole, Lowe and Phillips)

cities such as Shanghai, Guandong, Beijing etc. demand in more provincial cities and the rural areas would be more difficult to determine. In any case it has been established that the growth of the business would be a long-term undertaking.

3 *Concentration*

A concentrated strategy is inevitable. Tackling China as an entity simply is unfeasible. Major conurbations would be the focus of attention.

4 *Channels*

One thing leads to another. A concentrated strategy would dictate the channel choice. Control of the channel is essential in this developing market especially as the method of distribution is via direct marketing. Warehousing, physical distribution and logistics are key factors in profitability.

5 *Capacity to pay*

Again Amway would investigate fully the appropriate segment community prior to commercialisation. The emerging affluent middle class act as influencers to the working class who would be the majority in the longer-term.

6 *Currency*

Mindful of the fact that the local currency is not fully convertible and may not be particularly stable (inflation in China is moderately high), Amway must and will recognise the pitfalls of dealing in it. However the company has vast experience in dealing in unstable markets and will plan accordingly.

7 *Contractual agreement*

It is recognised that the Chinese way of doing business is different to western practices. Amway must examine the appropriate way of doing business – liaising with local political officials and dignitaries as well as business people. Should corruption be an issue Amway must exercise the necessary caution.

8 *Choices*

The detail market entry strategy will be discussed later but Amway will consider balancing the **Risk** against the **Benefits**. Again the concentrated strategy will enable Amway to evaluate this stage by stage in its development.

9 *Communication*

Western communication channels i.e. advertising media are less highly developed in China, although advances are taking place rapidly. Modern technology has taken hold and television ownership is increasing. However the company will evaluate carefully the available channels and take full account of Guanxi and the impact of internal communication/word of mouth i.e. the Chinese way of doing things. The communication channel availability again links closely with the concentration on urban areas.

10 *Commitment*

Amway has this in abundance. The management of the company no doubt fully appreciates the scale of the task and what success entails.

11 *Caveats*

Other considerations include a full appreciation of the political, policy and taxation laws affecting both internal taxation and repatriation of profits to the USA.

12 *Culture*

This has been deliberately left to the last. An understanding of culture and the sensitivities surrounding it is the single most important strategic consideration, Fifield & Lewis loosely define culture as 'the very way we do things around here'. It is therefore the customer who is the central figure in determining success. Everything must be considered only in as much as it impacts on the beliefs and values of the customer. Anything less will invite failure. It is no use being product or operationally led – the customer is the centre of the company.

Question 1(b): answer

Introduction

Within the given time constraints of the examination period it is not feasible to prepare a marketing plan in any detail. What follows is an outline of the plan only, putting into perspective the implementation issues that would require more detail, thought and consideration.

At the outset it is vital to recognise that in 5 to 10 years planning horizons would be established and therefore clear, definable, measurable objectives would have to be established. Guandong is a stepping stone to a 300 million adult/housewife market.

It would be apparent that Amway would conduct an international marketing audit prior to the launch.

The Marketing plan outline that follows takes the form largely of brief almost 'bullet points', as a result of time constraints in the examination. The format is that of the 7 P's.

Product

- Great care is to be taken to match the product profiles to customer needs. This is fundamental to success and the statement does not need defending.
- Size, variety and especially packaging and labelling etc. would all require investigation.
- Consideration of appropriate testing (product research) would be relevant to a market with limited experience of the product portfolio. It is very likely that 'learning by doing' would be the best approach as formal product testing procedures familiar to western consumers might be totally inappropriate.
- Consideration to checking out indirect/substitute products and the strength of the entrenchment of existing consumer habits.
- Thought surrounding concentric rings of a product in terms of what the customer is buying (benefits of features) would be appropriate (for concentric rings ref. Kotler). The identification of what values the customer really is buying into is essential.

Price

- It is known that discounting and low price strategies equate to negative (fly-by-night operators).
- The Chinese customers take pride in buying brands.
- These two factors suggest a skimming pricing strategy.
- Additionally there is the corporate recognition of positioning Amway as the market leader, with Amway adopting a geocentric status not necessarily in the actual price but in price positioning. This strategic aspect of pricing increasingly important to multinationals/global corporations.
- Other factors impacting on pricing are long-term payback, speed of entry into the market and other logistical requirements: transportation, distribution, warehousing etc.

- It is not known just how price-sensitive the market is and Amway would need to carry out some customer testing but essentially Amway should price its products at the top end of what the market will bear.

Place
- A major consideration is if there is a lack of traditional retail outlets.
- Amway will need to think carefully and create their own distribution i.e. customer access. Being the world leader in 'member-get-member' direct marketing, the company can establish the appropriate route probably without too much difficulty. But cultural relevance will set the tone and it may be that alliances will have to be made with local politicians.
- Straightforward door-to-door canvassing is culturally unacceptable but Guanxi is acceptable. Amway deviously build on this and recognise the value of family and friends and the need to train everyone.

Promotion
- Push strategy will be the most appropriate customer communication interface given the circumstances of the market.
- Direct selling has been established as the way to success. It is cost-effective, believable, culturally relevant, the chain of communication is relatively short, direct and manageable (with care).
- However other marketing communication tools are also important. They can set the agenda, create awareness and position the company as the leader in the market. They can also assist greatly in creating the demand, for example, although household penetration of television may not be high, the medium may be appropriate for positional reasons and also because viewers may be the 'influencers' in the market (ref: new product innovation diffusion curve).
- Outdoor advertising/billboards would also be appropriate as they highlight brand – corporate values.
- In terms of sales promotion, discounting is probably inappropriate but cross-selling will undoubtedly work.
- Finally, public relations is very important as a culture of Guanxi i.e. word of mouth is very effective and relevant.
- Other considerations from the promotional perspective are the selection of the appropriate language (Mandarin). The tone of voice and the implementation of the marketing communication would have to reflect the values of the customer, e.g. translation of text would have to be done very carefully.

People
- The key to success (alongside the products). Everything that has been written underpins this fact.
- The issues are recruitment, training, motivation and retention of employees.
- Actually they are not employees but must be addressed and viewed as **Partners**.
- Training is the most important consideration.
- Middle management and front end contacts must be local and they will have an important say in the development of the product portfolio and the entire marketing programme so that flexibility is maintained in a fickle market-place.
- People will be the main marketing communication vehicle and public relations will feed off this.
- Also important are consistency of the message, protection of values and the development of standards, all developed and reinforced by training.
- It is therefore apparent that Amway must invest in a powerful training division whose director would warrant a board position.

Process
- The operational side of the business requires great care.
- Order servicing, call frequency, method and timing of deliveries requires a professional organisation and one that is in tune with customer requirements.

- The operational process must be consistent and systematic in order to succeed.
- Factors to consider also include depots (number and where placed) the costs – both fixed and variable; ordering cycles linked to production processing; payment procedures and methodology with cash flow implications etc.
- None of this is easy, but Amway is equipped to handle it. In an underdeveloped market Amway would need to establish and implant its corporate standards of customer service, setting the benchmarks for the industry but remaining conscious of cultural considerations.

Physical evidence
- Product support material, packaging delivery etc. will reflect the company position as the market and global leader.
- Dress code and all sales and marketing material will play their roles in delivering the right message.

Finally there is one more important point:

Control
- Controls are the building blocks of planning.
- It is essential that the appropriate mechanisms are firmly in place before launch.
- Attitudes and customer surveys. Plotting 'satisfaction' and negatives would be carried out on a regular basis monitoring both customer needs and market trends.

Kings Supermarket Inc. (June 1996)

Marks & Spencer (M & S), a giant UK retailer, has pioneered the selling of chilled food under the brand name St. Michael (pronounced Saint Michael). Now M & S plan to sell similar chilled food products in the United States through its recently acquired supermarket chain, Kings Supermarket Inc.

History

From simple beginnings 100 years or so ago, M & S has expanded to become the leading UK retailer, with 260 plus stores. Its core product(s) forming the basis of its success has been clothing – ready to wear garments for all the family. Its strategy and positioning has been to offer exceptional value for money. M & S has never sold on a price promotion platform. Discounting is unheard of as was until recently advertising and other marketing communication activity. M & S and its brand name St. Michael have become synonymous with quality and value. Shoppers of all social classes frequent the company's stores. Mrs Thatcher, when Prime Minister, shopped there regularly.

Having created a reputation in the clothing market M & S began to look for new challenges. Noticing the rise of food supermarkets, M & S decided to diversify away from their core business (clothing) and enter the food market. Their strategy was not to compete 'head to head' with the supermarket giants but instead to develop niche markets – again repeating their formula of exceptional value for money and ignoring price competition. They have been successful, standing today as number 3 or 4 in the food supermarket pecking order. Operating within their existing clothing stores it was quite impossible for the company to offer customers a comprehensive range of food products – in any case they had no desire to do so. The method of entering the food market was through offering a limited range of products that were different, exciting and which genuinely met consumer needs. Spearheading this challenge were 'complete meal' dishes, single servings. The meals were **not** frozen (such products existed in other supermarket chains) but CHILLED. Chilled food is freshly prepared and needs to be heated or lightly cooked before serving i.e. there is no defrosting process. The range of dishes chosen were semi-exotic as opposed to everyday ones. For example Sezhuan Chicken, Prawn with Spring Onion and Ginger, Aromatic Crispy Duck are among the selection, priced variously between £2.50 and £6.99 – and this for a single serving. So they are not cheap, nor are they designed especially for family eating. Rather the stereotyped customer is a professional person with a busy life-style who after a hard day at work can enjoy a 'special' meal without the bother of preparation. Very few consumers shop exclusively at M & S for food but rather use the store to augment the purchase of everyday items. (However as the formula has been successful M & S have extended their range of products to include some of the more mundane products such as bread.) Using the chilled meal concept as a bridgehead strategy has proven very successful for M & S's diversification programme.

Will it work overseas?

M & S are now examining the potential to repeat the formula in the United States through its subsidiary Kings Supermarkets. But transporting the UK concept to the US is not simple. Consider the following aspects:

1 **The US consumer** – The American customer may be more unconventional, seeking a wider range of dishes than their British counterparts. Nutritional issues are possibly more important. Lo-fat, Hi-fibre stickers are commonplace – something that M & S has not had to worry about. The choice of dishes attractive to the UK customer may not have similar appeal. For example Sezhuan Chicken, may have no appeal to US customers.

2 **Substitutes** – US supermarkets stock other varieties of take-home and premium easy-to-prepare foods. The traditional US 'deli', (delicatessen) together with salad bars and in-store bakeries offer a wide range of alternatives making chilled food less appealing.

3 **Price** – Chilled food is marketed as semi-exotic, or even gourmet (e.g. Crispy Duck) and is accordingly premium priced. This may limit the US market to certain up-market neighbourhoods e.g. Lower Manhattan in New York. Moreover, traditionally US food is cheaper than its UK counterpart.

4 **Shopping habits** – Whilst the UK trend to food shopping is towards out-of-town superstores visited once a week, Marks & Spencer's appeal is to those who top up their weekly shop with daily purchases of chilled and fresh foods. Will the US customer be interested in a daily shopping routine, e.g. picking up the chilled meal on the way home from work?

5 **Competition** – Other US food giants are also interested in the chilled food concept. Campbells, General Foods, Kraft and even Nestlé have entered this area. There is no virgin market opportunity here.

6 **Logistics and suppliers** – are just two further considerations. Chilled food spoils easily unless a constant temperature is maintained. Shipping from a central base to 264 stores in the UK is feasible, but the US is far bigger. Operating and maintaining a distribution network would be more difficult and costly. In moving to the US, the company would need to develop new suppliers with the consequent quality control issues – and in a new food category.

7 **The St. Michael brand** – In the UK consumer confidence in the company and its brand is second to none. Getting consumers' trust in the new concept of chilled food was not a problem. But in the US awareness levels are zero, and in any case the company has chosen to launch under King's brand name.

M & S have retained your services as a marketing consultant to address the overall task of launching into the US market. The issue is strategic, not tactical and your initial thoughts include an audit of the marketplace.

PART A

Question 1

(a) What particular steps would you recommend M & S to take **before** entering the US market? **(25 marks)**

(b) On the basis of the information provided in the case what would be your recommended outline action plan for launching into the US market? (Should you wish to make any assumptions, these must be stated clearly). **(25 marks)**

MARKS & SPENCER plc
The launch of chilled food into the US. market
June 1996

Prepared for M & S Management
By: Marketing Consultant

Contents
- Background to the brief
- Question 1a The investigations of the market
  - environment
  - culture
  - competition
  - company
  - consumer segmentation
  - positioning
  - summary
- Question 1b Outline launch considerations
  - pre launch
  - test market
  - launch

Question 1(a): answer

Background to the brief
- Marks & Spencer (M & S) has acquired Kings Supermarket.
- M & S, as a major UK retailer has adequate funds, management and marketing exercise.
- It has successfully pioneered chilled food in the UK and is the category leader. It has "redefined" the UK market.
- M & S has the corporate vision and ambition to be a world leader in retailing, with prepared food products playing an important role in its portfolio.
- The company in the UK is positioned as the provider of quality products offering value for money. It is not a discounter.

What is not known is whether the successful innovation of semi-exotic (in UK consumer terms) chilled food is transferable into the US market. This report sets out in 2 stages:

(a) An investigation into the tasks to be undertaken before entering the US market (Question 1a).

(b) An outline marketing plan, in strategic terms to enter the market (Question 1b).

(a)   The investigation prior to entering the market (Question 1a)
So as to understand the international marketing process, it needs to be viewed schematically from the first decision-making process through to implementation and control. Fifield and Lewis in their *International Marketing Strategy 1998–99* (Butterworth-Heinemann) present this in a flow chart model which is modified here as the method of entry, and the selection of the market has already been decided.

Time precludes a full explanation of the above model, but it is self evident given the circumstances of the case that:

1   Any decisions must be based on solid and reliable market information on the potential for the organisation, including an in-depth analysis of the competition. Success in what is quite evidently a highly competitive and crowded market-place can only come about from the adoption of a sustainable competitive differential/advantage. The adoption of, and its recognition by the consumer of a superior competitive positioning is essential.

2   A clear understanding by everyone in the organisation, of the company's goals and objectives and their role in creating success.

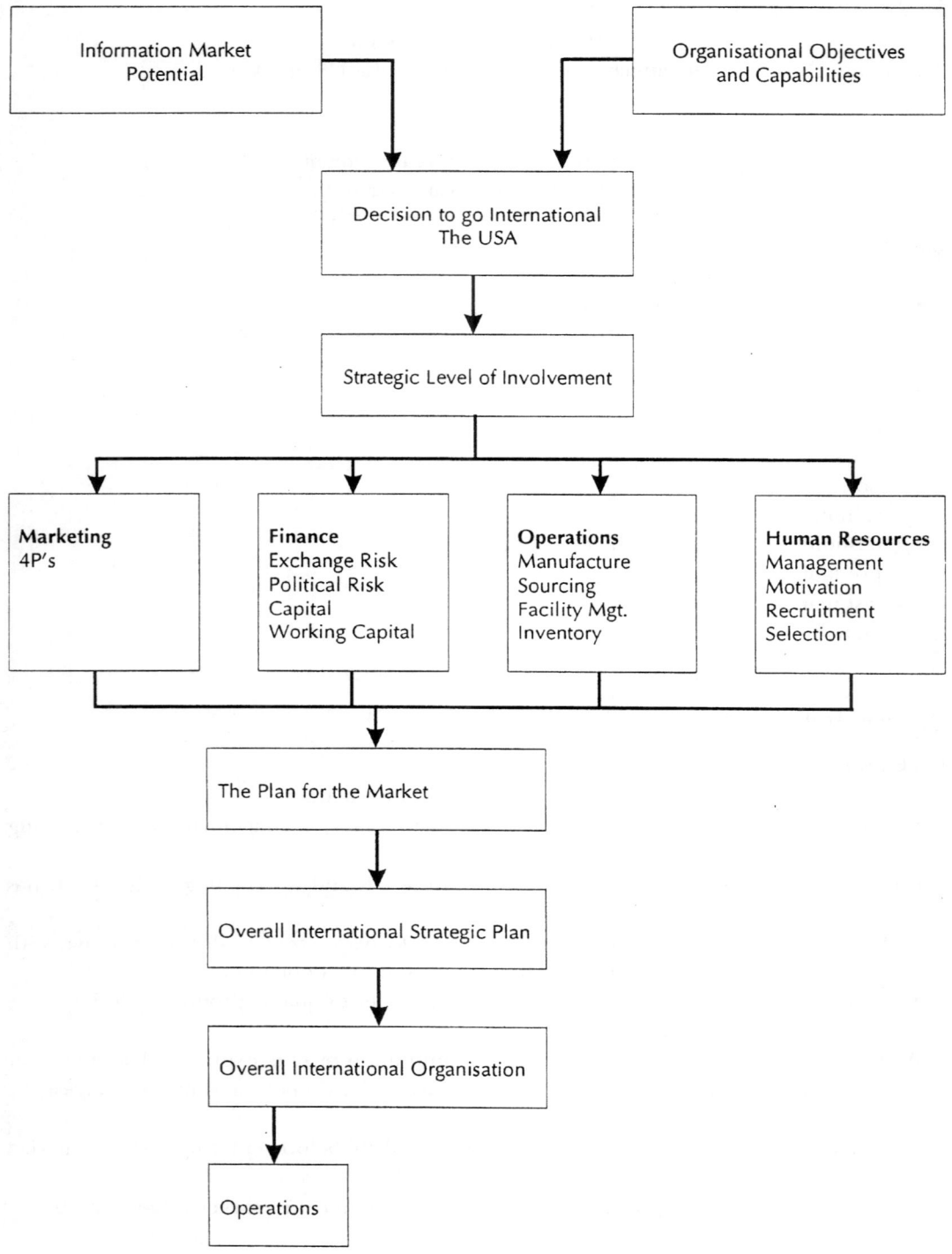

3   Perhaps the most important step is the Strategic Level of Involvement. This is the first strategic decision the organisation must make on its route to internationalisation, i.e. how deeply involved it must be to compete successfully in the market-place. This decision will determine (at least in the short to medium term) the marketing, financial, operational and human resource strategies that have to be considered and employed. This case demands a wider understanding of the principles of international business and is not simply about the manipulation of the 4 or 7 P's of the marketing mix.

It has already been stated that information is essential to success, as is a rigorous appraisal of the company. This knowledge must then be refined and used in developing appropriate segmentation, targeting and positioning as the basis for the successful entry into the market-place via the development of an appropriate marketing strategy and operational follow through.

Set out below are the stages of the investigation.

Stage 1

ENVIRONMENTAL AUDIT
Macro factors affecting the market and the organisation.

Political
Although superficially the US is an "open government" economy, future developments in the formation of the Triad, i.e. the 3 major trading blocks of the US, EU, and SE. Asia may well see a fortress mentality emerging which could have a detrimental effect on trading, via entry restrictions, repatriation of profits etc. Unlikely but not impossible.

Economic
There is some evidence of polarisation in the economy with the gap between the rich and the poor widening as industry restructures, and technology drives out workers fulfilling routine tasks. This might have an impact on purchasing power, particularly in the market for premium price convenience food.

Social
Changing demography, work patterns (part-time, more women working etc.) are already, and will increasingly alter the patterns of purchase as well as the nature of meal consumption. The US may well be at the cutting edge of these changes influencing the dynamics of family life. Something like 40% of all meals consumed in the US are taken "on the move".

Technical
Besides impacting on the pattern of consumption – car snacking for example, technology is having a huge impact on the supply side via EPOS; JIT shortening planning and delivery horizon, thus reducing costs dramatically. Such developments will have a favourable effect but only if the organisation is on top of them.

Stage 2

Culture
The US and the UK are 2 countries divided by a common language. There is very little synergy between the two. Ethnography, historical development and the whole range of the components of culture are different, e.g.

- religious beliefs
- role of family and friends in relationships
- education
- motivational forces
- home ownership
- peer group patterns
- beliefs and norms on social issues, choice and freedom etc.
- aspirations
- mobility and communications
- eating patterns
- the role of the 'meal' in society.

Not only do these vary by ethnic grouping, but they vary considerably by state/region. Texas is nothing like New Brunswick. It cannot be overstated that a deep understanding of what drives customer needs and wants will underpin success.

Stage 3

Competition
I have already commented on the notion of the Sustainable Competitive Advantage; Being First to Market; Redefining the market. This can only be achieved if first the competition is analysed – and not just from a "hard" perspective, i.e. volume, value, financial, distribution data, but perhaps (no not perhaps – definitely) from the perspective of their relative positioning in the mind of the consumer segments. Positioning exercises are often the key to identifying the competitive advantage. Perception is reality to your customers.

Stage 4

Company audit

Once the environment audit is completed, M & S should turn their attention to an honest evaluation and appraisal of its resources and skills – both physical and psychological; organisational and motivational.

This again is crucial to success. Too frequently companies are seduced by overseas potential – but fail due to lack of management skills (not necessarily marketing) and commitment. From what is known of M & S they have sufficient of both. However, history tells that they have never made a success in their Canadian venture, broke-even after around 6 years in France, not yet fully succeeded in their US clothing business (Brookes Brothers). The point being made is that being a mega success in your home market with superb management does not guarantee automatic success internationally!

Stage 5

Consumer segmentation

Finding the right segment and not attempting to speak to the whole market will prove to be a potentially tricky task in the US. Its cultural diversity and lack of homogeneity represents both a barrier to success, but also a great opportunity to both create and establish a new niche – redefining the market-place. M & S is advised to use local research agencies and to adopt recently developed research techniques, such as ethnography (living with the problem) in order to highlight the nuances of consumer behaviour. As an example, Toyota sent a host of company executives to live in the USA for 2 years as part of the development of the luxury car; the Lexus. They discovered, among other things, that the "clunk" of closing the car door was a very important consideration in the purchase decision. God is in the detail! – and there is nothing more detailed than food. So qualitative research is the key.

Stage 6

Positioning

Uniqueness in the mind of the consumer is essential. 'Me-too' products rarely succeed unless they are discounted with the corresponding effect on profitability. This, "specialness" is what creates branding. It may be a physical attribute but is all too frequently created by skilful marketing. I have written sufficient evidence on this point earlier to signify its importance.

Summary

These stages of investigation and analysis will form the basis of the development of the long-term marketing strategy from which the largely tactical decision of the marketing mix will emanate. This, then is the basis from which to begin the launch.

Question 1(b): answer

The information contained in the case is insufficient to produce a marketing plan of any detail. Question 1a emphasises the need for a careful investigation before entry takes place. All one can do at this stage is to consider some of the basic issues that would need to be addressed using the components of the marketing plan.

Pre-launch

Having identified the opportunity it is advisable that M & S undertake a careful step by step programme of new product development. They will need to create a hypothesis and test it, via a comprehensive research programme, utilising the full NPD process as explained by such authors as Wilson, Gilligan, Pearson, in the recommended text for the Planning and Control syllabus. In addition to focusing on the chosen Segment/Target Market the entire marketing mix will need testing prior to launch.

- Composition of the range.
- Packaging.
- Pricing.
- Distribution – precise location, both geographic (place) and in-store.

- Promotion – the development of an ideal positioning leading to the creation of the brand identity and image. Please note that the choice of its name is important here. Birds Eye, a much respected marketing company within Unilever once launched a product in the USA called, something like Faggots in Gravy with disastrous (if humorous) effect as faggots has a different connotation to the UK interpretation.

Coincidentally, M & S must investigate all aspects of the logistic, operational, financial and human resource issues. Referring to the first model in the report, Fifield and Lewis link success in international marketing to the integration of the elements of business strategy and operations (true of all marketing but especially internationally). The delivery mechanism and the supply chain is an integral part of the marketing plan. Logistics distribution are especially critical in short shelf life products. Additionally, great care will need to be taken in the choice of suppliers in delivering quality products, quality control, consistency and total service. It may be the case that initially M & S might consider serving and servicing the US market from the UK for "getting it right first time" is critical to success. Mistakes in the product end of the total service often invites immediate disaster and failure. It might seem far fetched, but M & S serve their French food outlets from the UK, shipping fresh bread and sandwiches daily [these 2 products are the company's biggest sellers in France]. McDonalds place such great importance on the product, that they frequently open in new markets, with supplies airfreighted in from overseas. They did this in their UK test stores.

Test market

Having "perfected" the offer via careful pre-launch research, the next stage is to test market in selected stores that reflect the appropriate neighbourhood containing the identified target market. M & S can learn from this, as it is very unlikely that the pre launch research will have covered every eventuality. Very careful monitoring and emphasis on qualitative research techniques should be employed. M & S should not rely on store sales alone for its evaluation.

The test market will utilise and embrace the full range of marketing motivation techniques to create awareness, trial (extremely important in a development such as this), repeat purchase techniques etc. It may be that the company may also use the most recent database marketing techniques to lure, and seduce selected individuals with a predisposition to innovation in the development of the marketing plan.

Obviously the company will carefully monitor competitive response and, in fact, anticipate the likely fight back.

Launch

It is too premature to consider specifics but as an indication of likely intent (this is often dangerous as it is too easy to impose self reference criteria on a market and its customers) the company might consider:

- Concentrating on key cities e.g.
  - East Coast nucleus such as New York, Philadelphia, Boston.
  - Central Nucleus; Chicago, St. Louis.
  - West Coast nucleus; Los Angeles, San Francisco, San Diego.

Whatever route is taken, carefully stage managed expansion is imperative. No one would contemplate a coast to coast launch as the supply side could not cope.

- Launch with a small (or restricted) range, building consumer knowledge and adding variety following experience in production, quality control, distribution and other logistics. Also continuous assessment and re-evaluation of consumer preferences (indicated improvements) of a limited range is more manageable and realistic in a "different" market.
- One should not overlook the effect that would need to be placed on the qualitative or "soft" factors in marketing, i.e. the 'People' part of the mix. Training and educating staff from the store level upwards is vital. For example, McDonalds Director of Training has a major position on the company Board of Directors – Nothing is left to chance, nor

should it be at the M & S launch. Again, training the supply side as well as internal company personnel is important.

- Whilst there are other points in the development of the marketing plan, sufficient guidance has been given to indicate the breadth of the task to be undertaken, and notification that marketing (international marketing) is not simply the manipulation of the 4 or 7 elements of the mix, but has wider ramifications that lead down from corporate strategy.

TZ Pipes (December 1995)

The executive training room at TZ Pipes was full with young and ambitious managers. The week long training programme was concerned with 'Developing an Improved International Culture at TZ Pipes'. The topic under consideration at the moment was international marketing strategy. One part of the day was concerned with the type of organisation that would be most suitable for TZ. The other part of the day would look at strategic options and their implementation.

The day started with a series of charts giving information about different countries in the world. Some of that information compared country size by population, by Gross National Product, by past and forecast growth rates. Additionally the charts attempted to compare the amount of cultural difference between the UK and the various countries under discussion.

The distribution of company sales was as follows: UK 28%, other countries in Europe 23%, Middle East 21%, Far East 11%, Africa 8% and South America 9%. The TZ Pipes market in Africa was to the sub-Saharan region and was dependent upon foreign aid and World Bank programmes.

TZ manufacture iron pipes and fittings for the water and gas industries. TZ export pipes to most parts of the world with the exception of North America and to China. Sales in 1995 were in line with the company forecast of £68 million. This was a nine percent increase over 1994.

Until now the company has relied on the sales and marketing efforts of David Jones and the export team of ten people, based at company headquarters just south of London. Direct contact with the market has been achieved through the use of agents and distributors. In order to generate growth for the future David Jones is considering changing to other approaches.

TZ Pipes have to cope with the technical specifications set out by the national organisations responsible for approving the standards of iron pipes for water and gas. Technical standards vary around the world. This is partly because of different climatic conditions, for example to cope with extreme heat in the Middle Eastern countries of Saudi Arabia and Kuwait. It also relates to different views about what are appropriate levels of performance and safety.

TZ Pipes is anxious to expand its international sales considerably. It is one of the larger companies in its field although many companies supply this market when viewed in world terms.

In the role of one of the managers on the training programme identify options and make recommendations on:

PART A

Question 1
How TZ Pipes should investigate market opportunities.   **(25 marks)**

Question 2
What TZ Pipes should do to develop a more international organisation and culture within the company   **(25 marks)**

Question 1: answer
Brief Observations (Where are we now?)

TZ is a biggish Company with a turnover of £68 million in 1995. It is acknowledged to be among the larger firms in the industry.

TZ is successfully exhibiting sales growth at 9% in 1995 and is on target to achieve budget.

TZ has considerable International experience, and has a degree of Internationalisation; but its sales performance overseas is not particularly strong and these remain major market opportunities unfulfilled. Sales figures indicate:

UK   28% = £1 9.0m
Rest of Europe 23% = £15.6m
Mid East   21% = £14.3m

Thus 72% of turnover is in these 3 regions.

The Far East 11% (£75m) is substantially underdeveloped, as is Africa and South America.

Markets not yet addressed include China and USA, and – in all probability – India.

Although there is information concerning local standards and culture, it is likely that the industry is/will become more global in the future, as Multinational Corporations develop global standards. It is therefore vital that TZ be established in all major markets.

TZ's level of Internationalism is low. It is ethnocentric and is export-led, with a team of 10 UK based Export Sales Managers.

To take advantage of opportunities, TZ needs to change its focus, reorganise its management, and become more International in its culture.

The Key Tasks

1 Find and exploit market opportunities.
2 Re-focus; reorganise its culture.

Investigating market opportunities

Before considering this question it is important that TZ recognises the value of creating a 5-year Corporate Business plan, and within it should be contained goals/objectives year by year. The company would be unwise to leap into new markets without taking stock of the notion of what kind of Company it wishes to be in the medium term (5 years). This business plan will form the framework for market/country development, and also be the benchmark for controls. It will also establish the organisational imperatives vital for TZ's future success.

The major methodology is to establish International segmentation, whereby groups of countries can be brought together in a series of clusters so that TZ can focus on a strategy of market concentration. Whilst the most appropriate method of investigation is Harrell & Kiefer's model, it is important to refer to Kale & Sudharshan's work in this area. Their argument is that a Company such as TZ should segment markets on the basis of customers, not countries – seeking out clusters of decision-makers in relevant industries with broadly similar needs, wants, purchase motivations, etc. It would appear that water and gas co-operation meet this criteria (albeit with some local differences). But the similarities outweigh the differences which can be accommodated at the tactical level. The Harrall & Keifer model below would identify Primary, Secondary & Tertiary opportunities.

Market Attractiveness

TZ's Compatibility with Market

	P	S	T
S	T	
T		

It is very important to recognise that the initial screening is designed to locate clusters of customers. It is also important to note that in countries as large as China, USA, etc., clusters may be found within the country. The market attractions would include:

- Size of market (industry not the country).
- Degree of sophistication (ability to handle the equipment etc.).
- Ability to pay (including international facilitators e.g. world bank).
- Level of competition (local and the multinationals).
- Clustering of the industry in a country.
- Accessibility (tariffs, government 'openness' to foreign companies, etc.).
- Political/economic risk.
- Degree of local differences, due to climate etc.

The list could be continued but there is sufficient criteria here to provide evidence of market attractiveness.

A second aspect of the market investigation is the creation of a Management Information System – in line with the 5-year plan. MIS is a long-range planning tool, and in this case should place SLEPT factors at the heart of the 'indicators' triggering TZ's future activities.

A third factor in the market investigation process is the investment in fostering government relationships at the appropriate level. This could be done initially under the auspices of the UK government – trade missions etc. – and the acquisition/creation of database knowledge relating to future industry/market developments. It is clear from the case study that the decision to invest in oil and water infrastructure is frequently taken at senior Governmental level, and therefore TZ needs to be represented at this level in order to secure the business. A following point to this is that in implementation and execution, partner selection is crucial, and it may be that TZ has to change its 'modus operandi' in the future.

Question 2: answer

Concluding Q1, with a comment on organisation was deliberate, for the strategic development of the Company is inextricably linked to its organisational pattern and the path it takes in changing its culture to match the strategic plan, and the business growth through market development. To become a world-class Company, TZ needs to change its focus from being ethnocentric and export-led, to having a greater knowledge of customers, competitors and currency. The factors that are essential to this change of culture are becoming more customer focused by moving the Company's decision-taking from London to the centre of the cluster/segments identified and developed via the Harrell & Kiefer and Kale & Sudharshan models described in Q1. Putting it succinctly, TZ needs to establish a number of regional hubs based around a key distribution, design, planning, and operational centre, which will control all business and marketing activities in the region. Taking the Far East as an example, Singapore would be a likely centre, covering ASEAN, with over 300 million population embracing 7 countries which are growing at an annual rate of c.8–10%. Gas and water infrastructure are very important to the development of ASEAN, and the member countries are keen to co-operate and collaborate on major industrial initiatives in the field in which TZ operates. In China, key hubs would develop around Guandong and Shanghai along the coastal strip, with later development inland (c.5 years hence).

Time: the competitive differential. TZ needs to begin planning this sea-change in culture with immediate effect, otherwise other major corporations will seize the market. Once established as the preferred supplier/installer, it is extremely difficult for others to break into the purchase cycle. Once a gas/water main is laid, it tends to stay there for decades, and the future ongoing business is replacement parts and after-sales service. So there is only a 'one time' opportunity. To seize it, TZ should start employing new people with International marketing experience (not export knowledge).

It should change its entire Export Department into the International Marketing Division, with relocation of existing Export Teams out to these newly identified regions, investing in training so they become more knowledgeable of the market – by that, I mean the customers and the key influences (Government Officials, etc.).

TZ needs to get closer to its intermediaries, distributors and agents, and involve them in the planning process. They must become business partners and be seen as the natural extension of the supply chain. They should not be seen as bolt-on accessories of the Organisation. They need to be motivated, supported, and trained in the TZ way of thinking. Key TZ International Marketing executives would probably be located within the key distributors. Distribution needs to be organised around the hub strategy, and needs to agree to co-operate and collaborate in the development of a regional business plan. This is not easy to achieve, as distributors (and agents) are often independently minded. Nevertheless, great efforts must be made along this collaboration route – unless TZ proposes to abandon its existing distribution methodology and go for wholly owned subsidiaries, which is totally unfeasible at this stage, but might be part of either a 10-year programme or part of a change in distribution strategy in developing new markets. But either could be done in the short term. TZ simply does not have the expertise.

So the new organisational strategy is based upon TZ being more regiocentric. It is perhaps worth summarising the key points:

- The Organisation should be based around customers and include Governments, major consortiums and other multinational organisations involved in infrastructure contracts.
- TZ must establish partnerships at all levels. This a 'long term' planning horizon industry where trust, relationships and back-up logistics matter. Relationships are vital, adding further emphasis to the regiocentric approach.
- TZ must be positioned as an 'insider', to quote Kenichi Ohmae.
- TZ must get closer to its intermediaries, abandoning the 'them and us'. Develop partnerships.
- Leadership is an essential ingredient. The Board of Directors must seize this initiative, and change must come from the very top. All key personnel must be part of the re-orientation, and the Company must reorganise with a Board Director(s) taking responsibility for the restructuring. Personnel, marketing, operations and finance are all inextricably linked in the change to regional hubs. Engineers must talk to customers in their markets and help them plan their requirements.
- Radical change is essential to achieve this, and future plans should include detailed analysis of:

  (a) Formulation of joint ventures, either with existing distributors or new partners in new markets.
  (b) Manufacturing within the designed regions, once the critical mass is established. With £14.3m turnover in the Far East and its recognised fast growth-rate, a decision might not be that far away. It would further establish TZ as an "insider". On the other hand, Europe – with £15.6m turnover – would probably be rather better served from the UK, as distribution logistics within the EU are fast and inexpensive.
  (c) Steps should now be taken to consider strategic alliances with key players. This could be a vital ingredient in opening up markets such as China, India, USA etc. The alliance could be with other global players, or key organisations in the 'local' market. China, and also Russia, Ukraine and other Eastern European markets not mentioned in the case, have great potential; but strategic alliance would be necessary to gain entry on distribution, and agents are virtually non existent.

Pivovar Brewery (Czech Republic) (June 1995)

The world beer market is dominated by a few large companies with global or near global brands. Major players include Anheuser-Busch of the US, Kirin of Japan, and Carlsberg and Heineken in Europe. European countries with a long beer-drinking tradition still have many smaller breweries, however, serving regional and local markets. Even in the United States, the domination of such giants as Anheuser-Busch is tempered by a growth of micro-breweries serving niche markets, and many foreign brands are imported.

The Czech Republic is situated in Central Europe and was formed in 1993 when Czechoslovakia split into the Czech and Slovak Republics. The former Communist regime collapsed bloodlessly in 1989 and democracy was established. It has a population of 10 million, the highest per capita beer consumption in the world (exceeding even that of

Germany) and a long and proud tradition of brewing. Beer is drunk by men and women of all ages, although wine is also very popular. Economic restructuring during the change to a market economy has reduced disposable income, however, and former strict price controls are gradually being relaxed, making consumers very price-conscious, at least in the short term. Marketing research has only begun since 1989. There is some over-capacity in the Czech brewing industry.

The Pivovar brewery is situated near Brno, the second largest city. The brewery is the tenth largest in the Czech Republic, though small by international standards. The ownership of the brewery is currently changing. In 1948 the brewery was nationalized when Communism was established in Czechoslovakia. With the return of democracy, the principle of reprivatization was established, but owing to the complicated pattern of ownership it was decided not to return the brewery to any of the previous owners, but to hand it over to Brno City Council, by whom it will be privatized.

The products

The brewery products are bottled beer and draught beer (in barrels). Bottled beer accounts for 46% of output and draught beer 54%. Bottles are of 0.3 litre size (80% of bottled output) and 0.5 litre size (20%).

The beer produced is principally a pale lager beer in two alcoholic strengths, 10° (about 3.8% alcohol by volume) and 12° (about 4.5% alcohol). Recently (1991) a dark beer of 3% alcohol by volume has been introduced, and there are plans to produce other new products, including a 'lite' beer, an alcohol-free beer and a strong Pilsner type beer. Bottled beer is pasteurized, but draught beer is pasteurized only for export.

Brewing followed the classic lager method till recently. The brewery has now begun to modernize the plant with the introduction of conical fermenters. It is estimated this will produce savings in the order of 15% of total production costs. Some of the older equipment may be retained for speciality and short-run beers. Independent blind tastings show no loss of quality with the new system.

Distribution

Until 1990 distribution was handled principally by three State distribution companies, but these have now ceased to operate. As a result Pivovar, like many other companies, is having to handle its own distribution. A number of depots have been built or taken over in the main sales regions. In an increasingly competitive market, quality and speed of delivery of orders are essential differentiating factors. Pivovar has a good reputation because it can currently supply any order within 24 hours, and has gained new custom recently. The brewery has its own fleet of trucks to deliver locally and to supply its depots.

Selling and marketing

Unlike the UK, but like most others worldwide, the Czech beer industry is not vertically integrated, and breweries only own a small number of outlets. Pivovar owns one pub in Brno but otherwise competes for contracts with other breweries in the area. Supply agreements with pubs and shops are usually contracted annually, and the price is fixed for that year. Pivovar now offers its customers for draught beer a technical service for maintenance of its dispense equipment as an added incentive. The delivered price of beer is 140% of production cost, giving a gross margin of 40%. Pivovar prices are just above average currently. Pivovar has retained its logo unchanged since the 1930s. Promotion is principally below-the-line, through point-of-sale material, beer mats, bottle openers and promotional posters. The posters were developed through a local Czech agency.

Pivovar used to export 20% of production to other countries of the Eastern bloc. The break-up of Comecon and the economic crisis in Russia have resulted in the loss of these markets. Former trading partners, including Slovakia, have introduced tariff barriers to protect their domestic producers. New export markets are therefore being sought, with a target of 30% of total production. The logistics of beer transport allow export of barrels to neighbouring countries and bottled or canned beer all over the world. Beyond a certain level, however, it is easier to license production through foreign breweries, though whether a licensed beer retains all its intangible values is debatable. Czech beer conforms to the German 'Reinheitsgebot' purity standard and has a good reputation there. Czech beer is also sold in the UK in supermarkets and off-licences, and in pubs (usually through alliances with UK brewers) and has a 'heritage' quality image.

Question 1

(a) Wishing to expand into international markets Pivovar have retained your services as an international marketing consultant. Taking full account of the information in the case, write a brief report examining the different ways in which Pivovar might expand its sales revenue and profits from international markets together with the implications for each choice. **(25 marks)**

(b) Pivovar have been approached by a major player in the global beer market with a view to acquiring the company. In the event of the take-over succeeding, what advice would you give the new owners in marketing the Pivovar brand globally? **(25 marks)**

Background information to candidates

Question
The question subdivides into a number of separate parts. Most notable you are asked to (i) identify the different ways in which Pivovar can expand sales revenue and profit whilst (ii) discussing the implications for each choice. The following answer is intended as a guideline only and may not be the definitive or complete answer (no such thing exists). Rather, the mini-case, because of its lack of hard facts, is a scenario which allows you to demonstrate the *process* of international marketing principles. Further points to consider are:

1 Adopt the role of a consultant employed by Pivovar. Consultants get paid for making recommendations – so make them and justify them. Set out clear aims and objectives and devise appropriate strategies.
2 Adopt a report format – the question demands it!
3 Always begin with general observations. Interpret the case – it plays an important part in shaping your answer.

Question 1(a): answer
The company has set specific goals. They are:

Aim
The current owners are Brno City Council, who have been given the brief to privatize Pivovar, i.e. they are seeking to sell it.

Objectives

1 To expand into overseas markets.
2 To expand sales revenue and profits.
3 To export 30% of production.

These goals are perceived to be limited and the terms of reference employed are short-term rather than five-year planning horizons.

The task

1 To examine different ways of achieving the objectives.
2 To consider the implications of each choice.

General observations: What do we know?/Where are we now?

1 Pivovar is in a change situation. At home it enjoys a good reputation.
2 The market is limited in scope for growth and there is some overcapacity.
3 The market is increasingly price-sensitive.

4 Pivovar is a modest sized organization – tenth largest in a country of 10 million population.

5 Its resources, management, finance, production etc. are in short supply.

6 Its marketing expertise is virtually non-existent; its pricing cost plus and not market based.

7 Its international know-how is also nil. It once 'exported' 20% of its production to Comecon countries but all of that has disappeared.

8 The products themselves are good in both the original and new formulation and Czech beer has a high reputation, which might be exploitable internationally.

Key assumptions

Bottled beers, in particular, have recently become fashion products in the majority of the world's sophisticated, post-industrial and industrialized economies. They attract premium pricing (part of their appeal) and are positioned as lifestyle products drunk by the upwardly mobile, e.g. the UK has seen Japanese, Mexican, Australian, German, Spanish, Thai and Singaporean, even Korean, beers selling well in the past decade.

The strategic options

It is important to recognize the scale of the task and balance it with the resources and skills of the company. Pivovar is seeking a 30% uplift in production earmarked for overseas markets – this is perceived as a short-term goal. This increase in production must also be profitable in the short term. Pivovar has no real option available other than positioning itself as a *niche* player in what is a massive industry, namely brewing beer. Understanding this is the key to the selection of options.

Strategic option 1   To be positioned as a 'classic' lager to consumers who perceive themselves to be enthusiasts. In the short term, priority should be given to identifying and prioritizing EU countries simply because of logistics, distribution and the learning curve. To these consumers, it is very likely that the country of origin effect is important. The product must be Czech produced. The product could and should be market-based in its pricing – and a premium price positioning should be sought as part of the criteria of choice for country/market entry gaining additional revenue and **Profit**. To achieve this it must be sold in bottles with distribution via supermarkets and other appropriate retail outlets together with restaurant, pubs, bars, cafés etc.

Implications stemming from Option 1 include:

- Care should be taken in selecting markets where consumers' profiles match the niche positioning – those who view Pivovar's classic Czechness as a benefit, a point of differentiation, are delighted to pay more!
- Distribution and logistics require careful partner selection, e.g. in the UK a major brewer with strong distribution networks and capable of distributing, selling and, importantly, promoting Pivovar.
- To achieve success, close liaison, planning, positioning and branding of Pivovar is vital. Pivovar does not have the skill base and would need to outsource this expertise to its partner and in return should secure guarantees/commitment to firm orders.
- This last point is essential so that production can be planned for.
- Logistics also require careful pre-planning and should be managed with precision as the retail trade (of all sorts) operates on low stock levels, JIT being everyday custom and practice. Being 'out of stock' guarantees lost sales and is unacceptable in this consumer demand-driven/niche-oriented segment of the beer market, known for its fickleness.
- The downside of this option is that the segment can be fashion-based, frivolous and potentially short-lived (or at least with short product life cycles). However, this may not concern Brno City Council, whose aim is increased profitability leading to the sale of Pivovar.

Strategic option 2   To export draught lager to neighbouring countries, e.g. Germany and Austria, both of whom are high consumption markets and who may well recognize the excellence of the Czech brewing industry.

Implications of this option are that it may be more difficult to penetrate an already well-established market where draught drinking habits may be entrenched.

- Additionally, the revenue flows may not be high, i.e. it may be more difficult to persuade potential customers to pay more.
- Usurping and overturning established brands usually requires financial underpinning and there is little evidence that monies are available. Who in Germany and Austria would want to invest in this option?
- To succeed, Pivovar would have to create a niche and unless a suitable partner could be found the option is unlikely to succeed. Doing it alone is not a viable alternative. Pivovar simply does not have the resources or the time to build market penetration.

Strategic option 3   Further into the future, to develop licensing agreements with brewers in more distant countries, i.e. outside the EU. These, in fact, could be anywhere.

Implications   This route is dependent on consumer acceptance that the country of origin effect is unimportant in the selected countries.

- However, with the world becoming a global village by the day, consideration must be given to the dilution and devaluation of the brand values in those countries where the country of origin may be of paramount importance in positioning terms.
- Licensing always has an element of risk in terms of product quality.
- Controlling the product position and its promotion is also difficult.

Additional implications of the internationalization of Pivovar

1 International expansion should be planned with deliberation and care. There is a learning curve to be experienced.
2 Pivovar should not try all three strategic options simultaneously. It should proceed stage by stage sequentially.
3 Of the three options, I would recommend starting with option one. It has the advantage of greater profitability.
4 At all times the international management of Pivovar should be planned. Control and evaluation procedures must be in-built to this development.
5 Promotional positioning across the chosen countries should be considered with a strategic perspective, i.e. one single positioning should be adopted with variations in execution allowable to meet consumers' perceptions in different countries. An international marketing communications company should advise on this, even though Pivovar may not have the financial clout to fund the creation of a Eurobrand. The basic building blocks and policy should none the less be established. From the perspective of a future sale of the company, a prospective purchaser will pay more for a Eurobrand than a series of unconnected positionings.
6 To have any reasonable chance of success Pivovar must, as a matter of urgency, create an international marketing division advised by myself as a consultant on a retainer for a two- to three-year period of engagement.

Question 1(b): answer

As a general comment, the world is becoming a global village. Major multinationals are increasingly seeking to buy brands and in particular brand values that can transfer internationally/globally. If they do not buy them now, they may not be available for purchase in the future (i.e. bought by competitors). It is generally less risky to buy a brand than develop one from zero. Should Pivovar receive a generous offer it should accept, for 'going it alone' in today's fiercely competitive drinks market, dominated as it is by multinationals, risks failure. Few independents will survive (gloomy but true!)

Advice to the new owners

1 Consolidate Pivovar's positioning. It is Czech, home of brewing excellence. Research carefully the country of origin effect. This should be done *before* purchasing the

company. Is Czechness inseparable from the source? If so, it limits the international product range to bottles as it is probably too expensive to ship bulk beer.

2 Retain the logo and its heritage/classic statement (assuming research is conducted internationally to ensure its acceptance, i.e. it is not offensive/negative in key beer drinking markets).

3 Create an international *brand*. Market Pivovar with single-minded rigour and develop a global positioning. Seek out consumer similarities and build brand values around this, accepting that differences will exist in execution and implementation.

4 Establish a clear list of countries, ranking them in priority for market entry, matching country attractiveness with company compatibility (here it is Pivovar's strengths of Czechness and heritage against country attractiveness). It is assumed the multinational has the capability to launch a new product virtually anywhere. Seek out clusters of markets in which Pivovar can be sold, possibly on a geographic basis.

5 Learn by doing. Decide whether to pioneer the world commercialization via a 'lead markets' strategy, possibly experimenting in smaller markets before launching into larger ones, e.g. USA. (This strategy is debatable, for time may be of the essence.)

6 If overseas production is acceptable, integrate production with other overseas facilities. Cut costs!

7 Ensure that in the purchase agreement key Pivovar personnel are retained – they may well hold the key to product quality.

8 In terms of positioning based on heritage, Pivovar should endeavour to remain niche-orientated. Moving to a mass appeal stance might devalue the brand – but research would determine this.

9 Having said the above, move quickly, be flexible, yet remain focused and ambitious.

10 Plan, evaluate and control everything!

World Freight Services (December 1994)

World Freight Services (WFS) was established in the 1920s to transport export business from the UK to a variety of destinations. Over the years WFS expanded to achieve a turnover of £76 million in 1993, employing well over 1000 people, mainly in the UK. WFS is one of a small number of large freight services companies in the UK. It has an important share of the European market but is not significant in other world markets.

The basis of WFS's business is a strong UK collection and delivery service; a worldwide freight-forwarding capability that includes all documentation and customs clearance requirements; a fast scheduled groupage service for both exports and imports to 51 locations in 15 different countries in the European Economic Area. WFS also runs a fast and direct scheduled groupage service to the Gulf (Saudi Arabia, Oman, United Arab Emirates, Bahrain, Kuwait and Iran) and to Japan.

In 1988 WFS carried out a thorough audit of their activities. Several issues emerged as significant threats. The start of the Single Market in the European Community would reduce customs and documentation requirements. The anticipated growth in intra European Community trade would help to offset some of the considerable loss (about 25 per cent of WFS revenue and profits) of customs clearance and documentation work. The opening of the undersea tunnel between the UK and France would again reduce demand for the freight services specialist. In addition, the more general developments in the integration of ownership among the buyers of freight services and among the providers of freight services would change the whole nature of customer service.

The difficulties forecast in 1988 had occurred by 1994. Unfortunately, the impact of the recession during the early 1990s compounded these difficulties, resulting in less demand for freight services. At the same time, competitors were putting pressure on WFS's margins by dropping prices and putting in low price quotations.

The marketing team at WFS was planning to use the country attractiveness/competitive strength matrix to aid its international marketing planning. They were unsure about which elements were appropriate to measure attractiveness and competitiveness in their market. In the countries in which scheduled and groupage services were offered, WFS had a considerable investment in storage and equipment, although its overseas risk exposure was minimized by the careful selection of agents and joint venture partners. The other parts of WFS's business: freight service provision through deep-sea, air-freight, complete documentation services and freight management and consultancy services could include almost any country or client in the world. In practice, however, most of WFS's business related to UK clients.

Question I

(a) What are the main strategic options available to WFS in international markets? Examine how you could use country attractiveness/competitive strength and other analytical techniques to improve WFS's international marketing strategy. **(25 marks)**

(b) Examine the particular difficulties that WFS would be likely to experience in implementing its international marketing plans. **(25 marks)**

Question I(a)

What are the main strategic options available to WFS in international markets? Examine how you could use country attractiveness/competitive strength and other analytical techniques to improve WFS's international strategy. **(25 marks)**

Note: Read both questions carefully. Question 1 is multi-dimensional and breaks into three sub-parts:

- What are the main strategic options?
- Demonstrate country attractiveness/competitive strength
- Show your knowledge of other analytical techniques.

The final line in Question 1 establishes that the question is strategic and not tactical. Candidates should write a balanced answer.

Question 1(b) asks you to examine particular difficulties in implementation. Your effort should be specific to the case and not a general overview of implementation of international marketing plans.

Question I(b)

Examine the potential difficulties that WFS would be likely to experience in implementing its international marketing plans. **(25 marks)**

Question I(a): answer

General observations

WFS is a mainly UK-based organization of considerable size. It has strong European representation but is weak elsewhere. Its current position is that the environment in which it operates is fast changing; in particular, events in Europe have created serious erosion in sales (–25 per cent) *and profit*. So the central issue is clear and unambiguous: WFS must change or die (albeit slowly):

1 WFS must replace lost business
2 WFS must expand into new areas of business.

Main strategic options

Before answering the question it is perhaps worth outlining briefly the nature of the business. WFS is a service organization serving the needs of a diverse customer base. In fact it is the interface between two groups of customers. As such, WFS must be flexible in what it offers so that both parties are satisfied.

The next stage is to set some clearer objectives before establishing the strategic directions. The information in the mini-case suggests the following.

Objectives

1 Improve efficiencies in existing markets to protect margins and enhance profitability
2 Develop new markets broadening the business base, particularly in markets where margins might be generous

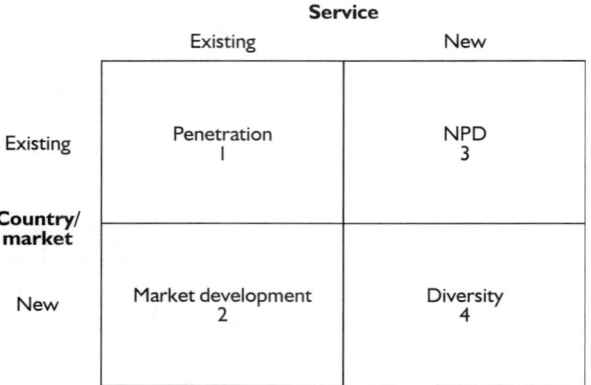

Figure 15.3

3 Develop new products in line with the changing customer dynamics, i.e. finding out what it is customers need and want in a fast-changing world.

The proposed model for exploring strategic options in line with the declared objectives is Ansoff (modified) (Figure 15.3). Dealing with each:

- *Penetration* (1)   As an urgent priority WFS must consolidate and strengthen its position in Europe (EU). It is the core business. Failure to address changes and challenges here will result in further accelerating decline.
- *New market/countries* (2)   WFS is good at what it does. It is efficient and is successful with a range of products/service offers. It is a big player currently restricted in geographic coverage. It should expand into new markets. This is priority No. 2 in terms of strategic options.
- *New product development (NPD)* (3)   This always takes time to develop. Customers would need considerable researching. However, this is an important area as the freight service market is one that is undergoing rapid change as technology drives the business and customers are requiring faster and higher service levels. NPD is seen as a priority No. 3 – one for the medium term. The medium term in this context means 2–3 years, as in this business you are either 'up with the game' or you are not a player!
- *Diversification* (4)   Acquisition could and perhaps should be considered. WFS is a major player – it has assets and if it needed to move quickly to counter a change in the business environment it could do so. But for the moment it is not considered a top priority.

Country attractiveness/competitive strength

The approach taken is to consider the implications of strategic Option 2, i.e. market development. What is important is that WFS matches its strength with that of market/country needs – or rather with that of the customers in a given market. With much of the world to choose from it is vital that WFS develop a systematic approach in order to narrow its options from many to few. Having identified and prioritized key market opportunities, further in-depth analysis and research into customer needs would be implemented.

WFS strengths

In the first place we might consider (briefly) WFS strengths, which are considerable:

- Strong UK collection and delivery
- Worldwide forwarding including documentation and customs
- Fast scheduled groupage to 51 locations and 15 European countries
- Fast groupage to the Gulf and Japan
- Managed risk exposure overseas.

Further detail would be given by WFS to prioritize those strengths and match them to countries/markets to create the best possible 'fit'. Again research would be required initially via secondary research to establish this.

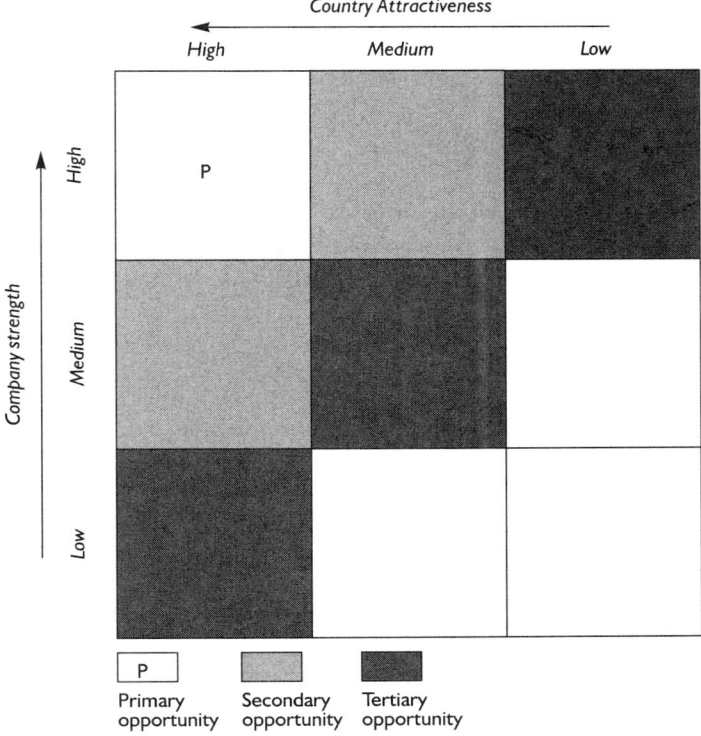

Figure 15.4

The basis for establishing the criteria of country attractiveness would be an analysis of SLEPT factors, e.g.

- Social: culture, language, religion
- Legal: country specific such as foreign ownership
- Economic: rate of growth, business sophistication, size, etc.
- Political: tariffs, other barriers, etc.
- Technology: infrastructure, speed of entry.

A recently developed model that would aid identification of 'best opportunities' is Harrell and Kiefer (1993) (Figure 15.4):

- *Primary* opportunities represent the best fit strategically, i.e. the best opportunity to develop long-term business. Having identified these WFS would then embark on a thorough research programme.
- *Secondary* markets that have either a higher risk factor, or obstacles to entry would require considerable costs in time, personnel and money. These markets would be handled pragmatically with WFS responding to and being proactive but from a distance. They would be markets earmarked for greater future involvement as WFS gained experience in dealing with them.
- *Tertiary* – high risk and/or low return. There is absolutely no reason not to do business in these markets but each contains situations that would be considered on an individual basis. Short-term profit would be the business driver not long-term investment. No serious investment would be considered and no research of any scale considered.

Other analytical techniques

There is no one way that is absolutely correct in assessing potential markets. Briefly, other models might be considered appropriate, e.g. the General Electric/McKinsey approach which is similar to the method described in Question 1(b). Alternatively, the model created by Gilligan and Hird (1985) could be applied in which markets/countries are screened in terms of existing, latent and incipient demand and the firm's products graded on their competitiveness. Finally, it is worth mentioning that other methodologies might include:

- Demand pattern analysis
- Accessibility/profitability/market size analysis
- Analogy estimation (more suitable for Third World countries than to WFS's core customers)
- BERI – Business Environment Risk Index.

Michael Porter's work on generic strategies and his five forces could also be applied. Time precludes addressing the mechanics of the above; they are simply mentioned as alternatives.

Question 1(b): answer

The question is broad based. In the absence of a specific marketing plan it is difficult to be objective or indeed be overspecific in terms of addressing the question. However, it is possible to identify a number of individual particular difficulties that WFS might encounter.

Identification of difficulties

- Identification of the appropriate (specific) key product/service offers that international customers might want, i.e. the service ↔ customer match
- Adapting to the changing business environment impacting on the freight industry, i.e. adaptation to meet the SLEPT factors
- Speed of implementation. This is a fast-response industry
- The ethnocentric orientation of WFS
- The creation and development of a balanced international organization
- The need to find and keep non-UK clients
- Financing the change in company orientation
- Issues of monitoring and control.

Dealing with each in turn (briefly):

1 *Identification of service ↔ customer match*   WFS acts as a service facilitator. There is no physical product. The company interfaces between two customers. Success is about responding to their needs, quickly and efficiently. It is truly a business where being 'close to customers' is paramount. Identifying precisely what customer service levels are appropriate and what customers are prepared to pay is vital in expanding this business. (Unprofitable business can be got anywhere.) Careful research among customers and a critical review of competitors is essential in getting the service offer right. Flexibility is keynote as customers want/demand a customized service. WFS will need to invest in market research and information technology.

2 *Adapting to the environment*   Following on from above, it is essential that WFS monitor the SLEPT factors via an MIS/MKIS. Without specifying details it is apparent that the freight industry is highly competitive and, increasingly, customers succeed or fail on the basis of delivering on time. In a marketplace where products are often similar the cutting edge in determining success is service response. WFS in its marketing plan must take full account of this, e.g. technology is driving the marketplace. Next-day delivery anywhere in the world is commonplace. The manner in which a product is delivered becomes critical.

3 *Speed of implementation*   This is a further endorsement of the previous point. Just-in-Time (JIT), bulk break, cutbacks in inventory levels all affect profitability. A firm that can enhance customers' profitability by fast response will win the battle. WFS will need to accelerate its already successful activities. To do so will require investment in Information Technology.

4 *Ethnocentricity*   WFS is basically a UK operation. To be successful long term on the international front requires establishing a network around the world. This requires a change of orientation from ethnocentric to polycentric operations with responsibilities devolved. There is no other way that WFS can overcome the difficulties mentioned in points 1–3. Furthermore, to speed up international development WFS will need to find suitable partner organizations and establish either a series of joint ventures or strategic alliances.

5 *Balanced organization* Again following on, WFS will need to establish a balanced organization. This will require a careful re-examination of its management structure with leadership and control implications. On the marketing front WFS will need to create an international marketing structure with clear lines of communication, responsibilities and control.

6 *Finding and keeping non-UK clients* To succeed in its ambitions WFS must set in place a process of identifying potential customers. Again careful research and investigation is the key. A polycentric staff would have greater knowledge, insight and contacts in overseas markets. Market research would also be usefully employed as would international marketing communications. How else would potential customers know of the existence of WFS? Establishing overseas market research operations and overseas marketing communications expertise is another difficulty to be considered.

7 *Finance* Establishing a wider international organization would have an impact on the short-medium-term profitability. But WFS has no option other than to commit resources. Entering new markets and creating international networks is expensive.

8 *Control* This is a major issue. Consideration of the previous seven points makes it obvious that WFS is addressing major difficulties. Establishing benchmarks, objectives and performance standards of all kinds is essential. Measuring them, establishing feedback channels and the development of control mechanisms is a prerequisite for the success of WFS.

Examiner's comments

No answer to questions of this nature is complete. Candidates may well add to this list of difficulties. However, it is important to recognize that in international marketing, issues other than ones dealing with the marketing mix are very relevant.

Glossary of terms

4Ps/7Ps   See the marketing mix.

Advertising   Any paid form of non-personal presentation of ideas, goods or services by an identified sponsor.

Ansoff matrix   A model used for identifying the product and market alternatives open to an organization. This involves focusing upon existing and new products and existing and new markets.

Balance of payments   The record of all a country's external transactions in a given period, usually twelve months.

Benchmarking   The analytical process through which an organization's performance is compared with that of its competitors.

Boston Consulting Group (BCG)   The management consulting group which developed the Boston matrix, which makes use of relative market share and the rate of market growth to analyse the product portfolio. Products of SBUs (see below) are categorized as *cash cows, stars, dogs* or *question marks*.

Bottom-up planning   An approach to planning in which individual business units develop their own objectives and strategies. These are then agreed by corporate management, which then adopts a hands-off approach and requires only that the targets are achieved.

Brand/branding   The name, symbol or design used to identify the products or services of a producer and differentiate these from those of competitive producers.

Capability   'A firm's capabilities relate to the distinctive competencies that it has developed to do something well and a company is likely to enjoy a differential advantage in an area where its competencies outdo those of its potential competitors' (Dibb, Simkin *et al*).

Central planning   An economic system in which the government makes all major economic decisions, e.g. the now defunct Communist block.

Cluster   Geographically proximate collection of related businesses, industries and countries. But can incorporate countries with similar buyer characteristics.

Competitive advantage   Those factors which allow the firm to compete (more) effectively in the marketplace.

Competitive information system (CIS)   The formal system that is used to collect, analyse, evaluate and disseminate within the organization information on the firm's competitors.

Competitive stance.   The basis on which an organization chooses to operate and compete in the market place. Michael Porter argues that there are essentially only three generic bases of competition: cost leadership, focus (market niching), and differentiation.

Competitors   Those organizations with which the firm interacts, directly and indirectly, in the fight for sales.

Concentrated marketing   The focusing of the marketing effort upon just one or two of the available market segments.

Consumer   The user of the product or service (see also Customer).

Contingency planning   A plan of action which will be implemented only if events outside the parameters of the accepted plan begin to emerge.

Contract manufacture   The manufacturer or assembler of goods on behalf of a company usually in a foreign market.

Cost leadership   One of Michael Porter's three generic strategies, which involves pursuing a strategy based on the development of the lowest cost structure in the industry.

Culture   The sum total of beliefs, knowledge, attitudes of mind and customs to which people are exposed in their social conditioning. Comprises beliefs and values, customs (and laws), artefacts, and rituals. Perhaps best summed up in the phrase 'the way we do things around here'.

Customer   The buyer of the product or service (see also Consumer).

Desk research   The collection of secondary data in marketing research.

Differentiated marketing   The development of a different marketing mix for each segment.

Differentiation   One of Michael Porter's three generic strategies, which involves making the product or service different from others on the market by developing one or more unique features or by developing a package of benefits which others do not offer.

Direct exporting   Exporting to overseas customers, who might be wholesalers, retailers or users, usually involving agents or distributors.

DMU   Decision-making unit, i.e. the group of people in a business who decide whether to buy a product.

Dumping   Sale of goods in an overseas market at a price lower than would be charged in the home market. Alleged dumping has been an excuse for protectionist measures particularly by the US and EU against companies from Japan and the Third World, to protect national/ regional firms. Examples abound in consumer electronics industries.

ECGD   Export Credit Guarantee Department; UK government department which provides guarantees to banks on behalf of exporters. Renamed NCM post privatization.

Economies of scale   Reductions in costs as output increases. Can be referred to in production terms and other functions.

ECUs   European currency unit; notional unit of account for settling amounts in different currencies; its value is based on a weighting of European currencies.

Effectiveness   The appropriateness of an action or 'doing the right job'.

Efficiency   A measure of how well an activity is performed ('doing the job right').

Environment   The marketing environment is made up of a series of *micro* forces (suppliers, customers, competitors, the public at large and the distribution network) and *macro* forces (political, economic, social, cultural, demographic, legal and technological factors).

Environmental analysis   The process of identifying the various forces within the environment, determining their likely patterns of development and assessing their implications for the organization.

Ethics   The set of moral principles and values that guide an individual's conduct.

Ethnocentrism   In international marketing terms, overseas operations are viewed as secondary to domestic operations and created as 'clones' of HQ operation. In cultural terms, it implies attitudes of cultural superiority, i.e. HQ knows best.

EU (European Union)   Consisting of fifteen European nations, formerly called the European Community (EC).

Exchange rate   The price of a currency expressed in terms of another currency (e.g. £1 = DM2.56).

Exchange risk   The risk that the monetary value of a transaction when translated/remitted in the home currency will differ from what was anticipated, as a result of changes in the rate of exchange, if the transaction occurred in a foreign currency.

Focus   One of the three generic strategies identified by Michael Porter, which involves concentrating the marketing effort upon a particular segment and then competing within this either through cost leadership or a differentiated approach.

Foreign currency pricing   Pricing your goods in foreign currency, hereby risking the potential exchange rate change.

Formal organization   The stated and explicit structure of an organization which determines the hierarchy, the division of labour, job specifications and hence the basis of the relationships between individuals and departments.

Former Eastern Bloc country   A previous 'satellite' of the Russian state, where the legacy of communism has not been totally replaced.

Franchising   Popular in retail and service industries, the franchisee supplies capital and the franchiser supplies expertise, a brand name and promotion. Examples worldwide include Body Shop, McDonalds.

GATT (General Agreement on Tariffs and Trade)   Organization which promoted free trade on a multilateral basis between members. Now superseded by the World Trade Organization (WTO).

General Electric multi-factor model   An approach to portfolio analysis which categorizes SBUs on the basis of industry attractiveness and business strength.

Generic strategies   See Focus, Cost leadership and Differentiation.

Geocentrism   The organization views the whole world as a market and standardises accordingly. A philosophical viewpoint where in management terms 'the best person for the job' is appointed, e.g. Alex Trottman (Scottish) is CEO of The Ford Motor Company and Tony O'Reilly (Irish) runs H. J. Heinz.

Geodemographics   An approach to segmentation which classifies people by where they live. The rationale for this is that 'birds of a feather flock together'.

Global brand   Single brand name for a product (e.g. Coca-Cola).

Global company   'The global corporation is an organizational form that makes no distinction between domestic and international business.' (Terpstra). This term is rarely used precisely, and many so-called global firms are dominated in one way or another by domestic considerations. A global company may be multidomestic, multinational or transnational in outlook and operation.

Global sourcing   Obtaining raw materials or subcomponents from companies worldwide.

Globalization   'Globalization of markets' (Levitt, 1983) is an expression which relates first to demand: tastes, preferences and price-mindedness are becoming increasingly universal. Second, it relates to the supply side: products and services tend to become more standardized and competition within industries reaches a worldwide scale. Third, it relates to the way firms, mainly multinational corporations, try to design their marketing policies and control systems appropriately so as to remain winners in the global competition of global products for global consumers (Usunier).

Goals down/plans up planning   An approach to planning in which corporate management establishes the broad planning parameters in terms of targets, but then allows the business unit to decide how these will be achieved.

Gross domestic product (GDP)   A measure of the value of the goods and services produced by an economy in a given period, usually twelve months.

Gross national product (GNP) GDP plus the rewards from investments.

INCOTERMS These are standard shipping forms for dividing costs of carriage between buyer and seller. FOB or Free on Board means that the buyer does not pay the price of transporting the goods from factory/warehouse to the ship. Another popular Incoterms is CIF Carriage Insurance and Freight.

Indirect distribution The use of intermediaries, such as wholesalers and retailers, to supply a product to the customer.

Indirect exporting Use of intermediaries such as export houses or specialist export management companies.

Informal organization The social dimensions and relationships within a business. This is sometimes referred to as 'the oil which allows the wheels to go round'.

Insideration Building up a production and distribution network from scratch, alone or with local cooperation in a local market. Being seen as a 'local' organization from a management perspective and more importantly from the customers viewpoint.

Invisible trade The exporting and importing of services (as distinct from physically visible goods).

JIT (just in time) A technique for the organization of work flows to allow rapid, high quality, flexible production whilst minimizing manufacturing waste and stock levels. An item should not be made or purchased until it is needed by the customer or as input into the production process. It is considered that Toyota popularized this technique in the 1980s.

Joint venture Arrangement whereby two or more firms create a separate company for financial, manufacturing and marketing purposes and each has a share in both the equity and the management of the business. Popular with protectionist governments in developing countries.

Lesser developed country (LDC) Relies heavily on primary industries and/or commodities (mining, agriculture, forestry, fishing) with low GDP per capita, and poorly developed infrastructure.

Lifestyle segmentation 'A person's pattern of living as expressed in [their] activities, interests and opinions . . . [it] portrays the "whole person" interacting with his or her environment. Lifestyle reflects something beyond the person's social class . . . or personality . . . [it] attempts to profile a person's way of being and acting in the world' (Kotler).

Managerial culture The basic assumptions and beliefs that are shared by members of the management team and which determine the organization's view of itself and its environment.

Market challenger Firms which adopt an aggressive stance by attacking the market leader or others in the industry in order to strengthen their position and possibly gain leadership.

Market follower Firms which avoid direct confrontation with others in the market are generally willing to accept the current market structure and status quo, and react to the initiatives taken by others. (Note: followers may follow others closely by responding quickly, or at a distance in that they respond only at a much later stage.)

Market leader Although the market leader is typically seen to be the largest player in the market, an alternative (and, in many ways, better) approach involves seeing the market leader as the firm which, by virtue of its proactive stance, determines the nature, bases and intensity of competition within the market. In this way, others are forced to respond.

Market nichers Firms which concentrate their efforts upon a small and often specialized part of the market.

Marketing assets The capabilities possessed by the organization which managers and the marketplace view as beneficially strong. These include customer-based assets (brand image and reputation), distribution-based assets (the density and geographic coverage of the dealer network), and internal marketing assets (skills, experience, economies of scale, technology and resources).

Marketing audit   A formal review of the organization's products, markets, customers and environment.

Marketing channels   The 'sets of interdependent organizations involved in the process of making a product or service available for consumption' (Kotler).

Marketing effectiveness review   A framework for measuring the organization's marketing capabilities and performance by making use of five dimensions: the strength of the customer-oriented philosophy, the degree of integration within the marketing organization, the adequacy of marketing information, the firm's strategic orientation, and levels of operational efficiency.

Marketing information system (MkIS)   'A system which consists of people, equipment and procedures to gather, sort, analyse, evaluate and distribute needed, timely and accurate information to marketing decision makers' (Kotler).

Marketing mix   The set of controllable variables that the organization uses to influence its target markets and determine demand. Although the mix has traditionally been seen to consist of four principal elements (the 4 Ps of product, price, place and promotion), others have been added to this in recent years, leading to the 7 P's; the three additional elements are physical evidence, process management, and people.

Marketing planning   The process of identifying, evaluating and selecting the organization's products, services and markets, and how the organization is to operate within each sector of the market.

Marketing research   The process of gathering, recording and analysing market-related information. This typically involves making use of published or secondary data and the collection of problem-specific data (primary research).

MIS/MKIS   Marketing information system.

Multinational company   Company with direct investment (operations/facilities) in more than one country: i.e. they are more than just exporters. Most multinationals have a close involvement with the home country. *See also* Global company.

NAFTA (North American Free Trade Agreement)   A treaty agreeing to reduce trade barriers between the US, Canada and Mexico; launched in 1994.

Non-tariff barriers   Non-physical barriers, sometimes called invisible barriers, to the import of goods other than taxes on imported goods. Include quotas, restricted entry points (e.g. a French government's requirement that imports of Japanese video cassette recorders should all be routed through a small customs post in Poitiers), government restricted prices, etc. Some non-tariff barriers are informal and regarded by exporters as underhand.

Objectives   Measures of desired achievement which are used as the basis of planning and a measure of performance.

OECD   Organization for Economic Cooperation and Development.

Overseas export agent   Agents do not take title to goods, but are normally paid by commission. Recent EU rules have meant stricter regulation of agreements between agents and principals.

Pareto (80/20) distribution   A frequency distribution with a small proportion (say 20 per cent) of the items accounting for a large proportion (say 80 per cent) of the value/resources.

Performance-importance grid   A tool used for measuring marketing, financial, manufacturing and organizational performance against the background of the market importance of each dimension.

Personal selling   An oral presentation with one or more prospective purchasers for the purpose of making sales.

PEST   The acronym for the Political, Economic, Socio-cultural and Technological forces within the organization's environment.

Planning   The setting of objectives and the identification, evaluation and selection of the strategic and/or tactical actions needed to achieve them.

Polycentrism   Subsidiaries are established in overseas markets, with their own objectives, strategies, plans, promotional budgets, etc. A philosophical viewpoint that proposes that local management knows best – the opposite of Ethnocentrism.

Portfolio analysis   The approach to planning and management of the product range, which involves recognizing the nature of the interrelationships between strategic business units and then making investment and marketing decisions that are designed to maximize the performance of the range as a whole rather than that of the individual SBUs.

Positioning   The relative competitive stance adopted within a target market.

Price takers/price makers   Price takers are those organizations which, by virtue of a weak market position, lack of an offensive strategy, absence of distinguishing features, or few resources, simply accept the prices set by others in the marketplace. Price makers, by contrast, are those which, because of their size, competitive stance, aggression, resources, or strong selling propositions, are able to determine not only their prices but also those of other firms in the market.

Primary data   Data collected for a specific market study and designed to help answer a particular question.

Product life cycle (PLC)   A model of product and market evolution which suggests that products and markets have a finite life and that during this life they pass through a number of distinct stages (these are typically *introduction, growth, maturity* and *decline*). As the product goes through these, the nature of the strategy needed to support and develop the product should reflect this, with emphasis being given to different parts of the marketing mix.

Protectionism   Discouraging imports by raising tariff barriers, imposing quotas, etc. in order to favour home/domestic producers.

Publicity   The non-personal stimulation of demand for a product or service or business unit by planting commercially significant news about it in a published medium or obtaining favourable presentation of it upon radio, television or stage that is not paid for by the sponsor.

Purchasing power parity   The theory that, in the long run at least, the equilibrium exchange rate between two currencies is that which equates the domestic purchasing power of each. For example, US$2 = £1 will represent equilibrium if $2 will buy the same amount of goods in the US as £1 will buy in the UK.

Quota   Restriction in the number of items that may be imported into a market (import quotas) or in rarer cases, exported from a market (export quotas). Import quotas are used unofficially to restrict imports of Japanese cars into the European Union.

Relationship marketing (RM)   The conscious attempt to develop long-term and mutually beneficial relationships with customers. This contrasts with transaction marketing, which tends to view each transaction separately.

Resource audit   The identification and evaluation of the internal and external resources available to the organization.

Sales promotion   Those marketing activities, other than advertising, personal selling and publicity, that stimulate consumer purchase, such as displays, shows and exhibitions, demonstrations and various non-recurrent selling efforts not in the ordinary routine.

Scenario planning   The process of identifying and planning for possible alternative futures.

Secondary data   Market data that is not collected directly by the user nor for a problem-specific purpose. Examples include government and sector reports.

Segmentation   The sub-dividing of a market into distinct and homogeneous sub-groups.

Services   Distinguishable from products in that they are most often produced as they are consumed and cannot be taken away or stored.

Seven-S framework   The model developed by Peters and Waterman which illustrates that strategic capability is influenced not just by the 'hard' Ss (strategy, structure and systems), but also by a series of 'softer' Ss (skills, style, staffing and shared values).

Short-termism   Preference supposed to exist in the UK, US and similar business cultures, as opposed to Japan or Germany, in which short-term results take priority over long-term strategic outlook.

SLEPT factors   Mnemonic for Social, Legal, Economic, Political and Technological features in a firm's environment.

Societal marketing concept   An extension of the traditional definition of the marketing concept in order to take greater and more specific account of the consumer's and society's well-being.

Socio-cultural   The mix of social and cultural factors in the environment (demographics, lifestyle, social mobility, attitudes and consumerism).

Stakeholders   A person or group with a direct or indirect interest in an organization, its activities and outcomes.

Strategic business unit (SBU)   A single business or collection of related businesses which might feasibly stand apart from the rest of the organization and which offer scope for independent planning.

Strategic drift   The gap that emerges between what the organization is offering and what the market wants.

Strategic grouping   The process of plotting the position of the various players within the market on the basis of the similarities and differences that exist in the type of strategy being pursued.

Strategic wear-out   The tiredness or staleness of corporate and marketing strategies.

Strategy   The course of action to achieve a particular objective.

Stuck in the middle   Although Michael Porter identified three generic strategies (*see* Generic strategies; Cost; Focus and Differentiation) and argued that firms need to adopt a distinct competitive stance, many organizations fail to identify, develop or exploit a meaningful position. The result is that they end up 'stuck in the middle', in the sense that they have no obvious or communicated selling proposition and hence there is little reason for customers to do business with the firm.

SWOT   The analysis and assessment of the firm's strengths and weaknesses (in essence, the firm's capabilities) and the opportunities and threats in the marketplace.

Tactics   The development of resources within a strategy.

Take-over/acquisition   The acquiring, by a firm, of a controlling interest in the assets of another's company. A way of buying into a market, e.g. Nestlé take-over of Rowntree.

Targeting   The choice of market segments at which the marketing effort is to be aimed.

Tariff   A tax on imported goods, either by volume or value.

Test marketing   The process of measuring market response to a new product or service by piloting it within a small area which is seen to be representative of the market as a whole.

Top-down planning   An approach to planning in which corporate management sets the objectives and maintains a close involvement with both the development and implementation of the strategy and tactics.

TQM (total quality management)   An approach to production, and also management, aimed to prevent defective manufacture and to promote continuous improvement.

Trade fair   Trade fairs are events at which many firms display their wares to other businesses. One of the most important routes to new customers in international markets.

Transfer price   The price at which goods or services are transferred from one subsidiary of a company to another or from HQ to subsidiary or even vice-versa. The extent to which costs and profit are covered by the price is a matter of policy. A transfer price may, for example, be based upon marginal cost, full cost, market price or negotiation. Transfer pricing is important in global businesses sourcing components from many countries and is seen by some as a means of avoiding taxation.

Transnational company   This term is used in a variety of contexts, and might be taken to mean global company or multinational company. Its true meaning is that of a company that sees no natural boundaries and markets as though the world (or large regions of it) is one marketplace.

Undifferentiated marketing   A broad-brush approach to marketing, in which the market is not sub-divided into segments.

Unique selling proposition (USP)   A product/service feature or benefit which others are not currently able to offer. Assuming that the USP is meaningful to customers, it provides a basis for differentiation.

VALS (values and lifestyles)   An approach to market segmentation which classifies people on the basis of nine value lifestyle groups.

Value chain   The relationships between the value-creating activities within an organization which, if managed effectively, are capable of creating a competitive advantage.

World Trade Organization (WTO)   Successor to GATT, formed in 1995.

Index